ISBN 978-1-332-46856-0
PIBN 10126533

# 1 MONTH OF
# FREE
# READING

## at

## www.ForgottenBooks.com

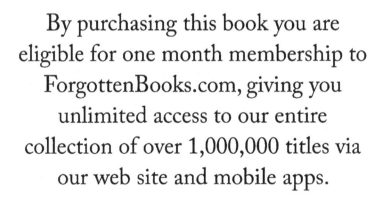

By purchasing this book you are eligible for one month membership to ForgottenBooks.com, giving you unlimited access to our entire collection of over 1,000,000 titles via our web site and mobile apps.

To claim your free month visit: www.forgottenbooks.com/free126533

# ULTIMA THULE;

OR,

# A SUMMER IN ICELAND.

BY

RICHARD F. BURTON.

𝔚ith 𝔥istorical 𝔌ntroduction, 𝔐aps, and 𝔌llustrations.

VOL. I

WILLIAM P. NIMMO.

LONDON: 14 KING WILLIAM STREET, STRAND;
AND EDINBURGH.

1875.

EDINBURGH:
PRINTED BY M'FARLANE AND ERSKINE,
ST JAMES SQUARE.

# DEDICATION.

Trieste, *March* 1875.

My dear Sir,

Be pleased to accept this very inadequate return for the varied information with which you have favoured me, and for all your hospitality and kindness to me at Edinburgh and elsewhere.

You are so well known as a traveller in Iceland, and as a warm and generous friend to the Icelander, that you will not be held responsible for my over freedom of speech, nor for any unpopular opinions expressed in the pages honoured by bearing your name.

Pray believe me,

Yours very sincerely,

RICHARD F. BURTON.

Robert Mackay Smith, Esq.,
ETC., ETC., ETC.,
EDINBURGH.

" SIGNOR, non sotto l'ombra in piaggia molle
    Tra fonti e fior, tra Ninfe e tra Sirene;
   Ma in cima al l'erto e faticoso colle,
    Della virtù riposto è il nostro bene:
   Chi non gela, e non suda, e non s'estolle
    Dalle vie del piacer, là non perviene."

—TASSO, xvii. 61.


" NOT among nymphs and sirens, founts and flowers,
   Not in voluptuous herbage in the shade;
But on the toilsome steep where valour towers
   Alone, O Prince, our supreme good is laid;
Who from the paths of pleasure will not raise
   His thoughts; nor freeze nor sweat, arrives not there."

—JAMES.


" IN somma, ho avuto sempre mai d'avanti agli occhi quelle sante leggi della Storia, di non osar dire il falso, né temer di dire il vero; e mi lusingo di non avervi contravenuto."

—ABBATE CLAVIGERO.

# PREFACE.

ACCORDING to the fashion of the day, this volume should have been published two years ago, shortly after my return from Iceland. The truth is that before the second third had been written, I found a large fallow of pre-historic study, the Castellieri of Istria, and I could not help putting hand to the work at "Iceland's" expense. But this much of delay is, methinks, a disadvantage rather in popular prejudice than in point of fact. The loss of freshness brings with it not a little gain. Whilst all the scenes and events of a journey, during and immediately after its progress, appear like an unartistic sketch, confused and without comparative distance; time gives perspective, and relation of details, and distinction of light and shade. Moreover, in treating of Iceland there is present danger of misleading the reader, unless due reflection correct hasty work. The subject is, to some extent, like Greece and Palestine, of the sensational type: we have all read in childhood about those "Wonders of the World," Hekla and the Geysir, and, as must happen under the circumstances, we have all drawn for ourselves our own Iceland—a distorted and exaggerated mental picture of what has not met, and will not meet, the eye of sense. Moreover, the travellers of the early century saw scenes of thrilling horror, of majestic grandeur, and of heavenly beauty, where our more critical, perhaps more cultivated, taste finds very humble features. They had "Iceland on the brain," and they were wise in their generation: honours and popularity await the man who ever praises, the thorough partisan who never blames. But not the less our revulsion of feeling requires careful coercion: it always risks under-rating what we have found so much over-valued, of tinging neutral-hued sobriety with an angry flush of disappointment.

I went to Iceland feeling by instinct that many travellers had prodigiously exaggerated their descriptions, possibly because they had seldom left home. "The most difficult and expensive country in the world" would certainly prove cheap and easy after the Andes and the Haurán. What could be made of "giddy rapid rivers" at most three feet deep, and if deeper provided with ferries? Yet the "scare" had succeeded in making a deep impression: one tourist came to Iceland prepared to cross the streams "in buff," and firmly determined on no account to climb a scaur. "The ruts are only one danger of Icelandic travelling, *the* danger is crossing the streams," says a modern author—how his descriptions were derided by a couple of English officers who had ridden about the Himalayas! What could I think of the "stupendous precipice of Almannagjá," of the "frightful chasm," of the "dreadful abyss, causing the most disagreeable emotions," when also told that men ride up and down the side? Yet another says, "rush for your life" from the unfortunate Strokkr; whilst we are actually threatened with perils of polar bears—half-starved wretches floated ashore upon ice-floes to be slaughtered by the peasants with toy scythes before they can stretch their cramped and numbed limbs. The "horrific deep chasms" of the Reykjavik-Hafnafjörð road, and the popular sketches, affected me with extreme incredulity. A friend described to me life in Iceland as living in a corner, the very incarnation of the passive mood; and travelling there as full of stolid, stupid risks, that invite you to come and to repent coming, not like the swiftly pursuing or treacherously lurking perils of tropical climes, but invested with a horror of their own —such was not my experience.

Shortly after returning to England, I published, in the columns of the *Morning Standard* (October to November 1872), two letters for the benefit of intending tourists and explorers. Written in the most sober and realistic style, and translated into many of the languages of Europe, they gained for me scant credit at home. " Old Identity" again kicked against the goad of " New Iniquity," and what could I expect? Mackenzie and Henderson, who *would* " feast wondering eyes" upon everything and everybody, had set the example of treating Iceland as an exceptional theme. They found followers: even the hard-headed Scot gallops between Reykjavik and Thingvellir along the edge of a " dreadful precipice," where I saw only the humblest ravine; and travellers to the age-weary, worn-out Geysir rise at midnight in their excitement to sing those " grand old psalm-tunes, such as York and the Old Hundredth." Need it be said that Mr Cook's pilgrim-tourists have done exactly the same thing in the Holy Land?

My matter-of-fact notions were set down as the effects of " Peter Porcupine," over-" combativeness," and the undue " spirit of opposition" that characterises an Objector-General, with the " morbid object of gaining popularity by stating something new" —a hasty judgment, which justifies me in writing these volumes, and in supporting my previously expressed views. I can appeal for confirmation to the dozen intelligent English tourists who were in Iceland at the same time as myself: all united with me in deriding their previous conceptions, and in forming the estimate here offered to the public.

My plan throughout this volume has been as follows: The
reader, not the critic, is assumed to know as little about the
island as its author did before visiting it; and the first impressions are carefully recorded, not only as a *mise en scène*, but for
conciseness' sake, so that only differences, not resemblances, may
require subsequent notice.  Thus the capital and its environs are
painted at some length, whilst most authors simply land at the
little port, and set out at once for the interior.  The cruise to
the north coast, and the "Cockney trip" to Hekla and the Geysir
are related with less circumstance, but I have added itineraries,
as such details have not yet appeared in English.  The journey
through the eastern country claims considerable space.  Critics
tell us that African travellers have so much trouble to reach the
Unexplored Regions, that they are apt to report all they see at
wearying length, and to empty the contents of their journals
upon the public.  But every mile of new, or even comparatively
new, ground deserves careful topographical notices: let the
general reader "skip" such photos if he likes, but let them be
written at least for the purpose of future comparison.  Again,
the Icelanders may complain, like the Swiss, that, whilst their
country has become a touring-field to Europe, scant attention
is paid to themselves.  I have endeavoured to remedy this
grievance by ethnological descriptions; and though it has been
my desire to speak of things, and states of things, not of persons,
it has been impossible at times to avoid personalities.  And,
whilst a wanderer knowing only enough of the language to express his humble wants, whose travels have been limited to a
single fine season, has little right *ex cathedrâ* to pronounce, even
in this scanty community, upon religion and politics, upon commerce and civilisation; he is fully justified in quoting as his
own the judgments formed by consulting experts and authorities,
upon whom his experience, and that "sixth sense" developed

by the life-long habit of observation, have taught him to rely.

There is still much to be done in Iceland, and I flatter myself that the fifteenth chapter, which shows my only attempt at actual exploration, will supply adventurous men with useful hints. The geography, especially of that huge white blot, the south-eastern part, is unknown; and a tyro can be usefully employed there in collecting specimens of botany. The meteorology, again, is highly interesting—does the cold in the " Insula quæ glacialis dicitur" increase, as some have supposed, the effect of the " precession of the equinoxes, the revolution of the apsides, variations in the excentricity of the earth's orbit," etc. ? Or has it increased at all since Saga times? Evidently it would be most interesting to compare the Icelandic glacier-formations with those of Switzerland; and to determine if the rules laid down by the " De Saussure of Great Britain," the late Professor David Forbes, by Professor Tyndall, and by Mr Whymper, the conqueror of the mighty Matterhorn, are here applicable. As anthropologists, we ask why a people once so famed for arms, if not for arts, has almost disappeared from the world's history—is the change caused by politics or religion; is it the logical sequence of monarchy or " media," of icy winters, of earthquakes and volcanoes, of pestilence and famine ? We are curious to learn why a noble poetry should have ceased to sing. And as we have dwelt upon the past, so we would speculate upon the future of the Scandinavian race, which is supposed to be tending to reunion in its old homes, and which, as it enlarges its education, will, like the Slav, take high rank in the European family.

The main object of the book, however, has been to advocate the development of the island. Sensible Icelanders freely confess that the life-struggle at home is hard, very hard, and that the " Alma Mater " is a " Dura Mater," but they have not

suggested any remedy for the evil.   I hold three measures to be
absolutely necessary; the first is the working of the sulphur
deposits—not to mention the silica—now in English hands; the
second, a systematic reform of the primitive means and appliances with which the islanders labour in their gold mines, the
fisheries; and, thirdly, the extension of the emigrating movement,
now become a prime need when the population is denser than
at any period of its thousand-year history.   Concerning that
" make-shift," the pony traffic, and the ill-judged export of sheep
and black cattle, ample details will also be found.

No care has been omitted in securing for these pages as much
correctness as the reader can expect.   Mr Robert Mackay
Smith, of Edinburgh, whose name I have placed, with permission,
at the beginning of this volume, obliged me with the details of
his own travels.   Dr Richard S. Charnock, whose extensive reading and access to libraries fit him well for the task, assisted me
in the Introductory Section, which treats of Thule.   Mr Gwyn
Jeffreys kindly examined my little collection of shells; Mr
Alfred Newton was good enough to suggest hints concerning a
possible " last of the Gare-fowl;" and Mr Watts, of Vatna-, or
rather Klofa-, Jökull fame, gave me a list of his stages.   My
fellow-traveller, Mr Alfred G. Lock of Roselands, kept me
thoroughly well posted, at great trouble to himself, in ephemeral
literature concerning Iceland.   When preparing my manuscript
for the press, I found that the notes showed various lacunæ and
want of details resulting from lack of time: Mr Jón A. Hjaltalín
of the Advocates' Library, Edinburgh, whose name is sufficient recommendation, consented to become my *collaborateur* in
working up the Introduction; and Mr A. H. Gunlögsen has
revised the sheets in my absence from home.   Of the late Dr
Cowie I shall speak in another place.   Mr Vincent courteously
placed his paper on " Sulphur in Iceland," at my disposal; and

Mr P. le Neve Foster, Secretary of the Society of Arts, allowed me to borrow from it or to reprint it. Mr William P. Nimmo has brought out the book in the most handsome and liberal form. I thank these gentlemen from my heart, and, at the same time, I warn my readers that all sins of commission and omission occurring in these pages, must be charged upon the author, and the author alone.

Allow me to conclude this necessary preliminary ramble with the lines of good "old Dan Geffry:"

> " For every word men may not chide or pleine,
> For in this world certain ne wight there is
> That he ne doth or sayth sometime amis."

# CONTENTS.

## INTRODUCTION.

### SECTION I.

#### OF THULE.

### SECTION II.

#### PHYSICAL GEOGRAPHY OF ICELAND.

### SECTION III.

### SECTION IV.

#### POLITICAL GEOGRAPHY OF ICELAND.

VOL. I.   *b*

# SECTION V.
## ANTHROPOLOGY.

# SECTION VI.
## EDUCATION AND PROFESSIONS.

# SECTION VII.
## ZOOLOGICAL NOTES, ETC.

# SECTION VIII.
## TAXATION, ETC.

# SECTION IX.
## CATALOGUE, ETC.

## CHAPTER I.

PAGE

## CHAPTER II.

## CHAPTER III.

## CHAPTER IV.

## CHAPTER V.

# LIST OF ILLUSTRATIONS.

## VOL. I.

Horn (Cap Nord)

Straumnes
Fljot
Aðalvik
Grænahlið
Staðr

Ísafjarðurdjup

Jökulfjörd

Drange
Jökull

Súgundafjörðr
Önundarfjörd
Sauri
Dýrafjörðr
Hraun
Moldarar
Sandar
Núma
Arnarfjörðr
Jökull

Kópanes
Sdarða
Tálknafjörðr
Patreksfjörðr
Breiðavik
Tunga
Sandalkakldr
Saurar
Barðastrand

Staðr
Hrófberg
Þingrimsfjörð

Flatey
Svefneyjar

Vatternes
Gufudals
Tröllatunga
Heydjörd
Pell
Reykholt
Garpsdle

BROADFIRTH
BREIÐI FJÖRÐR

Búðardalr
Skard
Sælingsdalstunga
Bær
Bor

Diupeldarnes
Staðr
Hvamm

Önverðarnes

Stykkisholm
Hvamsfjör
Hjarðarholt

Saurar
Narford
Blöndulið
Randmed
Hrosholti
Kolbeinsstaðr
Hitardál
Reun

Snæfells
Jökull
Knor
Stabrstaðr
Trollakirki
Stapi
Gor
Eldborg
Staðarhraun
Langarbrekka
osshdl
Nord
Hjarðarho

Laungafjörðr

Akrar
Hvaleyar

FAXA FJÖRÐR

Hjörtsey
Alftanes
Skarðheiði
Saurbær
Melar

FAXFIRTH

Garðar
Reyniv

Whalefirth
Brautarhol

Viðey
Mostell
Lagofell
Gufunes

First Cruise and Excursion
Skagi
Reykjavik
Second Excursion
Utskálar
Bessastaðr
Garðar
Hafnarfjörðr
Jöfr
Last
Hvalanes
Keflavik
Kallatjörn
Vigisfell

Njarðvik
Kurkjuvogr
Sveifluhals
Krisuvik
Gold
Staðr
Solvögr
Bær
Hiall
Zijr
Stranda

Reykjanes

Fuglasker
Eldey

# ULTIMA THULE;

OR,

# A SUMMER IN ICELAND.

---

## INTRODUCTION.

### SECTION I.

### OF THULE.

But is Iceland " Ultima Thule?"

The author hopes to make it evident that " Thule " was used according to date in five several senses—a sufficient reason for the confusion which has so long invested the subject. It has been well remarked that no place is more often mentioned by the ancients than the " island hid from us by snow and winter;" and yet, that no position is more controverted.[1] There has been a " King of Thule," and now there is a " Princess of Thule,"—but where and what is " Thule?"

It will take some time to clear up the darkness which has been heaped by a host of writers upon " Thule," and we will begin by distributing the debated word.

*Firstly*, It was attributed poetically, rhetorically, and per synecdochen, to the northern " period of cosmographie," and to its people, real or supposed.

*Secondly*, It was applied to Iceland, and to Iceland only, from the earliest ages of its exploration.

---

[1] " Mirum de Tyle, quæ inter occidentales ultima fertur insulas, quod apud orientales tam nomine quam naturâ sit famosissima ; cum occidentalibus sit prorsus incognita," says Giraldus Cambrensis, chap. xvii., p. 98, ed. T. F. Dimock, M.A., Lond. 1867.

# ULTIMA THULE;

OR,

# A SUMMER IN ICELAND.

## INTRODUCTION.

### SECTION I.

### OF THULE.

BUT is Iceland "Ultima Thule?"

The author hopes to make it evident that "Thule" was used according to date in five several senses—a sufficient reason for the confusion which has so long invested the subject. It has been well remarked that no place is more often mentioned by the ancients than the "island hid from us by snow and winter;" and yet, that no position is more controverted.[1] There has been a "King of Thule," and now there is a "Princess of Thule,"—but where and what is "Thule?"

It will take some time to clear up the darkness which has been heaped by a host of writers upon "Thule," and we will begin by distributing the debated word.

*Firstly,* It was attributed poetically, rhetorically, and per synecdochen, to the northern "period of cosmographie," and to its people, real or supposed.

*Secondly,* It was applied to Iceland, and to Iceland only, from the earliest ages of its exploration.

---

[1] "Mirum de Tyle, quæ inter occidentales ultima fertur insulas, quod apud orientales tam nomine quam naturâ sit famosissima; cum occidentalibus sit prorsus incognita," says Giraldus Cambrensis, chap. xvii., p. 98, ed. T. F. Dimock, M.A., Lond. 1867.

*Thirdly*, In the centuries when imperial Rome extended her sceptre to the north of " the Britains;" it was given to the out-lying parts, Ireland, Scotland, the Orkneys, the Shetlands, and features known only to fabulous geography.

*Fourthly*, The later Roman writers prolonged it to the " Scania Island," modern Norway, Sweden, and Lapland. This Thule should be called " Procopiana."

*Fifthly*, Between the establishment ·of Christianity in Eng-land, and the official or modern rediscovery, the term Thule was once more, as of old, limited to Iceland.

## I.

## "THULE," POETICAL AND RHETORICAL.

The following are popular instances of Thule used in its first sense, the remotest part of the septentrional world, when it was a " fabulosa non minus quam famosa insula." Virgil has only one allusion to it (Georg., i. 30, 31):

> " Tibi serviat ultima Thule,
> Teque sibi generum Tethys emat omnibus undis;"

but his epithet has been consecrated by a bevy of succeeding poets.

Servius, commenting upon Virgil, explains:

" Thyle insula est oceani inter septentrionalem et occidentalem plagam, ultra Britanniam, Hiberniam, Orcadas;"

which is vague enough. He is afterwards more precise:

" At this island, when the sun is in Cancer, the days are said to be continuous without nights. Various marvels are related of it, both by Greek and later writers ; by Ctesias and Diogenes among the former, and by Samnonicus among the latter."

The work of Ctesias here referred to is little known : Thule would hardly enter into Persica and Indica (B.C. 400). Of Diogenes presently. Samnonicus Sorenus was a writer put to death by command of Caracalla (Notes and Queries, t. ii., v. 119, p. 301).

L. Annæus Seneca (ob. A.D. 65) first re-echoes Virgil in the celebrated " prophetic verses," whose sense has been extended to the New World:

> " Venient annis secula seris,
> Quibus Oceanus vincula rerum
> Laxet, et ingens pateat tellus,
> Tethysque novos detegat orbes,
> Nec sit terris ultima Thule."
>
> —*Medea*, 375, *et seq.*

Ammianus Marcellinus (ob. circ. A.D. 390) uses (History, lib. xviii., 6, 31) the adage, " Etiamsi apud Thulen moraretur Ursicinus."

Claudius Claudianus (flor. A.D. 395-408) sings:

> " Et nostro procul axe remotam
> Insolito belli tremeficit murmure Thulen !"
>
> —*De Bell. Getic.*, 203, *et seq.*

And—

> "Te vel Hyperboreo damnatam sidere Thulen,
> Te vel ad incensas Libyæ comitatur arenas."
>
> —*In Rufin.*, ii. 240.

Finally, we find in Aurelius Prudentius (nat. A.D. 348):

> " Ultima littora Thules
> Transadigit."

## II.

### STRABO, MELA, PLINY, PTOLEMY.

Entering upon the second phase of the subject, it is advisable to consider what has been written concerning Thule, by the four patriarchs of classical geography. With Strabo Thule is Iceland; in Mela it is indefinite; and to Pliny and Ptolemy it is part of Britain, with an *arrière pensée* of Iceland: of Pytheas and Eratosthenes we must also say a few words.

#### STRABO.

Strabo (nat. B.C. 54; Introduction, vol. i., p. 99, Hamilton and Falconer's translation, Bohn, 1854) tells us, § 2:

" Thence (*i.e.*, from the Dneiper) to the parallel of Thule, which Pytheas says is six days' sail north from Britain and near the Frozen Sea, other 11,500 stadia " [a measure which we will assume with Leake to be 700 = 1°].

## Again, § 3 :

" But that the Dneiper is under the same parallel as Thule, what man in his senses could ever agree to this ? Pytheas, who has given us the history of Thule, is known to be a man upon whom no reliance can be placed ; and other writers who have seen Britain and Ierne [1] (Ireland ?), although they tell us of many small islands round Britain, make no mention whatever of Thule."

## In § 4 :

" Now from Marseille to the centre of Britain is not more than 5000 stadia ; and if from the centre of Britain we advance north not more than 4000 stadia, we arrive at a temperature in which it is scarcely possible to exist. Such indeed is that of Ierne. Consequently the far region in which Eratosthenes places Thule must be totally uninhabitable. By what guess-work he arrived at the conclusion that between the latitude of Thule and the Dnieper there was a difference of 11,500 stadia, I am unable to divine."

In book ii., chap. 4, §§ 1, 2, he thus disposes of Pytheas ("by whom many have been deceived ") :

" It is this last writer who states that he travelled all over Britain on foot, and that the island is above 40,000 stadia in circumference. [2] It is likewise he who describes Thule and other neighbouring places, where, according to him, neither earth, water, nor air exist separately, but a sort of concretion of all these, resembling marine sponge, in which the earth, the sea, and all things were suspended, this forming, as it were, a link to unite the whole together. It can neither be travelled over nor sailed through. As for the substance, he affirms that he has beheld it with his own eyes ; the rest he reports on the authority of others. So much for the statements of Pytheas, who tells us besides, that after he had returned thence, he traversed the whole coasts of Europe from Gades to the Don. Polybius asks, 'How is it possible that a private individual, and one too in narrow circumstances, could ever have performed such vast expeditions by sea and land?[3] And how could Eratosthenes, who hesitates whether he may rely on his statements in general, place such entire confidence in what the writer relates

---

[1] The Iernis of Onomacritus (who is supposed to have written about B.C. 535, in the days of Pisistratus). Its authenticity is defended by Ruhnkenius (Epist. Crit. 2), and by Archbishop Usher (Ecclesiar. Antiq., chap. 16), while Camden (Britan.) has claimed the island to be England. Adrian Junius, a Dutch poet of the sixteenth century, quoted by Moore (History, chap. 1), thus alluded to Ireland having been known to the Argonauts :

> " Illa ego sum Graiis olim glacialis Ierne
> Dicta, et Jasoni puppis bene cognita navis."

We shall afterwards find Sibbald identifying Ierne with Strathearn.

[2] Consult the paper " On the Stade as a Linear Measure " by W. Martin Leake, Esq., Journal of the R.G.S., vol. ix. of 1839, pp. 1-25. The word Stadium or Stade does not appear in the index of the first twenty volumes ; and this is only one instance of the carelessness with which an essential addition to the Journal has been drawn up.

[3] We may ask in our turn what prevented him travelling with traders ?

concerning Britain, Gades, and Iberia?' Says he, 'It would have been better had Eratosthenes trusted to the Messenian (Euhemerus or Evemerus) rather than to this writer. The former merely pretends to have sailed into one [unknown] country, viz., Panchæa, but the latter that he has visited the whole of the north of Europe, as far as the ends of the earth ; which statement, even had it been made by Mercury, we should not have believed. Nevertheless Eratosthenes, who terms Euhemerus a Bergæan, gives credit to Pytheas, although even Dicærchus would not believe him.'"

In book ii., chap. 5, § 8, we have a further notice of Thule :

"It is true that Pytheas Massiliensis affirms that the farthest country north of the British Islands is Thule ; for which place, he says, the summer tropic and the Arctic circle is all one. But he records no other particulars concerning it ; [he does not say] whether Thule is an island, or whether it continues habitable up to the point where the summer tropic becomes one with the Arctic circle. For myself, I fancy that the northern boundaries of the habitable earth are greatly south of this. Modern writers tell us of nothing beyond Ierne which lies just north of Britain, where the people live miserably and like savages, on account of the severity of the cold. It is here, in my opinion, the bounds of the habitable earth ought to be fixed."

Finally, in book iv., chap. 5, § 5, we have the most important notice of all :

"The description of Thule is still more uncertain on account of its secluded situation ; for they consider it the northernmost of all lands, of which the names are known. The falsity of what Pytheas has related concerning this and neighbouring places, is proved by what he has asserted of well-known countries. For if, as we have shown, his descriptions of these is in the main incorrect, what he says of far distant countries is still more likely to be false. *Nevertheless, as far as astronomy and mathematics are concerned,*[1] *he appears to have reasoned correctly that people bordering on the frozen zone would be destitute of cultivated fruits and almost deprived of the domestic animals ;* that their food would consist of millet, herbs, fruits, and roots ; and that where there was corn and honey they would make drink of these. That having no bright sun they would thresh their corn and store it in vast granaries, threshing-floors being useless on account of the rain and want of sun."

The whole question evidently hinges upon the credibility of Pytheas Massiliensis, who travelled about the time of Alexander the Great. It has been ably argued, pro and con, by a host of writers, and in our day by the late Sir G. C. Lewis (Astronomy of the Ancients, p. 467, et seq.), and by Sir John Lubbock (Prehistoric Times, p. 59). But the dispute has not been settled. I would remark that the old traveller's account is consistent enough.

---

[1] Hipparchus ad Arat. (i. 5 ; confer Plut., iii. 17), also attests the scientific worth of Pytheas, and mentions how he explained the tides by lunar phases.

He appears to place Thule under N. lat. 66° (assuming, as Strabo does, the tropic at 24°), a parallel which would pass through the north of Iceland. He is quite right about the absence of fruits. His spongy matter may have been ice-brash, Medusæ, the German meer-lungen, or even pumice-stone, which modern travellers have found floating in such quantities upon the sea, within reach of volcanoes, that their movements were arrested. We read that about a month before the eruption of A.D. 1783, a submarine vent burst forth at a distance of nearly seventy miles in a south-westerly direction off Cape Reykjanes, and ejected such immense quantities of pumice that the surface of the ocean was covered with it to the distance of 150 miles, and the spring ships were impeded in their course. Also when Herodotus, a Greek—whose world embraced the Eridanus or Amber River, the Tin Isles, the Arimaspians and the Hyperboreans—could confound snow with feathers, Pytheas, a Marseillais, might be allowed some latitude in describing glaciers. Poverty has not prevented the most audacious journeys; and discovery has been mainly the work of individuals. Geminus (Isagoge, etc., cap. 5) opines that Pytheas was taken to Iceland against his will. The barbarians showed him where the sun set on the shortest day, and rose again after a short interval. Then the sea began to thicken "pulmonis marini (πνεύμονι θαλατ-τίῳ) simile." He afterwards heard that where the sun does not set, is the uttermost part of the world, and cannot be travelled over. Greek *outrecuidance* evidently hated to be taught by a kind of Gaul like Pytheas. Strabo, with his captious, bilious, and acrid criticism, is wrong, and Pytheas is right, in a highly important part of the question, the inhabitability of the island. In fact, sundry modern writers have declared that, as far as we have the means of judging, Strabo's predecessors, Pytheas and Eratosthenes, were more correctly informed than he was concerning the geography of the western parts of Europe.[1] The learned

---

[1] See Rerum Script. Hiberniæ (Prolog., i., xii.), quoted at the end of this section. Of Pytheas we know little, except that he was a Phocæan or Massilian Greek, who is supposed to have made two voyages between B.C. 350 and B.C. 300. In the first, he sailed round Albion and reached Thule. In the second, he set out from Gadira (Cadiz) to the Tanais, which is popularly supposed to have been the Elbe. Both his works, "On the Ocean," and the "Periplus," are lost. Even Strabo, who seems to have had "that charlatan Pytheas on the brain," does not deny his knowledge of astronomy, mathematics, and navigation.

Isaac Casaubon (Commentaries upon Strabo) thus decides the question clean against his author: "Thule—non esse aliam quæ Islandia hodie dicitur, facile doctis viris assentior." He adds that Eratosthenes held Pytheas to be an oracle, but when Polybius and others found his geography loose in points familiar to the Greeks, they pronounced him a liar, and rejected all he wrote.

I must therefore conclude that Pytheas, with all his fables, by Thule meant Iceland, and Iceland only; moreover, that he had acquired some knowledge of the island. Indeed Gosselin opined that both Pytheas and Eratosthenes had had access to the memoirs of some unknown ancient people to whom Europe and its seas were as well known as to ourselves. He argues that this people could not have been Babylonians, Phœnicians, Carthaginians, nor Egyptians. Bailly (Hist. de l'Astr. An., 1-3), entertaining a similar opinion, supposes them, after the fashion of the day, to be Antediluvians.

## MELA.

Pomponius Mela (A.D. 41-54; De Situ Orbis, iii. 6) is our next authority. After mentioning Britannia and Iverna, the thirty islands of the Orcades, the seven Hæmodæ (Shetlands) fronting Germany,[1] and the Scandinavian Isle held by the Teutons,[2] he says:

---

G. G. Bredow (Untersuchungen, etc., ii. 122-129, Altona, 1800), C. H. Tzschuckius (P. Melæ, lib. tres, Lipsiæ, 1806, vol. iii., pp. 223-230), and J. I. Pontanus (Chorographica Daniæ Descriptio, Amstelodami, 1631, folio, p. 741), give many references to Pytheas. See also Histoire Littéraire de France, i. 71, et seq.; Bougainville (Mémoires de Paris, xix. 146); D'Anville (Mém. de Paris, xxxii. 436, and his objections to the traveller having visited Iceland, 50, 441); Murray (Nov. Comm. Soc. Goetting, vi. 59-63, 82-86); Fournier (Hydrographie, 322, et seq.); and Wagner (Ad Guthrie Allgem. Welt. Gesch., xvi. 4). Forbiger (Handbuch der Alt. Geog., iii., Leip. 1848) also quotes a multitude of authors, including Mannert, Humboldt, and Lelewel (Pytheas u. die Geo. Sein. Zeit., s. 30).

[1] These are the Acmodæ of Pliny (iv. 30), which can only be the Shetlands. Salmasius identifies the Acmodæ, Hæmodæ, and Hebrides. Camden makes them different, and refers the Acmodæ to the Baltic. Parisot informs us that off the West Cape of Skye and the isle of North Uist (the nearest of the Hebrides to the Shetlands) there is a great gulf, which, being full of islands, is still called Mamaddy or Maddy—hence, possibly, the Greek Ἁι Μαδδάι, and the Latin Memodæ. According to Dr Charnock, the name in Keltic may be translated the "black head or hill," or the "hill of God."

[2] Mela's "Scandinovia" is one of six islands which are described rather as parts of a great peninsula than as regular "insulæ." Amongst their Sarmatian population are the Oænæ (egg-eaters), the Hippopodæ (horse-feet), and the Panoti (all-ears), whose existence is attested by credible travellers (Cf. p. 165, Geografia di Pomponio Mela, by Giovanni Francesco Muratori, Torino, Stamperia Reale, 1855).

"Thule fronts the seaboard of the Belcæ (alii Belgæ and Bergæ),[1] an island celebrated in the Greek poetry and in our own.    There, as the sun rises to set afar
off, the nights are indeed short; but during winter, as in other places, obscure;
in summer they are light, because throughout that season (the sun), already
raising himself higher (above the horizon), despite not being seen, yet illuminates
the nearest parts by his approaching splendour.    At the solstices there is no
darkness, because then (the sun), becoming more manifest, shows not only his
rays, but the greater part" (of his disc).

## PLINY.

The next authority is Pliny (nat. A.D. 23, ob. A.D. 79), who
makes Thule the northernmost British island.    Both he and
Cæsar (Bell. Gall., v. 13), placing Mona about N. lat. 66°, declare
that the sun does not set in summer, but perpetually disappears
during the winter solstice.    To the former phase Cæsar assigns
thirty days, Pliny six months (senis mensibus).    The great
natural philosopher mentions the Massilian traveller without
abusing him:

"Pytheas informs us that this is the case (i.e., the day lasting six months, and
the night being of equal length) in the island of Thule, which is six days' sail
from the north of Britain" (Nat. Hist., vol. i., book ii., chap. 77, Bostock and
Riley, Bohn, 1835).

In book iv., chap. 30, occurs:

"The most remote of all that we find mentioned is Thule, in which, as we
have previously stated, there is no night at the summer solstice, when the sun is
passing through the sign of Cancer; while, on the other hand, at the winter
solstice there is no day."

Again (loc. cit.):

"There are writers also who make mention of some other islands, Scandia,
namely, Dumna, Bergos, and, greater than all, Nerigos (or Nerigo, Noreg, i.e.,
Norway), from which persons embark for Thule.    At one day's sail from Thule,
is the Frozen Ocean, which by some is called the Cronian Sea."

Finally, in book vi., chap. 39, we find:

"The last of all is the Scythian parallel,[2] which runs from the Riphæan range

---

[1] Camden suggests that "Belcarum" was a clerical error for "Bergarum."    But
Mela places Bergæ on the confines of Scythia and Asia, and he joins the Caspian
with the Northern Ocean (iii. 5).

[2] To understand the full significance of this sentence, we must consult the
context.    The first "additional parallel," whose longest day was sixteen hours,

to Thule, in which, as we have already stated, the year is divided into days and nights alternately of six months' duration."

With these passages before us, it is easy to understand why popular writers generally assume Pliny's Thule to be the Shetland Isles. But he evidently confirms the account of Pytheas, and adds the significant detail about the Cronian or Frozen Sea. It is well established that the ocean south of Iceland is not icy, whilst the northern and western shores are often frost-bound.

## PTOLEMY.

Claudius Ptolemy, the Pelusian (flor. A.D. 159-161) notices $\Theta o\acute{v}\lambda\eta$ in nine places. After correcting (book i., chap. 20, §§ 7, 8,[1] = p. 17 [2]) the errors of Maximus of Tyre, he says (book i., chap. 24, § 4, = p. 19) : " Consequently also the parallel passing through Thule shall be laid down as $\nu$ $\beta'$ (52) sections from $\eta$ to $\zeta$ $\eta$, along the lines of latitude $\xi$, $o$, $\pi$." The same chapter (§ 6, = p. 20) tells us, " Also shall be comprehended the interval between $o$ and $\kappa$ southwards, that is, between the parallels passing through Thule and through Rhodes $\kappa$ $\zeta$ (27) sections." Thirdly, the same chapter (§ 17, = p. 22) continues: " $\kappa$, through which shall be described the line (of latitude) defining the north, and falling on the island of Thule." Fourthly, in the same (§ 20, = p. 22), we find : " And as $\tau\grave{o}$ $\mu\hat{\eta}\kappa os$ (the longitude) is commensurable with $\tau\grave{o}$ $\pi\lambda\acute{a}\tau os$ (the latitude), since upon the sphere whose great circle is five, of these the parallel passing through Thule is about $\bar{\beta}$ and $\delta'$ " $(2\frac{1}{4})$.

Book ii., chap. 3, § 32, = p. 28, establishes the position of Thule :

" And above them (the Orkades) is the (island of) Thule, whose—

---

ran through ·" the Daci and part of Germany, and the Gallic provinces, as far as the shores of the ocean." The second traversed " the country of the Hyperborei and the island of Britannia, the longest day being seventeen hours in length." The third is far more applicable to Iceland than to the Shetland or Færoe groups.

[1] C. Ptolemæi Geographia, edidit Carolus Fredericus Augustus Nobbe, Lipsiæ, 1843. A correct text.

[2] C. Ptolemæi, etc., libri octo, ex Bilibaldi Pirckeymheri translatione, Lugduni. 1535. When may geographical students hope to see a portable English translation of Ptolemy, and be saved the mortification of carrying about this uncomfortable folio? The work was proposed many years ago to the Royal Geographical Society, and was rejected, I believe, on the grounds of Ptolemy being a mathematical writer. The paragraphs in the text refer to the Greek, the pages to the Latin translation.

| | | | | | | |
|---|---|---|---|---|---|---|
| Western parts are in | . | . | E. long. (Ferro?) 29° | | N. lat. | 63° |
| The Easternmost being in | . | . | ,, | ,, | 31° 40' ,, | 63° |
| ,, Northernmost ,, | . | . | ,, | ,, | 30° 20' ,, | 63° 15' |
| ,, Southernmost ,, | . | . | ,, | ,, | 30° 20' ,, | 62° 40' |
| And the Mid Isle in, | . | . | ,, | ,, | 30° 20' ,, | 63° " |

The sixth book (chap. 16, § 1, = p. 113) tells us:

" Serica is bounded west by Scythia beyond the Imaus mountain, according to the line laid down ; on the north by an unknown land on the parallel passing through Thule ; on the east by regions also unknown, along the meridional line whose limits are :

$$\text{" E. long. } 180° \qquad \text{N. lat. } 63°$$
$$\text{,, } \quad 18° \qquad\qquad \text{,, } \quad 35° \text{ "}$$

Again we find (book vii., chap. 5, § 12, = p. 125):

" But the northern part is bounded by the parallel which is north of the equinoctial line 63 parts (*i.e.*, N. lat. 63°), and this is described through Thule, the Island. So that the breadth of the known world is 76° 25', or in round numbers, 80 degrees." [1]

Lastly (book viii., chap. 3, § 3, = p. 131) we are told:

" But the (Island) Thule has its greatest day of twenty equinoctial hours, and from Alexandria it is distant two equinoctial hours to the west." [2]

Thus Ptolemy's Thule is a long narrow island, 160 by 35 miles, and his description, despite the times in which he wrote, is applicable rather to North Britain and even to Iceland, than to Scandinavia. He is consistent in his assertions : (1.) That Thule is an island; (2.) That its northernmost point extends to 3° 17' south of the Polar circle (66° 32'); (3.) That it lies north of the Orcades.[3] Manifestly we cannot rely upon the longitudes, Ptolemy's first meridian being still *sub judice*. The late Mr

---

[1] Ptolemy assumes the southernmost part of the old world to be in S. lat. 16° 20' instead of S. lat. 34° 51' 12" (Cape Agulhas). Already in 1800, G. G. Bredow (loc. cit.), recognising the imperfect graduation, had reduced Ptolemy's N. lat. 57° to N. lat. 51° 15', and N. lat. 62° to N. lat. 55° 15'.

[2] Lemprière and other popular books, contain the following curious assertion : " Ptolemy places the middle of his Thule in 63° of latitude, and says that at the time of the equinoxes, the days were *twenty-four hours*, which could not have been true at the equinoxes, but must have referred to the solstices, and therefore this island is supposed to have been in 66° latitude, that is, under the Polar circle." La Martinière, of whom more presently (sub voce Thule), makes no such blunder. Ptolemy gives N. lat. 63° and *twenty hours*, in which he is followed by Agathemerus.

[3] It is suggested (Notes on Richard of Cirencester) that beginning with the Novantum Chersonesis (Mull of Galloway ?), in E. long. (Ferro ?) 21°, the latitudes were mistaken for the longitudes, hence Cape Orcas (Duncansby Head ?) was thrown to the east, E. long. (Ferro ?) 31° 20'.

Hogg suggested[1] that the zero of longitude was not, as usually assumed, at Ferro in the Fortunate Islands (W. long. (G.) 24° 23′ 40″ to 24° 34′), but at " S. Antonio, Cape Verd Islands " (read São Antão[2]) in W. long. (G.) 25° 2′ 40″ to 25° 25′ 45″—a change which would give in round numbers a difference of fifty miles.[3] Nothing more need be added upon this head. Pytheas and Eratosthenes evidently referred to Iceland; Mela did the same in making it front Bergen; Pliny heard of it when he relates that from Nerigos persons embark for Thule; and neglecting Ptolemy's latitudes and longitudes, his description tallies best with Iceland.

## III.

## THULE, PART OF GREAT BRITAIN.

Of Thule applied to some part of Great Britain we have a multitude of instances, which are ably and lengthily brought together by Sir Robert Sibbald.[4] Our writer begins by establishing the fact that the ancients connected the idea of darkness with the north.

" These places of Homer πρὸς ζόφον (ad caliginem), and οὐ γὰρ ἴδμεν ὅπου ζόφου (neque enim scimus ubi sit caligo), are by Strabo (ii. § 6) interpreted of the north, "Nescimus ubi sit Septentrio " (We know not where the north is).

He quotes Tibullus (nat. circ. B.C. 54; iv. 1, 154):

" Illic et densâ tellus absconditur umbrâ."

And Pub. Papinius Statius (nat. circ. A.D. 61; Sylv., iii., Ad Claudiam Uxorem, v. 20):

" Vel super Hesperiæ vada caligantia Thiles."

---

[1] " On some old maps of Africa, etc.," a valuable paper read before the British Association, August 1863 : Herr Kiepert is greatly indebted to it.

[2] The error "S. Antonio," for " São Antão," is not the learned Mr Hogg's ; it is common to Norie and other books on navigation.

[3] It is regretable that geographers lost the excellent opportunity offered by the Vienna Weltausstellung of 1873, to determine in congress a single *point de départ* of longitude for the civilised world. Now each nation has the pretension of making a first meridian of its own, consequently whilst geographical readers have a fair conception of latitude, that of longitude is especially hazy. I only hope we shall not lose sight of the desideratum in the Geographical Congress of Paris (1875).

[4] " A Discourse concerning the Thule of the Ancients," by Sir Robert Sibbald, vol. iii., Gough's Camden (Britannia, etc.) of 1787. See also Gibson's edition of Camden, Lond. 1695, and Frankfort edition, 1602.

Again (Sylv., iv. 4, 62):

"—— aut nigræ littora Thule."

And again (Sylv., v. 1, 90, 91):

"—— quantum ultimus orbis,
Cesserit et refluo circumsona gurgite Thule."

Strabo (book ii., chap. 4, § 8) is quoted to show by Pytheas, that Thule is "one of those islands that are called British," and we have seen Strabo's own opinion that it lies farther south than where the Massilian placed it. He quotes Catullus (B.C. 87; Ad Furium Carm., xii.):

"Sive trans altas gradietur Alpes,
Cæsaris visens monumenta magni,
Gallicum Rhenum, horribilesque ultim-
osque Britannos ;"

and Horace (i. 35, 30):

"Serves iturum Cæsarem in ultimos
Orbis Britannos ;"

to show that the Britons were the northernmost people then known. Due use is made of Silius Italicus (nat. circ. A.D. 25 ; Punic, lib. xvii., 417, 418):

"Cœrulus haud alitur cum dimicat incola Thule,
Agmina falcifero circumvenit arcta covino,"

for it appears from Cæsar's Commentaries, that the bluish colour and the fighting out of hooked chariots were in use among the inhabitants of Britain. Pliny also (N. H., iv. 30) treats of Thule in the same chapter where he treats of the British Isles, "ultima omnium quæ memoratum est Thule." Tacitus says (Agric. Vita, cap. x.) when the Roman navy sailed about Britain, "dispecta est et Thule."[1]

---

[1] The full passage of Tacitus is, "Hanc oram novissimi maris (the Deucale-donian Sea) tunc primum Romana classis circumvecta, insulam esse Britanniam affirmavit, ac simul incognitas ad id tempus insulas, quas Orcades vocant, invenit domuitque. Dispecta est et Thule" (alii "Thyle" and "Tyle") "quadam trans : nix et hiems appetebat ; sed mare pigrum et grave remigantibus : perhibent, ne ventis quidem perinde attolli ; credo quod rariores terræ montesque, causa ac materia tempestatum et profunda moles continui maris tardius impellitur." Plutarch tells us (Life of Cæsar) that the very existence of such a place as Britain had been doubted. When Diodorus Siculus wrote (temp. J. Cæsar and Augustus), the British Isles were amongst the regions least known to the world : "Ἥκιστα πέπτωκεν ὑπὸ τὴν κοινὴν ἀνθρώπων ἐπίγνωσιν" (lib. iii.). Eusebius (nat. circ. A.D. 264) tells us in his Chronicon, "Claudius de Britannis triumphavit, et Orcades insulas

'Ireland, properly so called, was the first of the British Isles which got the name Thule, being the first that the Carthaginians met with as they steered their course from Cadiz to the west; and hence it is that Statius (Ad Claud. Uxor., lib. iii., v. 20) calls Thule 'Hesperia,' and it seems to be the same that is said by (the pseudo) Aristotle (Liber de Mirab. Auscult) to have been discovered by the Carthaginians when he speaks thus (lxxxv.):

"'In the sea beyond the Pillars of Hercules, they say, the Carthaginians found a fertile island uninhabited, abounding in wood and navigable rivers, and stored with very great plenty of fruits (*fructibus*) of all sorts,[1] distant several days' voyage from the continent.'

And Bochartus (Geog. Sac.) confirms this by what he observes, that an ancient author, Antonius Diogenes,[2] who wrote twenty-four books of the strange things (or Incredibilities) related of Thule,[3] not long after the time of Alexander the Great, had his history from the Ciparis Tables, dug at Tyre out of the tombs of Mantinea and Dercilis (Dercyllides), who had gone from Tyre to Thule, and had stayed some time there. But though this be the first Thule discovered by the Carthaginians, yet it is not that mentioned by the Roman writers, for they speak of the Thule which the Romans were in and made a conquest of, but it is certain they were never in Iceland properly so called.

---

Romano adjecit imperio." Orosius (circ. A.D. 415) adds (vii. 6, Hist. Adver. Pag., libri vii.), "Cognitæ insulæ erant forte et ante Claudium et sub Claudio, non quidem armis Romanis, sed mercatoribus, aut etiam eruditis, Mela teste." And Mela, who wrote in the days of Claudius, assures us (iii. 6), "Triginta sunt Orcades angustis inter se diductæ spatiis."

[1] The mention of fruits in this passage banishes the idea of Iceland.

[2] Diogenes of Apollonia flourished in the fifth century B.C., and also wrote περὶ φύσεως—concerning nature—a treatise on physical science. In the days when Hanno the Carthaginian, passing the Mediterranean Straits, explored the western coast of Africa, an event usually placed in the fifth century B.C., although Gosselin (Recherches sur la Géographie des Anciens) goes back as far as the tenth, Himilco (Pliny, N. H., ii. 67) was also sent to explore the remote parts of Europe. Sailing along the shores of Gadir, Tartessus (Tarshish), and Gallicia, he reached the Tin Isles. His Periplus, originally deposited in a temple at Carthage, was used by Dionysius, and was versified by Rufus Festus Avienus in the fourth century, in his iambic poem "De Oris Maritimis." He himself says :

" Hæc nos ab imis Punicorum annalibus,
Prolata longo tempore edidimus tibi."

And Dodwell justly observes (Dissert. de Peripli Hannonis Ætati): "Ea causa satis verisimilis esse potuit, cur tamdiu Græcos latuerit Himilco, etiam eos qui collegæ meminerint Hannonis."

[3] Τά ὑπερ Θούλης ἄπιστα. An abridgment is preserved by the learned Patriarch Photius in his Myriobiblion seu Bibliotheca.

"That they were in Thule appears from Statius (Sylv., v. 2, 54):

> " '—— quantusque nigrantem
> Fluctibus occiduis fessoque Hyperione Thulen
> Intrârit mandata gerens.'

Now the father of Crispinus, to whom he writes, was Vectius Bolanus, governor of Britain, A.D. 69, under Vitellius (as Tacitus informs us), which is clearly proved by the same poet (Sylv., v. 2, 140-143):

> " 'Quod si te magno tellus frenata parenti
> Accipiat—
> Quanta Caledonios attollet gloria campos !
> Cum tibi longævus referet trucis incola terræ ;
> Hic suetus dare jura parens.'

The words 'Caledonios' and 'trucis incola terræ' clearly show that by Thule is meant the north part of Britain, which was then possessed by the Picts, designed by the name 'Caledonios,' and by the Scots, designed as 'trucis incola terræ,' the same epithet that Claudian (De Bell. Get., 416) gives to the Scots in these verses :

> " 'Venit et extremis legio prætenta Britannis,
> Quæ Scoto dat fræna truci, ferroque notatas
> Perlegit exsangues Picto moriente figuras.'

And of this north part of Britain that verse of Juvenal (Sat., xv. 112):

> " 'De conducendo loquitur jam rhetore Thule,'[1]

is also to be understood. Of this the best exposition is taken from Tacitus (Agric., xxi.) :

> " 'Jam verò principum filios, liberalibus artibus erudire, et ingenia Britannorum studiis Gallorum anteferre, ut qui modò linguam Romanum abnuebant, eloquentiam concupiscerent.'

"Claudian (De III. Consul. Honor., 52-56) yet more particularly gives the name of Thule to the north part of Britain :

> " 'Facta tui numerabat avi, quem littus adustæ
> Horrescit Libyæ, ratibusque impervia Thule.
> Ille leves Mauros, nec falso nomine Pictos
> Edomuit, Scotumque vago mucrone secutus,
> Fregit Hyperboreas remis audacibus undas.'

---

[1] Juvenal here ironically describes the progress of Greek and Roman letters towards the barbarous north. The Britons are learning eloquence from the Gauls, and even Thule thinks of hiring a rhetorician.

And in these lines (De IV. Consul. Honor., 26-33) :

> " ' Ille, Caledoniis posuit qui castra pruinis,
> Qui medios Libyæ sub casside pertulit æstus,
> Terribilis Mauro, debellatorque Britanni
> Littoris, ac pariter Boreæ vastator et Austri.
> Quid rigor æternus cœli, quid sidera prosunt ?
> Ignotumque fretum ?  Maduerunt Saxone fuso,
> Orcades: incaluit Pictorum sanguine Thule :
> Scotorum cumulos flevit glacialis Ierne, '

where, by placing the Moors and Britons as the remotest people
then known, and mentioning the Scots and Picts as the inhabitants of Thule and Ierne, he demonstrates clearly that
Thule is the north part of the isle of Britain, inhabited by the
Scots and Picts.   For this Ierne, or, as some read it, ' Hyberne,'
can no way be understood of Ireland properly so called; first,
because Ireland can never deserve the epithet ' glacialis,'[1] since,
by the testimony of the Irish writers, the snow and ice continue
not any time there; secondly, the Romans were never in Ireland,
whereas, according to the above-mentioned verses, Theodosius
passed over the Friths of Forth and Clyde, called by him
' Hyperboreæ undæ,' and entered Strathearn, which to this day
bears the name Ierne; in which Roman medals are found, and
the Roman camps and military ways are to be seen—the un-
doubted testimonies of their being there; and therefore is so to
be understood in the same poet's lines upon Stilicho (see De
Laud. Stilich., lib. ii., 250-254), who was employed in the British
war :

> " ' Me quoque vicinis pereuntem gentibus, inquit,
> Me juvit Stilicho, totam cum Scotus Iernen
> Movit, et infesto spumavit remige Tethys.
> Illius effectum curis, ne tela timerem
> Scotica, ne Pictum tremerem.'

Now, Tethys in these verses, and the ' undæ Hyperboreæ ' in
the verses before mentioned, cannot be understood of the sea
between Scotland and Ireland, for Ireland lies to the south of
the Roman province, and the situation of the Scots' and Picts'

---

[1] For " glacialis," see Adrian Junius before quoted.  The high-sounding and
convenient epithet seems to have been applied to Ierne, as "ultima" to Thule.
If the Romans did not hold Ireland, at any rate they knew it well: " Melius aditus
portusque, per commercia et negotiatores cognita " (Tacit. Agricol., xxiv.).

country is to the north of it; for it was separated by the two Friths of Forth and Clyde from the Roman province, which clearly shows it was to be understood of them: the same thing that is also imported by the words 'Hyperboreas undas' and 'remis;' for these cannot be understood of the Irish Sea, which is to the south of the Roman province, and is very tempestuous, and cannot so well be passed by oars as the Friths of Forth and Clyde. And the same poet has put this beyond all doubt (in the verses before quoted, De Bell. Get., 416).

"For were it to be understood of the Irish Sea, then the wall and the 'prætenturæ' (*legio prœtenta*) should have been placed upon the Scottish shore that was over against that country, which is called Strathearn now, and is the true Ierne not only mentioned by Claudian, but also by Juvenal in these verses (I. Sat., ii. 160):

> " ' Arma quidem ultra
> Litora Juvernæ promovimus, et modò captas
> Orcadas, ac minimâ contentos nocte Britannos.'

"That this Thule was a part of Britain, the Roman writers seem to be very clear, especially Silius Italicus in the verses before quoted.

" But to make it appear which part of Britain the Thule was which is mentioned by the Romans, it will be fit to see to which part of Britain the epithets attributed by writers to Thule do best agree. First, then, it was a remote part, ' ultima Thule,' as if this were the remotest part of Britain; so Tacitus (Agric., xxx.) brings in Galgacus expressing it, ' We, the uttermost bounds of land and liberty,' etc. Then Thule was towards the north, and so was this country with respect to the Roman province; and, thirdly, it might deserve the name Thule (darkness), because of its obscure and dark aspect, it being in those days all overgrown with woods. Fourthly, the length of the day annexed to Thule; and, upon this account, it must be the country to the north and to the east of Ierne, by the verses of Juvenal before mentioned (V. Sat., xv. 112).

"Another property of Thule given by Tacitus (loc. cit.) is that about it is 'mare pigrum et grave remigantibus,' which agrees indeed to the sea upon the north-east part of Scotland, but not for the reason that Tacitus gives, *i.e.*, for want of winds, but because of the contrary tides which drive several ways, and stop not only boats with oars, but ships under sail.

"But Thule is most expressly described to be this very same country that we treat of by Conradus Celtes:

> " ' Orcadibus quâ cincta suis Tyle et glacialis
>   Insula.'

"This same epithet Claudian (see p. 15) gives to Ierne, when he calls it ' Glacialis Ierne; ' and this Thule he makes to be encompassed ' suis Orcadibus,' which isles lie over-against it; and a little after he gives it the like epithet with ' mare pigrum.'

> " ' Et jam sub septem spectant vaga rostra Triones
>   Quà Tyle est rigidis insula cincta vadis.'

And afterwards he makes the Orcades to lie over-against this Thule, and seems to have in his eye the skerries and weels in Pictland (Pentland?) Frith in these lines:

> " ' Est locus Arctoo quà se Germania tractu
>   Claudit, et in rigidis Tyle ubi surgit aquis,
>   Quam juxta infames scopuli et petrosa vorago
>   Asperat undisonis saxa pudenta vadis
>   Orcadas has memorant dictas a nomine Græco.' [1]

"But the clearest testimony of all we owe to Arngrimus Jonas (Specimen Islandicum, A.D. 1593),[2] when he brings in the verses of Fortunatus (lib. viii., cap. 1), who sings of St Hilarion (ob. A.D. 372):

> " ' Eloquii currente rotâ penetravit ad Indos,
>   Ingeniumque potens ultima Thule colit.'

---

[1] In Icelandic " Orkn " and " Orkn-selr " are applied to a seal. (Compare Lat. *orca*, supposed to be the grampus : Cleasby.) Pliny makes *orca* a kind of dolphin (*D. orca*), and *orec* or *orc* is the Gaelic form; hence Cape Orcas, which is popularly identified with Dunnet Head, the extreme northern point of Scotland. We have no need to derive " Orkneys " from εἴρκω (*coercio*), these isles breaking and restraining the force of the raging waves; or from " Erick " or " Orkenwald," or any other " Pictish prince famous there at its first plantation."

[2] The Crymogæa (Sive De Reb. Isl., Hamb. 1593) of this learned Icelander will be found analysed in Purchas, vol. iii., and Hakluyt, vol. i.   His principal argument is very unsatisfactory : " If Iceland is taken to have been the classical Thule, it must have been inhabited in the days of Augustus, which is contrary to the chronicles of the island."   This author's chief objection is thus stated by himself : " Si etenim Islandia idem esset cum Thule, rueret totum hujus narrationis fundamentum de Islandia A.C. 874 habitari primum cæpta ; " an objection which will be considered elsewhere.   Meanwhile I prefer the opinion of the equally learned Pontanus, who says of Iceland : " Non heri aut hodie quod dicitur fuit frequentata, sed habuit indigenas suos multa ante sæcula."

"And then reckoning up the several nations enlightened by him, he mentions Britain amongst the rest:

> " 'Thrax, Italus, Scytha, Persa, Indus,
> Geta, Daca, Britannus.' [1]

"To which he adds, 'From whence it may fairly enough be inferred that either Britain or (as Pliny will have it) some island of Britain was the *ultima Thule.*' And afterwards, 'To confirm the opinion of Pliny and his followers, who will have some of the British Isles, or particularly, that farthest in the Scottish dominions to be Thule, I must acknowledge that the history of the kings of Norway says the same thing, in the life of King Magnus, who, in an expedition to the Orcades and Hebrides and into Scotland and Britain, touched also at the Island of Thule and subdued it.'

"By all this, I think, it appears sufficiently that the north-east part of Scotland, which Severus the emperor and Theodosius the Great infested with their armies, and in which, as Boethius[2] shows us, Roman medals were found, is undoubtedly the Thule mentioned by the Roman writers; and this also, if we believe the learned Arngrimus Jonas, was meant by Ptolemy, where he saith, that, to the twenty-first parallel drawn through Thule by Ptolemy, the latitude answers to 55° 36', so that our country in those ancient times passed under the name of Thule and Hibernia, and the 'Hiberni et Picti, incolæ Thules' are the same people who were afterwards called Scots.[3]

"I shall only add one remark more, and that is, that we need not have recourse for the rise of the name Scot, to the fabulous

---

[1] According to Dr Charnock, he speaks only of the Sacæ, the Persa, and the Britannus.

[2] Dr Bosworth (Anglo-Saxon Dict.) quotes Boethius (29, 11): "Oth thæt iland the we hatath Thyle, thæt is on tham northwest ende thisses middaneardes thær ne bith nawther ne on sumera niht, ne on wintra dæg" (To the island which we call Thule, that is on the north-west end of this middle earth, where there is neither night in summer nor day in winter). Cardale (1, 166) also: "Thonne be norðan Ibernia is thæt ylemede land thæt man hæt Thila" (Thence to the north of Ibernia is that island which men call Thila). See also Orosius, 1, 2.

[3] The author here settles offhand a point disputed *ad infinitum.* Dr Charnock has shown that Scotland was at one time called Igbernia, Hibernia (the classical name of Ireland, corrupted from *iar-in*, the western isle), and from the end of the third to the beginning of the eleventh century, *Scotia* was used exclusively to indicate Ireland.

account of the monks who bring it from Scota, Pharaoh's daughter, married to Gathelus; since without that strain, if it be granted that the country was once called Thule, which in the Phœnician language signifies 'darkness,' we have a very fair reason for the name Scotia, which signifies the same in the Greek tongue. And it is very well known that it was usual with the Greeks (who next to the Phœnicians were the best navigators) not only to retain the Phœnician name of the place, but likewise to give one in their own language of the same import; and since the learned Bochartus has very ingeniously deduced the Greek name of the whole island, Βρετανικὴ, from Bratanack and Barat anac,[1] in the Phœnician tongue signifying 'a land of tin' (which the Greeks not only reduced to their own termination, but likewise called the British isles [2] Κασσιτερίδες, that is, 'lands of tin,'[3] which is the signification of the Phœni-

---

[1] برّة النّك (Barrat el Tanak), "tanak" being the Arabic for tin.—Dr Charnock in his various writings (Local Etymology, etc.), after referring to the derivation of Britannia from the Punic ברת אנג, barat-anac, the land of tin or lead ; and the Hebrew ברא, bara, in Pihel, to create, produce ; quoting Camden, Owen, Clarke, Borlase, Bochart, Boerhave, Shaw, Bosworth, and Armstrong, gives the following suggested derivations of the name from the Keltic, viz.: from its inhabitants, the *Brython;* from *brit, brith,* of divers colours, spotted (ברד, *brd,* pl. ברדים, *brdim,* spots, spotted with colours) ; *bràith-tuinn,* (the land on) the top of the wave ; from *Yuys Prydain,* the fair island ; from *Prydyn,* son of Aez the Great; from *bri,* dignity, honour ; from *Brutus,* a fabulous king of Britain ; from *bret,* high, *tain,* a river ; but Dr Charnock inclines to derive the name from *bret-inn,* the high island. It need hardly be said that the Tin Islands (Cassiterides) contained no tin; like Zanzibar, they were probably a mere depôt where the Phœnicians met the savages of the interior.

[2] In the following verse of Catullus (Carm. 27) :

" Hunc Gallæ timent, hunc timent Britanniæ,"

we find " Britain " used to denote the whole of the British Isles.

[3] Kassiterides is Aryan not Semitic ; the metal in Sanskrit being *Kastīra,* which, like the Arabic *Khasdīr,* may be from the Greek. The Scilly islands were also called Æstrumnides, a name which occurs in R. Festus Avienus (loc. cit.):

" Ast hinc duobus in sacram, sic insulam
Dixere prisci, solibus cursus rati est.
Hæc inter undas multum cespitem jacit,
Eam que latè gens Hibernorum colit.
Propinqua rursus insula Albionum patet.
Tartesiisque in terminos Æstrumnidum
Negociandi mos erat Carthaginis
Etiam colonis, et vulgus inter Herculis
Agitans columnas hæc adibant æquora."

All this, be it remembered, is borrowed from Punic sources. Therefore Hibernia is explained by Bochart as "nihil aliud quam ultima habitatio," and Keltic Ierne is translated the " uttermost point."

cian and Greek names); we may take the same liberty to derive
the Greek name Scotia from Phœnician Thule;[1] but this is so
fully treated of in the 'Scotia Antiqua,' that I need say no
more."

To these authorities may be added Silius Italicus (lib. iii.,
597), who manifestly places "unknown Thule" about Scotland:

> " Hinc pater ignotam donabit vincere Thulen
> Inque Caledonios primus trahit agmina lucos."

R. Festus Avienus (Descr. Orb. Ter.), metaphrasing Dionysius,
treats of Thule when speaking of Britain, and yet gives "the
unknown island" an Arctic day:

> " Longa dehinc celeri si quis rate marmora currat,
> Inveniet vasto surgentem gurgite Thulen;
> Hinc cùm plaustra poli tangit Phœbeïus ignis
> Nocte sub inlustri rota solis fomite flagrat
> Continuò clarumque diem nox œucula ducit."

We have also the testimony of Richard of Cirencester (Ricardus
Coronensis, ob. circ. A.D. 1401), who tells us (De Situ Britanniæ)
that in the time of the later emperors, " Thule" was applied to
Valentia or Valentiana, the district between the wall of Severus
and the rampart of Antoninus, including the south part of Scotland, Northumberland, and a portion of Cumberland.

It might have been supposed that the distinct mention of the
Orcades and Hebrides[2] by Pliny (N. H., lib. iv., cap. 30), and
by Ptolemy (lib. ii., cap. 3, § 32, = p. 28), would have barred their
claim to the classic title. This is far from being the case.
John Brand (A Brief Description of Orkney, etc., Edin. 1701,
Pinkerton, iii., p. 782), after quoting Claudian and Conradus

---

[1] The Greeks were in the habit of borrowing their geographical terms from the
indigenæ, not from the Phœnicians. Yet Dodwell is hardly justified in rejecting
Hanno's Periplus because Greek names occur instead of Phœnician. I have
already derived their Erythræan Sea from the Sea of Edom, and the Sea of Him-
yar (of which the root is ﺣﻤﺮ, redness); and the "Mountains of the Moon"
from Unyamwezi, still shortened on the coast to Mwezi, the general name for the
moon in the great south African family of languages. Dr Charnock (Local Etymology) says, "Scotland is the land of the Scoti, who by some have been considered as identical with the Σκύθαι, Scythæ, who may have been named from their
great skill in the use of the bow, their principal weapon," and he gives O. Teut.
scutten, scuthen, archers; Gael. sciot, an arrow, dart.

[2] Surely there is no reason why Macpherson should derive Hebrides from
Ey-brides, islands of St Bride or Brigida, the Vesta of the North.

Celtes, with others who call Thule " Britannicarum insularum septentrionissimam," thus disposes of Iceland :

" I greatly doubt if ever the Romans had the knowledge of Iceland, their eagles never having come and been displayed to the north of Scotland or Orkney. ' Imperii fuerat Romani Scotia limes,' saith the great Scaliger. Ptolemy will have it to be among the Isles of Zetland ; and Boethius, our historian (Boethius, in p. 740, also in p. 755, which quotes from his life of Mainus, king of Scots), distinguisheth between a first and a second Thule, calling Ila the first, and Louisa the second, which are reckoned among the isles called Hebrides. ' Ptolemæus inter Schethlandicas insulas, quæ ultra Orchades sunt, aut proxime Norwegiam sitam vult, haud quaquam propter immensam intercapedinem intelligi potest, nos autem Ilam (Islay ?) primam Leuisam (Lewis) Hebridum præstantissimam secundam Thulen vocamus.' But I am inclined to think that although some might design a particular place by the Thule, yet generally by a synecdoche, usual with the Roman authors, they might denote all those places remote from them to the north, and especially Britain and the northern parts thereof, whither their arms did come."

The Shetland claimants take another line of argument. Eutropius (A.D. 330-375, lib. vii.) makes the emperor Claudius, during his invasion of Britain (A.D. 43) annex the Orkneys: " Quasdam insulas etiam ultra Britanniam, in oceano positas, Romano imperio addidit, quæ appellantur Orcades." Pliny, they say, endorses Pytheas Massiliensis, who writes that Thule is six days' sail north of Britain. Tacitus (loc. cit.) declares that Agricola sailed round Britain, conquered the Orcades, and saw Thule. The latter cannot be the Orcades or Hebrides, because both are mentioned by Pliny, and as their northerly point is not so far north as Cape Wrath, they could hardly be described as " ultra Britanniam." Caithness and other parts of Scotland are put out of court, since they are all to the south of Orkney, and therefore not beyond it. The Færoes and Iceland are excluded, because they were both too distant to be visited by the frail galleys of the Romans, unaided as they were, either by the compass or the science of navigation, and they could not possibly have been seen from Orkney. The same arguments apply to the Norwegian coast, which also is not an island, and is not situated north of Britain.

By this " process of elimination," we are compelled to conclude that Shetland, and only Shetland, justifies the descriptions and allusions to the " Ultima Thule" contained in the Latin classics.

It consists of islands which, viewed from afar, might be mistaken for one. It lies north of the Orkneys, from some parts of which Foula the Fair Isle, or the bluff of Fitfulhead, can be seen in clear weather. A passage of six days would be a fair average in the primitive barks of the Romans, who were never much distinguished for seamanship. The more positive proofs are the Roman coins found in the country, according to Dr Hibbert (Description of the Shetland Islands, Edin. 1822), and the ruins of a fortification in the island of Fetlar, which the same authority declares to be a Roman camp.

It need hardly be observed that all these arguments are insufficient, and that the utmost they prove is the determination by Agricola and his men, that the venerable Thule was part of the Shetlands. Probably they saw only the loom of land to the north, and identified it with the "period of earth." Possibly they might have been swayed by the verbal resemblance of Foula, which may be seen from the Orkneys: it is evidently Fogla or Fugla-ey, and the same desire to clear up a foggy point of geography, which made Abyssinian Bruce discover the sources of the Nile in the fountains of the Blue River, found Thule in "Fowl-isle."[1] The opinion, however, has found supporters. Gaspar Peucerus (De Terræ Dimensione) declares that the Ptolemeian Thule is to be recognised in the Shetlands, which he heard "the sailors call Thilensel" (Fugl-insel ?). Cellarius (Geog. Ant., ii. 4) discovers Thule in the island of Hjaltland (Shetland), or in the Færoe group, "quæ in eâdem fere latitudinem sunt." He is followed by Probus (Com. on Virgil, ii. 358), who makes Thule the farthest of the Orcades; by the philosopher Petrus Ramus (de la Ramée); by Johannes Myritius, who rather cleaves to the end of Britain; by the learned Vossius, who prefers the Hebrides or Orcades; by Buchner (Ad Tacit. Agric., cap. 10); by Camden, by Gosselin, and others. Stephanus Byzantinus says: "Thule insula magna in oceano sub Hyperboreas partes, ubi æstivus dies ex viginti horis æqualibus constat, nox verò ex quatuor. Hyberna verò dies à contrario." This calculation would place Thule three degrees south of the Polar circle, and would better suit the Færoe

---

[1] Compare "Fulham" (volucrum habitatio), the home of fowls.

archipelago (N. lat. 61° 23′ to 62° 26′ 40″). Forcellini understands Cellarius also to refer to the Færoes; De Kerguelen Tremarec (Voyages) opines for Iceland.

## IV.

## THULE = SCANDIA.

It has been seen that Pliny (Nat. Hist., iv. 16) apparently separates Norway from Thule; moreover, that Ptolemy (ii. 3) confirmed by Agatharcides and Stephanus Byzantinus (lib. i., in extremis), whilst pointing to North Britain and to Scandia, or Scandinavia, in his time held to be an island,[1] and little known to the civilised world, adds details which rather belong to Iceland. On the other hand, it is evident that during the later Roman empire, Thule was applied to Scandinavia.

Procopius, the Byzantine historian (nat. circ. A.D. 500), leaves no doubt upon this point. He devotes to it a considerable space (lib. ii., De Bello Gothico, c. 15), and his account will be little abridged. After relating how a party of Heruli, when conquered by the Longobardi, passed through the lands of the Slavini, the Varni (Οὐάρνοι, al. Harmi), and the Dani (Δάνοι, al. Dacæ), till they reached the ocean, he makes them take ship and settle at Thule:

"The island is ten times larger than Britain, and far to the north.[2] The greater part of it is desert. The inhabited region contains thirteen great peoples, each governed by its own king. A curious phenomenon is reported from that

---

[1] Celsius, indeed, arguing from the universal concensus of the classical geographers, believes in the former insularity of Scandinavia; the secular upheaval of the coast, which in parts still continues, may account for its annexation to the continent. Thus Skáni and Skáney (the -ey answering to the Latinised -avia), the modern term applied to Scania, the Scandinavia of Pliny and subsequent geographers, is still given only to the southernmost point of the great northern peninsula, the first district known to the Romans.

[2] M. Bruzen La Martinière (Grand Dictionnaire Géographique et Critique, fol., La Hage, 1738, and Venice, 1741) runs this sentence into the next, and makes the greater part of northern Thule barren. The text is the reading adopted by the splendid edition of Claudius Malvetus (Greek and Latin, Venetiis, 1729), and by the Latin translation, Basiliæ ex officinâ Ioannis Hervagii (anno 1531, pp. 92-94, and not divided into chapters). As regards the Heruli, whom Procopius calls Ἐρούλοι, we find in Stephanus Byzantinus (fifth century) Ἐλούροι; in Sidonius Apollinaris (fifth century, Carm. 7):

"Cursu Herulus, Hunnus jaculis, Francusque natatu;"

and in Zonaras (twelfth century) Ἀιρούλαι.

place: every year, about the summer solstice, the sun remains forty days above the horizon. Six months after this there is a night of forty days, a time of sorrow, when all intercourse and business are at an end. I (says Procopius) was greatly desirous of seeing this marvel for myself, but the opportunity was ever wanting. I therefore asked those who had been there how the sun rises and sets. They told me that for forty consecutive days, the sun lights the island; sometimes from the east, at other times from the west; but that when he returns to the same point where he appeared, a single day is counted. During the season of forty nights, time is measured by the moon. When thirty-five of these long and lasting nights have passed, some of the people ascend the highest mountains, and give warning to those below that after five days more they will see the sun. The Thulitæ rejoice over the good news, and celebrate in the dark a festival which in ceremony exceeds all their others. Although this happens every year, still it would appear the inhabitants apprehend a total desertion of the sun.

"Amongst the barbarian peoples of Thule, none are so savage as the Skithifini (Σκιθίφινοι, al. Scritifini). Like beasts,[1] they ignore clothes and shoes; they drink no wine, and they eat nothing which the earth grows. Both men and women, who will not take the trouble of cultivation, occupy themselves exclusively with hunting, and the forests and mountains supply them abundantly with game. They eat the flesh, and, being without flax and wool, they wear the skins, which they fasten with sinews, having no knowledge of sewing. Also, they do not bring up their offspring like other people. The children of the Thulitæ are fed upon the marrow of beasts, instead of being suckled by their mothers. When the woman has been delivered, she wraps her babe in a skin, secures it in another, places some brains in its mouth, and sets out with her man for the chase, in which both sexes equally excel. The Thulitæ adore several gods and demons, some of whom they believe to inhabit the sky, others the air; some are on the earth and in the sea, whilst others of the smaller kind, affect the rivers and springs. They often offer sacrifices and immolate all manner of victims, the most acceptable being the first man captured in war; he is sacrificed to Mars (Thor?), the most powerful of all their gods. On these occasions they do not simply slay the victim, they either hang him to a tree, or roll him over thorns, or put him to death in some other way, choosing the most cruel.

"Such are the customs of the *Thulitæ*, amongst whom are the Goths (Γαυτοί), a fecund people that gave land to the Herulian immigrants. The remnants of this race who lived amongst the Romans, after slaying their king, sent their chief worthies to the island of Thule, for the purpose of finding if any of the royal blood there remained. The deputies were successful, and chose out of many one who pleased them the most. But as he died on the way, they returned (to Thule) and brought with them one Todasius (Τοδάσιος, al. Datis); this man was accom-

---

[1] La Martinière informs us that the Skithifini, Scritifini, or Scrithifinni of Procopius were the Scritofinni of Paulus Diaconus (sixth century), and the Crefennæ or Scretofennæ of Jornandes (sixth century). This Scandinavian tribe, according to Hermanides (Descriptio Norwegiæ, p. 46), held the country afterwards called Scredevinda or Scriticivinda, extending along the coasts of the Boreal Ocean from the confines of Finmark to the beginning of White Sea, and now included in Russian Lapland. The account of Procopius also tallies with those of the ancient Lapps.

panied by his brother named Aordus ("Αορδος) and by two hundred youths of the island."

This description of Thule is evidently great Scandinavia, not little Iceland. Hence Ortilius (Thesaurus sub voc.) D'Anville, who rejects Iceland; Farnaby, Schœnning (Von Nordich. Land in Neue Allg. Welt-Gesch, vol. xiii., p. 14, et seq.); Rudbeck, who understands Sweden; Murray (loc. cit.); Wedel (Alhandlung über die "Alt-Scandinavische Gesch.," p. 32, et seq.); Schlözer (Allg. Nordisch. Gesch, pp. 14, 16), Parisot, and other geographers, have referred the descriptions of Procopius especially to the Norwegian canton still called "Tyle-mark," or "Tile-mark." Maltebrun (iii. 6) prefers Jutland, on the continent of Denmark, part of which, he hears, is still termed "Thy" or "Thy-land." Calstron believed that all Scandinavia was meant. Celtes (Schardius, Basil ed., p. 59) makes Iceland "one of the isles of the ocean," together with Scandia, Dania, Suecia, etc. Adelung (Mithridates) supports the claims of Norway. Others go as far as Lapland, and even Greenland has not been without claimants to the honour. Yet in the sixth century, Jornandes (De Origine Actuque Getarum Liber, p. 393, Basle edition of 1531), after mentioning the thirty-four Orcades, says, "Habet et in ultimo plagæ occidentalis aliam insulam nomine Thyle, de quâ Mantuanus, Italia, 'tibi serviat ultima Thyle,'" and he carefully distinguishes it from the "ampla insula nomine Scanzia."[1]

## V.

## THULE = ICELAND.

It has been shown that the accounts of Pytheas, supported by details from Pliny and Ptolemy, refer only to Iceland. They are confirmed by the following authorities. In Caius Julius Solinus (A.D. 230; 2 vols. fol., Traj. ad Rhenum, 1689), we find Thule five days' sail from Orkney, and we cannot allow less than 100 knots for the δρόμος νυχθήμερος, or a total of 500 direct geographical miles; the run from northern Orkney to the south

---

[1] "Scana," in Adam Bremensis; generally "Scandia," and popularly derived from "Schön" and "aue." According to Cleasby, the Icel. "Skáney" is said to mean "borderland," and perhaps derived from "skán," a thin border, surface, etc.

coast of Iceland being about this distance. The Polyhistor, held an oracle in the Middle Ages, adds (chap. xx., 111):

"Inter multas quæ circa Britanniam sunt insulas, Thylen ultimam esse còmmemorat. In quâ æstivo solstitio dicit esse noctem nullam. Brumali verò perinde diem nullum."[1]

Orosius, whose history (London, 8vo, 1773) extends to A.D. 417, says:

"Tylen per infinitum à cæteris separatam undique terris in medio sitam oceano vix paucis notam haberi."

Isidorus Hispalensis (A.D. 600-636; Orig. Seu Etym., xiv. 6; Opera Omnia, fol., Parisiis, 1601) appears to repeat Pliny:

"Thyle verò ultimam oceani insulam inter Septentrionem et occidentalem plagam,[2] ultra Britanniam sitam esse describit, à sole nomen habentem, quia in eâ æstivum solstitium sol faciat, et nullus ultra eam dies sit. Ultra Thylen vèro pigrum et concretum mare."

The last sentence of the bishop being emphatically true in winter. Other authorities who identify Thule with Iceland, are Cluverius (Germ. Ant., ii. 39), Harduin and Dalechamp (Ad Plin.), Bougainville (c. 1., p. 152), Hill (Ad Dionys.), Penzel (Ad Strab.), Pontanus (Chorog. Dan. Descrip., p. 74), Isaac Thilo (Dissert., Lips., A.D. 1660), Gerhard Mercator, and Mannert (Geog., i., p. 78), to mention no others. Martin (Histoire des Gaules, i. 159) takes the Gauls to Iceland.

---

[1] The whole account of Solinus is interesting enough for detailed quotation: as regards Thyle being two days distant from Caledonia, and five from the Orkneys; the numerals are supposed to be clerical errors: "Multæ et aliæ Britanniam insulæ, e quibus Thyle ultima, in qua æstivo sole de Cancri sidere faciente transitum nox pænè nulla: brumali solstitio dies adès conductus, ut ortus junctus sit occasui. A Caledoniæ promontorio Thylen petentibus bidui navagatione perfecta excipiunt Hebridæ insulæ, quinque numero, quarum incolæ nesciunt fruges, piscibus tantum et lacte vivunt. Rex unus est universis: nam quotquot sunt, omnes angusta interluvie dividuntur. Rex nihil suum habet, omnia universorum: ad æquitatem certis legibus stringitur; ac ne avaritia divertat a vero, discit paupertate justitiam, utpote cui nihil sit rei familiaris: verum alitur e publico. Nulla illi datur femina propria, sed per vicissitudines, in quamcunque commotus fuerit, usurarium sumit. Unde ei nec votum, nec spes conceditur liberorum. Secundam a continenti stationem Orcades præbent: sed Orcades ab Hebudibus porro sunt septem dierum, totidemque noctium cursu, numero tres. Vacant homine; non habent silvas, tantum junceis herbis inhorrescunt. Cetera carum undæ arenæ. Ab Orcadibus Thylen usque quinque dierum ac noctium navigatio est. Sed Thyle larga et diutina pomona copiosa est. Qui illic habitant, principio veris inter pecudes, pabulis vivunt, deinde lacte. In hiemem compascunt arborum fructus. Utuntur feminis vulgo; certum matrimonium nulli. Ultra Thylen pigrum et concretum mare."

[2] Both Ausonius (Idyl. 12) and Statius (loc. cit.) make Thule to be "Hesperia," i.e., west of Britain. On the other hand, the Geographer of Ravenna (Pre Guido? v. 31) places his Thule east of Britain.

In the ninth century we have positive evidence that Thule had returned to its oldest signification, Iceland. The monk Dicuilus, who wrote in the year 825,[1] relates that thirty years before that date (A.D. 795) he had seen and spoken with several religious who had inhabited the island of Thule between February and August. He asserts that Iceland and the Færoes had been discovered by his countrymen; and his calculation of the seasons and the days at different times of the year, together with the assertion that a day's sail thence towards the north would bring them to the Frozen Sea, shows that "Iceland, and Iceland alone, could have been the island visited by the anchorites."

The Domesday Book of the north, the "Landnámabók," whose lists of 1400 places and 3000 persons were drawn up by various authors in the twelfth century, supported, according to Mr Blackwell (note, p. 189), "by other ancient Icelandic documents," simply states (Prologus, p. 2), "Before Iceland was settled by the Northmen there were men there called by the Northmen Papæ. These men were Christians, and are thought to have come from the west, for there were found Irish books, bells (biöllur), staves (baglar), and various other things, whence it is thought that they were Westmen," Irishmen—a name still preserved in the Vestmannaeyjar archipelago. Moreover, we learn that these relics were found in Papey (the Isle of the Papæ), a rock off the eastern coast, which still bears the same name, and at Papyli, in the interior; and finally, that "the Christians left the country when the Northmen settled there"[2]—the latter being pragmatical pagans.

Mr Blackwell concludes that these people were probably fishermen from the north of Ireland and the Western Isles of Scotland, who may annually have frequented the northern seas, and made Papey one of their winter stations. Mr Dasent (i., vii.)

---

[1] Another authority was Ari Froði (Ara Multiscius), one of the writers of the Landnámabók, who also tells us (c. 2, p. 10, in Schedis de Islandiâ, Oxoniæ, 1716, 8vo) that these "hermits" chose not to live with the heathen, and for that reason went away, leaving behind their books, bells, and staves.

[2] M. Mallet's Northern Antiquities (Bohn, 1859), p. 189, note by the editor, Mr J. A. Blackwell. Mr G. W. Dasent (The Story of Burnt Njal, Edin., Edmonstone & Douglas, vi., viii.) quotes Dicuili Liber de Mensurâ Orbis Terræ, Ed. Valckenaer, Paris, 1807; and Maurer, Beiträge zur Rechtsgeschichte des germanischen Nordens, i. 35.

more justly identifies them with the Papar or Culdees (?), a class
of churchmen who have left their traces in almost every one
of the outlying islands of the west. Under the name of " Papar "
we find them in the Orkneys and Shetlands, the Færoes and
Iceland; "and to this day the term ' Papey' in all these localities
denotes the fact that the same pious monks who had followed
St Columba[1] to Iona, and who had filled the cells at Enhallow
and Egilsha and Papa, in the Orkneys, were those who, according to the account of Dicuil, had sought Thule or Iceland that
they might pray to God in peace."[2]     These Culdees were

---

[1] Or Columbanus (nat. circ. A.D. 559); he was born about forty years later than
St Columbkill.

[2] The word "Culdee" is used by Dasent. It was reserved for a sub-learned and
ultra-disputatious Icelander, Mr Eirikr Magnússon, to assert at the Anthropological Institute (November 19, 1872), that Culdee is a "general term for men of
religious and monastic living, and that the epithet is derived from ' Cultores
Dei.'  The singular is simply the Erse ' Ceile De,' or ' servant of God.'"
    The following exhaustive note upon the Culdees was kindly forwarded to me by
Dr Richard S. Charnock :

"The Culdees anciently had establishments not only in Scotland and Ireland, but also
in England and Wales.  They were numerous in Scotland, and continued there from
the ninth century to the Reformation.  Chalmers (Caledonia) says the Culdees of
Scotland are not mentioned in history till about the beginning of the ninth century
(circ. A.D. 800-815), and their first establishment was at Dunkeld, under the bishop of
that see.  They were afterwards (circ. A.D. 850) placed at St Andrews, where they
had their chief establishment for many centuries ; and it is stated by Buchanan
that Constantine III., king of Scotland, who died in A.D. 943, spent the last five years
of his life in religious retirement amongst the Culdees of that city.  Chalmers states
that before the introduction of the canons regular of St Andrews (twelfth century),
the Culdees alone acted as secular canons in cathedrals, and as dean and chapter
in the election of bishops ; and that thenceforth both orders were joined in the
right until A.D. 1272, when it was usurped by canons regular.  He also says that
the Culdees of Brechin continued for many ages to act as dean and chapter of that
diocese, and according to Jamieson (History of the Culdees) the Culdees of St Andrews
elected the bishop of that see down to the election of William Wishart (1270), when
the power was abrogated ; but in those early times it appears that the bishops in many
sees in Scotland were of the order of Culdees.  In G. Cambrensis mention is made
of Culdees in the island of Bardsey, off the Welsh coast.  The annotator of the Annals
of the Four Masters (A.D. 1479) says, ' By the Latin writers they were called Colidæi,
Culdei, Kelidei, and sometimes Deicolæ.'  The Colidei or Culdees are mentioned by
various other ancient writers, and by several Scotch historians, as monks in Scotland
as early as the fourth and fifth centuries.  But the statements of John of Fordan,
Hector Boethius, and others, are entirely contradicted by the learned Lanigan.  Smith
(Life of St Columbkill) and Jamieson (History) have maintained that they were Columbian monks, or members of that order instituted by St Columbkill at Iona, in
the Hebrides, and also in various parts of Scotland ; and they have represented these
Culdees as a very strict and religious order in those early times, from the sixth to the
twelfth century.  But Lanigan shows that these statements are erroneous, and that the
Culdees were not mentioned by the Venerable Bede or any other ancient ecclesiastical
writer as Columbian monks, nor in the works of Usher or Ware, nor in the five lives
of Columbkill published by Colgan.  Lanigan considers that the Culdees were first
instituted in Ireland in the eighth or ninth century ; and Aongus, surnamed Ceile De,
a celebrated ecclesiastical writer of the eighth century, author of Lives of Irish Saints,
etc., is supposed to have been a Culdee.  They are mentioned in the Annals of the
Four Masters and of Ulster (A.D. 920), in which it is recorded that Godfrey, king of the

not likely to spread, as they carried no women, but they left traces of their occupation in their cells and church furniture. The simple story told by Dicuil is eminently suggestive. Thus Thule became, probably for a second time, one of the "Britanniæ," the Isles of Britain; and we may consider the discovery a rediscovery, like the central African lakes, whence Ptolemy derived the Nile. When the rude barks of the eighth century could habitually ply between Ireland and Iceland, we cannot reject as unfit the Roman galleys, or even the Phœnico-Carthaginian fleets. The Periplus of Himilco was not more perilous than the Periplus of Hanno, and the Portuguese frequented the northern seas long before they had doubled Cape Horn. Berg-

---

Danes of Dublin, plundered Armagh, but he spared the churches and Colidæi. It appears from Lanigan and other authorities that the Culdees were not, strictly speaking, monks, neither were they members of the parochial clergy, but were a description of secular priests called 'secular canons,' and attached to cathedrals or collegiate churches termed prebendaries; and although bound by rules peculiar to themselves, they belonged to the secular clergy, and are to be distinguished from the canons regular, or communities of monks, who sprang up at a much later period, and officiated in the chapters of cathedral churches. The Culdees also sang in the choir, lived in community, and had a superior called 'Prior of the Culdees,' who acted as precentor or chief chanter. The principal institution of the Culdees was at Armagh, and, according to Usher and others, there were Culdees in all the chief churches of Ulster; and some of them continued at Armagh down to the middle of the seventeenth century. The Culdees had priories and lands in various parts of Ireland, particularly at Devenish Island, in Fermanagh, and at Clones, in Monaghan, both in the diocese of Clogher; also at Ardbraccan in Meath: and G. Cambrensis gives an account of the Colidæi who lived on an island in a lake in North Munster, which island was called by the Irish *Inis na mbeo*, or the 'Island of the Living' (or of cattle ?), from a tradition that no person ever died on it; it was afterwards called Mona Incha, and was situated about three miles from Roscrea, in the bog of Monela, in Tipperary. In the time of G. Cambrensis this island was a celebrated place of pilgrimage; and their residence was afterwards removed to Corbally, a place near the lake, where the Culdees became canons regular of St Augustine. Though the Irish Culdees were generally clergymen, yet some pious unmarried laymen joined their communities. There were also Culdees in Britain, particularly in the North of England, in the city of York, where they had a great establishment called the Hospital of St Leonard, and were secular canons of St Peter's Cathedral, as mentioned in Dugdale's Monasticon; and got some grants of lands in A.D. 936, during the reign of Athelstan, and continued at York at least down to the time of Pope Adrian IV., who confirmed them in their possessions. We also read in the 'Annals,' under A.D. 1479, that Pearce, son of Nicholas O'Flanagan, who was a canon of the chapter of Clogher, a parson, and a prior of the Ceile De, a sacristan of Devenish, and an official of Loch Erne (vicar-general of Clogher), a man distinguished for his benevolence, piety, great hospitality, and humanity, died after having gained the victory over the world and the devil. It would appear by the Annals of the Four Masters that Culdees were found in Ireland in A.D. 1601: 'O'Donnell having received intelligence that the English had come to that place (Boyle), was greatly grieved at the profanation of the monastery, and that the English should occupy and inhabit it in the place of the Mic Beathaidh (monks) and Culdees, whose rightful residence it was till then, and it was not becoming him not to go to relieve them if he possibly could.' At the Reformation, a little later, out of 563 monasteries in Ireland mentioned by Ware, and also in Archdale's Monasticon, it would appear that there was one belonging to the Culdees, viz., the Priory of Culdees at Armagh. See also Dr Jamieson's History of the Culdees, 4to, Edin. ; Maccatheus's History of the Culdees, 12mo, Edin. 1855 ; and Keith's Catalogue of Scottish Bishops, new edition."

mann had evidently no right to determine that Iceland was not
"Ultima Thule," *because*—(1.) The Romans were bad sailors; (2.)
They were in the habit of writing "Rome—her mark" wherever they went, whereas no signs of their occupation are visible
in Iceland; and (3.) Because Iceland was probably raised from the
sea at the time when the Vesuvian eruption buried Herculaneum
and Pompeii.

It is true that Roman remains have not yet been discovered
in Iceland, but this is a negative proof which time may
demolish; moreover, the same absence of traces characterises
the Papar occupation which we know to have been a fact. On
the other hand, Uno Von Troil speaks of a ruined castle near
"Videdal" (Viðidalr), some 200 perches in circumference, and
smaller features of the same kind on the glebe of Skeggestað,
near Langanes. Mr Henderson[1] declares of Hrutur's cave, or
rather caves—a vast apartment 72 feet long by 24 broad and 12
high, within which is a small recess 15 feet by 9, apparently a
sleeping place—that both " are said to have been cut by people
in former times."

We are, then, justified in concluding that we need no longer
question with Synesius, if such a place as Thule exists, or doubt
with Giraldus Cambrensis, whether it has yet been discovered.
We may follow A. W. Wilhelm (Germanien, etc., 1823), and
believe with the Teatro Grande Orteliano, "Islandia insula,
veteribus Thyle dicta, miraculis si quæ alia clarissima." We may
agree with Mannert that Iceland might have been discovered
by Pytheas the Phocæan, and even by the Carthaginians. We
may even support what appears to be rather an extreme opinion:

"Pytheam præterà increpat Strabo ut mendacem, qui Hiberniam et Uxisamam
(Ushant) ad occidentem ponit à Galliâ, cum hæc omnia, ait, ad Septentrionem
vergant. Itaque veteres geographi Hiberniæ situm definiunt meliùs quam
scriptoris seculi aurei Augusti, Himilco et Phœnices meliùs quam Græci vel
Romani" (Rer. Script. Hib., prol. i., xii.).

Moreover, it appears certain that the old tradition of Thule,
though different ages applied the word differently, was never

---

[1] Vol. i., chap. 8. This traveller did not visit the cave, but quotes from
Olafsson and Pállsson, p. 927.

completely lost; and that the Irish rediscovered the island before the eighth century, if not much earlier, when the official rediscovery dates from the ninth, and the earliest documents from the eleventh and twelfth.

The Venerable Bede (eighth century) speaks of Iceland under the name of Thyle, more than a hundred years before its official discovery by the Scandinavians; and Alfred (ninth century), in his translation of Orosius (p. 31), assures us that the utmost land to the north-west of Ireland was called Thila, and that it was known to few on account of its great distance. Yet even after the occupation of Iceland by the Northmen, we find in the literary world the same vagueness which prevailed in earlier ages. For instance, Isaac Tzetzes (twelfth century), in his notes on Lycophron, calls the fabled Fortunate Islands of the Greeks " the Isle of Souls, a British island between the west of Britain and Thule towards the east," which is impossible. But in the fifteenth century Petrarch has left us a valuable notice of the knowledge then familiar to men of letters (De Situ Insulæ Thules, epist. i., lib. iii., De Rebus Fam., vol. i., pp. 136-141, ed. 1869, J. Fracassetti, Le Monnier. Florentia). In reply to his own " Quæro quiânam mundi parte Thule sit insula?" he quotes Virgil, Seneca, Boethius, Solinus, Isidore, Orosius, Claudian, Pliny, and Mela. He could obtain no information from " Riccardo, quondam Anglorum regis cancellario "— Richard de Bury was probably too busy for such trifles. He learned something, however, from the " Libellus de Mirabilibus Hiberniæ, à Giraldo (Cambrensi) quodam aulico Henrici secundi, regis Anglorum." And after quoting this " scriptorum cohors," he thus ends with " pointing a moral "—" Lateat ad aquilonem Thyle, lateat ad austrum Nili caput, modò non lateat in medio consistens virtus," etc.[1]

Icelandic Thule was advocated by Saxo Grammaticus; but his opinion was strongly opposed by his commentator (Johannis

---

[1] This interesting letter was brought to the author's notice by Dr Attilio Hortis, Director of the Bibliotheca Civica, Trieste. This young and ardent scholar has published for the centenary festival of Petrarch (June 1874), certain political documents hitherto unprinted; they prove Petrarch to have been, like almost all the great Italian poets, a far-seeing statesman in theory if not in practice.

Stephanii, Notæ Uberiores in Hist. Dan. Sax. Gram. Soræ, ed. 1644, fol.). The words of the latter's preface are—"Ex opinione magis vulgari, quam rei veritate *Thylenses* ubique nominat Saxo, qui Islandi rectius dicerentur;" but he relies chiefly upon the controvertible arguments of "Arngrimus Jonas." Iceland was opposed by Gaspar Peucerus (De Terræ Dim.), by Crantzius (Præfatio in Norvagiam, borrowed from Nicolaus Synesius, epist. 148); by Abraham Ortelius (Theatrum Orbis and Thesaurum Geographicum), and by Philippus Cluverus (Germania Antiqua). The globe of Martin Behaim (A.D. 1430-1506) shows a certain knowledge of details: "In Iceland fair men are found who are Christians. The custom of its inhabitants is to sell dogs at a very high rate; while they willingly part with some of their children to merchants for nothing, that they may have sufficient to support the remainder. Item.—In Iceland are found men eighty years old who have never tasted bread. In this country no corn grows, and in lieu of bread dried fish is eaten. In Iceland it is the stock fish is taken which is brought to our country."

## THULE (ETYMOLOGY OF).

Perhaps the origin of "Thule" is ground more debatable and debated than even its geographical position.

"Some," says Sibbald, "derive the name Thule from the Arabic word Tule (طول = Túl), which signifies 'afar off,' and, as it were with allusion to this, the poets usually call it 'Ultima Thule;' but I rather prefer the reason of the name given by the learned Bochartus,[1] who makes it to be Phœnician, and affirms that it signifies 'darkness' in that language. Thule (צל) in the Tyrian tongue was 'a shadow,' whence it is commonly used to signify 'darkness,' and the island Thule is as much as to say, an 'island of darkness;' which name how exactly it agrees to the island so called at the utmost point to the north is known to everybody."

Others find Thule in the Carthaginian צל = "obscurity;" the Hebrew has צלל, and the Arabic ظل = "obscuravit."

---

[1] Bochart (in Chanaan, i. 40), quoting Diogenes and Dercyllides of Tyre, whose tables, according to Photius (loc. cit.), were dug up by order of Alexander the Great, explains Thule to mean in Phœnician "tenebrarum insula." But this etymology reminds us of the Semitic origin applied to Britain.

After using or abusing the Semitic tongues, we come to Greek, which puts forth three principal claimants: θόλος = fuscus color, caligo; τέλος, a goal; and τηλέ, procul. Meanwhile Isidorus (Orig. Seu Etym., lib. xiv., 6) derives Thyle, as has been shown, from the sun and its solstice. In the twelfth century, Suidas (Lex. sub voc.) makes Thulis (Θούλις) a king who reigned over Egypt and the isles of the ocean, one of which was called after his name.

Etymologists presently applied themselves to the Gothic languages and their derivatives; and they did not reject geographical resemblances. Pontanus (loc. cit., i., p. 746) asserts that the islands about the Norwegian coast were generally called Thuyle. Ortelius (Thesaur. and Theatr. Orbis, p. 103), relying upon Ptolemy's latitudes and longitudes, declares that "Thilir" was the term applied to the people of Norwegian "Tilemark;" the latter word is also written "Thulemarchia" (Johannes Gothus); "Thielemark," "Thylemark" and "Tellemarck" (Pontanus).[1] Not a few writers refer "Thule," as has been said, to "Thy" or "Thy-land," the extreme point of Jutland. The commentator on Saxo Grammaticus, before referred to, records a derivation of "Thule:"

"Quod vel instar *Tholi*, cujusdam orbis terrarum sit imposita, vel quod eo navigantes ad ploratum (tothülen Belgæ dicunt) proficiscerentur."

In p. 175 he becomes still more vague:

"Rectius itaque Velljus nostro, juxtà ac M. Christiernus Petri, primus Saxonis interpres, reddidere Blend aff Tellφe vel Blend aff Tylφe. Quænam verò iste sint insulæ, juxtà scimus cum ignarissimis."[2]

Prætorius (De Orbi Goth., iii. 4, § 3) deduces "Thule" from the

---

[1] The Icel. is Thilir, men of Thela-mörk, mark of the Thilir, the Norwegian country now called Thilemarken.

[2] Dr Charnock remarks that "Thule" is the name of a river in Glamorganshire, of a place in Silesia, and a town in Westphalia; also that "Southern Thule" was a title given to a part of Sandwich Island, the southernmost region discovered by Captain Cook in January 1775. Lt. Wilford's Pandit invented a Pushkara Dwipa under the Arctic circle, corresponding with modern Iceland. Camden (Britannia) warns us, not unnecessarily, against confounding the "insula in ultimis et extremis Borealis Oceani secessibus longè sub Arctico Polo," with the Indian "Tylis" or "Tylos" (Bahrayn?), of which St Augustine (lib. xxi. 5, De Civit. Dei) says, "Tylen Indiæ insulam eo preferri cæteris terris, quod omnis arbor quæ in eâ gignitur nunquam nudatur tegmine foliorum," doubtless alluding to the palm. Strabo, we believe, does not mention "Tylos;" Pliny refers to it in three places (Nat. Hist., vi. 32, and xii. 21 and 22).

Gothic "Tiel," "Teule," or "Tuole" (= τέλος, finis), meaning a
long distance, and denoting the remotest land; he doubts the
existence of the place, with D'Anville (Mem. de Paris, vol.
xxxvii., p. 439). Reinerus Reineccius (Reinech, Historiæ tam
Sacræ quam Profanæ Cognitio, Frankf. et Lipsiæ, 1685, and
Methodus Legendi, etc., Historiam tam Sacram quam Profanam,
Frankf. 1670) advocates the Saxon "Tell," meaning a limit—
limes septentrionis atque occidentis. Dr Charnock compares
the Saxon "Deel," a part or portion, and quotes Wachter (Gloss.
Germ.), who gives amongst other meanings of "Teil" (hod.
Theil), pars, portio, segmentum, and "teilen," i.e., dividere in
partes.

Torfæus (Hist. Norwegiæ, i. 5, p. 12) proposes a variety of
derivations. Wilhelm Obermüller (Wörterbuch, etc., Williams
and Norgate, Lond. 1872) would explain "Thule Procopiana,"
by Dal (a dale), or "Tulla," also written "Tolin" and "Tullin,"
a meadow or pasturage; and he remarks that Norwegian "Telle-
mark" or "Thilemark," is of the same descent. The Thracian
Kelts had a kingdom of Tyle, which here probably signified
"Dail," a fortress. When Pliny makes men sail from Nerigos to
"Thule," the latter might have meant Du-ile, "the little island,"
or perhaps "the dark ('dubh,' cloudy and wintry) isle."

Even the orthography of "Thule" is disputed, and there are
sundry variants—Thula, Thyle, Thile, Thila, Tyle, and Tila.
The popular Greek form adopted by Strabo, Ptolemy, Agathe-
merus, Isidorus, Jornandes (De Reb. Get., cap. 1, 1), Procopius (De
Bell. Goth., ii. 15) and Stephanus Byzantinus, is Θούλη, which in
Romaic would be pronounced "Thúle;" the ethnic being Θουλαῖος
(Thulæus), and Θουλίτης (plur. Θουλίται). The Latins (Mela,
Pliny, Tacitus, Anonymus Ravennæ, Martianus, Solinus, etc.)
seem to have preferred "Thule;" and Cluverius (Germ. Ant.,
iii. 39) rejects all others as barbarous. The learned and humorous
Salmasius (in Solin., cap. xxii.) declares that "Thyle" ought
never to be written, despite many good codices of Virgil, Pliny,
Jornandes, Isidore, the Anon. Ravennæ, and others, which give
Thyle and even Tyle, Θύλη and Θυλίτης; Æthicus (in Cosmog.,
p. 730), borrowing from Orosius, has "Tilæ;" Boethius (xx. 11),
"Tile" and "Đyle."

We here conclude the subject of Thule, "celebrata omnium litteris insula." To do it full justice, and especially to quote from the "cohort" of modern writers, would require a volume.

---

## SECTION II.

### PHYSICAL GEOGRAPHY OF ICELAND.

#### § 1. GENESIS AND GEOLOGY.

"Iceland owns its existence wholly to submarine volcanic agency" —such is the statement generally made by travellers and accepted by readers. The genesis of this "Realm of Frost and Fire;" this "fragment of earth white with snow, black with lava, and yellow with brimstone;" this "strange trachytic island, resting on an ocean of fire in the lone North Sea," where the "primary powers of nature are ever at war with one another," is compared with the efforts, vastly magnified, which in 1811 threw up from the waters Azorean Sabrina to a height of 480 feet above sea-level. And many have assumed as its exemplar the three-coned Nyöe (Nýey) that rose during the Skaptár eruption (1783), some thirty miles south-west of Reykjanes, and sank into a subaqueous reef before the end of the same year.[1]

This is true, but not the whole truth. The basis of Iceland was recognised by Baron Sartorius Von Waltershausen to be the Palagonite[2] which forms the foundation of volcanic tufas on Etna, the Azores, Tenerife, the Cape Verds, and other

---

[1] To which may be added, neglecting the "Automata" of classical and mediæval times (Pliny, i. 89 ; Ruspe, de Novis Insulis, etc.), Arons Island (1628) ; Sorca of the Moluccas (1693); the offsets of Santorin (1707); Stromöe (1783); Graham Island, near Sicily, which, in 1831, was thrown up to a height of 750 feet, and the three outliers of Santorin (1866). These little worlds enable us to study Earth in the art of parturition.

[2] From Palagonia in Sicily, where it was first described (1838) by that savant (see pp. 222-483, and 802, Dana's System of Mineralogy, Trübner, London, 1871). The specific gravity is 2·43, and the fracture mostly conchoidal. The distinguished chemist, Professor Bunsen (Sect. ix., § 1), who, succeeding in producing artificial Palagonite, gives it iron, either magnetic or peroxide, and "some alkali," a vague term : Dr W. Lauder Lindsay adds minor constituents, felspar,

Plutonic regions. It is known to the people as " Mó-berg," the *saxum terrestre-arenosum* of Eggert Olafsson, translated by the dictionaries Clay-soil, but generally used in contradistinction to Stuðlaberg,[1] hard stone, the basalts, basaltites, dolerites, and others of their kind. By the older travellers, as Henderson, it is termed sandstone, and *conglomérat-basaltique,* while not a few have confounded it with trachyte. In Iceland this mineral substance, rather than mineral, is a far more important feature than even in Sicily.

By virtue of its composite character and different colour, this hydrosilicate of alumina is a Proteus; massive and amorphous; crystalline, muddy, sandy, and ashy; friable, porous, and spongy like lava and pumice; granular, silicious, and arenaceous; heavy and compact like slatey clays; vitreous and semi-vitreous with the lustre of pitch-stone. It is as various in tint as in texture; usually ferruginous brown, dark brown or dun yellow; grey and slate-coloured; dark with hornblendic particles; pure white where it is converted into gypsum, clay marl, and limonite with the aspect of chalk, by exposure to the action of sulphurous acid; green tinged with olivine; garnetic-red; ochreous, the effect of iron; and at times showing a ferreous coat of pavonine lustre. Palagonite lava is often " of so deep a brick-red colour that it resembles an iron slag, were it not for its superior lightness."

Here, this Palagonite degrades to the yellow sand which contrasts so remarkably with the black Plutonian shore; there, in the lowlands it shows fissile strata horizontal like sand-

---

augite (hornblende), jasper, olivine, obsidian, hornstone, chalcedony, and zeolite. Professor Tyndall (Royal Institution, June 3, 1853) offers the following table:

| | |
|---|---|
| Oxide of iron, | 36·75 |
| Alumina, | 25·50 |
| Lime, | 20·25 |
| Magnesia, | 11·39 (not found by Dr Murray Thomson). |
| Soda, | 3·44 |
| Potash, | 2·67 |

100·00

In 1872, only a single and a very poor specimen of this highly interesting rock had found its way to the museum in Jermyn Street.

[1] From Stuðill, anything that steadies, a stud, prop, stay. A specific usage makes Stuðlar signify pentagonal basalt columns, and Stuðla-berg is a basaltic dyke (Cleasby). It is popularly opposed to Mó-berg, " a kind of tufa," properly Palagonite, from Mór, a moor or peat-fuel.

stone, and at times marly couches. It paves the soles of valleys and the floors of rivers; and it rises on the surface of the loftiest Heiðar (highland heaths), where earth is worn down to the very bone by rains, snows, and winds. Now it towers in huge cliffs and scaurs, irregular masses of rock overlying or underlying the traps; then it bulges into high belts of country, sierras and detached mountains, like Herðubreið and others which will afterwards be mentioned. Consolidated and in places crystallised by heat and high pressure, this produce of submarine volcanoes was elevated by the long continued action of quietly working forces, but it still displays its subaqueous origin. Firstly, it is a hydrate containing 17 to 25 per cent. of water; secondly, it is stratified as if formed of hardened ashes and modified lavas; and, thirdly, it contains broken mollusks[1] of marine types still existing, and the silicious skeletons of infusoria: a negative proof is that we never meet with it among volcanic tuffs subaërially deposited. In places it becomes an acute-angled breccia, enclosing basalts and lavas varying from the size of a pin's head to that of a man, or rounded conglomerates suggesting that the foreign matter was deposited in a shallow sea. The fresh appearance of the shells and the presence of infusoria also tend to prove that it was deposited in a heated, at least not in a gelid sea.

Professor Tyndall finds in Palagonite the first stage of the fumarole : " If a piece be heated with an excess of aqueous sulphuric acid, it dissolves in the cold to a fluid, coloured yellowbrown by the presence of peroxide of iron. On heating the fluid, the peroxide is converted into protoxide ; a portion of its oxygen goes to the sulphurous acid, forming sulphuric acid, which combines with the basis of the rock and holds them in solution." But the resultant springs show no trace of oxide of

---

[1] About ninety species of mollusk shells and the hard parts of echinoderms and crustaceæ have been found in the Palagonite of Sicilian Aci Castello. Lime, for the use of the shell-builders, enters into the composition of such tuffs generally, and the percentage depends upon the percentage of shells. Silica is extracted from it by carbonic acid and sulphuretted hydrogen ; and this mineral again depends upon the included quantity of infusorial skeletons. Professor Quekett, Dr Gulliver, and other authorities, have examined specimens of Icelandic Palagonite, in which they could not detect infusoria nor their skeletons, even after boiling in nitric acid.

iron which has been dissolved and has disappeared. "The very rock from which it was originally extracted, possesses the power of re-precipitating it, when by further contact with the rock, the solution which contains it has its excess of acid absorbed, and has thus become neutral. In this way, the aqueous sulphurous acid acts as carrier to the iron, taking up its burden here, and laying it down there; and this process of transference can be clearly traced to the rocks themselves."

Upon this Palagonite floor, the "Protogæa," or oldest formation, were laid immense tracts of sand and stratified ejections of "trap." According to Macculloch, "the word is a cloak for ignorance which saves the trouble of investigation." But it is still a general term for the older, lighter, less earthly and basic, and more crystalline forms than the basalts, containing intercalated pumice-tuffs deficient in shells, whilst the cavities abound in zeolites and amygdaloids.[1] Concerning the strike and dip of the trap-strata, which rise sheer from the sea, in grades and layers, steep, angular, and bare, and which outline the mural copings and stepped cones of the old coast and the jaws of the river-gorges, there are many conflicting opinions. Some hold that the strata all incline gradually and quaquaversally, more or less, towards the centre of the island; whilst others find that as a rule, they are horizontal. The expedition led by Prince Napoleon (1857) recognised convergence, and often a slope of 15° towards the grand foci of eruption that form the respective systems; for instance, the *inclinaison rayonnante* towards Snæfellsjökull. The author could lay down no rule, except that the steps, viewed in profile, especially from the gashes and torrent-beds, appear to recede rather than to project, to dip inland rather than seawards. The strata vary in number to a maximum of fifty; they are perpendicular courses separated by débris, and sometimes footed by déblai and humus, disposed at the natural angle—this regularity again suggests submarine deposition, and everywhere attracts the stranger's eye.

Professor Bunsen divides the rocks of Iceland, and probably those of most other volcanic systems, into two great groups: (1.)

---

[1] The word "trap" will be used in these pages to denote the lavas ejected by submarine volcanoes.

*Normal Pyroxenic*, the basalts and dolerites, whence silica is almost absent; and (2.) *Normal Trachytic*, abounding in that mineral. The basalts[1] are of two kinds, the true, rich in, and the basaltite, which notably wants, olivine. Both are either honey-combed with drusic cavities, or perfectly compact and fine-grained; the water-rolled pieces are soft, and smooth as marble. The basalts pass by almost imperceptible degrees into dolerites (green-stones) coloured by admixture of chlorite, and often containing iron pyrites. Of less importance as a geological feature, are the masses, veins, and crests of trachyte which pierce the Palagonites, the traps, and the basalts. The rock which is compared with the chain of the Puys (Auvergne), occurs, however, in an altered form at many places unsuspected by old travellers, and every explorer adds to its importance. From Reykjavik appear two gold-yellow and white-streaked peaks, associated with jasper and other forms of quartz. The Snæfellsjökull peninsula is also for the most part trachytic. The celebrated Baula (the cow), a cone rising 3000 feet high, contrasts the mechanic neatness of its whitey-grey pillars[2] with its red neighbour, Little Baula, and with the surrounding chaos of darkness; and heat-altered trachytes are found about Hekla and the Geysir. The green trachyte of Viðey, apparently tinted by chlorite, was found to contain silica, alumina, iron, and traces of magnesia. Daubeny, and a host of writers, assumed that a trachytic band, disposed upon a rectilinear fissure 200 kilometres long, bisects the island from south-west (Reykjanes) to north-east (Langanes), and represents the original Iceland, as the Longmynd and Stiper Stones are the nucleus of England. Moreover, the great centres of eruption, igneous and aqueous, were disposed upon this

---

[1] Until late years the general opinion was that all basalts are of igneous formation. The contrary has been supported by Mr H. P. Malet (Geogr. Mag., August 1874), to mention no others : he finds in that of Rossberg and the "Rowley Rag" vegetable, animal, and earthy particles which, passed through the fire, would have vanished in vapour. The distinction, therefore, between basalt and basaltic lava becomes fundamental. Granite, again, is by the same writer taken from Hutton and returned to Werner. The author could not but observe, when travelling in the basaltic Haurán, in that Bashan which, according to some, gave a name to the mineral, that the dried mud split under the sun into lozenges and pentagonal flakes (Unexplored Syria, i. 215). Upon this subject more will be said in Chapter XIV.

[2] Forchhammer considered this trachyte an unknown variety of felspar, and called it Baulite.

diagonal, flanked by the earlier Plutonic masses. Lastly, the modern volcanic chimneys were all theoretically opened in the old and new trachytic domes. M. Robert (1835) especially sought and failed to find the "trachytic band," and, since Von Waltershausen's visit, it has been determined that the material is the Palagonite floor traversed by the Geysir and by most of the active volcanoes.

The peculiar contrasts of the island are thus noticed by an old writer : "The king of Denmark is still master of Iceland, which is supposed to be the *Ultima Thule* of the ancients. The surface, though it is covered with snow, nevertheless contains burning mountains, whence issue fire and flames, to which the Iceland poets compare the breasts of their mistresses. It has also smoking lakes, which turn everything thrown into them to stone, and many other wonders which render this island famous." Iceland, like Tenerife, owes its present general contour to subaërial volcanic action of the post-Tertiary period, the secular growth of the detached regions overlying the pockets and foci of eruption, as explained by Von Buch, together with the gradual accretion, the gift of exit-chimneys and dejections from the Plutonic cauldrons. The normal pyroxenic was followed by the felspathic formations, trachytic, acid and pumiceous, which, though comparatively modern, still date from immense antiquity. The distribution into fire-vents (true volcanoes) and sand-vents (pseudo-volcanoes), will be noticed in a future page.

The lava is composed of trachytic (silicious) and doleritic (basic) ejections, varying in weight ;[1] the stone averages about half the specific gravity of granite, and in a molten state it flows at the rate of 50 to 100 yards per diem. When first cooled, the ejections are lamp-black; they are then tarnished by oxygen to brown; they become grey with lichens; and finally, the lapse of ages converts them into humus. To the latter process, Brydone, on Etna, assigned 14,000 years, and greatly scandalised our grandsires, who held sound opinions upon the date (B.C. 4004) empirically assigned to creation. We can hardly forget poor Cowper's poor verse, and poorer sense :

---

[1] See Chapter XI.

"Some drill and bore
The solid earth,and from the strata there,
Extract a register, by which we learn
That He who made it, and revealed (!) its date
To Moses, was mistaken in its age." [1]

The following is a list of the principal orographic features, Jökulls,[2] Fells (mountains), volcanoes, masses of Palagonite, snow-peaks, and true glaciers, which are rare. Gunnlaugsson's astronomical positions are given in Danish feet, and the former are reduced to the meridian of Greenwich by assuming Copenhagen to lie east 12° 34′ (Rafn, 12° 34′·7). The Danish foot is calculated at 12·356 inches English, or about 67 : 69.

The north-eastern quarter numbers fifteen points, ranging from 1000 to 3000 Danish feet, and the following ten exceed the latter:

|  | Dan. feet= | Eng. feet. | N. lat. | W. long. (C.) = | Greenwich. |
|---|---|---|---|---|---|
| Lambafell, | 3459 | 3562 | 64° 58′ 28″ | 26° 39′ 19″ | 14° 5′ |
| Herðubreið, | 5290 | 5447 | 65° 10′ 39″ | 28° 58′ 55″ | 16° 25′ |
| Gagnheiðarhnúkr, | 3009 | 3098 | 65° 13′ 35″ | 26° 53′ 42″ | 14° 20′ |
| Beinageitarfjall, | 3517 | 3621 | 65° 27′ 37″ | 26° 42′ 2″ | 14° 8′ |
| Dyrfjöll, | 3606 | 3713 | 65° 31′ 20″ | 26° 35′ 17″ | 14° 1′ |
| Smjörfjall, | 3859 | 3973 | 65° 36′ 40″ | 27° 24′ 6″ | 14° 50′ |
| Heljarfjall, | 3991 | 4109 | 65° 48′ 26″ | 31° 31′ 56″ | 18° 58′ |
| Rimar, | 4020 | 4139 | 65° 52′ 45″ | 31° 7′ 33″ | 18° 33′ |
| Ólafsfjarðarfjall, | 3272 | 3369 | 65° 58′ 34″ | 31° 31′ 8″ | 18° 57′ |
| Kaldbakr, | 3699 | 3810 | 66° 0′ 24″ | 30° 48′ 58″ | 18° 15′ |

In the south-eastern quarter, nine heights range from 1000 to 3000 Danish feet, and eleven rise higher, viz.:

|  | Dan. feet= | Eng. feet. | N. lat. | W. long. (C.) = | Greenwich. |
|---|---|---|---|---|---|
| Stórhöfði, | 4509 | 4643 | 63° 55′ 34″ | 29° 17′ 7″ | 16° 43′ |
| Staðarfjall, | 3782 | 3894 | 63° 57′ 55″ | 29° 12′ 51″ | 16° 39′ |
| Öræfajökull,[3] | 6241 | 6426 | 64° 0′ 48″ | 20° 20′ 16″ | 16° 46′ |
| Thverártindsegg, | 3668 | 3776 | 64° 11′ 14″ | 28° 46′ 12″ | 16° 12′ |

[1] The date "revealed to Moses" has long delayed the progress of science, and the 6000 years or so, still linger in the orthodox brains. The Hindus and the Moslems were far wiser, or rather better informed ; the latter provide for the countless Æons of the past by the theory of Pre-Adamite kings and races.

[2] The Jökull (plur. Jöklar) is explained passim. Suffice it here to say, that it is a mass of eternal ice formed by the enormous pressure of the superincumbent snow ; it is not correct, but it is decidedly convenient to render it by "glacier." The Fell (our "fell," pronounced Fedl or Fetl) is a single block or peak, and in the plural, a range or sierra ; it is mostly free from snow during the summer heats. Fjall (Fyadl, and plur. Fjöll) is the generic term "mons" and κατ' ἐξοχήν ; it is applied in Icelandic literature to the Alps.

[3] Here is the culminating point of the island, usually assumed at 6500 English feet, more than one-third higher than Vesuvius (4000 feet).

| | | Dan. feet=Eng. feet. | | N. lat. | W. long. (C.) = | Greenwich. |
|---|---|---|---|---|---|---|
| Birnudalstindr, | . | 4300 | 4428 | 64° 14′ 54″ | 28° 34′ . 1″ | 16° 0′ |
| Bakkatindr, | . . | 3316 | 3414 | 64° 20′ 50″ | 28° 50′ 22″ | 15° 47′ |
| Afrèttartindr, . | . | 3842 | 3956 | 64° 31′ 4″ | 27° 33′ 54″ | 15° .0′ |
| Búlandstindr, . | . | 3388 | 3488 | 64° 41′ 54″ | 27° 3′ 4″ | 14° 31′ |
| Snæfell,[1] . | . . | 5808 | 5964 | 64° 48′ 1″ | 28° 11′ 43″ | 15° 38′ |
| Kistufell, | . . | 3499 | 3602 | 64° 51′ 18″ | 27° 11′ 16″ | 14° 47′ |
| Lambafell, | . . | 3459 | 3561 | 64° 58′ 28″ | 26° 39′ 19″ | 14° 5′ |

In the north-eastern quarter, twenty points range from 1000
to 3000 Danish feet, and only three rise higher, viz. :

| | | Dan. feet=Eng. feet. | | N. lat. | W. long. (C.) = | Greenwich. |
|---|---|---|---|---|---|---|
| Illviðrahnúkr, | . | 3476 | 3579 | 66° 8′ 14″ | 31° 37′ 4″ | 19° 4′ |
| Hvammsfell, | . . | 3785 | 3897 | 65° 39′ 18″ | 31° 48′ 21″ | 19° 14′ |
| Mælifellshnúkr, | . | 3476 | 3579 | 65° 23′ 30″ | 31° 59′ 10″ | 19′ 25′ |

In the south-western quarter, thirteen points range from 1000
to 3000 Danish feet, and again only three rise higher, viz. :

| | | Dan. feet=Eng. feet. | | N. lat. | W. long. (C.)= | Greenwich. |
|---|---|---|---|---|---|---|
| Snæfellsjökull, . | . | 4577 | 4713 | 64° 48′ 4″ | 36° 25′ 8″ | 23° 51′ |
| Hekla,[2] . | . . | 4961 | 5108 | 63° 59′ 2″ | 32° 19 2″ | 19° 45′ |
| Eyjafjallajökull,[3] | . | 5432 | 5593 | 63° 37′ 2″ | 32° 16′ 18″ | 19° 42′ |

From these tables we see that the north-eastern and south-eastern
quarters contain not only the greatest number of heights, respectively twenty-five and twenty, exceeding 1000 Danish feet, but
also the apex of Iceland. The north-western, though generally
a high level, has only three master peaks, and the traveller's eye
soon determines the south-western to be the lowest of all. It
may here be remarked that the islanders have names for the
mountains, peaks, and even blocks, as well as for the valleys,
whereas the Arabs, as a rule, name only their wadys.

Upon the points above named,

> "Nix jacet et jactam nec sol pluviæque resolvunt
> Indurat Boreas, perpetuamque facit."

The snow-line above the tableland (1500 to 2000 feet) varies
according to position and formation of ground from 2000 to 3500 [4]
feet over sea-level. The mean has been laid down at 2830 feet.

---

[1] Usually assumed at 6000 English feet.
[2] Generally exaggerated to 5700 English feet.
[3] Popularly reckoned at 5900 English feet.
[4] This is about the forest limit of Scandinavia (2500 feet). The spruce fir first
disappears, the Scotch fir rises a few hundred feet higher, and the highest is the
birch, common and dwarf (*Betula alba* and *nana*).

Iceland, as far as it is known, contains few true glaciers. The best known of the Skriðjöklar, *glaciers mouvants,* the "vacillating jökuls" of Henderson (i., pp. 237, 265), protruded by the thrust from behind and above, are the southern offshoots of the great Klofajökull. Two have been often described—the Skeiðarárjökull and the Breiðamerkrjökull. Concerning these ice masses, which are confined, as far as is known, to the southern and the south-eastern shores, and which slope gently to the sea, it is generally believed in Iceland that the congealed tracts are diminishing. Professor Tyndall observed the same in the Mer de Glace, and Mr Freshfield on the Caucasus, where the excess of consumption over supply threatens to make the "gletchers" mere spectres of their former selves.

We now approach the modern formations, the volcanic tracts which overlie the plateaux of Palagonite, trap, and trachyte, and the valleys of elevation and erosion which cleave their masses. As usual throughout the world, the fire-vents are confined to the neighbourhood of the sea and lakes : the centre of Iceland is the Sprengisandur (bursting sand),[1] a black " Ruba' el Kháli." In many places the trap terraces have become a wall, over which great gushes of modern lavas have poured down towards the ocean—stone models of the waters which stream down the valleys, and which spring in cataracts from step to step.

Again, it is asserted, with premature generalisation, that the volcanic vents trend, as a rule, from north-east to south-west— a corollary of the " trachytic-band" theorem. The principal systems, which are the following, do not bear out this disposition, and it is probably true only of the south-western part of the island, which was first examined by travellers. Beginning from the north-west, we have the following list of eight great systems.

1. The Dranga[2]-Glámu system in the great palmated projection, the former lying north-east of the latter.

---

[1] Sprengisandur; from "sprengja," to burst, to split (in an active sense) ; "að sprengja hest," to burst a horse, to ride it till it bursts. This is the reason of the name : the Sprengisandur has so few halting places, that there is a danger of working the horse to death before coming to a station. It is generally and erroneously translated "springing," *i.e.,* wind-blown, sands. The Ruba' el Kháli ("empty fourth," or quarter) is the great Arabian Desert.

[2] Drangr, = a lonely, upstanding rock ; in popular lore, rocks thought to be giants turned into stones.

2. The Leirhnúkr, Krafla, and Heiðarfjall, near the Mý-vatn Lake. They anastomose, by the Ódáða-hraun, with the Vatnajökull and the Skaptár—the direction being north to south.

3. The Snæfellsjökull (Western Jökull) runs distinctly from west to east, ending at the sea-shore.

4. The Hofsjökull, including the Arnarfells branch to the east, and the Blágnýpujökull to the south-west. Occupying the centre of the island, it approaches the Túngnafellsjökull, an outlier of the Vatnajökull system to the south-east; and westward, it almost touches the north-eastern extremity of the long Reykjanes line.

5. The Hekla system, which the old theory of fissures connected with Etna. It lies on a parallel, a Palagonite ridge about 2000 feet high, extending from west to east through the Torfajökull, to the banks of the Skaptá.

6. The Vatnajökull, whose apex is Öræfa, the whole measuring some 330 miles in circumference, and occupying an area of 3000 to 4000 square geographical miles: stretches upon a parallel, and is connected by· a meridian of lava-run with No. 2.

7. The Katla, or Kötlu-gjá system, again, is not linear, but disposed in a group at the southern extremity of Iceland. The principal items are the Mýrdals, Eyjafjalla, Merkr, Goðalands, and Tindfjalla Jökulls. This great mass is generally known as the Eastern Jökull, opposed to the Western or Snæfells.

8. The Reykjanes system is apparently the only diagonal which extends from the Fire Islands north-eastwards to Skjaldbreið, and to the snow mountains, whose northernmost point is Eyriksjökull. Its items are the Láng, the Ball, the Bláfells, the Geitlands, and the Ok.

Mr Keith Johnston, sen., and other authorities, give the following list of volcanic eruptions which have occurred during the present century.[1]

---

[1] The total number of recorded eruptions between A.D. 894 and 1862 is given by Baring-Gould, Introduction, xxi.-xxiii. There have been eighty-six from twenty-seven (reckoned in round numbers to be thirty) different spots, and the intervals of repose have varied in Hekla from six to seventy-six years; in Kötlu-gjá from six to three hundred and eleven. Such is the statement generally made. The fact is, however, that the exact number of the eruptions is not known, as the annals are more or less confused. The number of volcanic foci in Iceland is popularly and roughly laid down at twenty, and of these three are called active—

1. Aust-Jökull (an indefinite term for the great Eyjafjalla system), in December 1820 to June 1822, and January to June 1823.

2. Mýrdals Jökull (or rather Kötlu-gjá) in 1823, from 26th June, covered about a hundred square miles with sand and ashes.

3. Skeiðar Jökull began to erupt February 13, 1827, and did considerable damage. ·No record of this outbreak is to be found.

4. The submarine eruption off Cape Reykjanes took place in 1831.[1]

5. Hekla, in September 2, 1845(-46), broke out the twenty-sixth time, according to popular writers, throwing up ashes, which fell in the Orkneys, and which gave the first intelligence of the event.

6. Kötlu-gjá again was slightly active, vomiting ashes and water in May 1860, its thirteenth eruption.

7. It has been generally assumed that on March 23, 1861, the Öræfajökull broke its long rest, and the smoke is said to have tarnished silver at the distance of fifty miles. But Mr Jón A. Hjaltalín, who was in Iceland during that year, denies having heard of any convulsion, nor was it mentioned by the island papers. He adds, " What is spoken of in Metcalfe's book was a ' Jökul-hlaup.' "

An ash-eruption from Trölladýngjur is recorded in 1862, but accounts of it greatly vary. Mr Keith Johnston chronicles nine eruptions extending through nearly five centuries and a half—namely, the submarine volcano in the middle of Breiði Fjörð (A.D. 1345), Trölladýngjur (1510), Herðubreið (1716-17), "Krabla" (1724-25), Leirhnúkr (1730), Siðu Jökull (1753), Öræfajökull (1755), Hnappafellsjökull (1772), and Skaptárjökull (1783). And he further informs us that two great groups are active —Leirhnúkr, " Krabla," Trölladýngjur, and Herðubreið, [2]—all nearly on a parallel of latitude to the north-east; and Hekla,

---

Hekla, Katla or Kötlu-gjá, and the Vatnajökull volcano. It is a large proportion out of the total assigned to the world; the latter varies between the extremes of 167 and 300, showing the uncertainty of our present knowledge. Popular books speak of 2000 eruptions per century, or an average of twenty per annum.

[1] Smoke also appeared in the sea off Reykjanes, and pumice was thrown upon the shore during February 1834. This phenomenon was followed by an earthquake at Reykjavik, August 15-20, 1835.

[2] The formation of these four items will be explained in a subsequent page; they are very improperly massed together.

Aust Jökull, Mýrdals, and Öræfa, placed in a right-angled triangle to the south.

Concerning the unvisited volcano in the snows of the Vatnajökull, all procurable details will be found in the Journal. The author was surprised to find that not one of the known centres was in a state of activity, although every preconceived idea suggested that the summer of 1872 would be one of unusual perturbation.[1] Two days before the outbreak of Vesuvius (January 1, 1872), shocks began in the north-east of Iceland. On the after-

---

[1] The year after the author's departure witnessed an eruption of the Skaptárjökull, in the north-west corner of the Vatnajökull, but it lasted only four to five days. The following account appeared in the papers; nothing more has subsequently been learned about it. But how can this outbreak "witness against Captain Burton's assertion in the *London Standard*"—the same assertion which is here repeated in the text, and which was made in 1872 ?

"An Icelandic gentleman has kindly forwarded to us the following account of the eruption of the Skaptárjökull (announced by telegraph from Lerwick yesterday), as witnessed by him from Reykjavik, about 100 miles distant:

"'Reykjavik, March 23, 1873.

"'On Thursday, the 9th of January, about three o'clock A.M., we observed from Reykjavik a grand fire in east-north-east direction, and all agreed that it was "some neighbouring farm burning," with haystacks. The fire shot up like lightning, displaying beautiful evolutions in combination with the electricity above. Indeed, it was exactly like a fine display of rockets and wheels, and so bright was it, that during the dark morning hours we all thought it must be very close to Reykjavik. But when daylight dawned, and we could discern the mountains, we observed a thick and heavy column of vapour or steam far in the background, beyond all mountains visible, so it was clear that it was far off, and, according to the direction, it seemed most likely to be in Skaptárjökull, the west part of Vatnajökull—the great waste of glaciers in the east and south of the island. Morning and night this grand display was visible during the 9th, 10th, 11th, and 12th, and during the day the column of steam and smoke stood high in the sky.

"'When similar news came from east, north, and west, all came to the same conclusion, that it must be in Skaptárjökull—witnessing against Captain Burton's assertion in the *London Standard*—and according to the different points of observation, and the statement of our newspaper at Reykjavik, the position of the crater ought to be between 64° 7′ and 64° 18′ north lat., and 30° 45′ and 30° 55′ west long. from the meridian of Copenhagen.

"'In the east, near Berufjörð, as stated in the northern paper, some shocks were felt, and fire was seen from many farms. Ashes, too, had fallen over the north-east coast, so that pasture fields were covered so far that the farmers had to take their sheep into the huts and feed them. But the paper says : "In the south no earthquakes were felt, or noises heard in the earth, far or near, as far as Markarfljót (near Eyjafjallajökull). Nowhere has been observed any fall of ashes or dust, but all aver a bad smell was felt, and also here in Reykjavik in the forenoon of the 10th. The people of Landeyjar (opposite Westmann Islands) assert the same to have been the case there on the first day of the eruption, but here, at Reykjavik, it was not observed that day, but we felt the air very close, particularly on the 9th, from three to five o'clock in the afternoon, with some smell of sulphur and powder, very like the smell from a lately discharged gunbarrel."

"'No change was observed in the sun, moon, etc. The sky was clear all these days. The direction of the wind was from N.W.—W.S.W., and the weather fine. At Landeyjum the wind had been E.N.E. on the 10th, with a strong breeze,

noons of 16th and 17th April, Húsavik, a small comptoir to the east of Skjálfandi Fljót, suffered severely, as will appear in a future page. This immediately followed the fearful cyclone at Zanzibar (April 15), a phenomenon unknown in former times, which destroyed part of the town, and which sank most of the foreign and native craft,[1] doing damage estimated at £2,000,000. The earthquake at Húsavík also took place only thirteen days after the earthquake at Antioch (morning of April 3), which shook down two-thirds of the houses, and killed nearly one-third of the people. Moreover, shocks were reported at Accra on the Gold Coast, a town which had been almost destroyed some ten years before.[2] Followed (May 1) by the cyclone at Madras, which breached the pier, severely injured the city and suburbs, and wrecked eleven merchantmen, drowning many of the crew. Lastly came the report that the unseen crater in the untrodden snows of the Vatnajökull, whose smoke was first seen in August 1867, had again begun to "vomit flames."

Meanwhile the eruptions of Vesuvius continued till April 26, when a new crater built a hill in the Atrio del Cavallo, where only a fissure before appeared. Professor Palmieri, who stuck staunchly and gallantly to his observatory on the banks of the new Styx, reported that the mountain was sweating fire at every pore, and that after the showers of ashes and red-hot stones, and the discharges of lava and "boiling smoke," storms not less dangerous had begun to rage. These meteors, as a rule, occasion great floods, which, sweeping down the ashes and *rapilli* that cover the slopes, complete the ruins of the lands spared by the lava. During this eruption, a report was spread that the crater of Vesuvius had become an electric pile; that strong currents,

---

and the column of steam got very high, and mist hid all the eastern horizon, but no fall of ashes took place.

" 'This eruption lasted only four or five days, and is not likely to have done any damage to inhabited parts or pasture grounds, except in so far as the fall of ashes might hurt the sheep.

" 'The weather has been very changeable during the whole winter, but very little snow has fallen in the southern part of the country. The cod-fishing has been very favourable when the boats have been able to go out. During the stormy weather some fishermen were lost. On the 1st of March we had a very heavy fall of snow, but since then the weather has been mild but rather stormy.' "

[1] It was reported that there were a hundred wrecks, the "Abydos" alone being able to ride out the storm.

[2] I have given an account of this event in "Ocean Highways," February 1874.

generated by the violent ejections of the crater, showed themselves in lightnings, flashing with a dry and hissing sound from the great trunk of smoke and ashes; and, finally, that an earthquake might at any moment shake Naples to its foundation. This abnormal electricity may explain the meteorological peculiarities of the spring of 1872, even in England, where May behaved itself with the leonine violence of March. The great Pacific earthquake (August 1867) and the tremendous and unusual storm which simultaneously visited the eastern coast of South America, to quote no other instances, showed that, whilst similar effects usually are of limited extent upon solid ground, they stretch to great distances at sea, and they may influence the atmosphere in the furthest regions of the world. Though we may accept only as provisional the geological theory which places volcanoes upon fissures or solutions of continuity in the earth's surface,[1] we must remember that on October 17, 1755, a fortnight before the earthquake which shook down Lisbon, the Kötlu-gjá fissure began the terrible eruptions that lasted for a year: at the same time the waters of Loch Ness were agitated; the British Isles were rocked by repeated oscillations, and shocks extended to Asia and to America. Again, in 1783, the Upper Calabrian earthquake (February 5 and 7, and March 28) was closely followed by the fearful phenomena of the Skaptárjökull.[2] Thus Nature appeared to have made in the summer of 1872 every possible arrangement for a grand pyrotechnic display; yet the author can positively assert that during the whole of his stay in Iceland not one of the twenty-seven to thirty great vents showed a symptom of activity. Indeed, only one was ever reported to be in existence, and that one has never been visited.

---

[1] The late Professor Forbes was the first to show that Iceland, the Færoes, the Hebrides, Ireland, and Iberia, are connected by a "continous tract of land, ranging from the Azores along the line of that belt of gulf-weed which exists between N. lat. 15° and 45°."

[2] This eruption is reported to have discharged a mass of lava greater in bulk than Mount Etna. According to Henderson (i. 274-289, who borrows from the account of Chief-Justice Stephensen), it destroyed 9336 human beings, 28,000 horses, 11,461 head of cattle, and 190,488 sheep. This mortality resulted either directly from the ejection of molten lava and stone showers, débâcles and aqueous lavas; or from pestilence, the effect of sulphureous and other noxious vapours; or from famine, the fish leaving the coast, and the pasturage being destroyed by erupted sand and ashes.

Professor Bunsen has shown that active volcanoes whose temperature is high, discharge sulphurous acid, whilst the dormant give forth sulphuretted hydrogen; hence the irregular and simultaneous appearance of these two gases which play a most important part in Iceland. "Let a piece of one of the igneous rocks be heated to redness, and permit the vapour of sulphur to pass over it. The oxide of iron is decomposed; a portion of sulphur unites with the iron which remains as sulphuret; the liberated oxygen unites with the remaining sulphur, and forms sulphurous acid. Let the temperature of the heated mass sink just below a red heat, and then let the vapour of water be passed over it: a decomposition of the sulphuret before formed is the consequence; the iron is reoxydised, and the liberated sulphur unites with the free hydrogen to form sulphuretted hydrogen. Thus the presence of two of the most important agents in volcanic phenomena is accounted for. These are experimental facts capable of being repeated in the laboratory, and the chronological order of the gases thus produced is exactly the same as that observed in nature."

The most remarkable features of the island, after the volcanic, are the Fjörðs,[1] or firths proper, conducting streams and admitting the sea; opposed to Víks and Vágrs, bights and bays, mere indentations of the coast. Though of igneous origin, they are compared with the granitic features of Norway, where a volcano is unknown, and yet where the shape becomes that of an *arête*, a fish's dorsal bone with regular ribs on both sides: this flat snow-capped ridge is "the keel" of the maritime population. The popular theory (Students' Manual of Geology, Jukes and Geikie, Blacks, Edin. 1872) is that the Fjörðs are glens once submerged, raised above water, and hollowed out by glaciers and by the various influences which come under the name of "weather." Glacial action is, we must own, distinctly traced in most parts of the island. But in many places, Berufjörð for instance, there is no room at the head of the dwarf amphitheatre for a glacier of any magnitude. As in the Færoe archipelago, these ravines are the rents and fissures which divided and

---

[1] Fjörðr, *plur.* Firðir.

fractured the first upheaval; and in Iceland they were bound together by the action of earthquakes and eruptions, ice and snow, wind and rain.  The greater gorges are found chiefly on three sides of the island.  The south-western shore, like that of Ireland, is digitated by gales, currents, and Greenland ice, and it abounds in " Út-ver," [1] the narrow-necked peninsulas of Norway.  The Síða, or sea-" side " to the south-east, is a long, narrow strip of habitable land between the mountains and the waters: here the Fjörðs were obliterated by the combined action of the Jökulls.  Under the name " Fjörðs " are also included immense bays, as the Faxa Fjörð, sixty-five miles across; the Breiði Fjörð, forty-five miles wide; and the Húnaflói, into which the Arctic Sea sends its unbroken swell, running forty-six miles deep and twenty-seven in diameter.  The western features are, as a rule, broad, with shallow sag: here, according to some,[2] was deposited the Surtarbrand[3] or lignite, and, like the driftwood of Kerguelen Island, it escaped incineration by subsequent eruptions from causes analogous to the operation of charcoal burning.  The northern firths are long and deeply indented, and the eastern are sharp and narrow, encased in walls of Palagonite, trap, and basalt.

The archipelagoes and solitary islands outlying Iceland are invariably small; and in places, as will be seen, the " stacks " and " drongs " form a " skerrý-guard;" almost a false coast.

Concerning a common feature of the interior, the Gjá (pron. *Geeow*, or like *ow* in fowl), rent, chasm, or fissure, details will be given in the course of the Journal.  Here it may be mentioned that it perfectly resembles the " Ka'ah " of the Lejá and the Haurán, and the Lava Fields in the Far West of North America, which lately sheltered the " Indians," and gave so much trouble to the Federal troops.

The surface of Iceland, where free from snow, and over which men travel, may be reduced to four general formations.

1. Loose, volcanic ashey sand, grey above and black below; often mixed with pulverised Palagonite; barred with white lines

---

[1] Út-ver in Icel. is an outlying place for fishing, etc.; hardly corresponding with the continental "udver."

[2] See Journal, chap. 5.

[3] Surtr, *i.e.*, the Black, an Eddic name of a fire-giant.

of salt and potash, and either erupted subaërially or formed under water, as the rolled stones and pebbles show. This feature is found best developed in the central and the north-eastern parts of the island; the Sprengisandur and the Stóri-sandur (Sahará or Great Sands) being the great examples. The hills and terraces are utterly barren, because they will not hold water: the lower levels, fed by percolation, bear the normal growth, and especially the wild oat.

2. Stone; chiefly Palagonite, trap, basalts, trachyte, lavas, and obsidians, the Μαῦρα λιθάρια of the modern Greeks. It is, how-ever, far safer travelling than the polished limestone of the Libanus, and an hour's ride over calcareous Kasrawán is more troublesome than a day in Iceland. Its greatest inconveni-ence is perhaps the sun: during a clear day it becomes, in Ice-landic phrase, "hot enough to make a raven gape." A fair specimen of the stone-country may be found between Reykjavik and Krísuvík.

3. Clay and humus, the former generally disposed in horizontal strata, the latter deposited by decayed vegetation upon the surface. These formations, the Geest-lands of Denmark, mostly extend round the hill feet, dividing them from the deeper levels of bog. They form essentially "rotten" ground; drilled with holes by frost, rain, and sun, and cut by gullies of all sizes, a plexus of wrinkles or gashes and earth-cracks, radiating from the highlands to the lowlands. When the path becomes a hollow way, sunk too deep for riding, rut-tracks straggle, as in the Brazil, over wide spaces and, after the vernal thaws, the traveller will find the "corduroys" of America and the "glue-pots" of Australia;" whilst in places scattered stones are so many traps for careless horses. Yet these clays and humus are the best paths and, after the sands, give the fairest chance of a gallop.

4. Bog in Iceland clothes the hill-sides, as well as the bottoms and the "flats," that is, any low alluvial land: it is easily dis-covered from afar by the dull-red tint of iron-rust and the snow-white spangles of cotton-grass. There are two forms of profile: one lumpy, tussocky, and what one traveller calls "hassocky," like the graves of a deserted churchyard; the other a plane, the swamp pure and simple; often flooded after rains, and in the

dries provided with two or three veins, into which animals plunge, struggle, and fall. These channels change so frequently that none but local guides are of use, and often the best path leads to the place which has lately become the worst. Instinct and experience do something, but not much, for man and beast: both naturally prefer running water to stagnant, and when the foremost is bogged, the followers seek a better place either higher up or lower down. On frequented lines the impassable places are provided with " Brúr," dykes or causeways of peat or stone, traversed by rude arches and flanked by shallow ditch-drains.

The Heiði, or high divide separating two river-valleys, is a "dry-land wave" ($\kappa \hat{\upsilon} \mu a \ \chi \epsilon \rho \sigma a \hat{\iota} o \nu$), varying from 1500 to 2000 and even 3000 feet in altitude. These ridges, especially during the mist and fog, snow and hail, wind and rain, are the horror of native travellers, and few venture upon the passage in foul weather. The profile is a harsh caricature of our Scotch and Irish moors and mosses, bogs and swamps, combining all the troubles of sand, stone, clay, and slush; whilst the marshes and drains are most troublesome to cross. " Carlines," or old women (Vörður and Kerlingar),[1] are built in places where transit must be made at all seasons; but they are often useless, as the streams shift their bottoms, and permanent paths cannot be traced on what is neither water nor good dry land. At the beginning and end of the travelling season, snow-*fonds* and veins, based upon compressed ice, streak the slopes and dot the hollows, whilst natural arches and bridges, under which savage torrents gnash and foam, must be crossed on horseback. Concerning the behaviour of the snow, details will be found in the course of the Journal.

Roads are made in Iceland, like those of Syria, by taking off, not as in Europe by putting on, stones. In the more civilised parts of the island they are represented by horse-paths, which are occasionally repaired, and by sheep-paths, which are left to themselves: they humbly suggest the " buffalo " track of the prairie, and the elephant tunnel of the African forest. Not a few show worse engineering and tracery than those of olden Austria; hence we find upon the map such pleasant titles as

---

[1] Englishmen would call them " old men."

Höfða-brekka[1] (head-brink or slope), Hálsavegr (neck-or-nothing way), Íllaklif (evil cliff), and Ófæra or Úfæra, Úfærð (the untravellable)—the latter often applied to short cuts over the seasands where the wayfarer is exposed to a cannonade from the heights.

## § 2. HYDROGRAPHY.

The hydrography of Iceland has several peculiarities. A glance at the map shows that the Sprengisandur is the keystone of the flattened arch, which, averaging 2000 feet in altitude, forms the centre of the island. From this point the main lines diverge quaquaversally, except to the south-east, where the huge white oval, denoting the Vatnajökull, bars the way, and forms a drainage-system of its own. Hence none of the streams are navigable above the mouth, and their magnitude, as well as the dimensions of their basins, are out of all normal proportion to the area of the island. The four head rivers—Hvitá,[2] Thjorsá, Jökulsá (western), and Skjálfjandifljót (shivering or waving flood)—range from 100 to 160 miles in length. The Thjorsá is 150 miles long, and falls 2000 feet in twenty leagues, carrying more water than the Hudson of New York. "White River" is a common local name, the effect of glacier detrition giving the milky aspect familiar to every traveller in Switzerland, and hence, probably, the muddy White Nile, as opposed to the clear Blue River. A more unusual feature is the Fúli-lækr (foul or stinking stream); the iron pyrites, where the stones are ground to powder, part with their sulphur, and the latter, uniting with the hydrogen, accounts for the unsavoury name. The Jökulhlaup, or "Snow-mountain leap," is the sudden débâcle and exundation which spring from the congealed masses, often with the irresistible might and the swift destruction of the true avalanche.

---

[1] Henderson (i. 127) translates "Höfdabrecka" by "Breakneck." Hálsavegr is from "háls," Scotticè "halse."

[2] A (fem.) at the end of a word means a water, as Temsá = Thames River: so the German Don-au is the Iceland Dóná, the Danube. The root may be traced through the Sanskrit *Ap*, the Persian ﺁﺏ, and the Latin *Aqua* to almost all families of European speech. Uncomposed, the Icelandic "Vatn" means water or lake.

The streams in the south-eastern corner are the shortest and
the most perilous, rising full grown from the glaciers, and
sweeping down fragments and miniature floes of ice. Henderson
is the first English traveller who forded and described the
Skeiðará and the network called the Gnúpsvötn. We may here
acquit him of excessive exaggeration : the natives of the eastern
coast, when travelling to Reykjavik, prefer the immense round
by the north to the short cut along the southern shore; and
when asked the reason, they invariably allege the dangers of the
snow-drains. In the course of the Journal we shall cross two of
the four head streams, and observe a water-power amply sufficient for the wants of a first-rate European people. The principal cataracts are the Oxará, the Seljaland Foss, the Goða
Foss, and the Dretti Foss, first visited by Baring-Gould. All
have been described by travellers, and the highest is the Hengi
Foss which we shall pass on the road.

Of the lakes (Vötn), we shall inspect the two largest, the
Thingvalla-vatn [1] and the Mý-vatn; and we shall sight a
multitude of tarns and ponds, single and grouped. One
peculiarity is noticed in many of the minor waters. In Iceland
it is emphatically untrue that lakes without drains are salt or
briny—a rule apparently applicable only to the temperate and
tropical zones. Whether the phenomenon in the north arises
from subterranean drainage through the fissures of the bed, or if
it be due to absence of saline matter in the area of drainage,
which is often modern lava too hard to be sensibly degraded, we
have no means of determining : perhaps there is a union of both
causes.

A remarkable feature is the abundance of warm water laid
on by the hand of Nature; the map shows upwards of two
hundred; and here perhaps the hottest springs of the Old
World are found. Suffice it to say at present that they are
divided into two main groups. The acidulous and acid-silica,
which redden litmus-paper, depositing gypsum and sulphur, do not

---

[1] In old vellums spelt invariably Vatz, Vaz, or Vazt, and Vass is the modern
pronunciation. Only in two instances not dating earlier than the twelfth century,
we find Vatr, with the r common to all Teutonic peoples, and showing its connection with Wasser and Water (Cleasby).

erupt: these are the "Öl-keldur" (ale springs) mentioned in the "Royal Mirror" of the twelfth century, and they are still locally and popularly distributed into three species. Some, like "martial" waters, inebriate from the abundance of carbonic acid gas; others when allowed to stand, part with their stimulating property; and others again when filled in rise elsewhere. The second class is the alkaline-silica, which restores the colour of litmus paper; it is often explosive, and it contains chiefly sodium and silica. In the valley of the Yellowstone River the springs are either (1.) Calcareous (alkaline), depositing carbonate of lime with sulphates of magnesia and soda, chloride of calcium, and a little silica; or (2.) Silicious (acid), containing 85 : 100 silica, chloride of magnesium, and only a trace of lime.

The Geysir (gusher)[1] is a spouting spring; the Reykirs (reekers) give forth steam; the Laug is a warm fountain which may serve as a bath; the Náma[2] (hole of hot water) is sulphurous and gaseous; the Hverr (cauldron), like its smaller congener the Ketill (kettle), is a tranquil, hot, and even boiling well or pool, it is also applied to mud springs; and the Makkaluber (the Italian "Salsa," or "Hofetta," and the American "Mud-puff") is a miniature volcano of hissing, boiling bolus. Further details concerning the names and natures of these features will be given in the Journal.

## § 3. CLIMATE.

The "cold of Iceland" is as proverbial as the "deserts of central Africa," and both sayings are equally based upon unfacts. "Iceland, where the cold and winter are perpetual, and the cold scarce to be endured," is what we read. But those who travel in the island find—(1.) that even in winter the temperature is rarely severe; (2.) that there are two distinct climates, on the north coast and in the southern country; and (3.) that the air, however unpleasant, is exceptionally wholesome.

1. The isotherms by no means follow the circles of latitude.

---

[1] Paijkull translates the word "to ascend violently." It is derived from aδ gjósa, to gush. Max Müller (Science of Language, Longmans, 1862) derives it from the root which gives ghost, geist, gust, yeast, gas, etc.

[2] The dictionary gives only Náma or Námi, a mine or pit, for this word of general use.

The cold lines swerve away from, instead of passing through, Iceland, and show none of that severity which characterises Greenland and the northern parts of British America. As has long ago been observed,[1] the isotherm of F. 32°, the freezing point of water, which is that of Akureyri, varies 14° between southern Asiatic Russia (N. lat. 56°) and northern Norway (N. lat. 70°).

The mildness of the insular climate, and that of the easterly winds, which are too clear to come from warmer waters, are popularly attributed to the "great Gulf Stream." This sea-river, we are told, "sweeping up from the south, brings with it a store of heat to bless the islanders, and so materially affects the island that in the south of Iceland the winter is not more severe than in Denmark." The Gulf Stream is generally supposed to strike the south-western angle, and to flow along the southern shores; while others make it bifurcate off Reykjanes, hence one part subtends the north-western point or Land's End of Iceland, where it meets the Polar and Arctic current, the other half embraces the southern shore, and both meet in the north Atlantic arm separating Iceland from Norway. Dufferin's map shows the popular belief: the true Florida current, sweeping past the southern shore of Iceland, forks about Spitzbergen, sending off a branchlet to the west, and ends south of Novaya Zemlja. On the other hand, Dr Carpenter contends that the real " River in the Ocean" dies out in the mid-Atlantic. According to Dr Joseph Chavanne of Vienna (Mittheilungen, No. vii., 1874), the northern arm of the Gulf Stream, which flows between Bear Island and Novaya Zemlja, touches the northern coast of Asia, and eastward of the New Siberia Islands joins the western drift of the Kurosiwo. The other northern branch, which subtends the western coast of Spitzbergen and the Seven Islands, is submerged between the Polar currents, to reappear at the surface farther northward, and thence to lave the shores of the Arctic continent: the latter is thus washed by two warm streams, rendering the existence of perennial ice a sheer impossibility.

We may fairly question the existence of the Gulf Stream along the southern Icelandic shore, and doubt its bifurcation

---

[1] Lyell's Principles of Geology, vol. i., p. 241, 11th edition. A fuller notice of this isotherm (32° F.) is given in Baring-Gould's Introduction, pp. xxx., xxxi.

and subsequent reunion. This is not the place to discuss the subject of ocean circulation, a "discovery equal to that of the circulation of the blood," first made by Professor Lenz of St Petersburg in 1845, based upon the second voyage of Kotzebue in 1823-26, and independently by Dr Carpenter during the cruise of the "Porcupine" (1869). Their aqueous movement corresponding with the aërial; and the mass of thermal equatorial waters travelling towards the poles, whilst the counter current sets in the inverse direction, would account for many phenomena yet unexplained, but it is still *sub judice lis*.[1] We may remark that the comparatively shallow seas between the British Islands and Iceland must accumulate heat, and that this fact perhaps suffices for what has been attributed to the Gulf Stream and to the general circulation. Thomas Bartolin (Acta Medica Havn. ad annum 1673) mechanically explains away the necessity of the former: " Aqua Insulas Ferroenses allabens, quamquam per se frigida sit, salsitudine tamen suâ, ex perpetuo motu, plerumque producit hyemem temperatam." Hence the waters of Niagara are colder above than below the falls, and the ocean is warmer after a storm.

Practical men, especially mariners, in Iceland vigorously deny the existence of the Gulf Stream.[2] Captain Tvede, an intelligent and observing Dane whom we shall meet in the eastern regions, considers that the theory, like judicial phrenology and a host of pseudo-sciences, became popular because it generalises, formalises, and simplifies facts. He declares that a Gulf Stream, if

---

[1] The question is of vast practical importance. Upon it hinges the decision whether future Polar voyages, so necessary to the advanced study of electrical phenomena, to mention no other, shall take the route by Smith's Sound or by Spitzbergen. For the battle of the Gulf Stream and Polar current between the Færoes and Iceland, see the Mittheilungen, xvi. (Nos. vi. and vii. of 1870), where the Gulf Stream is made to show 36°·5 F. as far as Novaya Zemlja, and to enter the Polar basin with diminution of temperature. The two distinct strata, the warm (40°-80° F.), and the heavier and more saline cold (about 35° F.) in the channel of the Færoes towards Scotland, have been described by Drs Carpenter and Wyville Thomson, the last time at the British Association, Sect. E, August 22, 1874.

[2] The author and his late friend F. F. Steinhaeuser, were never satisfied with Admiral Maury's "Ocean River," even though this ῥοὴ ὠκεανοῖο flowed more rapidly and was a thousand times larger than the Mississippi—larger, indeed, than "all the rivers of the globe put together." Like the Pacific Kurosiwo or Black Stream, off Japan, it always suggested the idea of being only the main artery, the most important and noticeable part of a great whole.

it existed, would entangle the Greenland icebergs, and carry them to the southern coast of Iceland, which never happens. He asserts that a few miles south of Ingólfshöfði the Sea River is still warm, but that instead of striking the shore it trends directly north-eastwards to western Norway, sweeps round the continental North Cape, and here meets the icebergs from Spitzbergen and Jan Mayen. He has found himself in an ice-dock floating in water which showed 35° F. '

Captain Tvede kindly gave me the following series of observations:

1. June 19, 1867: thermometer in water 46° F. outside of Hrollaugseyar, 6 miles east of Ingólfshöfði, 48° F. 3 miles south-east of ditto, and 47° F. 20 miles west of ditto.
2. June 20: thermometer 47° between Portland and the Vestmannaeyjar, 47° F. 12 miles west of the Vestmannaeyjar.
3. June 23: thermometer 46° in the Breiði Fjörð, off Stykkishólm.
4. June 24: 43° outside of the Dýrafjörð, and 43°-43°·50 outside of the Ísafjörð.
5. June 25: 38° off the Húnaflói, and 43° off Cap Nord.
6. July 1: 40° off the Axarfjörð.
7. July 4: 39° off the Langanes (north-eastern point of Iceland).
8. July 6: 40° off Viðivik, and 42° outside of Borgarfjörð.
9. August 4: 46° 16 miles south-east of Langanes.
10. August 6: 42° in the Testilfjörð, western side of Langánes.
11. August 10: 38°·50 off Hornnes, and 39° same day off Gerpir, 4 miles south of Hornnes.
12. August 19: 44° off Dalataur, entrance of Sydisfjörð.
13. August 21: 44° off Héradsflói.
14. August 22: 42° to north, with Kollumúli bearing south-west, 44° at sea.
15. September 1: 41° off Berufjörð.

The subjoined figures are the means of observations taken every fourth hour on board the "Jón Siggurðsson" steamer, in which the author voyaged (June 26 to August 5, 1872) between Hafnarfjörð and Grafarós:

|   | Air. | Water. |   |
|---|---|---|---|
| 1. | 12°  (C.=53°·6 F.) | 10°  (C.=50°   F.) | at Reykjavik. |
| 2. | 11°  (C.=51°·8 F.) | 8°·5 (C.=47°·3 F.) | at Flatey. |
| 3. | 13°  (C.=55°·4 F.) | 9°   (C.=48°·2 F.) | at N. lat.66°30′, W. long.(G.)24°. |
| 4. | 9°   (C.=48°·2 F.) | 5°·8 (C.=42°·4 F.) | at N. lat. 66°10′, W. long. 23°12′. |
| 5. | 14°·5 (C.=58°·1 F.) | 8°·8 (C.=47°·8 F.) | at Borðeyri. |
| 6. | 14°·5 (C.=58°·1 F.) | 8°·3 (C.=46°·9 F.) | at Grafarós. |
| 7. | 11°  (C.=51°·8 F.) | 6°·8 (C.=44°·2 F.) | at Cap Nord. |
| 8. | 11°  (C.=51°·8 F.) | 8°·5 (C.=47°·3 F.) | at N. lat. 65° 8′, W. long. 23° 24′. |

Both series tend to show the capricious variation of temperature (from 38° to 48° F., and from 48°·2 to 58°·1 F.), where the summer sea is subject to the influx of a little snow-water, and none of the regularity which might fairly be expected from a " gulf-stream."

2. Every book of travels from Horrebow and Mackenzie to the present day, has given notices of the climate of Iceland.[1] The mean temperature of the Iceland year between 1828 and 1834, has been laid down at 3°·42 Reaumur (= 39°·7 F.). The annual average of Copenhagen is assumed at 46°·8 (F.) ; the maximum, observed in the shade, being 94°, and the minimum about 19° (F.). That of Montreal stands at 6°·30 Reaumur (= 46°·2 F.). The winters in Iceland are colder than in Montreal in October and November (both included) ; warmer from December to March, and again cooler from April to December. Eyjafjörð (N. lat. 65° 40') is more genial than Cumberland House (N. lat. 53° 57'), and much warmer than any place in its own parallel. The almost nightless summers from June to August, which must affect the respiration of plants, gather caloric, and the sun at that season fails to heat only at a very obtuse angle, when the rays are intercepted by a thicker column of air. The equatorial current which prevails in occidental England for eight or nine months during the year, as the south-wester in Iceland, must greatly modify the climate. Old travellers assure us that the sub-surface is frost-bound throughout the year; this takes place only after a succession of hard winters and ungenial summers— even the cellars are rarely frozen in winter if care be taken to close the doors. Mr Vice-Consul Crowe (first Report on Iceland, 1865-66), asserts that "the average temperature of the earth is about 4½° Reaumur all the year round."

Reykjavik, the capital of Iceland (N. lat. 64° 9'), enjoys a

---

[1] The most extensive are those of M. Victor Lottier (Physique, etc.), printed in the Gaimard work, and containing three parts : I. Observations of magnetism— declination, inclination, diurnal variation and intensity. II. Meteorology— barometer and thermometer ; force of winds, Aurora Borealis, etc. III. Miscellaneous observations ; astronomical phenomena ; tides ; remarks on maps and stations of the expedition. The Smithsonian Institute has published many studies of the Icelandic climate : in Scotland, also, as will presently appear, much has been done.

more genial climate than any place whose temperature is recorded between the parallels of 55° and 85° (N. lat.), except
only St Petersburg (N. lat. 59° 56′) and Sitka Sound (N. lat.
57° 3′). The mean of the year is but 1° (F.) less than that
of St John's, which lies 16° farther south. The winter corresponds with that of Illukuk, 10° to the south, and the summer is much hotter. Humboldt's mean temperature, 40° F., is
generally adopted, although some reduce it to 39°·4, and even
to 39°. He makes February, the coldest month, average 28°·22,
and July, the hottest, 56°·3—a difference of over 28°, which
others reduce to 27°. He fixes the winter mean at 29°·1; the
spring at 36°·9; the summer at 53°·6 (in Berghaus' Atlas, 50°);
and the autumn at 37°·9. Dillon (pp. 167, 168), during the
severest season of half-a-century, saw the mercury as low as 10°
(F.), in February; and Pliny Miles (p. 55) declares that the
thermometer seldom falls below 12° or 18°.

It will be remembered that the annual mean of climates,
where civilisation is highest, represents in Europe 52° (F.), and
the zone is 15° north and south of N. lat. 40°, an undulating
belt of 30° arching towards the equator and the poles. Including its protraction eastward and westward, it contains $\frac{95}{100}$ths of
the white races, and almost all the greatest development.

Certain valuable "notes on the distribution of animals avail-
able as food in the Arctic regions," compiled by Herr Petermann,
and published in the Journal of the R. Geog. Society (vol. xxii.),
enable us to compare the thermometer in the south and in the
north of the island. "Reykiavig" (N. lat. "64°·08") is placed
between New Herrnhut and Fort Reliance, whilst Eyjafjörð
(N. lat. 66° 30′), stands between Fort Hope and Winter
Island.

The figures are as follows:

| | Spring. | Summer. | Autumn. | Winter. | Annual mean. | Difference Sum. & Wint. |
|---|---|---|---|---|---|---|
| 1. New Herrnhut, | 26°·15 | 39°·28 | 26°·50 | 14°·30 | 26°·83 | 24°·48 |
| Reykjavik, . | 37°·04 | 53°·54 | 37°·94 | 29°·18 | 39°·43 | 24°·36 |
| Fort Reliance, | ,, | 12°·21 | ,, | −16°·97 | 16° (?) | ,, |
| 2. Fort Hope, . | −4°·73 | 39°·59 | 13°·93 | −25°·09 | 5°·96 | 64°·68 |
| Eyjafjörð, . | 28°·10 | 45°·80 | 34°·46 | 20°·84 | 32°·30 | 24°·96 |
| Winter Island, | 6°·35 | 31°·80 | 17°·58 | −20°·47 | 8°·82 | 52°·27 |

Ranged according to seasons and months, the figures stand :

### SPRING.

New Herrnhut in February (coldest), 22°·10 in March 21°·65 in April 24°·80
Reykjavik    ,,             28°·31    ,,    29°·86    ,,    36°·46
Fort Reliance  ,,       −18°·84    ,,   −6°·14    ,,    8°·23
Fort Hope         −26°·68    ,,  −28°·10    ,,  −23°·95
Eyjafjörð           18°·50    ,,    20°·66    ,,    27°·50
Winter Island  ,,    −23°·99    ,,    10°·72    ,,    6°·48

### SUMMER.

New Herrnhut in May,  32°·0 in June, 40°·10 in July, (hottest), 40°·33
Reykjavik    ,,     44°·80    ,,    51°·58    ,,    56°·19
Fort Reliance  ,,    36°·03    ,,    ,,    ,,
Fort Hope      ,,    17°·88    ,,    31°·38    ..    41°·46
Eyjafjörð      ,,    36°·14    ,,    43°·52    46°·94
Winter Island  ,,    23°·29    ,,    23°·17    35°·36

### AUTUMN.

New Herrnhut in August 37°·40 in September, 34°·03 in October, 32°·90
Reykjavik    ,,     52°·86    ,,    46°·45    ,,    36°·91
Fort Reliance  ,,    ,,     ,,     ,,    20°·70
Fort Hope      ,,    46°·32    ,,    28°·57    ,,    12°·56
Eyjafjörð      ,,    46°·94    ,,    43°·16    ,,    34°·34
Winter Island  ,,    36°·86    ,,    31°·61    ,,    13°·25

### WINTER.

New Herrnhut in November, 15°·80 in December 11°·75 in January 9°·05
Reykjavik    ,,     30°·45    ,,    29°·41    ,,    29°·82
Fort Reliance  ,,    13°·44    ,,  −17°·07    ,,  −25°·00
Fort Hope      ,,    0°·68    ,,  −19°·27    ,,  −29°·32
Eyjafjörð      ,,    25°·88    ,,    18°·32    ,,    25°·70
Winter Island  ,,    7°·88    ,,  −14°·24    ,,  −23°·17

Dr Joseph Chavanne, before alluded to, gives the following table of the wind temperature at Reykjavik, showing the deviations from mean:

### WINTER.—Mean Temperature − 1·8.

| N. | N.E. | E. | S.E. | S. | S.W. | W. | N.W. | Max. | Min. | Diff. |
|---|---|---|---|---|---|---|---|---|---|---|
| 3·6 | −2·2 | +1·3 | +4·1 | +3·7 | +1·1 | −1·4 | −2·9 | E. 68, S. +4·4 | N.—3·6 | 8·0 |

### SUMMER.—Mean Temperature + 11·0.

| N. | N.E. | E. | S.E. | S. | S.W. | W. | N.W. | Max. | Min. | Diff. |
|---|---|---|---|---|---|---|---|---|---|---|
| 0·0 | +0·5 | +0·1 | +0·2 | +0·3 | −0·7 | −1·0 | −1·3 | E. 30, S. +0·7 | W. 35, N.—1·6 | 2·3 |

Thus the climate of southern Iceland is insular and not excessive. We have a notorious instance of the same dis-

position in England. With us Devonia represents the south-
western coast of Iceland, and justifies Carrington's high praise :

"Thou hast a cloud
For ever in thy sky ; a breeze, a shower
For ever on thy meads. Yet where shall man,
Pursuing spring around the globe, refresh
His eye with scenes more beauteous than adorn
Thy fields of matchless verdure ?"

The northern climate of Iceland, distant only 3° or 180 direct
geographical miles, is distinctly continental; the difference
ranging between 14° and 17° (F.). This is easily accounted
for by the Arctic current, by the proximity of Polar ice, and by
the prevalence of northern and north-western winds, which, in
south Iceland as in Palestine, drive away rain. Whatever dis-
crepancy of opinion there may be concerning the Gulf Stream,
there can be none about the cold drift which, between Greenland and Iceland, measures some fifty miles in breadth, and
many hundred feet in depth. Hence the north-western digita-
tions are more subject to floes and bergs than the Breiði Fjörð,
which again is oftener invested than the Faxa Fjörð, the latter
being rarely beset more than once during the century. According to Uno Von Troil, the sea-ice, now so rare, came regularly
in January with the north-eastern gales, and was never far from
the north-east coast. At present the season is about April and
even later.

In the north, according to Metcalfe (p. 152), the winter is
much keener, and the summer is proportionally milder than in
the south; some observers deny the truth of the latter part of
the proposition, and make the hot months average about the
same figure. The snow often begins with October and lasts till
mid-May when the temperature stands at a mean of 35° (F.).
For Akureyri Baring-Gould (quoting the Almanak um Ár 1863),
gives the year as 32° (F., freezing point = Eyjafjörð), the
winter as 20°·7, and the summer 45°·5. He therefore determines that, while the mean of Reykjavik is very nearly that
of Moscow, Akureyri almost corresponds with Julianshaab in
Greenland.

At Stykkishólm on the mid-west coast (N. lat. 65° 4' 44",

and W. long. (G.) 22° 43′ 17″), observations have been taken by Hr A. O. Thorlacius for nearly thirty years. The gross results are given in the following table, taken from the Journal of the Scottish Meteorological Society, iii. 148-304:

MEAN TEMPERATURE OF THE MONTHS AT STYKKISHÓLM, during the Years 1845-71.

| | Jan. | Feb. | Mar. | April | May | June | July. | Aug. | Sept. | Oct. | Nov. | Dec. | Aver. |
|---|---|---|---|---|---|---|---|---|---|---|---|---|---|
| | 28·1 | 26·9 | 27·8 | 33·1 | 39·8 | 45·6 | 49·1 | 48·2 | 44·0 | 37·7 | 33·1 | 30·4 | 37°·0 |
| Highest mean, . | 33·0 | 34·7 | 40·1 | 41·9 | 43·8 | 50·5 | 53·1 | 51·8 | 48·7 | 43·9 | 38·4 | 37·4 | 39°·8 |
| Lowest mean, . | 17·2 | 13·3 | 12·4 | 19·8 | 31·4 | 41·5 | 44·2 | 43·0 | 37·2 | 32·5 | 26·4 | 24·0 | 29°·7 |

Mr A. Buchan, the learned Secretary of the Scottish Meteorological Society, has printed in the same Journal (1873, pp. 304-307), the following highly interesting notice on the climate of Iceland, and especially of Stykkishólm, which appear to have great differences of temperature in the same months of different years.[1]

"The mean annual temperature of the twenty-six years (1845-71) is 37°·0. The highest annual mean of any of the years was 39°·8 in 1847, and the lowest 29°·7, giving thus the enormous difference of 10°·1. This very low annual mean of 29°·7 occurred in 1866 under very exceptional circumstances, which were detailed by Mr Thorlacius in a letter 15th October 1866. Spitzbergen ice surrounded Iceland on the north and north-east coast from January to the close of August in a greater or less degree, and did not wholly disappear till about the middle of September. Its effect on the temperature of the summer was therefore perceptible. What enormous masses of ice filled up the ocean north of Iceland may be conceived from the fact that, in clear weather, its gleaming appearance could be observed from Stykkishólm twenty geographical miles, not only during the day but also at night. The depression of temperature which followed was very great, amounting on the mean of the year to 7°·3; of the nine months from January to September to 8°·1, and of February and March to 14°·5. Leaving, then, this exceptional year out of account, the next lowest annual mean was 33°·6 during 1859. Hence the coldest year fell short of the mean annual temperature to the extent of 3°·4, and the warmest year exceeded it by 2°·8.

"With 1859 began a marked diminution of temperature. For the previous thirteen years the annual mean was on each, except 1848 and 1855, above the average—the mean of these thirteen years being 38°·2, or 1°·2 above the average. For the next thirteen years the mean was only 35°·8. Thus the first half of the period was 2°·4 warmer than the last half.

"As regards the annual mean of temperature, the lowest (26°·9) occurs in February, and the highest (49°·0) in July—the difference between the coldest and the warmest months being thus 22°·1. The three coldest months are January, February, March, the mean temperature of which is 27°·6, that of

---

[1] The author has been unable to find at Trieste, the publications of the "Smithsonian Institute."

December being 2°·8 higher.  In the northern part of the British Isles, and at
the western station of the Atlántic, these are also the three coldest months, but
the difference between their mean temperature and that of December is comparatively small, whereas in the south-east and interior of Great Britain,
December, January, and February are the three coldest months.

"In the extreme north of the British Isles, the warmest month is August, and
the temperature of September, if it does not exceed, is nearly equal to that of
June.  But at Stykkishólm, July is the warmest month, and the temperature of
September is 1°·6 colder than that of June.  Another point of difference between
Iceland and Scotland is that at Stykkishólm, the mean temperature of April and
that of November are the same, viz., 33°·1, whereas in Scotland April is 44°·7
and November 40°·3, or April is 7°·4 warmer than November.

"Hence the striking peculiarity of the climate of this part of Iceland is :
During the cold half of the year the seasons are longer delayed than in any part of
Great Britain.  At Greenwich the mean temperature of April, as compared with
November, being 6°·5 warmer; at York, 4°·9 ; at Aberdeen, 3°·9 ; at Bressay,
Shetland, 0°·8 ; but at Stykkishólm, 0°·0.  On the other hand, during the
summer months the seasons at Stykkishólm are not delayed as in Shetland and
Orkney, but resemble in this respect the eastern district of Great Britain.

"The great annual increase of temperature takes place from April to June—
the increase of April being 5°·3, of May 6°·7, and of June 4°·8, and the great
annual decrease from September to November—the decrease of September being
4°·2, October 6°·3, and of November 4°·6.

"But the most remarkable feature in the Icelandic climate is the great
differences which occur in the temperature of the same month from year to year.
This is seen in the highest and lowest temperature of each month during the
twenty-six years.  Thus, as regards March, the mean temperature in 1846 was
40°·1, but in 1866 it was only 12°·4, thus showing a fluctuation of 27°·7 in the
mean temperature of March.  The mean monthly fluctuation in the first four
months of the year amounts to 22°·9, and for the whole twelve months 14°·9.
As regards Scotland, the largest difference for any month during the past fifteen
years was 11°·4—the temperature of December 1857 being 44°·9, and of the same
month 1870 being 33°·5.  In Scotland, the average of the whole twelve months
is only 7°·1, or less than half of Iceland.  These singular fluctuations of temperature are readily explained by the position of Iceland with respect to the Arctic
regions on the one hand, and to the Atlantic with its warm currents on the other.
As more than usual prevalence of easterly winds rapidly and greatly depresses the
temperature by bringing to its coasts the cold, if not also the frozen regions.  On
the contrary a prevalence of south-westerly winds disperses the cold, and pours
over the island the genial warmth of the Atlantic.  This fluctuating character of
the season is frequently very disastrous, it being evident that such summers as
that of 1866, whose mean temperature was only 42°·9, will well-nigh altogether
prevent the growth of vegetation."

The veteran observer Hr Thorlacius has laid down the following rule: " The great and sudden diminution of pressure which
characterises the winter months is the outstanding feature of the

meteorology of Iceland."[1]  The barometric mean during twenty-five years at 37 feet above the sea is 29·602. There are two annual maxima of pressure, the greater in May and the lesser in November; whilst the minima are in January and October. The average yearly rainfall closely agrees with the lower parts of the Scottish Lothians—between 1856-68 the mean was 26·81 inches; the maximum (1868) being 34·23, and the minimum (1867) 21·28. The greatest amount fell in autumn and winter—in October 3·16 inches, and in May 1·41. The amount of melted snow, annually registered, ranges from 4 to 12 feet; the mean of twelve years is 7·43; the maximum (1863) is 12·21, the minimum (1867) 4·76. The snowy days average 82 per annum, and the greatest falls are in January, 1·40; in February, 1·34; in December, 1·24; and in March, 1·18. During seven of the twelve years no snow appeared in June; during ten none in July; during eleven none in August; and during five none in September. The severest storm remembered was in 1868; snow began on January 15, and lasted till the end of March, making 7·14 inches. With one or two exceptions, Greenland ice annually showed itself at Stykkishólm between 1859-69. Thunderstorms were very variable. None were registered between February 1860 and August 1861 (included), but sixteeen during the six months between November 1853 and April 1854. Of 111 thunderstorms in twenty-three years nearly half were in December (twenty-five) and January (twenty-seven); two occurred in May and July, none in June and August. In the Færoes, also, thunderstorms are wintry, not summery: the reason seems to be that when the peaks are bare, electricity is equally distributed; but when they are invested with snow, a bad conductor, the local congestion relieves itself by discharges. Thunder is said to sound, as we might expect, unusually loud, the effect of rocky hill and stony dale.[2]

---

[1] Old writers declared that the mercury habitually rose higher in Norway and Iceland than in England and France; moreover, that the air particles being more compressed and heavier, diminished the weight of objects. Thus, we are assured, 1000 lbs. of copper at Rouen = 1010 at Throndhjem.

[2] The author did not see a thunderstorm during his stay in Iceland. As regards reverberation, he remarked on the Camerones Mountain, when above the electrical discharges, and when free from the echo of earth, that the lightning was followed only by a short, sharp report, without any "rolling."

3. The climate of Iceland, if not pleasant, is assuredly one of the most wholesome. All the English travellers upon the island in the summer of 1872 agreed that Anglo-Indians on "sick leave" should prefer a tour in the north to the debilitating German Bäder, or to the fantastic hydropathic establishments which are best suited to riotous health. Consumptive patients, and those suffering from constitutional and nervous debility, have of late years been diverted to the dry, cold, and bracing air of Canada, instead of the parts preferred by their fathers—Montpelier, with its dreadful *Vent de bise;* Pau, where the people describe their year as eight months of winter and four of *l'enfer;* Pisa, where Johannum and Barahút—the hot and cold places of punishment—seem to meet; and bilious Madeira, with its enfeebling, warm milk-and-water air, which may relieve the one-lunged, but is sadly trying to those with two. In Iceland throughout summer the stimulus of light is never wanting; rich, oily fish can always enter into the bill of fare; and the evidence is in favour of "free ozone," whose absence has accounted for the presence of cholera.[1] Hence phthisis hardly appears amongst the diseases of the islanders, although, when transported to warmer regions, they are as liable to it as natives of more genial climes. And whilst in Russia an overcoat may be necessary during the height of summer, in Iceland tourists walk about bare-headed at midnight.

There is a regular tide round the island, ebbing (Icel. fjara) and flowing (Icel. flóð) according to the rule of six hours. It sets into the Fjörðs, but in the offing it subtends the shore. According to old observers, these movements are stronger at the full and change, and strongest at the equinoxes. As every wind must blow more or less from the sea, those which pass over the least expanse of land bring rain condensed by the cold heights. Upon the coast there is a kind of daily trade following the summer sun's course, like that known in Norway.[2] Cyclones are ap-

---

[1] Ozone is utterly absent during the Sharki or Scirocco of Syria, and the trying effects of the east wind upon the constitution are well known to every resident. This is the more curious as it exists in the adjoining desert, when in the Nile valley and in the oases it is comparatively deficient. It has lately been proved to be everywhere more abundant in winter than in summer.

[2] It is there called Soel-far Vind (sun-faring wind); hence Sól-gangs veðr

parently wanting, but history records the most violent volcanic hurricanes; mountain squalls are the rule, and the smoke-gale of water-dust reminds us of the Continental Gauskuld, caused by the Finn-Lapp Magician sending forth his fly. In Iceland, as all the world over, the uplands are warmer than the lowlands—a fact well known to the ancients, but apparently puzzling to the modern traveller. "What is remarkable," says Henderson (i. 104), " I found the temperature of the atmosphere twelve degrees warmer in this hyperborean region than it was below in the valley." Yet it is easy to understand that whilst heated air rises, cold sinks; moreover, that, as a rule, there is more water, and consequently more evaporation, in lowlands than in highlands.

The mists (Mistar) are of the three kinds described by the Rev. G. Landt (Færoe Islands, London, Longmans, 1810): (1.) Skadda, or white cumulus on the hill-tops, supposed to show wet weather; (2.) Bolamjorkie, the vapour-belt which girdles the mountain flanks; and (3.) Mokyer (Icel. Thoka), the common fog of England.[1]

The Aurora Borealis, which the pagans held to be an emanation of the Deity—a nimbus encircling some mighty brow—and in which Greenland sees ghosts playing with walrus' heads, is expected to appear in mid-August, but of course not so splendidly as in winter. The author never saw either streamers or zodiacal light. Uno Von Troil (p. 54) makes the former show from all quarters, but especially from the southern horizon. Metcalfe (p. 385) asserts that it ranges from north-east to south-west, and there is a popular idea that the focus is more easterly than it was a decade ago. In the Færoes it flashes either from west and north-west to east, or from east and north-east to west. The streamers are bluish-yellow, gold-coloured, and red; rarely

means weather of the sun's course. The normal continental winds are (1.) the Land-south (south-east), warm, and therefore called Korn-moen, or the mother of corn; (2.) the north-east, termed Hambakka because it melts snow from the hill-tops; (3.) the Haf-gul (sea cooler), the west wind or sea breeze of the tropics, blowing from noon till midnight; and (4.) the Land-gul (land cooler), the east or land breeze, lasting from 2 A.M. to 10 A.M.

[1] Mr J. A. Hjaltalín remarks, "Thoka is equivalent to the English fog, and Sjólæða (sea creeper) is the mist which lies on the surface of the water, leaving the hill-tops clear. These are the only Icelandic names known to me."

blue, green, and scarlet.   The latter are called Lopt-eldr[1] or lift-fire, which shows the sky aflame.   It comes with strong winds and drifting snows, and, as in most hyperborean parts, it betokens great carnage over the place where it rises.   Icelanders can no longer make the aurora draw nearer by whistling to it.

The Alpen-glow, also called the evening aurora, is often a glorious spectacle when the reflection of the blood-red west, showing that the sun has just set, falls upon craggy hill and lowland slope, lighting up every house and field to a distance of five or six miles, and washing colour over the daguerrotyped outlines, usually so hard and sharp.   When distant objects seem near in most countries men predict rain, here the rule apparently fails.   The " Vetrar-braut," or course of winter (Milky Way), is by no means so bright as some travellers have described it.   In heathen times its appearance was used to forecast the hard months, especially as fortune-telling was part of the great autumnal feasts and sacrifices.   The author never saw in Iceland the phosphorescent water supposed to betray the presence of electricity and ozone, nor the *fulgor brutum seu spurium* of romantic meteorologists.   The rainbow (Icel. Regnbogi Nikuðs,[2] or of " Old Nick ") is of course common; the twilights strike the stranger from the northern temperates as being unimportant like those of the tropics; and there is a name for the mirage or heat-reek, Hillingar, or Upp-hillingar, when rocks and islands look as if lifted (" up-heaved ") from the level of the sea.   The common meteors are the Moorild or moor-fire of Norway (*ignis labentes seu fatui*), here called Hrævar-eldr[3] and Snæljós.   Castor and Pollux in Christian times either became Saint Elmo's (San Telmo's) flames, or connected themselves with Saints Nicholas and Clare; hence the Corpo Santo, and hence our " corpusance," frequently observed by the circumnavigator Pigafitta (A.D. 1519-1522).   The old English sailor regarded them as Will-o'-the-wisps intimately related to a certain Davy Jones.   The others are the Gýgjar-sól

---

[1] The term is also applied to lightning, and to meteors generally.   Hooker corrupts it to " Laptelltur," and he has been copied into many a popular book.

[2] The word is written Nikuðr and Nikuðs, Hnikar and Nikarr : originally a title of Odin, it has survived in the Icel. Nykr, a nick or water-goblin in the shape of a grey sea-horse, with inverted hoofs; and in the German Nix, a nymph or water-fairy.

[3] Or a " carrion lowe " (Cleasby).

(gow-sun) or Auka-sólir, mock sun (parabolia); and paraselenæ or lunar halos, with Rosabaugr, or storm-rings, literally "sleet-rings," the effect of minute ice spiculæ, or, perhaps, metallic particles, in the upper air refracting the light, and producing rainbow-hued circles and ovals, which often bisect one another. Water-spouts, the typhons of the Greeks, caused by the suction of clouds highly charged with electricity, have been observed. We read of fireballs or shooting-stars (Viga-hnöttur or Stjörnuhrap); of electric flames and red-hot globes (volcanic bombs) discharged with loud detonations during eruptions; and the people still believe in the " fire-vomiting" of their craters. Modern science explains the phenomenon by the reflection of the brilliant, glowing, glaring lava and the red-hot scoriæ, upon the dust and ash column, and upon the " smoke-clouds," which are really steam and other vapours. Yet M. Abich declares that in the Vesuvian eruption of 1834, he distinctly saw the flame of burning hydrogen, and this, indeed, might be expected.

As has been observed, the year of grace 1872 was exceptional. It opened with the finest weather till the equinox, after which it broke and strewed the ground with four feet of snow. Rain endured till the last quarter of June, but the rest of the travelling season was absolutely delightful. Mild east winds prevailed at Reykjavik, and the warmth of the " sirocco," as it was called, set the citizens speculating upon the possibility of an eruption in the interior. After July 11th the sky was that of Italy for a whole fortnight. The autumn was rough, with heavy gales from northeast to east, and from south-east to south-west; there were also hard frosts about mid-November, after which the weather became as mild as in 1871. Dr Hjaltalín, Land-Physicus or Physician-General of Iceland, was inclined to think that the summers were waxing warmer in Snowland, as they are growing, or are supposed to grow, colder in Scotland.

The travelling season of 1873 was very raw and dry. From the 20th of June to the 20th of July strong north winds prevailed, and from the 16th to the 18th of July there was a considerable fall of snow. August was tolerably rainless, but cold, and winter set in in earnest about the 20th of September.

## § 4. CHRONOMETRY.

In these hyperborean regions the light season and the dark season represent the "dries" and "rains" of the tropical zone. The gradual changes from winter to summer, and *vice versâ*, known as spring and autumn, can hardly exist when the frost often binds the ground till mid-June, and reappears in latter August.[1] Thus the Edda of the old Northmen (Vafthrûðnismál, Thorpe's trans., st. 27) very rightly distributes the year into only two parts:

> " Vindsval hight he
> Who Winter's father is,
> And Svâsud Summer's." [2]

The ancient heathen year contained 364 days (12 × 30 + 4 Auka-nætr, or Eke-nights) : [3] the remaining day, with its fraction, was gathered up into an intercalary week, called Summer-eke, or Eke-week, introduced by Thorstein Surt (the black) about the middle of the tenth century. Of old it was inserted at. the end of summer every sixth or seventh year, which then numbered 191 days. The Gregorian style inserts it every fifth or sixth year. Thus 1872 is marked the "first year after Sumarauki;" the years 1860, 1866, and 1871 being years with "Sumarauki." New style was not adopted till A.D. 1700.

The light months technically began with the Thursday preceding April 16,[4] O. S., = April 26, N. S. On that day children received their Sumar-gjöf (summer presents), which take the place of our Easter gifts. The season consisted of 184 days (30 × 6 + 4 Auka-nætr); the eke-nights being inserted before midsummer, which parts the season into two halves, each

---

[1] Even at Trieste, which is the heart of the temperates, with the parallel of 45° passing near it, there is an autumn, but no spring, the weather changing at once from cold to heat.

[2] Svasuðr, the name of a giant, the father of Summer. See the Edda.

[3] The way of counting amongst the old Scandinavians and Teutons was complex and curious, as they had no indeclinable numeral adjectives from twenty to a hundred (*i.e.*, 120): the word "tigr," a ten or decade, was a noun like Hundrað and Thúsund. Thus 41 was called 4 tens and 1, or "1 of the fifth decade;" 45 was "half the fifth tenth;" and 48 was "4 tens and 8;" or going back (like the Lat. un-de-viginti and duo-de-triginta) "5 tens short of 2." In the fourteenth century "tigr" began to lose its character as a substantive (Cleasby).

[4] Mr Dasent says the Thursday between April 9 and 15 (O. S.).

of three months. Thus in the Iceland almanac for 1872, Sumar-dagr-fyrsti (first summer day) fell on Thursday, April 25; the Auka-nætr ranged between July 24 to 27; Miŏ-sumar was on July 28; and Sumar-dagr-síŏasti (last summer day) happened on October 25. In modern usage the time from April to October is reckoned by the Sumar-vikur (summer weeks), the first, second, seventh, and twentieth; and the calendars mark every Thursday, during the light season, by the current number of the week. The "travelling time" extends from the Invention of the Cross (May 3) to St Bartholomew's Day (August 24). Meteorologically, summer opens with July. The winter, or dark half of the year (Vetr), began on the Saturday before St Luke's Day (O. S.), or that Saint's Day if a Saturday; and, like the summer, lasted twenty-six weeks. The Vetrar-dagr-fyrsti (first winter day) for 1872 and 1873 corresponds with Saturday, October 26. The following are the names of the months (Mánuŏr or Mánaŏr):

1. JANUARY— Icelandic, *Mörsugr*, "fatsucker;" Anglo-Saxon, *Æftera* (second) *Giuli* (Yule), from the turning or tropic of the sun; Old Danish, *Julemaaned*.

2. FEBRUARY—Icel., *Thorri*; A. S., *Sol monath*, from offerings made to the sun; O. D., *Blidemaaned*, or "blythe month."

3. MARCH—Icel., *Gói*;[1] A. S., *Rhed-monath*, "travel-month," or "month of the goddess Rheda," to whom warlike sacrifices were offered; O. D., *Törmaaned*, or "Thor's month"—hence Lucan (Phars., lib. i.):
   " Et Taranus Scythicæ non melior ara Dianæ."

4. APRIL—Icel., *Einmánuŏr*; A. S., *Eostre monath*, "Easter month," from the goddess Eostre; O. D., *Faaremaaned*, "fair month," or "sheep month."

5. MAY—Icel., *Harpa*, or *gaukmánuŏr*,[2] "cuckoo month," or *saŏlid*, "sowing season;" A. S., *Trimilchi*, because the sheep were milked thrice a day; O. D., *Maimaaned*, taken from the classics.

---

[1] Modern, *Góa*.
[2] "Gaukmánuŏr," according to Guŏbrandr Vigfusson, from the middle of April to the middle of May. Gaukr is the Scotch gowk, the cuckoo. Hrossa-gaukr, "horse cuckoo," is the green sandpiper, from its peculiar cry (Cleasby). In Sect. 7 the word will be found to have another meaning.

6. JUNE—Icel., *Skerpla*, or *egglið*, "egg-season," or *stekklið*; A. S.,
Ærra. (first) *Liða*, "serene sea;" O. D., *Hömaaned*, or
"hay month." The 3d to 5th of June are called *Fardagar*,
"flitting-days," because then householders change their
abodes.

7. JULY—Icel., *Sólmánuðr*, "sun-month," or *Selmánuðr*, "saeter
month;" A. S., *Æftera Liða*; O. D., *Ormemaaned*, or
"worm (lumbrici) month."

8. AUGUST—Icel., *Hey-annir*, or "time of haymaking," which
ends about the middle of next month; A. S., *Weide
monath*, "pasture month," or *Wenden monath*, "tare
month;" O. D., *Hoestmaaned*.

9. SEPTEMBER—Icel., *Tvímánuðr*; A. S., *Haleg monath*, or
"holy month;" O. D., *Fiskemaaned*.

10. OCTOBER—Icel., *Haustmánuðr*, "harvest or autumn month,"
or *Garðlagsmánuðr*, "the month for building fences;"
A. S., *Winterfyllath*, or "winter-full;" O. D., *Sædemaaned*,
"seed-month."

11. NOVEMBER—Icel., *Gormánuðr*, "gore-month," or "slaughter-
month;" A. S., *Bloth monath*, "sacrifice-month;" O. D.,
*Slagtemaaned*, "slaughter month."

12. DECEMBER—Icel., *Frermánuðr*, "frost month," or *Ýlir*,
"howler," from the howling storms; A. S., *Ærra Giuli*
(first Yule); O. D., *Julemaaned*.[1]

There is a quaint way of numbering the month-days by the
knuckles of the closed fist, which denote the longer, while the
intervals represent the shorter divisions, a *memoria technica*,
thus taking the place of our mnemonic lines, "Thirty days hath
September," etc. This "Dactylismus Ecclesiasticus,"[2] concerning

---

[1] According to the old Icelandic computation of time, as given in the Almanak,
Heyannir was the first month, and began the 25th of July; II. Tvímánuðr; III.
Haustmánuðr; IV. Gormánuðr; V. Frermánuðr; VI. Mörsugr; VII. Thorri;
VIII. Gói; IX. Einmánuðr; X. Harpa; XI. Skerpla; XII. Sólmánuðr, ending
on the 20th of July. From July 21st to 24th are called Aukanætur. The names of
the months VII. to IX. are still popularly known. For the rest, the Icelanders count
by winter weeks and summer weeks, when they do not use the common names of
the months. The terms given by Finnur Magnússon in Specimen Calendarii,
*e.g.*, Miðvetrarmánuðr, Föstuinngangsmánuðr, are never used, and it cannot be
seen that they ever were known to the people.

[2] See the Icel. treatise called "Fingra-rím;" rím=computation, calendar: A. S.
rím, and ge-rím.

which Bishop Jón Arnason wrote, is possibly what Uno Von
Troil means (p. 118), " They make use of an art to discover the
sun by their fingers."

The heathen week consisted of " Fimts " (pentads), whence,
probably, the sacred pentagonal star of Odinism; and six of these
formed the month. Thus the year was composed of seventy-two
weeks, a holy number (= 2 × 36, or 6 × 12). This old style
lingered long after the introduction of the planetary heptad, and
lasts in such expressions as " There are many turns of the
weather in five days (a fimt), but more in a month." Yet the
week (vika) was already in use about the middle of the tenth
century. Bishop John, who died in A.D. 1121, induced Iceland
to adopt the hebdomadal division, and the ecclesiastical names
of the days, as they survive in Spanish and Portuguese, e.g.,
Feria secunda, etc. Here we recognise, with the exception of the
two first, the familiar Quaker custom:

SUNDAY is *Sunnu-dagr*, or *Drottins-dagr*, " the Lord's day."

MONDAY—*Mána-dagr*, modern Icel. Mánu-dagr.

TUESDAY—*Thriði*, or *Thriðju-dagr*, " third day."

WEDNESDAY—*Miðviku*, contracted to *Miðku-dagr*, the Germ.
*Mittwoch*.

THURSDAY—*Fimti-dagr*, or " fifth day."

FRIDAY—*Föstu-dagr*, " fast-day," the O. Swed. *Vor Frudag*,
" *le jour de Nôtre Dame*," who took the place of Freya.

SATURDAY—*Laugar-dagr*, " bath day," as in the times of England before " tubbing."

The old Icelandic names of the week days were : Sunnudagr,
Mánadagr, Týsdagr (from Týr, Tuisco, the one‑armed god of
war), Óðinsdagr, Thórsdagr, Frjádagr, and Laugar or Thvátt dagr
(" washing-day," *i.e.*, Saturday).

Both Iceland and the Færoes have preserved the classical and
Oriental system of dividing into watches (Icel. Dagsmark, *plur.*
Dagsmörk, " day's marks " [1]), corresponding with the " Pahar "
still used throughout Hindostan. They ignored the hour, which

---

[1] Dagsmark, " day-mark," means both the space of three hours (*trihorium*) and
the mark by which this period is fixed.

would have been too troublesome and minute. Wanting time-
pieces, they used sundials (Sólskifa) and sand-glasses. The
rudest form was the peak or cairn, whose shadow noted the
time : the same system still prevails amongst the Bedawin. By
the sun also they learned to calculate the periods of ebb and
flow, and the southern altitude of the luminary denoted the
meridian. In winter evenings time was marked by the position
of the Pleiades, called, *par excellence, the* Stjarna (star). The
other constellations found useful at night were Örvindals-tá
(toe of Orwendel, = Rigel Orionis ?); Thjaza augu (the eyes
of Thiassi, = Castor and Pollux ?); Reið Rögnis (Charles' Wain,
the Wain of Rögn or Odin; whence also Ragna-rök, the twilight
of the gods and doom of the world); and Loka-brenna (Sirius,
Loki's fire, also referring to the final Odinic conflagration).

The Færoese divide the day into eight öktur (Icel. eyktir)
and sixteen half-öktur, the word Okt being shortened from
octava.[1] The Icelanders reckon nine like our seamen, the additional one being a " dog-watch," formed by dividing the 180
minutes into two. Their names are :

1. *Nátt-mál*, or night-meal to 9 P.M.
2. *Miðnætti*, to midnight.
3. *Ótta*, from midnight to 3 A.M.: " hana-ótta " is cock-crow.
4. *Miður-morgun*, also called *Hirðis-rismál*, " the rising time
   of the shepherd," to 6 A.M.
5. *Dagmál*, day-meal to 9 A.M. (*hora tertia.*)
6. *Hádegi*, or *Hiðr-dagr*, " high-day " till noon.
7. *Mið-mundi*, first dog-watch from noon to 1.30 P.M.
8. *Nón*, in olden times also *Eykt*, second dog-watch from 1.30
   P.M. to " nona," or 3 P.M.
9. *Miðr-aptn*, or mid-afternoon to 6 P.M.

The shortest day in the south averages five hours,[2] and the
longest is everywhere twenty-four.

As will appear in the Journal, Iceland preserves the Hebrew
style of beginning the civil day with evening, not with midnight

---

[1] Others derive it from vika, a week.
[2] Dillon reduces it at Reykjavik to three, and he found the sunlight during
Christmas little lighter than our twilights; but the winter was worse than usual.

like the rest of Europe. So Tacitus (cap. ii.) of the Germans:
"Nec dierum numerum, ut nos, sed noctium computant;" and
the older ecclesiastical law reckoned the greater feasts from the
nones or evenings of the preceding days. The hours are frac-
tioned after the English-Norwegian, not the German fashion:
thus 3.30 would be called "half (after) three," instead of "half
(to) four" (halb vier). Similarly our seamen when heaving the
lead sing out, "And a half three," *i.e.*, three fathoms and a half.

## § 5. SUMMARY.

Iceland has the general contour of Ireland with the eastern
side turned round to face the Arctic Pole. It is a square, cut,
furrowed, and digitated by the violence of the northern, the
north-eastern, and the south-western winds and waves; and its
shape is regular, and unsupplied with ports only in the south,
where, like Sicily, it is least exposed to weather.

The "little white spot in the Arctic Sea" is the epitome of a
world generated by the upheaval and the eruption; dislocated
and distorted by the earthquake, and sorely troubled and
tortured by wintry storms, rains, snows, avalanches, fierce
débâcles, and furious gales. The far greater portion, the plateau
above the seaboard, has a weird and sinister aspect; verging
on the desolation of Greenland, and lacking the sternness and
grandeur of nature in Norway. And nowhere, even in the
fairest portions, can we expect the dense forest on the Alp, "up
to the summit clothed with green;" the warbling of birds, the
murmurs of innumerous bees, the susurrus of the morning
breeze, or the melodious whispering of the "velvet forest:"
their places are taken by black rock and glittering ice, by the
wild roar of the foss, and by the mist-cloud hung to the rugged
hill-side. We may not look for that prodigality of colour with
which sun and air paint the scenery of the happier south. The
first impressions recorded by travellers are the astonishing
transparency of the atmosphere, the absence of trees, the
metallic green of the grass-fields, the pink and purple sheen
of the mountain heaths, the sharp contrast of Ossas and warts,

of ice and fire-born rock; and the prevalence of raw-white and dull-black hues, like gulls' feathers strewed upon a roof of tarred shingles, in fact the magpie suits of snowy jökull and sable fell.

Despite the almost hyperborean latitude, the frequent oases— Wadys or Fiumaras—of admirable verdure, soft and secluded from the horrors of loose sand and black lava, have suggested reminiscences of the Arabian wildernesses, whilst the caravans of ponies, the "dromedaries of the glacial desert," add a special feature of resemblance.

The "general glance" of southern travellers is perhaps too gloomy. It was hardly fair of the ancient Icelandic poet (tenth century) to call his native island a "gallows of slush," or for the modern Icelandic parson to describe it as "nothing but bogs, rocks, and precipices; precipices, rocks, and bogs; ice, snow, lava; lava, snow, ice; rivers and torrents; torrents and rivers." Cleasby crudely assures us that "the whole of Iceland may be said to be a burnt-out lava field, from eruptions previous to the peopling of the country." Henderson says rudely: "The general aspect of the country is the most rugged and dreary imaginable;" he quotes Jeremiah about a region "where all life dies, death lives, and Nature breeds all monstrous, all prodigious things;" and he dwells with apparent gusto upon the "doleful and haggard tracts," through which it was his "privilege" safely to pass. Baring-Gould repeats: "The general aspect of Iceland is one of utter desolation." Forbes gives an even more gloomy picture of repulsive deformity. One might be reading in these travellers a description of St Magnus' Bay:

> "For all is rock at random thrown,
>   Black waves, blue crags, and banks of stone; ·
>     As if were here denied
>   The summer sun, the spring's sweet dew,
>   That clothe with many a varied hue,
>     The blackest mountain side."

The harsh name "Iceland," which took the place of the far more picturesque and correct "Snæ-land," predisposes the wanderer to look upon this northern nature with unfriendly glance; but it is strange how her beauties grow upon him.

Doubtless the scenery depends far more upon colour and complexion than in the genial lands of the lower temperates. But, during the delightfully mild and pleasant weather of July and August, seen through a medium of matchless purity, there is much to admire in the rich meads and leas stretching to meet the light-blue waves; in the fretted and angular outlines of the caverned hills, the abodes of giant and dwarf; in the towering walls of huge horizontal steps which define the Fjörðs; and in the immense vistas of silvery cupolas, "cravatted" cones, and snow-capped mulls, which blend and melt with ravishing reflections of ethereal pink, blue, azure, and lilac, into the grey and neutral tints of the horizon. There is grandeur, too, when the Storm-Fiend rides abroad; amid the howl of gales, the rush of torrents, the roar of water-falls; when the sea appears of cast-iron; when the sky is charged with rolling clouds torn to shreds as they meet in aërial conflict; when the pale-faced streams shudder under the blast; when grim mists stalk over the lowlands; and when the tall peaks and "three-horns," parted by gloomy chasms, stand like ghostly hills in the shadowy realm. And often there is the most picturesque of contrasts: summer basking below, and winter raging above; peace brooding upon the vale and elemental war doing fierce battle upon the eternal snows and ice of the upper world.

Finally, there is one feature in Iceland which assumes a grandeur of dimensions unknown to Europe—the Hraun or lava stream. The "rivers of stone," like those of water, bear no proportion to the size of the island. The western arm of the Skaptárfellshraun, for instance, is nearly forty-eight miles long by ten of breadth at the lower end; and there are thousands of square miles covered by the Ódáða-hraun or Terrible Lava Stream. Every fantastic form, save of life, is there, and we cannot wonder if the peasant peoples them with outlying men or brigands. In a word, the student of Vulcanism must not neglect Iceland.

## SECTION III.

## HISTORICAL NOTES.[1]

The author has no intention of troubling his readers with the normal "historical sketch," which is usually an uninteresting abridgment—"compendium, dispendium,"—handed down from traveller to traveller. But it may be useful as well as interesting to dwell upon both extremes of the island annals; upon the beginning which is a disputed point, and upon the end which is still causing so much movement.

The Landnámabók (i. 1) briefly relates how, "according to some, Naddodd the Viking, in the days of Harold Fairfax, when sailing from Norway to the Færoes, was driven westward, and came upon the eastern coast of the island which he called Snæland;" how the Swede Garðar Svafarson, after the earliest circumnavigation, named it Garðarshólm, and established Húsavik; how Elóki Vilgerðarson, a mighty corsair (hèt Víkingr mikill) found ice investing the northern coast (A.D. 868) and gave the island its present grim and grisly title—"Greenland" being more kindly treated for advertising purposes, "a good name would

---

[1] Synopsis of dates :
A.D. 860 (861, Uno Von Troil). Iceland touched at by Naddodd. About this time (862), the Scandinavians, according to Nestor, founded the Russian empire.
,, 864. Garðar Svafarson built the first house in " Garðarshólm."
,, 874. First official colonisation of Iceland by Ingólfr Arnarson.
,, 877. Gunnbjörn discovered the Gunnbjörnarsker and coast of Greenland.
,, 929. Althing or Diet founded by Ulfljót.
,, 930-1300. Augustan age of literature under the aristocratic Republic.
,, 981-1000. Official discovery of the New World by the Northmen.
,, 982. Greenland visited by Eirikr Rauði (Eric the Red), father of Leifr the Lucky.
,, 986. First colony in Greenland established by the same. In 1124 the Bishop's See was placed at Garðar.
,, 1262-1264. Iceland incorporated with Norway.
,, 1380. ,, ,, ,, Denmark.
,, 1477. Iceland visited by Columbus.
,, 1540-1551. Lutheranism prevailed over Catholic Christianity.
,, 1800. Althing abolished.
,, 1843. ,, re-established.
,, 1845. ,, first met at Reykjavik.
,, 1874. First Constitution granted to the island on the date of its Millenary after Ingólf's settlement.

induce people to settle there;" how Flóki's companion Thórólf, describing it as a place where butter dropped from every plant, the northern equivalent of "flowing with milk and honey," gained the nickname of Thórólfr Smjör (Butter Thorolf); and finally, how Ingólfr, banished for murder, accompanied by his foster-brother and friend, Leifr, or Hjör-leifr (Leif of the sword), Hróðmarsson, settling in A.D. 870-874, the latter was murdered by his Irish thralls—an agrarian outrage which has since happened to many a landlord in the Emerald Isle. This official occupation of Ultima Thule took place shortly after King Alfred had defeated the Danes (A.D. 871): thus 1874 is the Millenary of Iceland colonisation, as 1872 was the Jubilee of Harold Fairfax, and as 1876 will be the Centenary of Freedom in the U.S.

But the Landnámabók proposes to itself a subject, the emigration of the pagan Northmen, who *nim'd* (Icel. "námu") the island,[1] and a few sentences, short and vague, are deemed sufficient for the older occupants. Later Scandinavian authors generally have satisfied themselves with repeating its statements, and have clung to a tradition which evidently does not date from ancient times. The argument relied upon by Arngrímr Jónsson has been often quoted; yet it appears far from satisfactory. The author is well aware of the difficulties to be encountered when supplementing the imperfect relation, and the "weight of tradition and historical circumstances" which lies in the way; he can hardly flatter himself with having succeeded, but he hopes that he has shown a case worthy of being taken in hand by some scholar who has leisure and inclination for the task.

The first modern writer who presumed to differ from the Landnámabók was, it is believed, Pontanus the Dane (loc. cit., Amstelodami, A.D. 1631, folio, p. 754). He gives the following extracts from the Bull of Pope Gregory IV., which he dates from A.D. 835, or thirty-nine years before the official date of discovery

"Ipsum filium nostrum, jam dictum Ansgarium et successores ejus legatos in omnibus circumquaque gentibus Danorum, Sueonum, Norvagorum, Farriæ,

---

[1] *i.e.*, Land-nim- (Germ. nehmen, "Corporal Nym," and modern slang, "to nim") book.

*Groenlandensium,* Helsingelandorum, *Islandorum,* Scritifindorum, Slavorum; necnon omnium Septentrionalium et orientalium nationum quocunque modo nominentur, delegamus et posito capite et pectori, super corpus et confessionem Sancti Petri Apostoli sibi suisque successoribus vicum nostram perpetuo retinendam, publicamque evangelizandi tribuimus auctoritatem," etc., etc.

Presently Pontanus quotes the following words from the Præcept of King Louis the Mild (regn. A.D. 814-840), son of Charlemagne, a document bearing date the year before the papal Bull (*i.e.,* A.D. 834):

"Idcirco Sanctæ Dei Ecclesiæ filiis præsentibus scilicet et futuris, certum esse volumus, qualiter divinâ ordinante gratiâ, nostris in diebus, Aquilonalibus in partibus, scilicet, in gentibus Danorum, Sueonum, Norvagorum, Farriæ, *Groenlandorum,* Helsinglandorum, Scritofinnorum, et omnium Septentrionalium et orientalium nationum magnum cælestis gratia predicationis sive acquistionis pateficit ostium, itâ ut multitudo hinc inde ad fidem Christi conversa, mysteria cælestia ecclesiasticaque subsidia desiderabiliter expetaret, unde Domino Deo nostro laudes immensas persolventes extollimus, qui nostris temporibus et studiis Sanctam Ecclesiam, sponsam videlicet suam, in locis ignotis sinit dilatari ac patefieri," etc.

Here it is possible that "Greenland," being mentioned with the islands and terra firma of Europe, may be the name of some district in the Scandinavian peninsula, and it has been suggested that "Iceland" may occur under similar conditions. In the Zeni Voyages, the Shetlands are called Estlanda, Eslanda, and Islande. But while a southern Shetland kept its place, the Shetlands were moved up to the north-east coast of Iceland, like the Orkneys to the south-east. He, therefore, who discovered the northern Shetlands, would also discover Iceland.

Evidently the first point is to consult an official copy of the Gregorian Bull referred to by Pontanus. The Very Rev. Father O'Callaghan, Principal of the English College, Rome, obliged the author with the following full extract:

*From the First Volume of the* BULLARIUM ROMANUM. *Printed at Turin,* 1857. Pages 279, 280.

"Confirmatio Sanctæ Sedis Hamburgensis in ultima Saxoniæ parti trans Albiam; cui Ecclesiæ Anscharius præficitur Archiepiscopus, datoque ei pallio, sibi subjectis gentibus apostolicæ sedis legatus constituitur.[1]

---

[1] Cointius Annal. Benedict. tom. viii., et Bollandus die 3 febr. in Comment. prævio ad vitam S. Anscharii, § xvii., Copenhagen, 1857.

### SUMMARIUM.

" Carolus Magnus Saxones ad Christi fidem perduxit—Hamburgensem sedem episcopalem constituit.—Anscharius [1] et successores Hamburgenses archiepiscopi legati sedis apostolicæ apud Danos, Sveones, Slavos, etc., delegantur.—Sedes Hamburg. vulgo d. archiepiscopalis efficitur.—Jus eligendi archiepiscopos penes Palatinos principes. — Anathema contra decreti hujus temeratores. — Pallium Anschario et successoribus.—Ad eundem Anscharium saluberrimæ adhortationes.

" Gregorius episcopus servus servorum Dei Omnium fidelium dinoscentiæ certum esse volumus, qualiter beatæ memoriæ præcellentissimus rex Karolus, tempore prædecessorum nostrorum, divino afflatus spiritu, gentem Saxonum sacro cultui subdidit, iugumque Christi, quod suave, ac leve est, adusque terminos Danorum sive Slavorum, corda ferocia perdomans docuit, ultimamque regni ipsius partem trans Albiam inter mortifera Paganorum pericula constitutam, videlicet ne ad ritum relaberetur Gentilium, vel etiam quia lucrandis adhuc gentibus aptissima videbatur, proprio episcopali vigore fundare decreverat. Sed quia mors effectum prohibuerat, succedente ejus præcellentissimo filio Hludewico imperatore Augusto, pium studium sacri genitoris sui efficaciter implevit. Quæ ratio nobis per venerabiles Ratoldum, sive Bernoldum episcopos, necnon et Geroldum comitem, vel missum venerabilem relata est confirmanda. Nos igitur omnem ibi Deo dignam statutam providentiam cognoscentes, instructi etiam præsentia fratris filiique nostri Anscharii primi Hordalbingorum archiepiscopi, per manus Drogonis Metensis episcopi consecrati, sanctum studium magnorum imperatorum, tam præsenti auctoritate, quam etiam pallii datione, more prædecessorum nostrorum roborare decrevimus ; quatenus tanta auctoritate fundatus prædictus filius noster, eiusque successores lucrandis plebibus insistentes, adversus tentamenta diaboli validiores existant, [2] *ipsumque filium nostrum iam dictum Anscharium, et succesores eius legatos in omnibus circumquoque gentibus Danorum, Sveonum, Northweorum, Farriæ, Gronlandan, Halsigolandan, Islandan, Scridevindum, Slavorum, nec non omnium septentrionalium, et orientalium nationum quocumque modo nominatarum delegamus, una cum Elbone Remensi archiepiscopo ; statuente, ante corpus et confessionem Sancti Petri, publicam evangelizandi tribuimus auctoritatem,* ipsamque sedem Nordalbingorum, Hammaburg dictam, in onore Salvatoris, sanctæque eius, et intemeratæ genitricis semper virginis Mariæ consecratam, archiepiscopalem deinceps esse decernimus. Consecrationem vero succedentium sacerdotum, donec consecrantium numerus ex gentibus augeatur, sacræ Palatinæ providentiæ interim committimus. Strenui vero prædicatoris persona, tantoque officio apta in successione semper eligatur : omnia vero a venerabili principe ad hoc Deo dignum officium deputata, nostra etiam auctoritate pia eius vota firmamus : omnemque resistentem, vel contradicentem atque piis nostris studiis his quolibet modo insidiantem, anathematis mucrone percutimus, atque perpetua ultione reum diabolica sorte damnamus, ut culmen apostolicum more prædecessorum nostrorum, causamque Dei pio affectu zelantes ab adversis hinc inde partibus tutius muniamur. Et quia te, carissime fili Anschari, divina clementia nova in sede primum disposuit

----

[1] " The Apostle of the North," a monk from the monastery of New Corvey, in Westphalia, who introduced Christianity to Denmark about A.D. 827.
[2] The words in italics are those quoted with variants by Pontanus, who, however, has added nothing to nor has he taken aught from the sense.

Marginal notes:
Carolus Magnus Saxo ad Christi fidem pe duxit; Hambur sem sede epi*s*copa constitui
Anschari et succes et successores Ha burgense archiep. legati Se Apostolic apud Da Sveo*n*es, vos, etc., delegant Sedes Ha burg. vul d. archie copa*l*is e tur. Jus elige archiepis pos pene Palatinos principes Anathem contra de ti huius temerato Pallium Anschari et succes ribus.

esse archiepiscopum, nos quoque pallio tibi ad missarum solemnia celebranda tribuimus, quod tibi in diebus tuis, uti et Ecclesiæ· tuæ perpetuo statu manentibus privilegiis uti largimur.   Idcirco huius indumenti honor morum a te vivacitate servandus est : si ergo pastores ovium sole, geluque pro gregis sui custodia, neque ex eis aut errando pereat, aut ferinis lanianda morsibus rapiatur, oculis semper vigilantibus circumspectant, quanto sudore, quantaque cura debeamus esse pervigiles, nos qui pastores animarum dicimur attendamus.   Et ne susceptum officium in terrenis negotiis aliquatenus implicare debeas ammonemus.   Vita itaque tua filiis tuis sit via; in ipsa si qua fortitudo illis inest, dirigant, in ea quod imitentur aspiciant ; in ipsa se semper considerando proficiant, ut tuum post Deum videatur esse bonum, quod vixerint.   Cor ergo tuum neque prospera, quæ temporaliter blandiuntur, extollant, neque adversa deiiciant ; districtum mali cognoscent, pium benevoli sentiant.   Insontem apud te culpabilem malitia aliena non faciat, reum gratia excuset ; viduis, ac pupillis iniuste oppressis defensio tua subveniat. Ecce, frater carissime, inter multa alia ista non sacerdotii, ista sunt pallii, quæ si studiose servaveris, quod foris accepisse ostenderis, intus habebis.   Sancta Trinitas fraternitatem tuam diu conservare dignetur incolumem, atque post huius sæculi amaritudinem ad perpetuam perducat beatitudinem.   Amen." [1]

Father O'Callaghan adds :

" I have carefully examined the fourth volume of the Bullandists, and find that they agree with Mabillon in omitting mention of Iceland and Greenland in their version of the Bull. [2]   The introductory commentary to the Life of St Anscharius (§ xii.), there given under the date of February 3, will suggest an explanation of the way in which the interpolation seems to have occurred."

The quotation of Mabillon (Acta Sanctorum Ordinis S. Benedioti, Sæculi Quarti, Pars Prima, 123, 124, fol., Venetiis, 1738) is as follows :

### BULLA GREGORII.

"Ipsumque filium nostrum, jam dictum Ansgarium Legatum in omnibus circumquaque gentibus Sueonum sive Danorum [*omitting the 'Norvagorum, Farriœ, Groenlandensium, Helsingelandorum, Islandorum, Scritifindorum,' of Pontanus*] nec non etiam Slavorum [*omitting 'nec non omnium Septentrionalium et orientalium nationum, quocunque modo nominentur, delegamus et posito capite et pectori,' of Pontanus*], vel in cæteris ubicunque illis partibus constitutis divina pietas ostium aperuerit, una cum Eboni Rhemensi archiepiscopo, statuentes ante corpus et confessionem Sancti Petri publicam evangelizandi tribuimus auctoritatem."

Furthermore, the Acta Sanctorum thus shortens the " Præceptum Ludovici Imperatoris":

---

[1] Data est hæc bulla post annum 834, quamvis ab aliquibus et præsertim a Pontano in rebus Danicis eo anno adscribatur.

[2] Here, again, the question is simply, "Has the Bull been tampered with or not?"   It would evidently be desirable to consult the earliest copies still extant, but unfortunately the author has no power of so doing at present.   The Bull of Pope Nicholas V. (A.D. 1448) should also be carefully inspected.   See p. 84.

"Idcirco Sanctæ Dei Ecclesiæ filiis, presentibus scilicet et futuris, certum esse volumus, qualiter divina ordinante gratia nostris in diebus, Aquilonalibus in partibus, in gente videlicet Danorum sive Sueonum [*omitting the ' Norvagorum, Farriæ, Groenlandorum, Helsinglandorum, Scritofinnorum, et omnium Septentrionalium et orientalium nationum,' of Pontanus*] magnum cælestis gratia prædicationis sive acquisitionis patefecit ostium."

It is curious to remark that the same tampering has been attributed to the Præcept as to the Bull, and it is not easy to divine the mode in which the double fraud was so successfully effected.

Mr Jón A. Hjaltalín, who owns to "grave doubts about the historical value of Danish chronicles recording dates of this period," supplies the following excerpts from the "Vita Sancti Anskarii, a Rimberto" (Archbishop of Hamburg) "et alio discipulo Anskarii conscripta" (before A.D. 876), "edidit C. F. Dahlmann, Prof. Göttingen." The editor's preface contains these words of

## INTRODUCTION.

"In edenda Anscharii vita hi codices et editiones subsidio fuerunt.
"(1.) . . .
"(2.) Codex Vicilini . . . textum exhibet ex eodem limpido quidem fonte manantem, sed consulta opera ita mutilatum et interdum interpolatum, ut facile suspiceris, ambitionem insatiabilem Adalberti archiepiscopi Bremensis, qui sub Henrico IV. imperatore patriarchatum septentrionis machinabatur, in hac fraude versatam. Recisa enim sunt, et ita quidem recisa, ut plane nihil deesse videatur, omnia, quæ de Ebonis, archiepiscopi Remensis, meritiis et legationis ejus in septentrionem susceptæ privilegiis verissime Rimbertus ex ore Anscharii excerpta scripsit, deest amissa cella Turholt, disceptatio interdioceses Bremensem et Verdensem unacum levamento damni quod Verdensis accepit, verbo omnia, quæ fideliter narrata ecclesiæ Bremensi detrimentum facere possent; contra addita dominatui Bremensi Islandia, quam Hibernicis quidem Anscharii ætate jam innotuisse nuper didicimus e Dicuilo, at plane tunc ignota Scandinavis et Germanis, æque ac Groenlandia, Færoeæ insulæ, reliquæque fraudulenter inculcatæ remotissimæ regiones."

## TEXT.

"Cap. 13. Et ut hæc omnia perpetuum suæ stabilitatis retinerent vigorem, eum honorabiliter ad sedem direxit apostolicam, et per missos suos venerabiles Bernoldum et Ratoldum episcopos ac Geroldum illustrissimum comitem omnem hanc rationem sanctissimo papæ Gregorio intimari fecit confirmandam. Quod etiam ipse tam decreti sui auctoritate, quam etiam pallii donatione, more prædecessorum suorum roboravit, atque ipsum in præsentia constitutum legatum in omnibus circumquaque gentibus Sueonum sive Danorum, nex non etiam Slavorum, aliarumque in aquilonis partibus gentium constitutarunt, unacum Ebone Remensi archiepiscopo, qui ipsam legationem ante susceperat, delegavit : et ante corpus et confessionem Sancti Petri apostoli publicam evangelizandi tribuit auctoritatem."

## EDITOR'S NOTE.

" Codex Vicilini hunc ita interpolatum exhibet locum, ut sublata plane Ebonis mentione, in majorem ecclesiæ Hammaburgensis gloriam nomina septentrionalium tunc inaudita adsuant, quæ fraus etiam latius serpsit interpolationibus ipsius bullæ papæ Gregorii : 'Gentibus Sueonum, Danorum, Farriæ, Gronlondon, Islondon, Scrideuindun, Slauorum, nec non omnium septentrionalium et orientalium nationum quocunque modo nominatarum delegauit. Et posito capite et pectore super corpus et confessionem Sancti Petri apostoli, sibi suisque successoribus vicem suam perpetuo retinendam publicamque evangelizandi tribuit auctoritatem' (Cod. Vicilinus). Manifesta utique interpolationum hujus loci et bullæ papalis fraus, quam ab Adalberto archiepiscopo, Adami Bremensi æquali, ad quem extremi venerunt Islandi, etc., profectam, cum Langebekio suspicamur" (G. H. Pertz, Monumenta Germaniæ Historica, tom. ii., p. 699).

## VITA S. RIMBERTI (Ex Codice Vicilino).
### Edidit G. H. Pertz.

"Imperator Hludowicus . . . extremam plagam aquilonarem ejusdem provinciæ ad hoc reservaverit, ut ibidem archiepiscopalis construeretur sedes, unde prædicatio verbi Dei finitimis fieret populis, Suenonum, Danorum, Norweorum, Farriæ, Gronlandan, Islandan, Scridivindan, Slavorum, nec non omnium septentrionalium," etc.

## EDITOR'S NOTE.

" ' Norweorum—Scridivindan,' hæc pro supposititiis habet Henschenius. Sed obstant diplomata ab imperatoribus summisque pontificibus ecclesiæ Hamburgensi concessa. 1. Hludowicus I. post Danos et Sueones etiam 'gentes Norweorum, Farriæ, Gronlandon, Halsingalandon, Islandon, Scridevindan, Slavorum et omnium septentrionalium et orientalium nationum' addit. 2. Gregorii IV. diploma eadem adjicit. 3. Charta Johannis X. pro Unni archiepiscopo a. 915 Norweos, Islandon, Scridevindon, Gronlandon. 4. Benedictus IX. in charta Adalberto archiepiscopo a. 1042 aut 1043 concessa 'Hislandicorum et omnium insularum his regnis adjacentium.' 5. Victor II. in diplomate a. 1055, Oct. 29, Islandon, Scridivindan, Gronlandon; et 6. Innocentius II., a. 1133, d. Maii 27, Farria, Gronlandon, Halsingaldia, Island, Scridivindan et Slavorem mentionem injecerunt. Hæc aliaque ejus ecclesiæ diplomata in codicibus diversis, uno, quem ante oculos habeo, Sæculi XIII. . . . altero Philippi Cæsaris quem codici Vicilini valde similem fuisse constat, occurrunt ; quorum de fide eo saltem non dubitare possumus, quod alia diplomata quæ hodie supersunt eorum exemplis hic adservatis congruunt. Igitur aut non unum sed quinque studio Adalberti archiepiscopi falsata credas, et tunc haud intelligeretur, cur Adalbertus multo majorem numerum reliquorum ecclesiæ suæ privilegiorum, ubi tantum de Danis, Sueonibus et Norweis aliisque septentrionalibus et occidentalibus barbaris nationibus sermo est, intactum reliquerit ;—aut omnia sana, et locum hunc ex charta Hludowici I. sincera in posteras omnes emanasse statuendum est. . . ." (G. H. Pertz, Monumenta Germaniæ Historica, tom. ii., p. 765).

Mr Jón A. Hjaltalín, who "admits that the subject is not fully cleared up," adds:

"We have only to do with the three documents first mentioned. (*See note* 1, p. 86.) Unless a copy of the letter of Ludvig and the Bull of Gregory, of a date anterior to the times of Adalbert, can be produced, I do not see any impossibility in all the copies mentioned, the earliest of which dates from the thirteenth century, being derived from a copy falsified by Bishop Adalbert; at any rate, if all the copies can be derived from a true one, as Dr Pertz seems to think, they can as well be derived from a false one. The Bullarium does not help us (we have only the older ones, not that of 834), as it does not state from what MS. the Bull is printed. But even if the Bull is proved true, which only can be done by producing the original, or at least a copy anterior to Bishop Adalbert, it would hardly establish the fact that Iceland was known by that name prior to its Norwegian discovery; for many of the names mentioned in these documents, such as Gronlondon, Scridevindon, and Halsingaldia, are perverted Norwegian districts, and I should be inclined to look upon Islandon in the same way. But, in my own mind, I am perfectly satisfied that Professor Dahlmann is right in pronouncing the interpolated passages as forgeries. In this case I prefer his judgment to that of Dr Pertz, as he has proved his intimate acquaintance with the subject in his eminently critical 'History of Denmark.'"

The following quotation from La Peyrère's "Account of Iceland," dated Copenhagen, December 18, 1644, and addressed to M. de la Mothe de Vayer (Churchill's Coll., vol. ii.), is quoted because it well expresses the opinion adverse to that generally received. Mr Jón A. Hjaltalín remarks of this amusing French traveller:

"Peyrère is no authority, either in this or in other statements. He wrote what he had been able hurriedly to gather together from Arngrímr Jónsson and Blefkenius, aided by conversation with sundry learned men in Copenhagen, and he confesses that he had scarcely time to peruse the writings of 'Angrim Jonas.' Consequently his account abounds in inaccuracies and blunders. It is evident that he had never heard of the Landnámabók, as he complains of Arngrím's not stating when Kalman and other Irish settlers came to Iceland. I have also grave doubts about his Danish chronicles. Arngrímr refutes Pontanus in his 'Specimen Islandiæ Historicum;' and Pontanus should have mentioned where he found his quotation, especially as it militates against everything that is known in the matter."

We may, however, be certain that in the following extract La Peyrère expresses the opinions popular at Copenhagen in the seventeenth century:

"*Angrim Jonas*,[1] as it seems, would not be so averse, to allow that *Iseland* is the same with the Ancient *Thule*, provided he could be convinced, that that Isle was

---

[1] In p. 432 (loc. cit.) we are told that *Angrim Jonas* is "erroneously call'd *Arngrim* by some"—it need hardly be said that the real name is Arngrímr Jónsson.

inhabited before the time of *Ingulph;* wherefore, tho' I have said enough upon this Head for the Satisfaction of unbyass'd Persons; yet will I not think it beyond the purpose, to alledge some undeniable Reasons for the Proof thereof, *viz.,* That *Iseland* was Inhabited before that time. I have by.me two Chronicles of *Greenland* written in *Danish,* one in Verse, the other in Prose. That written in Verse, begins with the year 770, when it says *Greenland* was first discovered. The other assures us, That the Person, that went first from *Norway* into *Greenland* pass'd through *Iseland,* and tells us, expressly, That *Iseland* was Inhabited at that time; whence it is evident, that *Iseland* was not first of all Inhabited in the year 874."

"*Angrim Jonas* will perhaps object, That my *Danish* Chronicles don't agree with that of *Iseland,* which says, That *Greenland* was not discovered till the year 982; nor inhabited till 986. But I must tell him, That my *Danish* Chronicles are founded upon the Authority of *Ansgarius,* a great Prelate, a Native of *France,* who has been acknowledged the first Apostle of the Northern World. He was made Archbishop of *Hamborough,* by *Lewis the Mild,* his Jurisdiction extended from the River *Elbe,* all over the Frozen Sea; the Emperor's Patent, constituting the said *Ansgarius* the first Archbishop of *Hamborough,* are dated in the year 834, and were confirmed by Pope *Gregory* IV.'s Bull in 835. The true Copy, both of the Patent and of the Bull, are to be seen in the 4th Book of *Pontanus* his *Danish* History of the year 834, where it is expressly said in the Patent, That *the Gates of the Gospel are set open, and that Jesus Christ had been revealed both in* Iceland *and* Greenland; for which the Emperor gives his most humble Thanks to God."

"Two Inferences are to be made from thence: First, That *Iseland* was inhabited by Christians in the year 834, and consequently 40 years before the arrival of *Ingulph* there: Secondly, That *Greenland* was inhabited by Christians in the same year, 834. Which agrees with my *Danish* Chronicle, where the first discovery of *Greenland* is fix'd to the year 770.[1] *Angrim Jonas* being put to a *nonplus,* tells us, That he questions the authority of the Bull of Gregory IV. alledged by *Pontanus,* which he would fain make us believe, is supposititious; but to be plain with him, I think he has taken a Notion of maintaining the Credit of his Native Country, by adhering too strictly to the Authority of its Chronicles; whereas it would have been more for his Reputation, not to have insisted so much upon that Authority, than to rob this Isle of the glory of its Antiquity; who is so ignorant, as not to know, that the Age wherein *Ingulph* lived, was not very barbarous? The *Goths* having carried the same together with their Arms throughout all *Europe;* whoever should go about to persuade me, into a Belief of all what is inserted in the Ancient Chronicles of these barbarous Ages, might as soon make me believe the

---

[1] Popular history, it has been seen, attributes the exploration to Eirikr Rauð (Eric the Red) in A.D. 982, some five centuries before the days of Columbus. Captain Graah, of whom more presently, speaks of a papal Bull by Nicholas V., who in A.D. 1448 declares Christianity in Greenland to date from 600 years back, thus removing the colonisation to A.D. 848. We have ample materials for determining the exact limits of the Northmen's explorations by their precising the length of the day. For instance, at Vínland the sun at the winter solstice was above the horizon from Dagmál (7.30 A.M.) to Eykt (4.30 P.M.), which gives nine hours = N. lat. 41°.

Romances of *Oger* the *Dane*, or the Four Sons of *Aymon*, of the Archbishop of *Turpin*, and other such like nonsensical Stories relating to the same time."

A fair collateral testimony is given by that conscientious writer, Uno Von Troil (p. 224):

"Thus I go further back with regard to the eruptions of fire in Iceland than the common tradition among the vulgar people there, who believe that the first inhabitants of the country, whom they suppose to have been Christians and Irishmen, were so much oppressed by the Norwegian colonists, that they were forced to leave the country, to which they first set fire to revenge themselves."

And Iceland still contains many traces of its old colonists— Welsh, Hebridian, and Irish. The places occupied by the former are known by the general term Kumbravágr. Arngrim Jónsson mentions one Kalman from the Hebrides (Land. II. i. 51), who first settled in Kalmanstunga or "Doab" of Kalman, the western part of Iceland; and Patrick (Patrekr Biskup, Land. I. xii. 23), a Hebridian bishop, is known to history as having sent the materials of a chapel, which was afterwards built at the base of the Esja mountain; hence Patreksfjörð in the north-west. The signs of the Irish are most numerous,[1] and possibly they supplied "Raven Floki" with food during the two years which he passed in the far north. Such are Briánn or Bran, Melkorka, Nial or Njáll, Konall (Connell), Kormak and Kjartan, Íraá (Irish River); the Írafell, or Irish fell, in the Kjósar Sýsla; and the Írarbuðr, or Irish booths, in the Hvammsfjörð. Hence we can explain the fables of history which have been regarded as simple fabrications. Geoffrey of Monmouth makes Prince Arthur, in A.D. 517, subdue Iceland with an army of 60,000 men. Hence, too, another writer attributes its recovery to Malgo, king of Britain; whilst a third alludes to the mixture of Finns and Scandinavians before the official rediscovery of the island.[2]

---

[1] The Dictionary (iii. 780) gives forty-nine Keltic names in the Landnámabók only, neglecting the Orkneyinga, or Iarla, Saga, and the Njála.

[2] Mr Jón A. Hjaltalín remarks: "The large number of Irish settlers in Iceland after Ingólf do not prove anything concerning a previous settlement. No one denies that Iceland was visited by the Irish previous to the Norwegian discovery. No proofs, however, have been as yet brought forward to show that a settlement was made more extensive than that spoken of in Landnámabók, and by Ari Fródi. The great bulk of the settlers were Norwegians; the rest were Danes, Swedes, and Irishmen." (See Landnámabók; Lambert, 'Αρχαιονομία, fol. 137, p. 2; and Encyclopedie des Gens du Monde, vol. ii., p. 60.)

Within sixty years after the first settlement by the Northmen, the whole was inhabited; and, writes Uno Von Troil (p. 64), " King Harold, who did not contribute a little towards it by his tyrannical treatment of the petty kings and lords in Norway, was obliged at last to issue an order, that no one should sail to Iceland without paying four ounces of fine silver to the Crown, in order to stop those continual emigrations, which weakened his kingdom." The stock phrase of the Landnámabók (ii. 12, 92) is, " Fyrir ofríki Haralldar Konungs "—" For the overbearing of King Harold." But posterity has done justice to Pulchricomus, the Fair-haired Jarl, who, following the example of Egbert, brought under a single sceptre the quasi-independent reguli and heads of clans: the latter remind us of nothing more than the thousand kinglets, each with a family all kinglets, the ridiculous King Boys and King Pepples of Western Africa.

Before the tenth century had reached its half-way period, the Norwegians had fully peopled the island with not less, perhaps, than 50,000 souls. A census taken about A.D. 1100, numbered the franklins who had to pay Thing-tax at 4500, without including cotters and proletarians. The chiefs, who were also the priests, lived each upon his own "Landnám," or lot, which perhaps he had seized from another. Once more like little kings, they intermarried; they left their possessions to their families; they assigned lands to new comers; and they raised revenue from their clients and freedmen, serfs and slaves. They brought with their language and religion their customs and records; they claimed all the influence which could be commanded by strength and valour, birth and wealth; and they had no common bonds of union save race and religion. The three castes were sharply distinguished, like the four of the Hindús. The first was the Goði, priest and lord, including a rare Jarl, and Hersir (baron). The two latter, descended from *Hersir* and *Erna*, are described like our " Barbarians," as having fair hair, clear complexions, and fine piercing eyes: their duties in life were riding, hunting, and fighting. Secondly came the progeny of Afi and Amma; the Thanes, Churls, Karls, or free peasants: their florid, red-haired sons were Stiffbeard, Landholder, Husbandman, and Smith; and their daughters, Prettyface, Swanlike, Blithespeech, and Chatterbox.  Last in the list were the Thralls, begotten by Thræl, son of Ái and Edda, upon Thý: for offspring they had Plumpy, Stumpy, Frousy, Homespun, Sootyface, and Slowpace, the latter a very fruitful parent; and their daughters were Busybody, Cranefoot, Smokeynose, and Tearclout.

But Iceland was already too populous for this "leonine" state of society.  In the brave old days when ancient mariners were ancient thieves, the roving islandry throve by piracy and discovery; but the settled Udallers (Óðalsmenn) must have felt that some tie was necessary for the body politic.  The Höfðingja-stjórn, or aristocratic republic, was initiated by the establishment of the Althing,[1] and by the adoption of Úlfljót's oral law in A.D. 929-930.  This annual assembly, at once legislative and judicial, was supreme over the local "Things,"[2] comitia or meetings which, independent of one another, and unchecked by a supreme court, could not do justice between rival nobles and franklins.  With the Althing was introduced a kind of President, under whom the Icelandic commonwealth at once assumed shape and form.  His title was Lögsögumaðr, or Sayer of the Law, and his functions resembled in important points the commoner, who began in A.D. 1377, to speak to (and not for) our Lower House.[3]

---

[1] Some foreigners erroneously write for Althingi, "Allthing," which would be pronounced Atl- or Adl-thing.  *Al-* is from *allr*, all, the highest possible degree, *e.g.*, Al-máttigr, Almighty.  *All-* is right or very, *e.g.*, All-vitr, right clever (Cleasby).  The following is a synopsis of the most important events in the history of this famous Diet:
A.D. 965. Reform (bill) carried by Thord Gellir, who organised the courts and settled the political divisions of Iceland.
,, 1004. Institution of the Fifth Court (of Appeal).
,, 1024. Repudiation of the King of Norway's attempt to annex Iceland.
,, 1096. Tíund or tithes introduced.
,, 1117-18. The laws codified, written down, and adopted by the Althing.  This code was afterwards called Grágás.
,, 1262-64. Submission to the King of Norway.
,, 1272. Second written code (Járn-siða) introduced.
,, 1280 (?). Third written code (Jóns-bók) introduced.
[2] Traces of some two hundred Things remain in the "Standing Stones" of Great Britain.  Mr Dasent, from whose study of the Iceland republic (Introduction, etc., Burnt Njal, pp. li.-lxvii.) these lines are abridged, shows our *meeting* to be "Mót-Thing," a public gathering of the district freeholders; as *Husting* is "House-Thing," an assembly of householders.  In Norway the Things were founded by Hákon, son of Harold Fair-hair, and the conquest over the Jarls was at once followed by the constitution.
[3] Sir Thomas Hungerford in 1377 was the first Speaker, and Sir John Busby in 1394 was the first Speaker formally presented for royal approval.  These officials were the mouth-piece of the House, and by no means so called on the *lucus-a-non-lucendo* principle.

Still Justice walked *pede claudo*. All suits were to be pled in the Thing nearest the spot where the cause of action arose, and plaintiffs perforce sought redress in the enemy's country, where violence was ready to hand. Thord Gellir, about a generation afterwards, caused the island to be divided into Quadrants, or Tetrads (Fjórðungr), and each of these to be subdivided into Thriðjungr ("ridings"), three judicial circles (Thing-sóknir), whose inhabitants were bound to appear at a common meeting. Causes were set on foot at the Spring-Thing (Vár-Thing), thence they were carried in appeal to the Quadrant-Thing (Fjórðunga-Thing), which must not be confounded with the Quadrant courts (Fjórðungsdómar) at the Althing; and, finally, if judged fit, to the Diet. Moreover, in each subdivision were established three chief temples (Höfuðhof), corresponding with our mother or parish churches, to which the most powerful Udallers holding priesthoods (Goðorð) were appointed. We shall presently find traces of this politico-religious supremacy of the pontiff in the parson of the nineteenth century.

Thus three priesthoods made one local Thing, three local Things one Quadrant-Thing, and four Quadrant-Things one Althing,—a grand total of thirty-six tribunals recognised by the Respublica. Every franklin was obliged to declare his allegiance to one of the priests, and to determine the community of which he was a member.

The next step was to separate the judicial from the legislative and executive attributes of the Diet. Hitherto there had been but one body at the Althing, the Lög-rétta,[1] combining the three functions. It now became exclusively legislative, the supreme power in the land, presided over by the Speaker, and consisting of forty-eight Goðar, who controlled all laws and licences. The judicial functions were distributed amongst the four Fjórðungs-

---

[1] The word is liable to misapprehension. It is used of the place as well as of the body sitting there; of the Sacred Circle (Vé-bönd) as well as of the lawmen who occupied it. Moreover, under the Commonwealth, it was the legislative session that met on the Lög-berg; and after the union with Norway it was the public court of law at the Althing considerably modified. The term is also variously derived from Rètt, a fence, a sheep-fold; or from Að rètta lög, to right (or make right) the law (Cleasby). Moreover, the Lög-berg (Hill of Laws) of the Althing was called Thing-brekka (Parliament brink, or high place) at the local assemblies.

dómar or Quadrant-courts of the chief assembly. Each of these took charge of the suits which, belonging to its division, were carried before the Althing.

Presently the State became master of the Church. The priest-hoods being limited to thirty-six, and new temples not being recognised by, nor represented in, the assembly, the old institutions would look rather to the central power than to their subjects. The Thingmen of the three established priesthoods, by the orders of the Diet, were gradually made to form one Vernal-court (Vár-Thing), and the Quadrant-Things became obsolete. Thus there was more of justice for suitors than when they were compelled to appear before a single priest and his dependants or parishioners.

The Vernal Thing, though only a tribunal of first instance from which an appeal lay, became an Althing on· a small scale. Each had its Thingbrekka, or Hill of Laws, whence notices were given; its Lögmaðr,[1] lagman, or lawman, who "said" the law from memory, and its general assemblies. Each also of the three priests, who presided in turn, named three judges, after the recognised principle, "three twelves must judge all suits;" and the three arbiters were bound to be unanimous. In addition to these courts were the tribunals called Autumn Leets (Leið),[2] held a fortnight after the dissolution of the Diet; here the calendar of the current year, and the new laws and licences of the past Althing, were published.

Under the new system the Court of Laws contained 39 priests $(3 \times 12, + 3$ for the Northlanders' Quadrant[3]); and, to counter-balance the three clerical extras, three laymen were chosen from each of the other Tetrads by the priests who represented it. Thus the whole number on the bench was 48 (39 + 9), and each

---

[1] Lög (i.e., "laws," used only in the plural; from "lag," a lay, layer, stratum) also signified the legal community or State.

[2] The Anglo-Saxon Leode, probably akin to June (ærra Liða) and July (æftera Liða); the Irish Fo-leith, and our modern "leet," properly the law-court of the hundred. In the Saga times (tenth century) the Leið was a kind of county as-sembly; during the rule of the Grágás (twelfth and thirteenth centuries), the Leið was held where the Vár-Thing used to sit, in common with all the three Goðar of the Quarter (Sam-leið).

[3] The Northlanders, by a provincial arrangement which the central authority hardly recognised, claimed four instead of three judicial circles (Thing-sóknir). The reason was, that the heads of houses east of the Eyjafjörð and west of the Skagafjörð, whose Quadrant-Things lay in the middle of the Tetrad, refused to ride so far.

of the 48 had two assessors. The Law Court, therefore, contained 144 (48 × 3) equal votes, and, including the Speaker, 145
voices. In later times the two bishops were added.

The four Quadrant Courts of the Althing (Fjórðungsdómar)
each numbered thirty-six judges, named as usual by the priest
out of the frequenters of his Thing: thus we find again the law
of three twelves, and the total of 144. Finally, in A.D. 1004,
about forty years after the institution of the four, was added the
Fimtar-dómr, or Fifth (High) Court of Appeal or Cassation,
suggested by Njáll Thorgeirsson, the hero of the "Nials-burning."[1]

Such was the artificial and complicated system which sprung
from the litigious nature of the Northern man. It was a
ponderous machine for the wants of some 50,000 souls, and
its civilised organisation contrasts strongly with the rude
appliances by which it was carried out, the barren wart and
the rough circle of "standing stones" on the hill-top where
the sessions took place.

A mighty change came over the island mind when Ólafr
Tryggvason (Olaf I., Trusty-son, killed during the same year at
the battle of Svoldur) induced, in A.D. 1000, the Althing to
accept Christianity as the national religion.[2] The old pagan
creed had become age-decrepit. After producing the Völuspá,
a poem, grand, noble, and ennobling in general conception, as
it is beautiful and perfect in all its parts, it engendered such
monstrous growths as the Fjöllvinnsmál (Fiolvith's Lay), a

---

[1] Nat. A.D. 930; converted to Christianity, 998, and murdered, 1014. Cleasby
derives "Fimtar" from "Fimt," the heathen week, a pentad or five days; whilst
the Swedish "Femt," a court before which one has to appear a "fimt" from the
citation, seems to have floated before the minds of the founders.

[2] Fat and ferocious Ólafr Helgi (Olaf II., or the Saint), when succeeding to the
throne of Norway, doomed to death and slavery, to exile and confiscation, all
who opposed the new faith. The blood of martyred pagans was not the seed of
their Church; and persecution, vigorously carried out, took, as usual, wide effect.
After his death at the battle of Stikklestad, he became the tutelar saint of
Norway, the "Lamb" of the calendar. His remains ranked as relics in the
ancient cathedral at Throndhjem, till Protestantism, or rather Lutheranism, under
Gustavus Vasa (A.D. 1527), and Christian II. (1536), replaced Romanism in the
Scandinavian peninsula. The Royal Order of Norway, founded in 1847 by the
late king, Oscar I., bears his name. London has boasted of four "St Olaves;"
and Tooley Street of the Tailors, according to Mr Peter Cunningham, notes the
site of the first church. To retain due reverence for such a "Saint," we must
believe with Pliny (Epist., viii. 24): "Reverere gloriam veterem, et hanc ipsam
senectutem, quæ in homine venerabilis, in urbibus sacra. Sit apud te honor
antiquitati, sit ingentibus factis, sit fabulis quoque."

mythological pasquinade abounding in *bizarreries,* and the Lokasenna (Loki's Altercation), all scoffs and sneers, an *epigramme moqueuse et grossière,* a kind of hyperborean *Guerre des Dieux.* The "great Sire of gods and men"[1] was dying or dead, a gloomy fate which equally awaits superhuman and human nature. The decline and fall of Odinism only repeated the religious histories of Palestine, Egypt, and India; of Greece and of Rome, whose maximum of effeteness has ever been at the period of the Christian invasion.

The faith of the Hindús, a modern people amongst whom we can best study the tenets and practices of the ancients called "classics," distinctly recognises Pantheus, the All-God.[2] The worshipper of Bramhá, Vishnu, and Shiva, still refers in familiar discourse to something above his triad of world-rulers; to a Paraméshwar (Chief Eshwara or Demiourgos), and to a Bhagwán or Giver of good, as if he were a Jew, a Christian, or a Moslem. Even the barbarous tribes of Africa are not without the conviction, as we see in the Nyonmo of the Gold Coast, and in the Nzambi Mupunga (Great Lord) of the Congo. But the God of ancient as of modern paganism was and is an unknown God—in fact, the UNKNOWABLE recognised by our contemporary philosophy, which seems to be returning to the natural instincts

---

[1] It was a classical dream which made Odin or Sigge (whence Sigtuna), and his followers the Æsir (minor gods), fly from Pompey in the days of Mithridates. It was a philological dream of Finn Magnússon's which identified Bragi with Bramhá, and the ferocious and sanguinary Odin with the moral and holy Buddha, the prototype of the Christian exemplar. The casual resemblance to the Etruscan Tina has not been more fortunate. Some one well remarks that "a man born about A.D. 333, and dying seventy-eight years old (A.D. 411), would, in respect to time, perfectly represent the personage whom the Scandinavians and the Anglo-Saxons call Odin and Woden, and who are the roots of their royal dynasties."

[2] This fact was not unknown to Bishop Warburton and to Lord Herbert of Cherbury. In the Egyptian hymn to Phthah we read: "Praised be thy countenance, Ruler of the World!" Ausonius thus explains the multitude of synonyms :

> " Ogygia ME Bacchum vocat ;
> Osirin Ægyptus putat ;
> Mystæ Phanacen nominant ;
> Dionyson Indi existimant ;
> Romana sacra Liberum ;
> Arabica gens Adoneum ;
> Lucianus Pantheum."

Those who see in ancient myths the eternal contest of sunlight and darkness ; of summer and winter, and, in the moral world, of intelligence and ignorance, will find strong confirmation in Eddaic poetry and prose.

of its childhood.   Moreover, in old Scandinavia the several
forms or eidola of the Deity, such as Oðin and Thor, Freyr and
Njördr, were confused as the systems of African Fetichism—
a confusion indeed by no means wanting in the civilised
idolatries of Assyria, of Egypt and India, of Greece and Rome,
and of Mexico and Peru, the New World representatives of our
" classical regions."

Curious to observe, however, the pagans had, like the
modern Gaboons, a form of baptism, water being probably the
symbol of the Urðar-brunnr (Weird or Fate-fount), and a regular
system of national expiation (Sónar-blót), annually performed
by prince-pontiff and lieges.

Presently Christianity came with its offer of a personal God,
an anthropomorphous Creator who, having made the creature
after His own image, was refashioned by the creature ; and the
change from vagueness to distinctness perfectly suited the spirit
of the age.   Yet, in Iceland, Thor[1] died hard because he was
essentially an Icelander; blunt, hot-headed, of few words and
of many blows.   The red-bearded one was not to be abolished
at once; "they called Paul Odin, but Barnabas they called
Thor:" the latter was long invoked by the traveller and the
soldier before deeds of "derring do;" whilst Jesus was prayed
to in matters of charity and beneficence.   "Hast thou heard,"
said the mother of Ref the Skáld, "how Thor challenged Christ
to single combat, and how He did not dare to fight Thor?"
We find the same phenomenon in the modern faith of the
Persian, who adores Allah, and who reveres Mohammed and
Ali, whilst he looks back with regret upon the goodly days
when his Persian deities, the gods and demi-gods of Guebrism,
gloriously ruled the land of Iran.

The transition from the turbulent and sanguinary Odinic system,
with its Paradise of war and wassail, to a religion based upon

---

[1] Properly written Thórr, a congener of the Mæso-Gothic Thunrs, the Thunder-
god who named our Thursday.   Whilst his golden-haired wife, Sif, who represented mother earth, with her sheaves of ripe grain, and the sanctity of wedlock
and the family, is wholly forgotten, this terrigenous deity still lives, as we shall
see, in modern Icelandic names.   It is usually said that Iceland, following Norway,
preferred Thórr, whilst the Danes paid the highest honours to Odin, and the
Swedes to Freya (Venus), or rather to Freyr, her brother, the sun-god, who presided over the seasons and bestowed peace, fertility, and riches.

mildness and mercy could not fail to bear notable fruit. The blithe gods who built Miðgarð vanished in the glooms of the sad "School of Galilee." Of the extreme craft and cruelty, the racial characteristics of the old Scandinavian, only the craft remained. A nation of human sacrificers now cannot bear to see a criminal hanged—he must be sent for execution to Copenhagen. The new faith, also, was adverse to the spirit of a free people: it preached over-regard for human life, and it taught fighting men *propter vitam vivendi perdere causas.* It weighed heavily upon the "secret and profound spring of society," as Ozanam describes the laws of honour in man, "which is nothing but the independence and inviolability of the human conscience, superior to all powers, all tyrannies, and all external force."[1] In fact, we may repeat in Iceland what Montalembert (The Monks of the West, p. 252) said of the ex-mistress of the world: "There is something more surprising and sadder still" (than all its pagan cruelty and corruption) "in the Roman Empire after it became Christian."

The first school, founded about the middle of the eleventh century, began to divert the national mind from arms and raids to art and literature. The Eddas and Sagas were committed to writing; and the Augustan age extended during the two following centuries, ending with the fourteenth. The islanders gave their own names, many of them very uncouth, to the festivals of the Church. Saints arose in the land. The best known to local fame was Bishop Thorlák (Thorlacius) Thorhallsson, who died in A.D. 1193. Though uncanonised, he was honoured by the dedication of a church at Mikligarð (the Great Fence), or Constantinople, for the use of the Waring[2] Janissaries. The *vigne du Seigneur* was split into two bishoprics, Skálholt (A.D. 1057), and Hólar (A.D. 1107). Hospitals were endowed, and no less than nine monasteries and nunneries were founded by the regular canons (Augustines), and by their most estimable brethren the Benedictines, whose annals command all our respect.[3]

---

[1] The reader may remember, in the late Rev. Frederick Robertson's Lectures to Working Men, a fine passage upon the same subject.

[2] *Væringi* (plur. *-jar*) *Warings*, or the name of the Scandinavian and Anglo-Saxon warriors serving as bodyguards to the Emperors of Constantinople.

[3] Of the monks proper (Icel. Múnkr, = μονὸς, monachus), only Benedictines

The following is a list of the religious houses built in Iceland:

The foreign Bishop Rudolph (ob. 1052) established the first monastery in Iceland in Bær, Borgarfjörð. It never had any abbot, and soon disappeared.

Bishop Magnús Einarsson (ob. 1148) bought the greatest part of the Vestmannaeyjar, and began to build a monastery there; after his death the institution came to nothing.

A monastery was instituted in Hýtardalr (circa 1166), but was dissolved before the year 1270. During its existence it had five abbots.

Jón Loptsson, the grandson of Sæmundr Fróði, built a house and a church at his estate Keldur (circa 1190), which he intended for a monastery; but owing to some quarrels with the bishop of Skálholt, it never was consecrated nor dedicated to its intended purpose.

Bishop Brandr of Hólar instituted a monastery in Saurbær in Eyjafjörð (circa 1200). It had two abbots, but it is never mentioned after the year 1212.

Of the monasteries permanently established, the earliest was

### THINGEYRAKLAUSTR.

Shortly after the installation of Jón Ögmundsson (1106) as bishop of Hólar, the season was so severe that no growth appeared when the people were assembled at the spring meeting (Vár-Thing, about the end of May) in Thingeyrar. The bishop made a vow to erect a monastery at the place, for monks of the Order of St Benedict. Soon after this there was a favourable change in the weather. It was not, however, until 1133 that the Benedictine monks fixed their abode there. The monks of Thingeyrar were celebrated for their learning, and several illustrious names are to be found among its abbots, e.g., Karl (ob. 1212), Oddr (ob. circa 1200), Gunnlaugr (ob. 1218), and many others. The twenty-third and last of the series died 1561.

### MUNKATHVERÁRKLAUSTUR.

This monastery, famous for its old documents, was founded by Bishop Björn Gilsson of Hólar in A.D. 1155. Its monks also were Benedictines. The twenty-fifth of its abbots embraced Lutheranism in A.D. 1551.

### THYKKVABÆARKLAUSTUR.

This monastery is also called the monastery in Ver or Álftaver. It was founded by one Thorkell Geirason, by the authority of Bishop Klœngur Thorsteinsson of Skálholt, in A.D. 1168. Its tenants were under the rule of St Augustine. The nineteenth and last abbot of this monastery went to Copenhagen in 1550, and was there converted to the Lutheran persuasion. This house had a famous library.

### FLATEYAR—HELGAFELLSKLAUSTUR.

Bishop Klœngur Thorsteinsson of Skálholt instituted a monastery in the island Flatey, in Breiðifjörð, in 1172. His successor, St Thorlákr, removed it to

---

were found in Iceland. They were accompanied by the regular canons of St Augustine. There were no "brothers" (fratres) or religious mendicants, as Dominicans and Franciscans; nor "regular clerks," as Jesuits, Theatines, etc., who date since the sixteenth century; nor secular priests united in congregations like Oratorians and Lazarists.

Helgafell, and dedicated it to St John. Its tenants followed the rule of St Augustine. The twenty-fifth and last abbot died shortly before 1550.

### VIÐEYARKLAUSTUR.

Founded by Thorvaldr Gissurarson, the father of Earl Gissur, and consecrated by his brother, Bishop Magnús of Skálholt, in the year 1226. Its tenants followed the rule of St Augustine. The eighteenth and last abbot embraced Lutheranism, and died in A.D. 1568. Earl Gissur here ended his days.

There were two priories in the island, viz. :

### MÖÐRUVALLAKLAUSTR.

Instituted by Bishop Jörund of Hólar in A.D. 1296. Its monks were Augustines. Seven of its priors are known, and the last died in 1546.

### SKRIÐUKLAUSTR.

Instituted towards the end of the fifteenth century. It only had four priors, who, it seems, followed the rule of St Augustine.

There were two nunneries :

### KYRKJUBÆARKLAUSTR.

Founded by one Bjarnharðr, at the application of Bishop Klœngur of Skálholt, and consecrated by him in A.D. 1186, on condition that its occupants should be nuns following the rules of St Benedict. The names of twelve of its abbesses are recorded.

### REYNISTAÐARKLAUSTR.

Founded by Bishop Jörund of Hólar in 1296. The sisters followed the rules of St Benedict. Ten of its abbesses are mentioned, and the last died in 1562.

The Skálds, or bards, who probably long retained their old paganism in new Christianity, distinguished themselves by word and deed in every northern court of Europe, and wandered as far as the Mediterranean shores. But the heart of the people was dying, and the national spirit had fled, never more to be revived. In A.D. 1024, the Althing bravely refused all connection with Norway. But, presently, the clergy, spiritually subject to foreign sees,—Bremen, Scania, and Throndhjem,—listened to the voice of the annexor, and thus traitors divided the island camp. They fostered jealousies between rival Udallers, whose implacable hatreds and blood-feuds converted the annals, like those of the Anglo-Saxons, into records of rapine and murder. The Althing shortly after A.D. 1004 had abolished the duello, a northern institution unknown to classic Greece and Rome; or rather, let us say; it abolished itself, when "trial by point and edge" had lost its old significancy as a formal and religious appeal to that God of Battles who defends the right. The Court

of Justice took the place of the Hólm-gang; and at times it was
silent in the presence of the sword and the firebrand, which, in
riotous frays, spared neither sex nor age. But gradually it developed every form of chicanery and law-devilry, in whose dark
labyrinths it is hard to see any improvement upon the "wild
justice of revenge." Its arts were jury-challenging; demurrers
aided by the jealousy of the judges, whose duty was to catch a
man tripping; the detection of flaws; attempts to split the
court (að vèfingja dóminn) and cause non-suits; false witness,
and the breaking of oaths those "sports of brave men and
terrors of fools." The law was made bankrupt by the tricks of
irrelevancy and by-play, by the special pleading, by the quib-
bling, the bribery, and the corruption of the tribunals. When all
failed, a petty massacre was sure to succeed; and as these proceedings arose from the captious litigiousness of the race, so
they long maintained the grievous trammels and shackles of so-
called legal principles.[1]

Thus in the middle of the thirteenth century, Hakon V., king
of Norway (reg. A.D. 1217-1264), was able openly to treat for the
surrender of Iceland liberty. After some three hundred years
of Udallism, the heroic island passed into foreign dominion by a
decree of the Althing under "Catillus," or "Catullus" (Kettill),
the last of the independent law-sayers or presidents. Modern
Icelanders, copied by strangers, stoutly and patriotically maintain that the relation of the two countries was an alliance, a
personal union, rather than a real union, or à priori a subjection.
It is certain that treaties were formally exchanged; that the
ancient laws and rights of property were secured; that free
commerce was stipulated; that Icelanders were made eligible to
hold office in Norway; and that any infringement of conditions
dispensed with the incorporation. But the hard facts remain
that a poll-tax, a tribute of sixteen ells of homespun cloth, was
imposed, and that a viceroy was appointed to govern the island.
Thus Liberty was palsied, and Independence gave place to the
status pupillaris. To dispute upon this independent allegiance
is only to debate a question of degree.

---

[1] As will be seen, modern law recognises, or rather compels, an official arbitration before causes can be brought into court.

The eighth and last of the Crusades, movements which began in A.D. 1188-1190, and ended in A.D. 1260-1275, was the first preached in Iceland (Hist. Eccles., i. 571), and it partially aroused the islandry from their apathy and habitual law-contests. But the effects were transient, save upon individuals. The physical history of the thirteenth century is chiefly remarkable for the widespread ruin caused by its terrible eruptions and desolating earthquakes. Now began the epidemics and epizootics which, from A.D. 1306 to A.D. 1846, number 134—viz., seven in the fourteenth, six in the fifteenth, twelve in the sixteenth, twenty-eight in the seventeenth, and forty-one in the eighteenth centuries, with several during the present. An unreformed pagan would have believed that the wrath of the olden gods weighed heavy on the land.

The same may be said of the fourteenth century, which also witnessed the calamitous annexation to Denmark.[1] After the death of Knut (Canute) in A.D. 1035, Magnús ascended the throne of Norway, and native sovereigns ruled till A.D. 1319, when the male line became extinct with Hakon VII. The Diet enthroned his daughter's infant son, Magnús Eiriksson, who, being already king of Sweden, had brought the Scandinavian peninsula and its dependencies under a single sceptre. But the union did not last. Magnús bestowed Norway upon his son Hákon, who was married to Margaret, sole daughter of Waldemar III., king of Denmark. The issue, Ólafr IV., succeeded to the throne of his grandfather in A.D. 1376, and to that of his father four years afterwards, thus incorporating Norway with Denmark. Dying a minor in A.D. 1387, he left both kingdoms to his mother, Margaret, by whose energetic rule the regency had been carried on, and she found no difficulty in setting aside the feeble pretensions of Albert of Mecklenburg. In A.D. 1397 the union or treaty of Calmar took place, and Iceland, which still maintained its modicum of independence, was once more trans-

---

[1] The author would by no means make the invidious assertion that the Danish treatment of colonies was worse than that of other contemporary nations. On the contrary, in Africa, India, and the West Indian Islands, it has been a favourable contrast to most of the rest. But Europe in the fourteenth century, and in the ages which followed it, presents a melancholy contrast with the refined and civilised usage of her settlements by Republican and Imperial Rome.

ferred without opposition to the triple crown of Denmark, Norway, and Sweden. The conditions of the annexation to Norway (A.D. 1264) were tacitly consented to by the Danish rulers when they succeeded to Iceland by marriage and inheritance. Yet "the Semiramis of the north" began by the usual contempt of stipulations: she repaid submission by perpetuating a poll-tax of half-a-mark per head, and, worse still, by establishing a royal monopoly of trade. The latter, confined to vessels licensed by the Crown, nearly secured for Iceland the fate which befell the lost colonies of Greenland. From this period till A.D. 1814, Denmark and Norway remained united, each, however, governed by its own laws.

The fifteenth century was as disastrous as that which preceded it. The Digerdoed, or Black Death, the Plague of the Decameron, had raged with prodigious violence about A.D. 1348, and it was followed by a winter which, destroying nearly all the cattle, left a purely pastoral country permanently upon the verge of utter ruin. A second pestilence, the Svarti Dauði, or Black Death, visited the hapless island; whilst English and other pirates, plundering and burning on the main, fortified themselves in the Vestmannaeyjar archipelago, despoiled the churches and farms of the coast, held the franklins to ransom, and sold the poor into slavery. And at last, in the middle of the sixteenth century, came the crowning blow, the introduction of Lutheranism.

Catholicism had sat lightly upon the remote spot verging on the hyperborean seas. The papal tithe (Páfa tíund) and Peter's Pence, imposed in A.D. 1305 by the king of Norway under pain of excommunication,[1] did not weigh heavy. At first the tax was one nagli (nail), or tenth of an ell, of Wadmal (Vað-mál) cloth, its equivalent being two fishes; and it never rose higher than ten ells of homespun per adult male. The sale of Indulgences, which accompanied the last and first crusade, was abolished in A.D. 1289. Celibacy of the clergy was introduced in Iceland by Thorlák Thorhallsson, who died in the quasi-odour of sanctity in 1193. After that date ecclesiastics were not form-

---

[1] Of this process there were two forms, which began to be passed (circa) A.D. 1180. Bann, or Meira Bann was E. Major; Minna Bann was E. Minor, whilst the interdict was called For-boð, the German Verbot.

ally married, but were not debarred from living with Frillur, or Fryllas, concubines, then generally called by the laity "holy women." As in Charlemagne's day, bigamy was not wholly unknown. A few took second wives, "*non libidinè, sed ob nobilitatem;* but the fierce temper of the Húsfreya, or *mater-familias,* must have made the arrangement uncomfortable. Thus it is said[1] Snorri Sturluson in A.D. 1212 married the daughter of Deacon Loptsson, who had a harem of concubines, one the child of a bishop. Jón Geirriksson, the Dane, popularly written "John Jerechini," bishop of Skálholt, in A.D. 1430, is also accused of being a buccaneer, a mere brigand, who could not write his name, which little drawback, however, did not prevent an attempt to canonise him after he was deservedly (?) lynched in A.D. 1433. Jón Arason, bishop of Hólar, is charged with keeping a mistress at the age of eighty.[2] But much of this may be sectarian exagger-

---

[1] This prudential reservation is the more necessary as most of our information comes from the enemy. Bishop Jón Ögmundsson had two wives, not at the same time, but one after another.

[2] "In the sixteenth century the Reformation was forced upon the people by the united kingdoms of Denmark and Norway; its progress was everywhere marked by blood, and even the Lutheran historian, Finn Jónsson, is unable to veil completely the atrocities which were committed. The venerable bishop of Hólar, Jón Arnason (*sic,* doubtless a clerical error), the last Catholic prelate, received the crown of martyrdom along with his two sons, uttering with his dying breath, 'Lord, into Thy hands I commend my spirit!'" Thus writes Baring-Gould (Introduction, xl.). Mr Jón A. Hjaltalín hereupon observes : "I must call attention to this quotation from Mr Baring-Gould regarding the introduction of the Reformation into Iceland. I cannot protest too strongly against it. *It is utterly false from beginning to end.* Every one who has the slightest acquaintance with the history of Iceland during the sixteenth century knows that Lutheranism was *not* forced upon the Icelanders. The Reformation movement was only encouraged by the king of Denmark. Old men, Bishop Jón Arason among others, were permitted to retain their former faith if they were willing to leave others equally undisturbed in the exercises of their religion. This fact is corroborated by the bishop's immediate descendants, who in everything glorified their ancestor as a martyr. Further, it cannot be shown that a single person lost his life in Iceland in connection with the introduction of the Reformation. The quarrel which led to the death of the bishop and his two sons arose from a dispute about the sale and occupation of a farm in the west. Bishop Jón Arason was an exact counterpart of the chiefs of the Sturlunga times ; he delighted to ride about the island with hundreds of followers, and to engage in fights and broils with every one who had any property to lose. That it was not religious zeal that devoured him or his sons may be seen from the fact, that in a letter to the chancellor of the king of Denmark (dated 10th August 1550) they say that 'their father the bishop, as well as themselves, are ready to keep the holy Evangelium, as His Majesty has ordered it to be preached everywhere in Iceland.' There is all probability that they would have come to an untimely end even if there had been no Reformation. The king had indeed ordered their arrest as disturbers of the public peace. He did not, however, order their execution. The responsibility for that act must rest upon the Icelanders who seized them, and mistrusted their ability to keep them in safe custody

ation, and in after-ages Protestant authors would not inquire too curiously if, as often happens in the present day, the priest was married before he was ordained. And, although we are told that a frequent entry at Councils was " Quoniam Dominus A. Episcopus scribere nescit, ideo ejus loco subscripsit, B.C."—which reminds us of many nobles and gentles who could " nocht write" in Scotland,—we must not forget that, in the thirteenth century, the Augustines attempted a vernacular translation of the Bible.[1]

Thus all the glow of faith and the fervid belief in the deifications of the family, in saints and martyrs raised above man's estate by supererogatory piety and virtue, and in the living and breathing *locum tenens* of the first apostle, was darkened by a system of semi-rationalism, which allows reason too much or too little scope; which arrogates to itself the unreasonable right of saying " Thus far shalt thou go and no farther," at the same time loudly professing its own fallibility; and which has succeeded fatally well in splitting the Church into a thousand fragments. A philosopher might have forecast the result from his study. Men unwilling to believe were relieved of a great load, and their energetic action was no match for the passive resistance of the many honest and pious souls who embraced the new form of faith. The Crown laid violent hands, as in England, upon the " Regalia Sancti Petri " (temporalities), which it transferred to its favourites; the religious houses were secularised, and the ecclesiastics had the choice either of banishment, or of conforming to what they held the teachings of a heresiarch.

Changes of religion seem to have been peculiarly unfortunate

---

until they could be brought before the proper tribunal. So far from anybody losing his life through the introduction of the Reformation, no one was even deprived of his liberty for a single hour except by Bishop Arason and his sons. I hope it was through crass ignorance only that Mr Baring-Gould penned such an extraordinary statement as the one quoted. Or is he able to name the people who suffered during the introduction of the Reformation, and to show trustworthy documents that they did thus suffer ? "

[1] Charges of national ignorance are favourites with the ignorant, and unhappily not only with them : the analphabetic state of Spain is pressed into active service by the English home littérateur, especially of the Evangelical or Low Church school. It sounds strange to one who has often met upon the outer bridle-paths men mounted on their mules, and diligently reading books and newspapers. And the superior civilisation of the Latin race is hardly to be measured by the three " R's," or by similar mechanical appliances.

in Iceland. The seventeenth century saw absolute monarchism extend from Denmark under Frederick III. to her distant dependency. Encouraged by the apathy and indolence of the islanders, the foreign pirates, English and French, redoubled their exertions; even the Algerines made a successful raid. The seventeenth century showed the epidemic of superstition which distinguished the descendants of the Pilgrim Fathers; an ignorant and fanatical interpretation of Jewish history caused the torturing and burning of many a witch and wizard, who probably were often only natural media, and mesmerisers or odylic sensitives. The eighteenth century (A.D. 1707) began with the small-pox, which killed 16,000 to 18,000 of the 50,000 islanders. In A.D. 1759, rigorous winters brought on a famine equally fatal to man and beast; of the former some 10,000 perished. In 1762 about 280,000 sheep died, or were slaughtered. In A.D. 1788 took place that first eruption of the Skaptárjökull, which has been described as the most appalling and destructive since authentic history began.

About the beginning of the present century, Iceland, under physical evils, monopoly, and misrule, fell to its lowest point. Greatly to the displeasure of the lieges, the two sees were reduced to one; the same took place with the colleges, and finally the Althing was abolished (A.D. 1800). The war between Great Britain and Denmark would inevitably have caused actual starvation, but for a humane order in council,[1] through the interest of Sir Joseph Banks, permitting the island to be supplied with the necessaries of life. In A.D. 1843, brighter days dawned. After a disuse of nearly half a century, the Althing was re-established; but it was only a shadow of its former self—a body of representatives whom the Home Government deigned to consult. Still, it roused the people to take interest in their own affairs. Finally, the proclamation of a constitution for Denmark (1848) produced effects which now are being matured.

The benefits of free and popular rule were offered by the Danish Government to Iceland. But the offer was based upon the supposition, indignantly repudiated in the island, that she was

---

[1] The document is quoted *in extenso* by Henderson (ii. 164-166), and by Baring-Gould (Introduction, pp. xlv., xlvi.).

subject to the Rigsdag;[1] and it was repeatedly refused, as falling
short of the royal promise made in 1848. Hence arose the
Radical party, whose extreme left, though disclaiming the idea
of separation, is distinctly republican. The author has compared it with the Home Rule movement in Ireland, warning his
readers, however, that there are salient points of difference; while
the absence of social and religious complications is all in favour
of the Scandinavian. The head of the party was and is the
highly distinguished scholar Hr Jón Sigurðsson; there is none
beside him, but "proximè accesserunt" Ex-Justice Benidikt
Sveinsson, Professor Haldór Friðriksson, Rev. Eiríkr Kuld, and
Jón Sigurðsson of Gautlönd, a farmer in the north. They complained that the king, whose rule at home was limited by the
Chambers, remained absolute in Iceland; that the constitution
did not place them on an equal footing with their fellow-subjects;
that they were governed by men living in Copenhagen, who
knew little of local requirements, and of a *doctrinaire* clique
which has done abundant harm. They described paternal rule
as equivalent to the rule of red tape; they distrusted the Danes
even *dona ferentes*, and they declared that there is still "something rotten" in a certain state. It was, indeed, evident that
the national Liberal party of Denmark, with the usual liberality
of "Liberals," aimed only at subjecting their Icelandic fellow-
subjects.

In vain the ministers of Frederick VII. offered what appeared
to the outer world the fairest terms—the establishment of an
Upper and a Lower House, and a settlement of all claims by a

---

[1] The Icelanders' view of the connection between their country and Denmark is
simply this : They declare the union, dating from 1264, and renewed in 1380, to
be personal, not real, and limited to both countries being under the same king.
The Rigsdag cannot therefore legislate for the Althing, and the constitutional
law of Denmark has never become that of Iceland. They consequently demand
that the Althing should have legislative and not mere counselling powers; that it
should sanction in the island the laws proposed by the Danes; and that the
minister who advises the Crown in Icelandic matters should be responsible to this
Diet. On the other hand, Denmark denies the validity of mediæval treaties, the
relations of the mother country and her dependency having been completely
altered by historical events; consequently Iceland is now an integral and insepar-
able part of the Danish kingdom, and the laws of Denmark must be valid in Iceland as in the other colonies. Iceland, they say, cannot claim any self-rule as
a right ; still, it may be desirable, on account of their peculiar circumstances, to
allow the Icelanders a voice in the management of their own affairs, subject, however, to the supervision and consent of the Rigsdag and the Home Government.

perpetual allowance of $60,000 per annum.[1] The Home-Rulers "totted up" all that the Danes *stole*, such is the mild word used,[2] from chalice to landed estate, with interest, simple and compound, for the last three centuries. These pretensions exceeded those of the United States in the Alabama affair: everything was placed to the debit of Denmark, nothing to her credit. But Hr Sigurðsson, the opposition leader, sensibly said, "The money claims are the most awkward to the Liberals, and pressing them is the best lever when moving for self-government." The Danes laughed at the idea of holding a constitutional country liable for the debts of absolute kings, contracted in A.D. 1550-1800, when Denmark herself was plundered, as well as Iceland, by irresponsible rulers. There was, however, this difference, that while Iceland was plundered to enrich Danes residing in Denmark, Denmark was plundered to enrich her own citizens. And Hr Sigurðsson was fated to win. Important events have happened since the author left the island. A public meeting, attended by delegates from every district, was held (June 26, 1873) at Thingvellir. Here it was resolved to use every effort either to end Danish rule in Iceland, or to obtain an extended constitution which should give the island a government of her own. Correspondents assured the writer that the movement passed off without undue excitement. "Hereditary bondsmen," know in those days that no physical blow need be struck, and that "every institution," to use the words of a well-known separatist, "can be modified or destroyed by the weapon of agitation, under the guidance of popular opinion."

At this preliminary to the opening of the Althing it was decided to send three delegates to Denmark, and to submit to the ministry a draft constitution, drawn up with the view of developing the island and its inhabitants. The two principal provisions were (1.) That Iceland should be connected with the home country by a "personal union only;" and (2.) That it should be governed

---

[1] It is popularly asserted that the Danish Government contributes $30,000 per annum for the support of Iceland. Upon this subject, see note at end of the present section.

[2] The author tried in vain to see the wording of the "little bill," and was assured that it had not been printed. It appeared in the *Allgemeine Zeitung*, Nos. 66, 84, 85, 101, and 102, of the 7th, 25th, and 26th March, and 11th and 12th April 1870. The article is entitled "Island und Dänemark," and is written by the historian Professor Konrad Maurer of Munich. See note at end.

by a Jarl, earl, or viceroy, with a minister or ministers responsible to the House of Representatives.

After the close of the meeting the Althing assembled at the usual place. Some of the more advanced kept, it is said, their seats when the usual cheers were given for the king; but no disloyal manifestation was made beyond rejecting almost all the bills brought in by the local government. The draft constitution was referred to a committee, which on July 28, 1873, reported in its favour, and added a resolution that the king should be requested to concede the following temporary arrangements as soon as possible, and not later than the next year:

1. That the Althing be at once invested with full legislative powers, and a new budget be submitted for its approval once in every two years, on the principle that no tax or impost shall be levied in Iceland for defraying expenditure incurred by the Danish Government.

2. That a special minister be appointed for Icelandic affairs, and that he be responsible to the Althing.

3. That this arrangement be valid for six years only, after which the entire constitution shall be laid before the Althing for its consideration.

On January 5th, 1874, after a struggle of thirty years, the new Icelandic constitution was signed by the king, and came into force on August 1st of the same year, the millenary festival commemorating the occupation of the Northmen. The original plan of the two houses has been carried out. The biennial Althing will consist of thirty members voted in by the people, and of six nominated by the Crown. The Upper House will contain the six royal nominees, and six others elected by the general body of the Althing from its members, duly returned by their constituencies; while the Lower House will number the remaining twenty-four. The vote is confirmed to officials, to ecclesiastics of every grade, to all university graduates, and even to students who sign themselves " Candidat" (B.A.). It is extended to citizens who lease farms, to those who pay a minimum of eight crowns a year in government taxes, and to the country people that contribute either cess or parish rates—evidently universal suffrage, excluding only women and minors, paupers and criminals. Every voter must be twenty-five years old, and of unblemished character; and he must have resided at least a twelvemonth in his electoral district. Any person who has a right to the franchise, who is thirty years of age, who has been domiciled in Iceland or Denmark for five years, and who is not in the employment of a foreign state, is qualified for election to the Althing. The session may not outlast six weeks without special royal assent, and provisions are made for extraordinary sessions.

The new constitution, which purports to regulate only home affairs, is a distinct improvement upon the old platform. The Secretary for Iceland is independent of the Danish Cabinet and Rigsdag, and becomes responsible to the king and to the Althing. This minister will be answerable for the maintenance of the constitution, and he will nominate for royal approval the chief local functionary. The governor's functions will be determined by his majesty, and constitutional complaints against him will be investigated by the Crown. Thus the Althing will enjoy certain legislative rights, and have some control over the administration of its country. Finally, as Iceland has no representative in the Rigsdag, and as she has never taken part in the legislature, nor in the general government of the empire, she will not contribute to the home expenditure.[1]

But the power of passing laws is not granted absolutely; it is subject to royal confirmation. The relative position of the Secretary for Iceland to the people, represented by the Althing, remains to be defined. Even less satisfactory are the arrangements concerning the local governor; his power and duties are not settled, and the Althing will have no voice in settling them. Hitherto he has mostly acted as a mere channel of communication between the island and the Copenhagen Cabinet, and the new constitution does nothing to remedy this evil. On the contrary, the king makes a special reservation concerning the expenses of the "highest local government of the island," meaning that the governor's salary will be dependent upon the Crown, and will not be discussed by the Althing with the rest of the budget. Thus the ruler becomes wholly independ-

---

[1] *Cela va sans dire :* for many years the island has been too poor to pay for the expenses of governing it. But see note at end of section.

ent of the ruled, and dependent only on the Secretary for
Iceland.   Again, the nomination of six members by the king
will have the effect, in case of disagreement between the Upper
and Lower Houses, of enabling the royal commissioners to frustrate
legislation simply by absenting themselves from the debates.
This is perhaps the weakest point of the new constitution; it
may be necessary in Denmark where the tone of the middle
classes is distinctly democratic and republican, but it is looked
upon and is protested against in aristocratic and conservative
Iceland as an affront to their loyalty.   And it can serve for
nothing but to create an artificial opposition and to strengthen
any minister or governor in anti-national or Danising measures.
The provision that the governor may sit in the Althing and
speak as often as he pleases, is distinctly unconstitutional; nor
is the paragraph concerning the fixed contribution and the
sinking contribution at all satisfactory.

The author ventures to predict, with due diffidence, that,
however liberal this constitution may appear, it will not satisfy
local requirements—it grants too much or it gives too little.
The next demand will be for the governor to be invested with
the full powers residing in the heads of British colonies,
supported by a local ministry, the latter virtually independent
of the Home Colonial Minister.   Denmark is, perhaps, not yet
sufficiently advanced in political education to grant the gift;
yet the experiment is worth trying.   If the demand be rejected,
the persuasion that Iceland has never thriven since Icelanders
lost their privilege of self-rule will steadily increase, and probably attain abnormal dimensions.   A school of politics has
now been opened to the people, and the new study will produce
special students.   Irrepressible malcontents, *intransigentes*, and
irreconcilables, who have trodden the path of separation, are
never easily brought back to the sleepy old highway of routine
rule; and the constitution has provided them with many
grievances, especially the doubts cast upon Icelandic loyalty
and good faith.   There are not a few European revolutionists
who, urgent for the general derangement of affairs, will hardly
disdain to " keep their hands in," even so far north.   An
Icelander in England flatly contradicted the assertion that a

republican or separatist feeling exists in Iceland.[1]  The "great public meeting" of 1873 expressed the latter, and what could a separated Iceland be or become except a republic? Not only "subversive philanthropists" but well-meaning and patriotic men will find subjection to a foreign secretary and a foreign governor intolerable when they wish to manage themselves. The "little bill" will still be a strong lever for raising popular passions. In the days when Ireland continues to "write and speak of '98," when Norway "strikes" as heavily as Great Britain, and when the Socialists breed troubles in Denmark where the International has been interdicted by the courts of justice, as a branch of the English society, the Icelandic Home Ruler is not likely to sit still—perhaps it is not desirable that he should.

Since the unhappy Dano-Prussian war we have heard little of Scandinavia in England, and we are apt to conclude that the Pan-Scandinavian idea is dead. It is not dead but sleeping; and while Pan-Slavism affects to slumber that it may gather vis and energy for decisive movements when the time for action comes, we still live in hopes of seeing a federal union of the great northern kingdoms, and to find Iceland taking her place as a minor but not an undistinguished member of the family. Scandinavian liberty, says Montesquieu, *est la mère des libertés de l'Europe*, and her free-born children have not lost and will never lose respect for the parent.

### NOTE TO SECTION III.

Since these lines were written, Christian IX., the first crowned head that ever sighted her shores, has visited Iceland upon the well-chosen occasion of her millenary festival. The courteous and parental bearing of the king has made its due impression. The lieges have taken a sensible view of the situation; they spoke in a conciliatory spirit, and satisfaction with the change from the former state of things seems to have been general. Even the anti-government party is thankful for what it has won,

---

[1] Hr Eirikr Magnússon in the *Standard* of December 1, 1872, et seq.

and hopes in course of time to win what it wants. "This is a good beginning," said a prominent member, "and, since we have got legislative powers, it is our own fault if we cannot get more."

The following statement was sent to me by Mr Jón A. Hjaltalín, who is responsible for his assertions. The paper thoroughly expresses the Icelanders' view of their financial relations with the Danish Government:

"The budget of Iceland for 1867-68 was :

| REVENUE. | EXPENDITURE. |
|---|---|
| $48,345  21 sk. | $79,682  56 sk. |
| 1868-69. | |
| $44,675  21 sk. | $63,929   8 sk. |
| 1869-70. | |
| $51,222  21 sk. | $77,361  24 sk. |
| 1870-71. | |
| $44,787  21 sk. | $65,865  72 sk. |

"This is the Danish statement of the annual budget for Iceland. Consequently it has been commonly said by Danes and travellers who have not been able to dive below the surface, that Iceland was the receiver of Danish bounty to the tune of something like $30,000 annually. It was, however, acknowledged by the Danish Chancellor of the Exchequer in 1845 that such was not the case, for in his report he said : ' It is perhaps doubtful whether we really contribute anything towards the support of Iceland. . . . It is true, certainly, that an annual sum is paid to the Icelandic treasury. . . . This payment cannot, however, properly be called a subsidy, because *the whole of the Icelandic revenues has not been paid into the Icelandic treasury* (but into the Danish treasury). . . . *The Icelandic treasury has also disbursed several sums* (at the command of the Danish Government), *which cannot be set down as expenses for Iceland.*' This is the gist of the whole dispute. Sums are not entered on the credit side of the Icelandic budget which Iceland has really paid into the Danish treasury. Thus an annual deficit is easily made out.

"Down to the middle of the last century the accounts of Iceland were kept clear and separate from those of Denmark. Then the Icelandic budget showed an annual surplus which found its way into the Danish treasury. After that date, the accounts of both were mixed up together, and for three quarters of a century (till 1825) the annual revenue and expenditure of Iceland cannot be properly ascertained. It is, however, known that several large sums, above the annual revenues of the island, were paid into the Danish treasury during this period. On the other hand, it cannot be shown that the annual expenses had risen above the former yearly average. When a separate account was again opened with Iceland, no notice was taken of the extraordinary sums paid into the Danish treasury on behalf of Iceland.

"To show the reader the chief items of the Icelandic budget, we will take the budget for 1870-71 :

| REVENUE. | | | | EXPENDITURE. | | |
|---|---|---|---|---|---|---|
| I. From the trade, | $12,600 | 0 | | I. Expenses of the administration and medical staff of Iceland, | $34,653 | 0 |
| II. ,, Crown property, . | 12,080 | 0 | | | | |
| III. ,, Royal tithes, | 3,750 | 0 | | | | |
| IV. ,, Repayment of loans, . | 8,192 | 15 sk. | | II. Expenses of the bishop and the educational establishments, | 27,212 | 72 sk. |
| V. ,, Sundries, | 8,165 | 6 | | | | |
| VI. Deficit, . . | 21,078 | 51 | | III. Sundries, . . | 4,000 | 0 |
| | $65,865 | 72 sk. | | | $65,865 | 72 sk. |

" It will be seen from the above that one of the chief items in the Iceland revenues is derived from Crown property in the island, which in round numbers now amounts to $12,000. This is entered in the annual budget to the credit of Iceland. In 1866, $175,037 had been paid into the Danish treasury for Crown property sold in Iceland at different times. Neither this sum nor its interest is, however, mentioned in the annual statements of Icelandic finances. But if Iceland has a right to the revenues derived from the Crown property still unsold, it has an equal right to the interest of the money paid for that which is sold. This sum, amounting to about $7000, ought to be added to the annual revenue, thus making the annual income from the Crown property $19,000 instead of $12,000. There are also several smaller items which ought to be entered on the credit side of the Icelandic budget.

" No. II. of the expenditure, viz. the salaries of the bishop and the professors of the colleges, and other expenses connected with the colleges, form a heavy item in the expenditure of Iceland, or, in round numbers, $27,000 annually. It is, however, not correct to charge this sum against Iceland unless an equal sum is entered on the credit side of the budget, because all the property supporting the two bishops and the two colleges of Iceland was sold according to a royal command of 29th April 1785, and the proceeds of the sale were paid into the Danish treasury on the understanding and implied promise of the king, that the expenses of these institutions were to be defrayed by the Danish treasury for the future. This sum is nevertheless annually charged against Iceland as if Denmark never had received any equivalent for it.

" The budget arranged according to the foregoing observations will be:

| REVENUE. | | | | EXPENDITURE. | | |
|---|---|---|---|---|---|---|
| I. From the trade, | $12,600 | 0 | | I. Expenses of the administration and medical staff of Iceland, | $34,653 | 0 |
| II. ,, Crown property, . | 19,080 | 0 | | | | |
| III. ,, Royal tithes, | 3,750 | 0 | | | | |
| IV. ,, Repayment of loans, . | 8,192 | 15 sk. | | II. Expenses of the bishop and the educational establishments, | 34,212 | 72 sk. |
| V. ,, Sundries, | 8,165 | 6 | | | | |
| VI. ,, No. II. Expenditure, | 34,212 | 72 | | III. Sundries, . | 4,000 | 0 |
| | | | | IV. Annual surplus, | 13,134 | 21 |
| Total, | $78,999 | 93 sk. | | Total, | $78,999 | 93 sk. |

"Thus it will be seen that the Icelandic budget, instead of showing a deficit of $21,078, 51 sk., has, when properly stated, a surplus of $13,134, 21 sk. The claims of Iceland arising out of these financial misstatements were partly recognised by the Danish Government in the Act of 2d January 1871, by which it was provided that $30,000 per annum should be paid perpetually from the Danish treasury to Iceland; and, in addition, an annual sum of $20,000 for ten years, after which period this latter sum is to decrease by $1000 per annum until it is extinguished.

"In conclusion, I will present the reader with the 'little bill' of the Icelanders against the Danish treasury. The rent of the Crown farms was always paid in kind, and the present money value of the articles paid as yearly rents for these farms at the time they were seized by the Crown is $41,055, 40 sk. When the rents of the still unsold farms are subtracted, there remains,

I. An annual claim against the Danish treasury for the balance,
amounting to     .     .     .     .     .          $27,855 40 sk.

II. The Icelanders' claim for loss of interest of money paid into
the Danish treasury for sold Crown property, the annual
sum of     .     .     .     .     .     .          6,900   0

III. For the rent of farms belonging to the bishop sees, and sold for
the benefit of the Danish treasury, calculated in the same
way as the rent of the Crown farms, the annual sum of     31,769 52

IV. For movable property belonging to the episcopal sees, and appropriated by the Crown, the annual sum of     .          2,400   0

V. For the trade monopoly, the annual sum of     .     .          50,800   0[1]

Total annual sums,     .          $119,724 92 sk.

"Thus the Icelanders consider themselves to have good claims on the Danish treasury for the annual sum of $119,724, 92 sk., or a round sum of $3,000,000.

"On the other hand, the Icelanders consider themselves bound to pay $20,000 annually towards the general expenditure of the Danish state (Report of the Royal Commission Appointed to Inquire into the Financial Affairs of Iceland, 1861, as communicated in the Thjóðólfr newspaper, xvii., pp. 101, 107)."

---

[1] It can be proved that the different sums paid into the Danish treasury by the various companies who rented the trade with Iceland from time to time (from 1602 to 1722) amounted at least to $2,000,000, and the revenue of Iceland has never been credited with this sum.

## SECTION IV.

## POLITICAL GEOGRAPHY OF ICELAND.

### § 1. General Considerations.

Iceland, we have seen, is the largest island in the North Atlantic, and one of the most considerable known to the Old World. Lying 130 direct geographical miles east of Greenland, 500 north-west of Scotland, and 850 west of Norway; distant 1000 miles from Liverpool, 1300 from Copenhagen, and 3000 from Boston, it is claimed as an Eastern dependency of the American continent which the Icelander first colonised. It has also been called a " singular fragment of Scandinavian Europe." Yet, geographically considered, it belongs neither to the Old nor to the New Hemisphere; it is a little continent of itself.

Formerly a considerable part of the island was made to enter the Polar circle, which, in some maps, passed through the northern third. On the other hand, the eastern coast was curtailed of its due proportions, being thrown too far west even in charts still used. Hooker, for instance, makes the longitude range from 10° to 12° west of Greenwich,—an extreme error of some two to three degrees.

Iceland extends from Portland, in N. lat. 63° 22′, to the North Cape, in N. lat. 66° 44′, covering 3° 22′ = 202 direct geographical miles of depth. The extreme longitudinal points are laid down between the north-eastern projection of Eskifjörð, in W. long. G. 13° 38′ (33′ ?), and the Point of Breiðavík, in 24° 40′ (36′ ?), or 11° 25′ of length, the degrees in this latitude being greatly reduced.[1] Thus the maximum depth would represent 186 geographical miles, which some writers increase to 190 and 192; and

---

[1] The degree of longitude in N. lat. 63° measures 2770·1 feet.

|    |    |    | 64° | ,, | 2674·9 ,, |
|----|----|----|-----|----|-----------|
| ,, | ,, | ,, | 65° | ,, | 2578·9 ,, |
| ,, | ,, | ,, | 66° | ,, | 2432·1 ,, |
| ,, | ,, | ,, | 67° | ,, | 2384·6 ,, |

instead of 6082 at the Equator.

the length 308, which are again extended to 313.   The circumference, measured from naze to naze, is variously given at 752 to 830 miles.   The superficial area has also been variously calculated.   Whilst Ólafsson gives .56,000 square geographical, and Egger 29,838 Danish, miles (15 = 1°), modern calculations have reduced it to 37,000, 37,388, and 40,000, the latter being generally assumed in round numbers.[1]   Thus Iceland is about five times instead of double, as certain writers supposed, the size of Sicily (7700 sq. geog. miles); about one-sixth larger than Ireland (32,511); nearly equal to Portugal (37,900); approaching the state of New York (46,000); two-ninths the extent of Sweden, and one-fifth the size of France.

The parallel of N. lat. 65°, which, roughly speaking, bisects Iceland, would pass westwards through Southern Greenland, cross Davis Straits, Fox-land and Fox-channel; the northern apex of Southampton Island, the Back River, the Bear Lake, and entering Eskimo-land, formerly Russian America, would leave Norton Sound to the south, and Prince of Wales Cape a few miles to the north.   Thence travelling over Behring's Strait, it would enter Asia a little south of East Cape, cut the two Siberias, the Tobolsk River, the Urals, the White Sea, and the Bothnian Gulf, and issue from Europe about Vigten Island, somewhat north of mid-Norway.   The antæcious oceans of the Old World contain no corresponding feature: the New Hemisphere shows immense uninhabited tracts — Graham's Land, Enderby's, Kemp's, and the Antarctic continent, which are probably continuous; with their outliers — South Shetlands, South Orkneys, and Sandwich Land.

The estimate of the habitable area was fixed at one-eighth by older writers.[2]   It is now assumed, with Paijkull, at one-tenth (4000 : 40,000).   Human life is confined to the larger islets, to

---

[1] Sir George S. Mackenzie makes the desert tracts of inner Iceland to number 40,000 square miles, a figure which still deforms Lyell's admirable Principles of Geology, 11th edit., vol ii., p. 454.   Mr Vice-Consul Crowe reduces the total area to 29,440 square miles (geog.), of which two-thirds are upwards of 1000 feet above sea-level, and only 4288 square geographical miles are covered with perpetual snow, whose line begins between 2000 and 3500 feet.

[2] The proportion of "boe," where barley can be cultivated in the Færoes, was, till very lately, 1 : 60 of outfield or pasture.

the vicinity of the more important sub-maritime lakes, to the sheltered valleys and river courses, below the plateau, and to the false coast. The latter, *eluvie mons deductus in æquor*, is formed by the débris and alluvium of the mountain walls washed down by rains, torrents, débâcles, and glacier-exundations, and subsequently elevated by earthquakes, which are supposed to be still raising the southern coast.[1] According to Gunnlaugsson and Ólsen, one-third is green or agricultural; there is a similar proportion of Heiðiland ; and the remainder is Úbygð (hod. Obygð) or desert—a chaos of sand-tracts and peat-swamps, lava-runs, and the huge masses of eternal congelation called Jökulls.[2]

The population was laid down by Barrow (1834) at 0·2 per whole area, and by Paijkull (1865) at 1·6 : being now assumed at 70,000, it would be 1·75. Paijkull makes 6·2 head the average of habitable ground, and for the reclaimed tracts he gives 17·5. The latter figure exceeds the mean of Africa, which is 16 to the square mile (viz., 192,000,000 head to 11,556,000 square statute miles), and it is three times greater than in the whole Western Hemisphere.

---

[1] The day is past when the " determinate lines of fracture," which resembled, the empirical parallelism and the pentagonal networks of mountains, connected Hekla with Etna—yet it was an improvement upon the theory which made both of them mouths of the Inferno. Evidence to the latter purport has been given in our law-courts. The earthquake district of Iceland was popularly supposed to include Great Britain, Northern France, Denmark, Scandinavia, and Greenland— regions of the most diversified formation. The theory seemed to repose for base upon isolated cases of simultaneity, possibly coincidents. But, as Dr Lauder Lindsay remarks, contemporaneity would suggest a vast extension of these limits. The (Lisbon) earthquake of 1755, for instance, extended from Barbary to Iceland, from Persia to Santos in the Brazil. The earthquake of 1783 was equally damaging to Calabria and to Iceland. Even in 1872, there were, as has been shown, almost simultaneous movements in Syria, Naples, and Iceland.

[2] Hooker tells us to pronounce Jökull " yuckull," which involves three distinct errors, especially in the double liquid, which becomes everywhere, except before a vowel, *dl* or *tl*, like Popocatape*tl*. Iaki is a lump of ice, a congener of the Pers. ξʋ, like our "ice," although Adelung derives the Germ. Eis-jöcher from the Lat. Jugum, and'translates "Excelsi Jökli " by " Montana Glacies." Jökull in Icel. primarily means "icicle, " a sense now obsolete. The signification "glacier" was probably borrowed from the Norse country Hardanger, the only Norwegian county in which "Jökull" appears as a local name ; and it was applied to the " Gletschers " of the Iceland colonies in Greenland. " The Jökull" *par excellence* is Snæfellsjökull.

## § 2. Divisions.

In early Norwegian days (A.D. 965) Iceland was distributed, like Ireland, into four quadrants, tetrads, or fourths (Fjórðungar), named after the points of the compass.   These were—

| | | |
|---|---|---|
| Austfirðinga-fjórðungr, | . . | Eastern Quarter. |
| Vestfirðinga- „ | . . | Western „ |
| Norðlendinga- „ | . . | Northern „ |
| Sunnlendinga- „ | . . | Southern „ |

Before A.D. 1770, one Amtmaðr governed the whole of Iceland ; in that year it was divided into two Amts (rules), the north-eastern and the south-western.   Thus the northern and the eastern quadrants, whose population was scanty, were placed for administrative purposes under a single Amt, the headquarters being at Friðriksgáfa, of old Möðruvellir, near Akureyri, on the western shore of the Eyjafjörð.   In 1787 the south-west Amt was divided into two, the southern and the western.   In 1872 it was proposed to unite the western with the southern tetrarchy, and to transfer the amtship of Stykkishólm to Reykjavik, the capital. Thus there will again be only two Amts under the governor, and this simplification may act well.

The official title of the highest official was Stiptamtmaðr; in Danish, Stiftamtmand.[1]   It has lately been changed, without, however, any other advantage of rank or pay, from High Bailiff to Governor-General (Landshöfðingi).   Formerly the military and naval services had a preference, and titled names were not rare : at present the post is given to civilians.[2]   The salary of this high official was $500 in 1772 ; it afterwards became $2000, and now it is $4000.

The four quarters were divided into Sýslur[3] (Dan. Syssel),

---

[1] The Icel. Stipti (Dan. Stift, and old Low Germ. Stigt) means a bishopric or ecclesiastical bailiwick.   Hence Uno Von Troil translates Stiftamtmand by "bailiff of episcopal diocese," and it gradually came to mean a civil governor.   Cleasby informs us (sub voce) that both name and office are quite modern in Iceland.

[2] Further details concerning the governor-general will be found in the Journal.

[3] The Sýsla (pl. Sýslur, and in compounds Sýslu) is derived from Sýsl, "business" —að sýsla, "to be busy."   As a law term, it signifies any stewardship held from

which are ever changing. For instance, the Gullbríngu and Kjósar have lately been united, politically as well as ecclesiastically; the same has happened to Mýra Sýsla and Hnappadals, whilst the vacancies have been filled up by the Vestmannaeyjar. Under the twenty-one Sýslur, cantons or counties, prefectures or sheriffdoms, are the 169 Hrepps or poor-law districts,[1] which are not like our ecclesiastic divisions. We have preserved in England the word, e.g., Rape of Brambor.

The following is a list of Sýslur and Hreppar, taken from the official documents which show the movement of Iceland in 1868.[2]

The Suður-umdæmið, or southern jurisdiction, contains 7 Sýslur and 48 Hreppar, viz.:

1. Austur-Skaptafells Sysla, }
2. Vestur-Skaptafells        „  } with 7 Hreppar.
3. Vestmannaeyjar                      , 1
4. Rángárvalla              „          „ 8    „
5. Árnes (not Arness)       „          „ 13   „
6. Gullbríngu and Kjósar    „          „ 9    „
7. Reykjavik                „          „ 1    „
8. Borgarfjarðar            „          „ 9    „

The Vestur-umdæmið contains 6 Sýslur and 55 Hreppar, viz.:

1. Mýra and Hnappadals Sýslur,     with 10 Hreppar.
2. Snæfellsnes (not Snoefells) Sysla,   „ 7    „
3. Dala                     „          „ 8    „
4. Barðastrandar            „          „ 10   „
5. Ísafjarðar               „          „ 14   „
6. Stranda                  „          „ 6    „

---

the king or bishop; in a geographical sense, it means a district, bailiwick, or prefecture. At present it answers to the Thing of the Icelandic Commonwealth (Cleasby).

[1] Not to be confounded with the Sókn, or parish proper. Cleasby is disposed to date the Rapes from the eleventh century, and he remarks that the district round the bishop's seat at Skálholt is called "Hreppar," showing that the house was the nucleus of the division.

[2] From pp. 703-909, the Skýrslur um Landshagi á Íslandi, vol. 4, Möller, Copenhagen, 1870, a portly octavo of 934 pages. Mr Longman's list of the Sýslas (p. 34, Suggestions for the Exploration of Iceland) was quite correct, except in point of orthography, but it is no longer so.

The Norður og Austur Umdæmið contains 7 Sýslur and 66 Hreppar, viz. :

| | | | | |
|---|---|---|---|---|
| 1. Húnavatns | Sýsla, | with 12 Hreppar. | | |
| 2. Skagafjarðar | „ | „ 12 | „ | |
| 3. Eyjafjarðar (Grimsey,etc.), „ | | „ 10 | „ | |
| 4. Suður-Thingeyjar | „ } | „ 12 | „ | |
| 5. Norður-Thingeyjar | „ } | | | |
| 6. Norður-Múla [1] | | „ 10 | „ | |
| 7. Suður-Múla | „ | „ 10 | „ | |

When the author visited Iceland (1872), the Bæarfógeti, or mayor of Reykjavik, was Amtmaðr for the southern quarter. Hr Christián Christiánsson ruled the north and east at Fríðriksgáfa, and Hr Bergur Thorberg, knight of the Danne-ʼbrog, had his headquarters at Stykkishólm on the western fourth. Now (1874), Hr Bergur Thorberg governs the southern and western quadrants, and Hr Christián Christiánsson, with the title of Justitsráð, the northern and the eastern. These officers are addressed as Hávelborni, and they receive the reports of the several Sýslumenn.

The Sýslumenn, or sheriffs, are the civil staff, the tax-gatherers and stewards as it were of the king; and appointed by the Crown. In order to obtain this office they must be graduates of the University of Copenhagen; they wear uniforms, a gold band round the cap, frock coats, waistcoats, and vests of blue broadcloth, with the royal button, and they may become ministers of state. They preside at the Hèraðthings [2] or annual county courts; they watch over the peace of their shrievalties; they officiate as public notaries; and they maintain the rights of inheritance. The Sýslumaðr in his judicial capacity, and chiefly when land-questions are to be determined, is occasionally assisted by four Meðdómsmenn (*concessores judicii*), who give suffrage and register proceedings; decisions are pronounced according to

---

[1] The Múla-Sýsla ("mull" county) was formerly divided into three parts, the northern, the central, and the southern, each with its Sýslumaðr. The present distribution dates from the year 1779.

[2] Hèrað (or Hierat) is the Scotch "heriot," a tax paid to feudal lord in lieu of military service. In Icelandic the Hèrað is a geographical district generally, and is specially applied to the river-basin of the Skagafjörð (Cleasby).

the vote of the majority.[1] He superintends elections. Formerly he could compel the lieges to repair the highways, and the law still obliges each landed proprietor to keep the rough fences upon his estate in good condition. A small sum called Vegabótargjald is also taken by the Sýslumaðr to pay for the necessary expenses of roads; unfortunately the *corvée* or robot of peasants has been abolished, and the means of transit are much neglected. A law compelling all sturdy vagrants and able-bodied paupers to work upon the highways is as much wanted in Iceland, as useful and productive employment for the hordes of soldiers who now compose the standing armies of Europe.

Under the Sýslumenn and appointed by the Amtmenn are the Hreppstjórar or Hreppstjórnarmenn, bailiffs and poor-inspectors with parochial jurisdiction. It is hardly to be doubted that the division into Rapes existed in heathen days, and Dr Konrad Maurer believes that they had organised poor laws and rules for vagrancy which the Christian bishops after-wards amended and expanded. In these days the Rape-stewards assist their civil and ecclesiastical superiors to manage the business of the Rape, to preserve public order, and to estimate cessable property according to the ancient custom of the island. They fix the poor-rate for each land-holder, and they especially attend to the condition and maintenance of paupers (Úmagar), who are no longer subject to the pains and penalties of that ancient code the Grágás (grey or wild goose).[2] Where the parish exceeds 400 souls, these minor officials usually number two to five. They are substantial yeomen who wear no distinctive dress. They and their children are exempt from taxation, and

---

[1] The sheriff does *not* attend parish meetings, he has no schools to inspect, for there are none, in fact he has nothing to do with education at all, that being the business of the parish priest under the superintendence of the prófastr (dean) of the district.

[2] The name of this Icelandic code of laws, which must not be confounded with the Grágás of Norway, is variously explained from the grey binding or from being written with a grey goose-quill. It was adopted in Iceland in A.D. 1118, and it contained a Lex de ejusmodi mendicis (sturdy vagrants) impunè castrandis. Some writers suppose that the Icelandic Commonwealth had written laws but no code. After the union with Norway the island received its first written code, the Iron-side, Járn-Síða (A.D. 1262-1272), and this was exchanged in A.D. 1272 for the Jónsbók, so termed from John the Lawyer who brought it from Norway. Uno Von Troil (p. 73) removes the date of the latter to A.D. 1272.

this is their only salary. The functions of the Amtmenn, Sýslumenn, and of the Hreppstjórar especially, will be greatly modified
when the law of May 4th, 1872, comes into operation during the
present year. A standing Hreppsnefnd, or a committee of three,
five, or seven, is to be elected in each Hreppr. This body is to
have charge of the poor, the sanitary conditions, and the
general business of the Hreppr, including the repair of roads.
It is also to levy the poor-rates and other cesses of the Hreppr.
The Hreppstjórar will be retained, but their functions are not
defined. A Sýslunefnd is also to be elected in each Sýsla, consisting of six to ten members; and the Sýslumaðr is *ex officio* a
convener or foreman of this committee. It is to have charge
of the roads, to manage the general business of the Sýsla, and
to exercise supervision over the Hreppsnefndir. Thirdly,
Amtsrað, Amt-Councils, consisting of the Amtmaðr and two
elected members, will audit and control all the accounts of the
Amt; will act as trustees of all public institutions and public
legacies, and will have supervision over the Hreppsnefndir and
Sýslunefndir.

## § 3. JUDICIAL PROCEDURE.

It is well known that trial by jury, the bulwark of Englishmen's rights, though fathered by English legal antiquaries upon
King Alfred, is a purely Scandinavian institution. According
to the Landnámabók (IL, ix., note, p. 83), the Kviðr plays a
considerable part in the republican history; and the form of
trial like our juries *de vicineto* appears in the thirteenth century.
As Mr Vigfússon remarks (Cleasby, sub voce Kviðr): "From
the analogy of the Icelandic customs, it can be inferred with
certainty that, along with the invasion of Danes and Norsemen,
the judgment by verdict was also transplanted to English ground,
for the settlers of England were kith and kin to those of Iceland,
carrying with them the same laws and customs; lastly, after
the Conquest, it became the law of the land. This old Scandinavian institution gradually died out in the mother countries[1]

---

[1] Mr Dasent, Introduction to Dict. (xlviii.), remarks that the jury was never
developed in Norway, and only struck faint root in the Danish and Swedish laws.

and ended in Iceland, A.D. 1271-1281, with the fall of the Commonwealth and the introduction of a Norse code of laws, whereas it was naturalised in England, which came to be the classical land of trial by jury."

Modern Iceland utterly ignores it, but, as in the United States, all freemen are familiar with judicial procedures, and public opinion, not to speak of the press, is a sufficient safeguard for a small community.

In criminal cases the Crown prosecutes, and the king must ratify capital sentences. Like the Cives of Rome, and very unlike the subjects of civilised Europe, Icelanders are not confined before trial, there being no houses of detention; but a criminal is kept either by the sheriff or the hreppstjóri, who is responsible for his being brought to judgment at an order from the court. By way of checking the litigiousness of the lieges, a regular system of arbitration is in force. The parish priest *ex officio* and one of his parishioners are the Forlíkunarmenn (reconciliators), and act as umpires; and a previous investigation of causes often quashes them.

It is only in administrative cases, *e.g.*, about paupers, etc., that there is an appeal from the decisions of the sheriff to the Amtmaðr. From the Sýslumaðr's court civil causes go for cassation directly to the Supreme Court (Konunglegi-Landsyfirrettur) of Reykjavik, which was instituted in A.D. 1800, when the Althing, which then had judicial as well as legislative and administrative functions, was abolished. The Royal Court consists of a Chief Justice (Justiciarius) and two assessors; the governor presides, but takes no part in the judicial proceedings. All three votes are equal, and the majority decides, thus making the judge and assessors jury as well as judges. The actual dignitaries are Hr Thórður Jonasson, Hr Jón Pétursen, and Hr Magnús Stephensen; the salaries are, $2816, $2016, and $1416. There are also two procurators (the English barrister and the Scotch advocate), Hr Páll Melsted and Hr Jón Guðmundsson, who edits the leading newspaper. Hr P. Guðjónsson, the church organist, is not

---

When asserting the jury to be purely Scandinavian, the author speaks of Europe, neglecting the admirable Panchayat system which arose in the village republics of Hindostan, and a multitude of other similar institutions.

a procurator although he occasionally conducts cases before the superior court.

At this Royal High Court of Judgment the evidence and pleadings of both parties are heard, and the Justiciarius, after taking the opinions of his assessors, pronounces his decision. For cassation, causes must then go to the Chancellerie, or Supreme Court of Judicature at Copenhagen.

---

## SECTION V.

## ANTHROPOLOGY.

Statistics—General Considerations—Personal Appearance —Character—The Family—Diseases.

### § 1. Statistics.

The constitution of society and the physical features of Iceland are peculiarly favourable to numbering the people. The island has no object either to diminish her total in order to avoid recruiting, and has scant interest in exaggerating it with a view to urban concessions and civic privileges. Between A.D. 1840-60 the census was quinquennial; since that time every decade has been deemed sufficient.

The following numbers are taken from various sources, and especially from the latest official figures in the Skýrslur of October 1, 1870:

O. Olavius Ponteppidan Thaarup, etc.

|  | S. Qr. | W. Qr. | N. & E. Qrs. | Total. |
|---|---|---|---|---|
| In A.D. 1703, | 18,728 | 15,774 | 15,942 | 50,444 |
| ,, 1769, | 17,150 | 13,596 | 15,455 | 46,201 |

In A.D. 1770 Uno Von Troil (p. 25) estimated the population at 60,000 souls, or about 10,000 more than sixty years after the Norwegian colonisation. In 1783 the total fell to 47,287, and in 1786 to 38,142 (Preyer and Zirkel, p. 483). Since the beginning of the present century we have exact and minute computations:

STATISTISK TABEL-VÆRK.

| | S. Qr. | W. Qr. | N. & E. Qrs. | Total. |
|---|---|---|---|---|
| In A.D. 1801, . . | 17,160 | 13,976 | 16,104 | 46,240 (47,207?) |
| ,, 1806 (Preyer and Zirkel, whereas Mackenzie assigns it to 1804), . . . . . . . | | | | 46,349 |
| ,, 1808 (Preyer and Zirkel; and Mackenzie, p. 280), . | | | | 48,063 |
| ,, 1834, (Dillon, unofficial, evidently "round numbers") | | | | 53,000 |
| ,, 1835, . . | 20,292 | 14,480 | 21,263 | 56,035 |
| ,, 1840, . . | 20,677 | 14,665 | 21,752 | 57,094 |
| ,, 1842 (Meddel., ii. 70), . . . . . . | | | | 53,000 |
| ,, 1845, . . | 21,364 | 14,956 | 22,238 | 58,358 |

SKÝRSLUR.

| | S. Qr. | W. Qr. | N. & E. Qrs. | Total. |
|---|---|---|---|---|
| In A.D. 1850, . . | 21,288 | 15,112 | 22,757 | 59,157 |
| ,, 1855, . . | 22,810 | 16,362 | 25,431 | 64,603 |
| ,, 1857 (Preyer and Zirkel), . . . . . | | | | 66,929 |
| ,, 1858 ( Do. ), . . . . . | | | | 67,847 |
| ,, 1860, . . | 23,137 | 16,960 | 26,890 | 66,987 |
| ,, 1865 (Vice-Consul Crowe), . . . . . | | | | 68,000 |
| ,, 1870, . . | 25,063 | 17,001 | 27,699 | 69,763 |
| ,, 1872 (estimated), . . . . . . . | | | | 70,000 |

while that of Madeira is 80,000.

The following table (Skýrslur um landshagi á Íslandi, v. 310, 1872) shows the increase of population during the present century down to 1870 :

From Feb. 1, 1801, to Feb. 2, 1835, increase 18·71 per cent.
,, Feb. 2, 1835, to Nov. 2, 1840, ,, 1·89 ,,
,, Nov. 2, 1840, to Nov. 2, 1845, ,, 2·55 ,,
,, Nov. 2, 1845, to Feb. 1, 1850, ,, 1·01 ,,
,, Feb. 1, 1850, to Oct. 1, 1855, ,, 9·21 ,,
,, Oct. 1, 1855, to Oct. 1, 1860, ,, 3·69 ,,
,, Oct. 1, 1860, to Oct. 1, 1870, ,, 4·14 ,,

The average rate of increase during the last century was very small: between A.D. 1703 and 1758 it was about one-fifth of 1 per cent. During the present age there has been, we observe, a tolerably regular progress with only three exceptions (A.D. 1835-40, A.D. 1845-50, and A.D. 1860-70). During this decade (1860-70) there has been a considerable failure, 4·14 per cent., or only 2·05 for each lustrum. In 1872, as will be seen, the number of males was 33,102; of females, 36,660. But throughout

Iceland the fluctuations have ever been so great as to reduce the value of " general considerations."

The following tables are compiled from the minute returns made to the Danish Government, and published in vols. i.-vi· of 1852-61, of the Meddelser fra det Statistishe Bureau, Copenhagen.

No. I.—Table showing the Population of Iceland and its Distribution on the 1st February 1850, and on the 1st October 1855.

| Districts. | No. of Families. | | Population. | | Increase, in hundredths. |
|---|---|---|---|---|---|
| | 1850. | 1855. | 1850. | 1855. | |
| **SOUTHERN AMT.** | | | | | |
| Reykjavik, . . . . . . . | 219 | 250 | 1149 | 1354 | 17·84 |
| Gullbríngu and Kjósar Sýsla,[1] exclusive of Reykjavik, . . . . . | 783 | 853 | 4519 | 4853 | 7·39 |
| The same, including Reykjavik, . | 1002 | 1103 | 5668 | 6207 | 9·51 |
| Borgarfjarðar Sýsla, . . . . . | 329 | 355 | 2097 | 2312 | 10·25 |
| Árnes Sýsla, . . . . . . . | 723 | 755 | 5018 | 5382 | 7·25 |
| Rángárvalla Sýsla, . . . . . . | 700 | 717 | 4766 | 4917 | 3·17 |
| Austr and Vestr Skaptafells Sýsla,[1] | 481 | 529 | 3340 | 3545 | 6·14 |
| Vestmannaeyja[2] Sýsla, . . . . | 91 | 98 | 399 | 447 | 12·03 |
| Total (Southern Amt), . . | 3326 | 3557 | 21,288 | 22,810 | 7·15 |
| **WESTERN AMT.** | | | | | |
| Mýra and Hnappadals Sýsla,[1] . . | 379 | 383 | 2410 | 2569 | 6·60 |
| Snæfellsness Sýsla, . . . . . | 512 | 526 | 2684 | 2825 | 5·25 |
| Dala Sýsla, . . . . . . . | 267 | 277 | 1923 | 2104 | 9·41 |
| Barðastrandar Sýsla, . . . . | 336 | 347 | 2518 | 2703 | 7·35 |
| Ísafjarðar[3] Sýsla, . . . . . | 508 | 545 | 4204 | 4589 | 9·16 |
| Stranda Sýsla, . . . . . . | 179 | 190 | 1373 | 1572 | 14·49 |
| Total (Western Amt), . . . | 2181 | 2268 | 15,112 | 16,362 | 8·27 |
| **NORTHERN AND EASTERN AMTS.** | | | | | |
| Húnavatns Sýsla, . . . . . | 556 | 639 | 4117 | 4637 | 12·63 |
| Skagafjarðar Sýsla, . . . . | 626 | 622 | 4033 | 4258 | 5·58 |
| Eyjafjarðar Sýsla, . . . . | 625 | 638 | 3965 | 4289 | 8·17 |
| Norðr and Suðr Thingeyjar Sýsla,[1] | 640 | 684 | 4453 | 5108 | 14·71 |
| Norðr-Múla Sýsla, . . . . | 405 | 473 | 3201 | 3754 | 17·28 |
| Suðr-Múla Sýsla, . . . . . | 391 | 416 | 2988 | 3385 | 13·29 |
| Total (Northern and Eastern Amts), . . . . . . | 3243 | 3472 | 22,757 | 25,431 | 11·75 |
| Total for all Iceland, . . . | 8750 | 9297 | 59,157 | 64,603 | 9·21 |

[1] Separated on Ólsen's map.
[2] Apparently combined with Rángárvalla Sýsla on Ólsen's map.
[3] Sub-divided into north and west by P. and Z., p. 480; Mck., p. 281.

No. II.—Distribution of the Population of Iceland according to ages in 1855.

| Ages. | Per cent. | Ages. | Per cent. |
|---|---|---|---|
| Under 20 years, . . . . | 42·315 | Between 50 and 60 years, . | 9·303 |
| Between 20 and 30 years, . | 19·485 | Between 60 and 70 years, . | 5·413 |
| Between 30 and 40 years, . | 11·886 | Over 70 years, . . . . | 2·463 |
| Between 40 and 50 years, . | 9·135 | | |

No. III.—Table showing the Means of Support of the Population of Iceland on the 1st October 1855.

| OCCUPATIONS. | PROVIDING SUPPORT. | | | SUPPORTED. | | | | | | TOTAL. | | | Percentage of Population. |
|---|---|---|---|---|---|---|---|---|---|---|---|---|---|
| | | | | Wives & Families. | | | Servants. | | | | | | |
| | Males. | Females. | Total. | Males. | Females. | Total. | Males. | Females. | Total. | Males. | Females. | Total. | |
| Ecclesiastics and teachers, . . | 196 | 7 | 203 | 399 | 623 | 1022 | 527 | 613 | 1140 | 1122 | 1243 | 2365 | 3·66 |
| Civil officials and employés, . . | 45 | 2 | 47 | 74 | 105 | 179 | 105 | 123 | 228 | 224 | 230 | 454 | 0·70 |
| Persons who live on their means, | 81 | 89 | 170 | 40 | 84 | 124 | 18 | 44 | 62 | 139 | 217 | 356 | 0·55 |
| Men of science and letters, . . | 29 | .. | 29 | 20 | 42 | 62 | 20 | 29 | 49 | 69 | 71 | 140 | 0·22 |
| Persons who live by agriculture, | 7063 | 618 | 7681 | 11,835 | 19,354 | 31,189 | 6112 | 7493 | 13,605 | 25,010 | 27,465 | 52,475 | 81·23 |
| Persons who live by the sea, . . | 980 | 86 | 1066 | 1090 | 1925 | 3015 | 465 | 509 | 974 | 2535 | 2520 | 5055 | 7·82 |
| Mechanics, . . | 199 | 27 | 226 | 133 | 219 | 352 | 59 | 73 | 132 | 391 | 319 | 710 | 1·10 |
| Traders and inn-keepers, . . . | 87 | 4 | 91 | 136 | 231 | 367 | 117 | 155 | 272 | 340 | 390 | 730 | 1·13 |
| Persons who work by the day, . . | 172 | 62 | 234 | 97 | 168 | 265 | 13 | 11 | 24 | 282 | 241 | 523 | 0·81 |
| Others who pursue no definite occupation, . | 162 | 123 | 285 | 67 | 172 | 239 | 20 | 42 | 62 | 249 | 337 | 586 | 0·91 |
| Receiving alms, . | 497 | 710 | 1207 | .. | .. | .. | .. | .. | .. | 497 | 710 | 1207 | 1·87 |
| Prisoners, . . . | 2 | .. | 2 | .. | .. | .. | .. | .. | .. | 2 | .. | 2 | 0·00 |
| Total, . . . | 9513 | 1728 | 11,241 | 13,891 | 22,923 | 36,814 | 7456 | 9092 | 16,548 | 30,860 | 33,743 | 64,603 | 100·00 |
| Percentage of population, . . | 14·7 | 2·7 | 17·4 | 21·5 | 35·5 | 57·0 | 11·5 | 14·1 | 25·6 | 47·8 | 52·2 | 100·0 | .. |

The following are the latest returns:

Table showing the Population of Iceland on the 1st October 1860 and 1870.

| Districts. | Number of Families. | Population. | | Increase and Decrease per cent. |
|---|---|---|---|---|
| | | 1860. | 1870. | |
| SOUTHERN AMT. | | | | |
| Reykjavik, . . . . . . | 356 | 1444 | 2024 | |
| Gullbríngu and Kjósar Sýsla, . . | 824 | 5001 | 5302 | + 13·7 |
| Borgarfjarðar Sýsla, . . . | 352 | 2251 | 2590 | + 15·1 |
| Árnes Sýsla, . . . . . | 772 | 5409 | 5891 | + 8·9 |
| Rángárvalla Sýsla, . . . | 689 | 5034 | 5201 | + 3·3 |
| Austr and Vestr Skaptafells Sýsla, . | 490 | 3499 | 3484 | − 0·4 |
| Vestmannaeyja Sýsla, . . . . | 885 | 499 | 571 | + 14·4 |
| Total (Southern Amt), . . | 3568 | 23,137 | 25,063 | + 8·3 |
| WESTERN AMT. | | | | |
| Mýra and Hnappadals Sýsla, . . | 373 | 2663 | 2765 | + 3·9 |
| Snæfellsness Sýsla, . . . . | 471 | 2869 | 2799 | − 2·4 |
| Dala Sýsla, . . . . . . | 285 | 2223 | 2190 | − 1·5 |
| Barðastrandar Sýsla, . . . . | 311 | 2727 | 2699 | − 1·0 |
| Ísafjarðar Sýsla, . . . . . | 518 | 4860 | 4895 | + 0·7 |
| Stranda Sýsla, . . . . . | 192 | 1618 | 1653 | + 2·2 |
| Total (Western Amt), . . | 2150 | 16,960 | 17,001 | + 0·2 |
| NORTHERN AND EASTERN AMTS. | | | | |
| Húnavatns Sýsla, . . . . | 623 | 4722 | 4906 | + 3·9 |
| Skagafjarðar Sýsla, . . . . | 614 | 4379 | 4574 | + 4·5 |
| Eyjafjarðar Sýsla, . . . . | 707 | 4647 | 5108 | + 9·9 |
| Thingeyjar Sýsla, . . . . | 715 | 5497 | 5746 | + 4·5 |
| Norðr-Múla Sýsla, . . . . | 487 | 4183 | 3885 | + 0·5 |
| Suðr-Múla Sýsla, . . . . | 442 | 3462 | 3480 | − 7·1 |
| Total (Northern and Eastern Amts), | 3588 | 26,890 | 27,699 | + 3·0 |
| Total for all Iceland, . . . | 9306 | 66,987 | 69,763 | + 4·1 |

The following is the official list of households for 1872:

In the Suðr-umdæmið (South Quarter) are 3568 households, with 11,835 men and 13,228 women.

| | | | | | | | |
|---|---|---|---|---|---|---|---|
| ,, | Vestr | ,, | (West ,, ) ,, 2150 | ,, | 7,981 ,, | ,, | 9,019 ,, |
| ,, | Norðr og Austr | . . | ,, 3588 | ,, | 13,286 ,, | ,, | 14,413 ,, |
| | | Total, . . . | 9306 | | 33,102 men and 36,660 women. | | |

According to Mr Vice-Consul Crowe (Report), during the average of ten years (1855-65) there was annually—

1 marriage for every .   .   .    143 persons.
1 birth for every    .   .   .     25   „
1 death for every    .   .   .     39   „
1 deaf and dumb for every   .   994   „
1 blind   .    .    .    .    .    320   „

In 1855 there were 202 blind and 65 born surd-mutes. In 1870 the former numbered 225 (160 men and 65 women), and the latter 50 (20 + 30).

In table III. (1855), we see that of 64,603 souls, 52,475, about three-fourths of the heads of families and those who provide support, lived by farming, that is, by cattle-breeding, whilst more than four-fifths of the entire population thus derived their maintenance. At the same time, 5055 were fishermen, and only 703 were traders, showing a primitive state of society. Mr Consul Crowe (Report, 1870-71) remarks: "Somewhat more than the 75 per cent. of the total population were engaged in sheep rearing and agricultural pursuits; and, notwithstanding the steady and lucrative nature of the fisheries, only about 10 per cent. were engaged in them." The mechanics may be further distributed as follows:

| | | | | | | |
|---|---|---|---|---|---|---|
| Bakers, | (in 1855) | 1 | proportion per thousand | 0·01 | in 1870 numbered | 2 |
| Coopers, | ,, | 35 | ,, | 0·55 | ,, | 17 |
| Gold & Silver } Smiths, | ,, | 80 | | 1·24 | | 21 |
| Blacksmiths, | ,, | 80 | | 1·24 | | 31 |
| Carpenters, | ,, | 61 | | 0·94 | | 12 |
| Masons, | .. | 6 | | 0·09 | | 2 |
| Millers, | | 4 | | 0·07 | ,, | 1 |
| Turners, | | 8 | | 0·13 | ,, | 1 |
| Boatbuilders, | ,, | 38 | | 0·59 | .. | 12 |
| Tailors, | | 27 | | 0·41 | | 10 |
| Joiners, | | 174 | | 2·69 | ,, | 56 |
| Saddlers, | | 46 | | 0·71 | | 15 |
| Weavers, | | 20 | | 0·30 | | 4 |
| Watchmakers, | ,, | 0 | | 0·00 | | 1 |
| Other industries, | ,, | 103 | | 1·59 | | 24 |

The following is a table of ages in 1870:

| Years. | MEN. | | | | WOMEN. | | | |
|---|---|---|---|---|---|---|---|---|
| | Married. | Unmarried. | Widowers. | Separated. | Married. | Unmarried. | Widows. | Separated. |
| 1 | ... | 801 | ... | ... | ... | 777 | ... | ... |
| 1-2 | ... | 1530 | ... | ... | ... | 1570 | ... | ... |
| 3-4 | ... | 1814 | ... | ... | ... | 1798 | ... | ... |
| 5-6 | ... | 1828 | ... | ... | ... | 1768 | ... | ... |
| 7-10 | ... | 3073 | ... | ... | ... | 3090 | ... | ... |
| 11-15 | ... | 3713 | ... | ... | ... | 3715 | ... | ... |
| 16-20 | 3 | 3693 | ... | ... | 39 | 3706 | ... | ... |
| 21-25 | 143 | 2374 | 2 | ... | 350 | 2301 | 14 | 3 |
| 26-30 | 843 | 1601 | 16 | 7 | 1031 | 1691 | 55 | 9 |
| 31-35 | 1224 | 814 | 44 | 12 | 1384 | 1046 | 126 | 17 |
| 36-40 | 1869 | 650 | 96 | 17 | 1867 | 916 | 226 | 31 |
| 41-45 | 1377 | 307 | 107 | 18 | 1225 | 523 | 289 | 22 |
| 46-50 | 1125 | 171 | 131 | 29 | 1067 | 350 | 343 | 23 |
| 51-55 | 751 | 100 | 114 | 17 | 623 | 232 | 361 | 24 |
| 56-60 | 501 | 83 | 111 | 4 | 456 | 204 | 359 | 10 |
| 61-65 | 424 | 67 | 154 | 6 | 360 | 203 | 383 | 9 |
| 66-70 | 341 | 64 | 208 | 7 | 282 | 208 | 494 | 8 |
| 71-75 | 178 | 42 | 174 | 2 | 130 | 113 | 346 | 3 |
| 76-80 | 70 | 10 | 126 | 1 | 50 | 60 | 206 | ... |
| 81-85 | 28 | 3 | 54 | ... | 16 | 24 | 88 | 1 |
| 86-90 | 5 | 1 | 12 | ... | ... | 7 | 15 | ... |
| 91-95 | ... | 1 | 1 | ... | 1 | 2 | 5 | ... |
| 96-100 | ... | ... | 1 | ... | ... | 2 | 3 | ... |
| Above 100 [1] | | none. | | | | none | | |
| | 8882 | 22,740 | 1361 | 120 | 8881 | 24,306 | 3313 | 160 |
| | | 33,103 | | | | 36,660 | | |

69,763

According to Mr Consul Crowe (Report, 1870-71), the proportion between births and deaths was:

---

[1] Dillon notices forty-one women who had passed ninety: the number has now greatly fallen off. There is a further decline from the days of Olaus Magnus, who informs us that "the Icelanders, who, instead of bread, have fish bruised with a stone, live three hundred years." The general longevity of Norway proves that the climates of the north, the *vagina gentium* of Jornandes, have nothing adverse to human life. In Scotland the census of 1870 gave a total of twenty-six centagenarians—nine men and seventeen women.

| Year. | Births. | Deaths. | Computed Population. | Percentage. |
|-------|---------|---------|----------------------|-------------|
| 1861 | 2525 | 2391 | 66,973 | + 0·20 |
| 1862 | 2693 | 2874 | 66,792 | + 0·27 |
| 1863 | 2648 | 2115 | 67,325 | + 0·80 |
| 1864 | 2760 | 2001 | 68,084 | + 1·13 |
| 1865 | 2757 | 2100 | 68,741 | + 0·96 |
| 1866 | 2662 | 3122 | 68,281 | + 0·67 |
| 1867 | 2743 | 1770 | 69,254 | + 1·42 |
| 1868 | 2449 | 1970 | 69,733 | + 0·69 |
| 1869 | 2177 | 2404 | 69,506 | + 0·33 |
| 1870 | 2276 | 1698 | 70,084 | + 0·83 |
| Total, | 25,690 | 22,445 | | |

The tables of 1855 gave an excess of 2865 women. Mackenzie (1801) shows 21,476 males to 25,731 females, or 4255 out of a total of 47,207. In 1865 the proportion of men to women was 1000 : 1093. In 1870 the conditions had improved, the surplus being only 3554 out of 69,763, a small percentage of waste labour.

It is easy to account for the preponderance of women, as well as their superior longevity, without entering into the knotty subject of what determines sex. They lead more regular lives, they have less hardship and fatigue, and they are rarely exposed to such accidents as being lost at sea or " in the mist." According to Mr Vice-Consul Crowe, in 1865-66, of every forty-two deaths one was by drowning.

There is a tradition that Iceland during its palmiest days contained 100,000 souls, but it seems to rest upon no foundation. On the other hand, the old superstitious belief that some fatal epidemic invariably follows an increase beyond 60,000, has, during the last few years, shown itself to be equally groundless. It is probably one of the *post hoc, ergo propter hoc* confusions so popular amongst the vulgar ; and, unhappily, not confined to the vulgar.

## § 2. General Considerations.

"The first inhabitants of the northern world, Dania, Nerigos, and Suæcia," says Saxo Grammaticus, repeated by Arngrímr Jónsson, "were the posterity and remnant of the Canáanites *quos fugavit Jesus latro*—expulsed from Palestine about A.C. 1500 by Joshua and Caleb." Duly appreciating the ethnological value of this tradition, we may remark that the occupation of Ultima Thule, which the ancients evidently held to be inhabited—*tibi serviat* must mean that there were men to serve—has not yet been proved. But Mongoloid or præ-Aryan colonies in ancient days seem to have overrun all the Old, if not the New World, and we must not despair of tracing them to Iceland.

The modern Icelander is a quasi-Norwegian, justly proud of the old home. His race is completely free from any taint of Skrælling, Innuit,[1] or Mongoloid blood, as some travellers have represented, and as the vulgar of Europe seem to believe. Here and there, but rarely, a dark flat face, oblique eyes, and long black horsehair, show that a wife has been taken from the land

> "Where the short-legged Esquimaux
> Waddle in the ice and snow."

In the southern parts of the island there is apparently a considerable Irish infusion; and we often remark the "potato face" and the peculiar eye, with grey-blue iris and dark lashes so common in outer Galway, and extending to far Tenerife.

It has been the fashion for travellers to talk of "our Scandinavian ancestors in Iceland," to declare that the northern element is the "backbone of the English race," and to find that Great Britain owes to the hyperborean "her pluck, her go-ahead, and her love of freedom."

That a little of this strong liquor may have done abundant good to the puerile, futile Anglo-Kelt, and the flabby and

---

[1] Innuit (Eskimo), like Illinois (from Illeni), means simply "a man"—a frequent tribal designation amongst savages. So Teuton and Deutsch, with the numberless derivations, are derived from Goth. Thiud, a people ; Alemanni from " All-men," and " German perhaps from Guerre-man " (Farrar, Families of Speech).

phlegmatic Anglo-Saxon, there is no doubt, but happily we have not had a drop too much of northern blood. The islanders are by no means slow to claim descent from the old Jarls of Norway and Sweden, whilst some of the peasantry have asserted, and, it is said, have proved, consanguinity with the Guelphs: this would make them Germans, like the Royal Family of Denmark, who enjoy only poetical and laureated connection with the " Sea-Kings." Those who reject these pretensions reply that every noble house emigrating from Scandinavia in the ninth and tenth centuries brought with it a train of serfs and thralls; for instance, Njál headed nearly thirty fighting men, serviles included, and Thráin led fifteen house-carls trained to arms. And genealogical statistics prove that while the Jarl's blood dies out, the Carl's increases and multiplies.

The Saga's description of Gunnar Hamondsson is that of a well-favoured Icelander in the present day : " He was handsome of feature and fair-skinned; his nose was straight and a little turned up at the end ('tip-tilted'); he was blue-eyed, and bright-eyed, and ruddy cheeked; his hair was thick and of good hue, and hanging down in comely curls." And Skarphèdinn Njálsson may stand forth as the typical "plain" Thulite : "His hair was dark-brown, with crisp curly locks; he had good eyes; his features were sharp, and his face ashen pale; his nose turned up, and his front teeth stuck out, and his mouth was very ugly."

The Icelander's temperament is nervoso-lymphatic, and, at best, nervoso-sanguineous. The nervoso-bilious, so common in the south of Europe, is found but rarely; and the author never saw an instance of the pure nervous often met with in the United States and the Brazil. The shape of the cranium is distinctly brachycephalic, like the Teuton who can almost always be discovered by his flat occiput and his projecting ears. The face is rather round or square than oval; the forehead often rises high, and the malar bones stand out strongly, whilst the cheeks fall in. A very characteristic feature of the race whose hardness, not to say harshness, of body and mind still distinguishes it from its neighbours, is the eye, dure and cold as a pebble—the mesmerist would despair at the first sight. Even amongst the "gentler sex" a soft look is uncommonly rare, and the aspect ranges from a stoney stare to a sharp glance rendered fiercer by the habitual frown. Hence probably Uno Von Troil (p. 87) describes the women as generally ill-featured. The best specimens are clear grey or light blue, rarely brown and never black; and the iris is mostly surrounded by a ring of darker colour, the reverse of *arcus senilis*. Squints and prominent eye-balls, in fact what are vulgarly called "goggle eyes," are common; and even commoner, perhaps, are the dull colourless organs which we term "cods' eyes." The "Irish eye," blue with dark lashes, is still found in the southern part of the island, where, perhaps, thralls' blood is most common. A mild and chronic con-junctivitis often results from exposure to sun-glare after dark rooms and from reading deep into the night with dim oil lamps. The nose is seldom aquiline; the noble and sympathetically advancing outlines of the Mediterranean shores will here be sought for in vain.[1] The best are the straight, the worst are offensive "pugs." Only in two instances, both of them men of good blood, I saw the broad open brows, the Grecian noses, the perpendicular profiles, the oval cheeks, and the chins full, but not too full, which one connects in idea with the Scandi-navian sea-king of the olden day. As a rule, then, the Icelandic face can by no means be called handsome.

The oral region is often coarse and unpleasant. Lean lips are not so numerous as the large, loose, fleshy, and *bordés* or slightly everted, whilst here and there a huge mouth seems to split the face from ear to ear. The redeeming feature is the denture.

---

[1] The discovery of Uriconium and of Roman remains throughout England, and even in London, during the last few years, strongly suggests that the beauty of the English race is derived from a far greater intermixture of southern blood than was formerly suspected ; and the racial baptism, repeated by the invasion of the Normans, must also have brought with it Gallo-Romans in considerable numbers. We can hardly doubt that the handsome peasantry of south-western Ireland is the produce of Spanish or Mediterranean innervation ; and a com-parison with the country people of Orotava in Tenerife, where the Irish have again mixed with the mingled Hispano-Guanche race, shows certain remark-able points of family likeness. On the other hand, except in certain parts of Great Britain, especially the Danelagh or Scandinavianised coasts and the counties occupied by the Angli and other Teutonic peoples, the English race remarkably differs from both its purer congeners, the homely Scandinavians and Germans. The general verdict of foreigners confirms its superior beauty, which, indeed, is evident to the most superficial observer.

The teeth are short, regular, bright-coloured, and lasting, showing uncommon strength of constitution. They are rarely clean when coffee and tobacco are abused, and they are yet more rarely cleaned. Doubtless a comparatively scanty use of hot food tends to preserve them. The jowl is strong and square, and the chin is heavy, the weak "vanishing" form being very uncommon. The beard is sometimes worn, but more often clean shaved off; it seldom grows to any length, though the mustachios, based upon a large and solid upper lip, are bushy and form an important feature. Thick whiskers are sometimes seen, and so are "Newgate frills," from which the small foxy features stand sharply out.

The other strong points are the skin and hair. The former is almost always rufous, rarely milanous, and the author never saw a specimen of the leucous (albino). The "positive blonde" is the rule; opposed to the negative or washed out blonde of Russia and Slavonia generally. The complexion of the younger sort is admirably fresh, pink and white; and some retain this charm till a late age. Its delicacy subjects it to sundry infirmities, especially to freckles, which appear in large brown blotches; exposure to weather also burns the surface, and converts rose and lily to an unseemly buff and brick-dust red. It is striated in early middle-age with deep wrinkles and it becomes much "drawn," the effect of what children call "making faces" in the sunlight and snow-blink. In the less wholesome parts of the island the complexion of the peasantry is pallid and malarious.

Harfagr (Pulchricomus) is an epithet which may apply to both sexes. The hair, which belongs to the class Lissótriches, subdivision Euplokomoi, of Hæckel and Müller (Allg. Ethnographie, 1873), seldom shows the darker shades of brown; and in the very rare cases where it is black, there is generally a suspicion of Eskimo or Mongoloid blood. The colour ranges from carrotty-red to turnip-yellow, from barley-sugar to the *blond-cendré* so expensive in the civilised markets. We find all the gradations of Parisian art here natural; the "corn-golden," the *blonde fulvide*, the incandescent ("carrotty"), the *flavescent* or sulphur-hued, the *beurre frais*, the *fulvastre* or lion's mane, and

the *rubide* or mahogany, Raphael's favourite tint. The abominable Hallgerda's hair is the type of Icelandic beauty; it was
"soft as silk and so long that it came down to her waist."
Seldom straight and lank, the *chevelure* is usually wavy, curling
at the ends, when short cut, as in England. The women have
especially thick locks, which look well without other art but
braiding, and many of the men have very bushy hair. As in
the negro, baldness does not appear till a late age, and perhaps
the Húfa (cap) by exposing the larger part of the surface acts
as a preservative; old men and women, though anile beauty
is very rare, are seen with grey and even white locks exceptionally thick. Canities comes on later than in Scotland and
Sweden, yet scant attention is paid to the hair beyond washing
at the brook. The body pile is as usual lighter coloured.

The figure is worse than the face, and it is rendered even more
uncouth by the hideous swathing dress. The men are remarkable for "champagne-bottle (unduly sloping) shoulders," "broad-
shouldered in the backside," as our sailors say. They are seldom
paunchy, though some, when settled in warmer climates, develop
the *schöne corpulenz* of the Whitechapel sugar-baker. They
have the thick, unwieldy trunks of mountaineers, too long for
the lower limbs—a peculiarity of hill-men generally, which
extends even to the Bubes of Fernando Po. The legs are uncommonly sturdy; the knees are thick and rounded, an unpro-
mising sign of blood; the ankles are coarse, and the flat feet are
unusually large and ill-formed, like the hands, a point of resemblance with the Anglo-Saxon pure and simple. Hence they
are peculiarly fitted for their only manly sport, besides skating
and shooting, "Glímu list:" this wrestling has a "chic" of its
own, though very different from the style of Cumberland and
Cornwall. The gait, a racial distinction, is shambling and un-
graceful, utterly unlike the strut of Southern Europe and the
roll of the nearer East; the tread is ponderous, and the light
fantastic toe is unknown. This "wabble" and waddle result
from the rarity of walking-exercise compared with riding and
boating, and from the univeral use of the seal-skin slipper. The
habit becomes a second nature: all strangers observe the national
trick of rocking the body when sitting or standing to talk, and

they mostly attribute it to the habit of weaving, when it is practised by thousands who never used a loom. The feminine figure is graceful and comparatively slender in youth, like the English girl of the "willowy type," but the limbs are large and ungainly. After a few years the "overblown" forms broaden out coarsely. Women do not draw the plough, as in Greece and parts of Ireland, but they must take their turn at all manner of field-work. The *Frauen-cultus*, said to be a native of Europe north of the Alps, has not extended here, at least in these days.[1] Hence the legs and ankles, hands and feet, rival in size and coarseness those of the men. As wives, they would be efficient correctives to the "fine drawn" framework and the over-nervous diathesis of southern nations. Cold in temperament, they are therefore, like the Irish, prolific, which may also result from the general fish-diet. Dr Schleisner, who resided in Iceland under the Danish Government, has proved the temperature of the blood to be higher than amongst other races. Assuming the average of Europeans at C. 36°·5 (= F. 97°·7), nine persons out of twelve exceeded C. 37° (= F. 98°·6): the maximum was C. 37°·8 (= F. 100°); the minimum was C. 36°·5, and the average was C. 37°·27 (= F. 99°·09).[2]

Intermarriage is so general that almost all the chief families are cousins; yet among several thousand the author saw only one hunchback, two short legs, and a few hare-lips. It is almost needless to say that the common infanticide of pagan days is now unknown, and that we must seek some other cause for the absence of deformity. It may be found, perhaps, in the purity of unmixed blood, which, mentioning no other instances, allows consanguineous marriages to the Jews, the Bedawin Arabs, and even to the Trasteverino Romans;[3] whereas composite and

---

[1] It appears probable that the reverence paid to women by the ancient Germans and Gauls arose from what Tacitus calls "some divine and prophetic quality resident in their women;" from the superstitious belief that the weaker sex was more subject to inspiration, divination, second sight, and other abnormal favours of the gods. The *Frauen-cultus* of the present age, which in the United States has become an absurdity, would be the relic and survival of this pagan fancy.

[2] The author cannot say whether due care was taken when making these observations. Amongst Englishmen, when the thermometer held in the mouth exceeds 98°·5, there is suspicion of fever.

[3] Marquis Massimo d'Azeglio observed this fact among the paviours and the wine-carters, who form almost a separate caste of the Trans-Tiber population.

heterogeneous races like the Englishman, the Spaniard, and especially the New Englander, cannot effect such unions without the worst results—idiocy and physical deformity.

As regards uncleanliness in house and body, it may be said that the Icelander holds a middle rank between the Scotchman and the Greenlander, and he contrasts badly with the Norwegian of modern days. Personal purity, the one physical virtue of old age, is, as a rule, sadly neglected. Concerning this unpleasant topic, the author is compelled to offer a few observations. The old islander could rival the seal: his descendant, like the man of Joe Miller, will not trust himself in water before he can swim. The traveller never sees man or woman in sea, river, or brook, though even the lower animals bathe in hot weather. It is a race *abominantes aquam frigidam*, and, even as pagans, their chief objection to Christianity was the necessity of baptism: they compounded for immersion in the Laug or hot spring,[1] and the latter is still, though very seldom, used. Washing is confined to the face and hands; and the tooth-brush is unknown like the nail-brush: the basins, where they exist, are about the size of punch-bowls. Purification by water, after Moslem fashion, is undreamed of. Children are allowed to contract hideous habits, which they preserve as adults; for instance, picking teeth, and not only teeth, with dinner-forks. Old travellers, who perhaps had not observed the cellarman in the wine vaults (London Docks) bore a hole and blow through it to start the liquor, record a peculiarly unpleasant contrivance for decanting the milk-pan into narrow-necked vessels; the same, in fact, adopted by the Mexican when bottling his "Maguey;" and "Blefkenius" alludes to a practice still popular amongst the Somal: it is only fair to own that the author never saw them. The rooms, and especially the sick rooms, are exceedingly stifling and impure. Those who venture upon an Icelandic bed may perhaps find clean sheets, but they had better not look under them. The houses, except in the towns, or the few belonging to foreign merchants, have no offices, and all that have, leave them in a horrible condition: there is no drainage, and the backyard is a mass of offal. Such

---

[1] Not always, as the common river-name Thvátt-á (wash or dip-water) proves.

is the effect of climate, which makes dirt the " poor man's jacket" in the north; which places cleanliness next to godliness in the sub-tropical regions, and which renders personal uncleanliness sinful and abominable to the quasi-equatorial Hindú. Nor must we forget that the old English proverb " Washing takes the marrow out of a man," still has significance amongst our peasantry.

## § 3. CHARACTER.

Appreciations of national character too often depend upon the casual circumstances which encounter and environ the traveller ; and writers upon Iceland differ so greatly upon the matter, that perhaps the safest plan will be to quote the two extremes.

The unfriendly find the islanders serious to a fault; silent, gloomy, and atrabilious; ungenial and morose; stubborn and eternally suspicious; litigious and mordant; utterly deficient in adventure, doing nothing but what necessity compels; little given to hospitality; greedy of gain, and unscrupulous in the *quocumque modo rem.* " Gaiety," says one, " seems banished from their hearts, and we should suppose that all are under the influence of that austere nature in the midst of which they were born."

Henderson (i. 34), who represents the bright side of the picture, enlarges upon their calm and dignified, their orderly and law-abiding character; he denies their being of sullen and melancholy disposition ; he was surprised at the degree of cheerfulness and vivacity prevailing among them, and that, too, not unfrequently under circumstances of considerable external depression. They are so honest that the doors are not locked at night in their largest town; strangely frank and unsophisticated; ardent patriots and lovers of constitutional liberty; fond of literature, pious, and contented ; endowed with remarkable strength of intellect and acuteness; brimful of hospitality, and not given to any crimes, or indeed vices, except drunkenness.

And, upon the principle of allowing the Icelander to describe himself, we may quote as an exemplar of character the following model epitaph: " To the precious memory of A., S.'s son, who married the maiden C., D.'s daughter. He was calm in mind; firm in council; watchful, active, his friends' friend; hospitable, bountiful, upright towards all, and the affectionate father of his house and children."

The truth is, that although isolation has, as might be expected, preserved a marked racial character, the islandry are much like other Northmen. During the pagan times, and indeed until the sixteenth century, we read "their chief characteristics were treachery, thirst for blood, unbounded licentiousness, and inveterate detestation of order and rule;" but we shall hardly recognise the picture now. They are truthful, and they appear pre-eminently so to a traveller from the south of Europe, or from the Levant. They have a sense of responsibility, and you may believe their oaths: at the same time, they look upon all men as liars, and they are as *desconfiados* (distrustful) as Paulistas or Laplanders—a mental condition apparently connected with a certain phase of civilisation. Compared with the sharp-witted Southron, they are dull and heavy, stolid and hard of comprehension as our labouring classes, without the causes which affect the latter. They cleave like Hindús to the father-to-son principle, and they have little at home that tempts either to invention, to innovation, or to adventure. They are a "polypragmatic peasantry;" the love of lawsuits still distinguishes the Norman in France after ages of separation from the parent stock. Even in private debate they obstinately adhere to the letter, and shun the spirit: an Icelander worsted in argument takes up some verbal distinction or secondary point, and treats it as if it were of primary importance. An exaggeration of this peculiarity breeds the *Querelle d'Allemand.*

Another peculiarity of the islandry is a bitterly satirical turn of mind, a quality noted of old. We rarely meet with a "Thorkel Foulmouth," but we see many a Skarphèdinn who delights and who takes pride in dealing those wounds of the tongue which according to the Arabs never heal. An ancient writer gives a fair measure of what could be done by Níðvísur [1] (lampoons),

---

[1] These satirical songs are known to the Greenlanders, who thus satisfy their malice, "preferring to revenge even than to prevent an injury." Yet, the Icelanders have a proverb, "Let him beware, lest his tongue wind round his head."

which never spared even the kings. They threatened Harold the Dane to write as many lampoons upon him as there were noses [1] in Iceland (Ólaf Tryggvason's Saga, xxxvii.), and escaped by magic from an invasion. Nor did they spare even the gods; for instance, Hjalti sings (Burnt Nial's Saga):

> "I will not serve an idle log,
> For one, I care not which;
> But either Odin is a dog
> Or Freya is a ———."

The term "Tað-skegglingar," Dung-beardlings, applied by a woman to certain youths whom she hated, caused a small civil war. When Dr Wormius was Rector Magnificus of the Copenhagen University, an Icelandic student complained of a libellous fellow-countryman. The poet, when summoned, confessed the authorship; contended that it contained no cause of offence, and, with characteristic plausibility and cunning, talked over the simple Vice-Chancellor. Thereupon the plaintiff in tears told the Rector that his fair fame was for ever lost, explaining at the same time the "fables, figures, and other malicious designs under which the malignity of the satire was couched;" and even the "spells and sorceries" which threatened his life. Thereupon Dr Wormius took high ground, and by citing certain severe laws against witchcraft, persuaded the poet to tear up his satire and never to write or to speak of it again. "The student was ravished with joy," because he had made his peace with a pest who could exceed in power of annoyance Aristophanes, Horace, and Juvenal.

The courage, steadfastness, and pertinacity of the Icelander are proved by his annals, and if he does not show these qualities in the present day, it is because they are overlaid by circumstances. As regards the relations of the sexes, we find nothing in the number of illegitimate children which justifies the poet in singing of the "moral north." [2] Iceland in fact must be reckoned amongst the

---

[1] Usually but erroneously translated "headlands," instead of "head of men."

[2] The popular assertion, "nothing can be more natural than that female chastity should be more prevalent in a northern than in a southern climate," is simply a false deduction from insufficient facts. It is a subject far too extensive for a footnote; we may simply observe that the Scandinavians have never been

"Littora quæ fuerunt castis inimica puellis ;"

and although she has improved upon the reckless licentiousness of the Saga days, ichthyophagy and idleness must do much to counterbalance the "sun-clad power of chastity." The "unsophistication" of the race is certainly on the wane; there are doubtless

"Honest men from Iceland to Barbadoes,"

but the islander is pre-eminent for a "canniness" which equals, if it does not exceed, that of the Yankee, the lowland Scotch, and the Maltese. And what he gains he can keep with a most tenacious hold.

The statistics of crime in Iceland are peculiarly unsatisfactory. As the Journal will show, many a man goes free who would be prosecuted and severely punished farther south. Traveller after traveller has asserted, "it is in a large measure to their widespread home education that we must attribute the fine moral character of the Icelanders;" and capital has been made of the fact that the old stone-prison became the Government House. The Danish Parliamentary Reports (p. 255, vol. xlvii. for 1837-1838) contain details concerning the number of persons arraigned and convicted, sentenced, and acquitted by the tribunals. During a period of seven years (1827-1834), there were but 292 indictments on the island; of these 216 ended in conviction; 20 cases were suspended; 32 were dismissed, and 56 were acquitted. Of the 216 convictions, 79 were for "carnal offences;" 86 for larceny; 15 for transgressing sanitarial laws; 5 for murder, and 31 for various offences, such as false-witness and receiving stolen goods. The last statistics in 1868 give 46 criminal cases (37 males, 9 females) for the whole island, and in 37 conviction and sentence followed; 34 were for theft, 1 for forgery; 2 for adultery, besides 29 were fined for disturbance of the peace and for offences against public order. There were also 57 cases of adultery and seduction; 24 of these were fined, and in 33 cases the fine was remitted (Skýrslur um Landshagi, v. 193, 1871).

---

distinguished for continence, nor are the northern more moral than the southern Slavs. In fact, the principal factor of feminine "virtue" seems to be race not climate. .

The suicide,[1] arson, and infant exposure of the republican and pagan ages are no longer heard of; vagrancy is hardly an offence; the state of the country prevents technical robbery; and forgery does not belong to its present state of civilisation. It is peculiar that almost all classes believe in and fear a tribe of outlaws or bandits who occupy the deserts of the interior—these are the days of Robin Hood come again.

## § 3. SOCIETY.

The social condition of Iceland has been compared with Lord Macaulay's pictures of the Highlanders a hundred and fifty, and of the English three hundred years ago—the differences are more salient than the points of resemblance. The proverb "Heimskt er heimaðlia barn" (homely is the housebred child) produced a habit of voyaging and travelling; and wide wandering made the homes centres of refinement: the same practice in the Hebrides astonished Dr Johnson. Unhappily it is now no longer the popular habit; it has gone the way of the manly exercises, bowls, quoits, swimming, and practising weapons, which distinguished the heroic age. With much aristocratic feeling there is no aristocratic order properly so called; the earl, the baron, and the clan-chief are equally unknown; whilst the parson, like the priest in Slavonic countries, is the modern pattern to the Thane or Churl. As in the United States, there is no gentlemen class except the liberal professions, and even the clergy until the present generation were farmers and fishermen, labourers, mechanics, and so forth, often poorer and shabbier than the laity. The official circles are too small to form a *beamten-kreis;* the squirearchy is represented by the franklins or peasant lairds, who no longer correspond with the ancient Udallers; the merchants are chiefly foreigners.

---

[1] "To go by the way of the rock" was the old pagan euphuism for self-destruction; and the modern Hindú, as the Girnár Cliff shows, preserves the practice of "Altestupor" and "Odin's Hall." Suicide is now, like the duello, extinct, and the few cases recorded in late history are looked upon as phenomena. We remark the same rarity of self-destruction both in Scotland and Ireland, a wonderful contrast to England, which, again, despite its ill-fame, shows favourably in this matter by the side of France.

Under these circumstances we can hardly expect much general refinement, nor the particular phase which produces men whose life consists in adorning society, and women born to wear diamonds and to be beautiful. Yet the Icelander, franklin or pauper, has none of the roughness and rudeness which we remark in the manners of the Canadians and of the lowland Scotch. "No tax is levied upon civility," and their mutual regard for one another's feelings, though sometimes carried to an inconvenient extent, is the essence of true politeness. The intercourse is rather ceremonious than "free and easy," and travellers deride such quaint mixture as "You lie, my blessed (or beloved) friend!" The abuse of mutual regard is a servile fear of making enemies; they often tamely put up with injuries, as the Brazilian submits to be plundered by a richer neighbour, and the Syrian swallows his wrath rather than offend one who may some day become a Pasha.

The Icelander is a large-brained and strong-brained man, essentially slow and solid in point of intellect, and capable of high culture, of wide learning, and of deep research. This lesson is taught by the whole of his literature; although the muse no longer sings of love and war, she is by no means mute —her turn is now the theological, the philological, and the scientific. Arngrímr Jónsson well describes his countrymen as "Ad totius Europæ res historicas lyncæi." But the islander never attains his full development except out of his own country, and this condition dates from past ages. Throughout the north, from England[1] and Val-land (France and Italy), to Mikligarŏr (Constantinople),[2] he has distinguished himself and proved

"That every country is a brave man's home."

---

[1] The reader has only to remember how much of Britain was Danish to understand the Snorra-Edda's express statement about Icelanders and Englishmen speaking the same tongue, "Vèr erum einnar tungu;" and Bartolin (Antiquitates Danicæ), "Eademque lingua (Norwegica seu Septentrionalis) usurpabatur per Saxonicum, Daniam, Sueciam, Norvegiam, et partem Angliæ aliquam."

[2] Their extensive travels gave them peculiar names for peoples and places, which are often somewhat puzzling. "Thýskr," a German, and Gerzkr, a Russian, are easy; but Samverskt (a Samaritan) is not so plain. Thus, also, we have "Enea" for Europe; "Hvítármannaland," or white man's land, and "Írland et mikla," Ireland the Great (the Irlanda el Kabíreh of Edrisi in the twelfth century), for South America; "Suŏurálfa" (i.e., southern half), for Africa;

Abroad, his emulation is excited, his ambition is roused, and his slow sturdy nature is stirred up to unusual energy. At home he can command no serious education, nor can he escape from the indolent and phlegmatic, the dawdling and absolutely unconditioned slowness of the country, where time is a positive nuisance, to be killed as it best can. In Iceland the author met several Danes, but only two Icelanders, who spoke good English, French, or German; it is far otherwise in Europe, and especially, we need not say, in England.

As the notices of emigration will show, Iceland, like Ireland, is instinctively seeking her blessing and salvation, the "racial baptism." One traveller records the "inexpressible attachment of the islanders for their native country." Their *Sehn sucht* in a mountainless land, and the. time-honoured boast, "Hið besta land solin skínr uppá" (Iceland is the best land upon which the sun shines).[1] So Bjarni Thorarensen sings, "World-old Iceland, beloved foster-land, thou wilt be dear to thy sons, as long as sea girds earth, men love women, and sun shines on hills." But all the people of all the poorest countries console themselves in the same way, and geographical ignorance confirms an idea which to the traveller becomes simply ludicrous: more-

---

"Great Sweden" for Eastern Russia; "Svalbarði" (discovered 1194), for Scoresby's Liverpool Coast (?); "Bjarmaland" for Permia, the land beyond the North Cape; "Sætt" for Sidon; "Njörfa-fjörð" for the Straits of "Gib;" Há-sterun for Hastings; and "Katanes" (boat naze), for Caithness. Some names are of ethnological value; for instance, "Bretland" for Wales; while Vendill or Vandill, the northern part of Jutland, preserves the name of the Vandals and the origin of Andalusia; and Garða-riki or Garða-veldi, the empire of the Garðar or Castella, tells us how the Russian empire was founded. So Suðr-menn (Germans) opposed to Northmen (Norðmenn), preserves the tradition of original · consanguinity. Others are useless complications, as Engils-nes, the Morea, and Ægisif ('Αγία Σοφία). The travestied names of persons are sometimes interesting, e.g., Elli-Sif (Scot. Elspeth) is Elizabeth, probably confounded like Ægisif, with Sif, the golden-haired wife of Thor, who lives in our gos-*sip*. Icelanders are not answerable for the mistake so general amongst foreigners which makes Níðar-óss (Oyce or ostium of the Nið River) an *alias* of Throndhjem, of old Thrándheimr, when it is the name of the ancient city occupying the position of the present town. The "Antiquités de l'Orient" (par C. C. Rafn, Copenhagen, 1856) well shows how Icelandic names were applied to the Byzantine empire, e.g., 'Εσσουπῆ (ei sofa, not to sleep), given to the first bar of the Dnieper; Οὐλβορσὶ (Hólm-fors or islet-force) to the second, and so forth.

[1] "This assertion of travellers never had any foundation in fact," says Mr Jón A. Hjaltalín, yet it is quoted by Henderson, the least imaginative, and, in such matters, the most trustworthy of men; and the Icelandic proverb says, "One's own home is the best home."

over, northerners, it need hardly be said, gain more by removal,
and therefore emigrate more readily than southerners. The
latter express themselves unmistakably:

*" Ἀνδρὶ γάρ τοι, κἂν ὑπερβάλλῃ κακοῖς*
*Οὖν ἔστι θρεψαντος ἥδιον πέδον."*

And "Ulysses ad Ithacæ suæ saxa properat, quemadmodum
Agamemnon ad Mycenarum nobiles muros; nemo enim patriam
amat quia magna, sed quia sua" (Seneca), They are happy at
home; why should they leave home?

The Icelander cannot be called degenerate. He is what he was.
But whilst the world around, or rather beyond him, has pro-
gressed with giant strides, he has perforce remained stationary.
His mother country forbids him to decuple the human hand
and arm by machinery; the enormous water-power of his rivers
is useless, and thinness of population bars out the appliances of
civilisation—how can he expect to hold a fair place in the race
of life? Moreover, like another small and heroic kingdom,
modern Greece, Iceland has suffered from ages of virtually
foreign dominion, not to say tyranny, and from restrictions of
trade, which, small as items, combined to form a system of
grinding oppression. His brightest days were those when, like
the Goth and Hun, the Arab and the Tartar, he devoted himself
to plundering the wealthy weak. But the times for these
nomad incursions are past, until at least China can renew them;
and he hopelessly sank when no longer able to harry the
southern islands, to break down London bridge, to plunder and
and massacre Luna, and to spread

"Beneath Gibraltar to the Lybian sands."

His future career is in his own hands, and improvement must
be sought in extended stock-breeding, in better use of the
fisheries, and in extensive emigration. With free institutions he
will bring to the task the same high and steadfast spirit which
distinguished him in his prime. Anthropologists justly object
to the popular theory of a nation degenerating, unless, indeed,
there be a mixture of foreign and inferior blood; but they see
everywhere in history the decline and fall of races, whenever the

stronger neighbouring peoples rise to the same or to a higher level of civilisation. The Roman and the Athenian still greatly resemble the conquerors of Europe and Asia, but in those days the Gauls and the Germans, the Scandinavians and the Britons, were mere barbarians, uneducated and undisciplined. Now all are on a level, and, as we saw in the late Franco-Prussian war, the physically strongest wins—the north beats, and will ever beat, the south.

The islanders, like their brother Scandinavians and the Teutons, had no idea of towns. We may apply to them the description of Tacitus (Germ., c. xvi.), "Nullas Germanorum populis urbes habitari satis notum est . . . colunt discreti ac diversi, ut fons, ut campus, ut nemus placuit." In Norway the first town, Níðar-ós, *par excellence* called Kaupang, was built by the two Olaves (Ó. Tryggvason or Trusty-son, and Ó. Helgi the Saint) in A.D. 994-1030; the real founder of cities was Olave the Quiet (1067-1093). Thus in old Norse codes the Town-law is an appendix to the Land-law. As late as 1752, Reykjavik was a single isolated farm.

It is strange how little the style of Iceland life has altered since the time (1767) when M. de Kerguelen wrote his short and lively sketch—it seems to be fixed like the language. As now, the island was divided into four provinces, of which each had eighteen to twenty counties, and every county fifteen to sixteen parishes. The Sýslur were under bailiffs, all subject to the grand bailiff (Governor), and to the sovereign council (Althing). The chief civil officer and the royal seneschal (treasurer), who collected the taxes, reported to a governor-general residing at Copenhagen—he is now represented by the minister for Iceland. There were two bishops, one for the south (Skálholt), and another for the north (Hólar); there is at present only one in the capital, but the people would willingly see, and will see, the older status restored.

The Iceland farm-house[1] was then, as now, a set of buildings scattered over the "tún," or infield. The abode was entered by

---

[1] As every traveller, from Uno Von Troil downwards, has given a plan and sketch of the Bær, the reader need not be troubled with them. The group of buildings composing the actual homestead is invariably built in a row: the front

a passage (Bæjar-dyr) six feet wide, with a cross-raftered roof,
and this "Skemma" was lighted by windowlets (Skjágluggi) of
"Himna" (membrane), transparent parchment of cattle's bladder;
by Likna-belgur, ewe's chorion; by Vats-belgur, sheep's amnion;
or by Skæna, inner membranes of the stomach, a little more
opaque, or, rarely, by bulls' eyes of glass.   They were not the only
tenements in the eighteenth century which had no light—

> " Save one dull pane, that, coarsely patched, gives way
>    To the rude tempest, yet excludes the day."

Fronting the common entrance was the Baðstofa (public room,
literally meaning bathroom), measuring fourteen ells by eight, in
which the household worked at dressing wool and weaving cloth.
It led to a bedroom, where the house master and mistress slept,
the children and servants occupying the garrets and cock-lofts.
On each side of the lobby were two rooms, the kitchen (Eld-hús,
opposed to the stofa or gynæceum), and the store-room or Búr
(our "bower," and the Scottish "byre"); the dairy and the guest-
chamber (Gestaskáli).   At present the entrance is usually faced
by the kitchen, and at right angles there is a covered gallery or
tunnel, upon which the doors open: thus the rooms are not
wholly dark, even when they lack glass, which is rare.[1]   The
outhouses (Úti-hús) were the stables, the stores (Geymslu-hús),
the byres, the sheep pens (Fjár-hús), the forge, and, sometimes,
the carpenter's shop.   The house (Bæjar-hús or Heima-hús) was
built of planks, which, coming from Copenhagen, were too expensive to be used as flooring.   The only fire was in a stove; the
fuel was of turf and cow-" chips," and the interior was never

---

(Hús-bust) faces south, towards the sea or the river, if in a valley, and the back
is turned to the sheltering mountain.   The strip of flagged pavement along the
front is called "Stétt;" the open space before it, "Hlað;" the buildings are
parted by a lane (Sund); the approach is termed "Geilar" or "Tröð," and the
whole is surrounded by the Húsa-garðr, a dry-stone dyke.

The Norse Skáli, or Hall of classical days, whose rude and barbarous magnifi-
cence was the result of successful piracy tempered by traffic, has clean vanished—
there is not a trace of one upon the island.   A ground-plan, section, and elevation,
are given in Mr Dasent's " Burnt Njal," but it is hard to say how much of it
came from the fertile brain of the artist, Mr Sigurðr Guðmundsson.   It was probably about as " desirable " a " residence " as the old Welsh manor-house, with
its stagnant moat and its banks or walls of earth.

[1] The author well remembers that at Hyderabad, in Sind, only one palace had
the luxury of glass, when we first occupied the city.

dry—the unrheumatic traveller will not find that damp of which the many complained. The furniture consisted of a table and chests acting chairs; Niels Horrebow, the Dane who saw everything *en beau*, added wainscots, glasses, and a variety of luxuries. Johann Anderson, afterwards burgomaster of Hamburg, by no means wore the rose-coloured spectacles.

"The people appeared mild, good-natured, and humane, but distrustful and *addicted to drink*. They were very fond of chess, and good coasting sailors, *but not very courageous*"—no wonder, considering their craft! They soon became infirm; they were old at fifty, and they rarely reached eighty. "Landsarsak" (Landfarsótt[1]) was the name given to all fatal illnesses usually arising from scurvy, wet feet, and want of exercise. Their hay was not housed, but heaped in stacks two yards square, upon raised mounds, at short distances, and covered with sloping turf to lead the rain into surrounding ditches. In summer food was of cods'-heads, boiled like all other provisions: in winter the peasants ate sheeps'heads kept in (fermented) vinegar of sour milk (Sýra), or in juice of sorrel (Súra),[2] and other plants, the mutton being sold. Bread was not the staff of life, being eaten only on high days and holidays, that is, at births, marriages, and deaths: the richer sort baked cakes, broad and thin, like sea biscuits, of black rye flour from Copenhagen.

The men dressed like sailors in breeches, jackets acting coats, and vests of good broadcloth, with four to six rows of buttons, always metal, copper or silver. The fishermen wore overalls, coarse smooth waistcoats, large paletots of sheepskin or leather, made water-proof by grease or fish-liver oil; leather overalls, stockings, and native shoes. The women were clad in jackets and gowns, petticoats and aprons of woollen frieze, over which was thrown a "Hempa," or wide black robe, like a Jesuit frock, trimmed with velvet binding. The wealthy added silver ornaments down the length of the dress, and braided the other articles

---

[1] Sótt is applied to physical, Sút to mental, sickness.

[2] More will be said concerning the several varieties of oxalis, which the people now seem to despise. Both wood-sorrel and meadow-sweet (*Spiræa*) were used by the poor of Ireland to heal ulcers (Beddoes, p. 47, on the Medical Use and Production of Factitious Airs). Uno Von Troil (p. 108) gives a long list of the popular anti-scorbutics.

with silk ribbons, galloon, or velvets of various colours. The ruff was a stiff collar from three to four inches broad, of very fine stuff, embroidered with gold or silver. The head-dress was a cone like a fool's-cap or sugar-loaf, two to three feet tall, kept in place by a coarse cloth, and covered with a finer kerchief. The soleless shoes of ox-hide or sheep-skin, made by the women out of a single piece, were strapped to the instep.

The wives were not so strong as the husbands, yet they had the hardest work in haymaking. Their labour was difficult, and they "kept their beds for a week." At baptism a bit of linen dipped in milk was placed in the babe's mouth, and the child was breeched at the end of two years.

## § 4. THE FAMILY.

Population was checked by not allowing marriage to a man who did not own a hundred of land or a six-oared boat in trim: this wholesome law, however, is becoming obsolete as the ferocious old code which prevented the propagation of paupers. The number of births is about 2940 to 2020 deaths per annum: thus the annual increase is 920, but the mortality of children is, or perhaps we should say was, disproportionate. In 1858, 489 upon the island died between the ages of 1 to 5, and 68 between 5 to 10—a total of 557. During the same year the number of illegitimate to legitimate births was 15 : 100 : this figure appears pretty constant, but rather on the increase than the reverse. In the early nineteenth century, Hooker gives 383 illegitimates in 2516 births = 15⅓ per cent. = nearly to 1 : 7—a high average, which he explains by the huddling together of families. Mr Vice-Consul Crowe (1866) gives 1 : 6·9 of births. Statistics of the years between 1860 and 1870 give 20 : 100, or 1 : 5. The Consular Report of 1870-71 asserts that "in every 100 births there were 17 of illegitimate children," and shows the following figures: 1866, 17·7; 1867, 16·7; 1868, 17·2; 1869, 16·2; 1870, 16·8.

Of 2937 children, only 48 were born (1858) of mothers under 20; 23 were legitimate, and 25 were not: 458 had mothers aged

20 to 25: 933, of whom 764 were born in wedlock and 169 were not, had mothers aged 25 to 30: the mothers of 703 new-born children were 30 to 35 years old; those of 549, from 35 to 40; those of 221 from 40 to 45; and, lastly, those of 25, from 45 to 50.

In the same year, 3 men committed suicide; 65 were drowned; 17 perished by accidents, and 1939 died of disease. The smallest number of deaths (128) occurred in February, the coldest month; and the greatest number (205) in July, the warmest.

There is little of novelty in the religious ceremonies accompanying baptisms, marriages, and funerals, which are those of the Augsburg rite; but there is something to say upon the subject of names. Until the middle of the last century, the surnames, as in olden Kent, were all patronymics or matronymics; such was the ancient fashion of Europe, especially of England and Germany, a custom still preserved by the great Slav race (*vich* or *ich*), and by the modern Greeks, who prefer -*poulo* and who almost ignore the ancient -*ides*. It is notorious how Linne (Linnæus), the prince of naturalists, was prompted by the growing use of family names to devise the generic and specific distinctions, which superseded a system cumbrous and intricate as that of a Chinese dictionary. In very thinly populated countries, where every man knew his neighbour, it was possible to be called Jón Jónsson [1] and Caroline Jónsdóttir, but so rude a plan would not serve elsewhere. We still find it in the country parts of Iceland, and, curious to say, the people are returning to the old fashion of taking the paternal name as surname. The matronymic, *e.g.*, Sveinn Ástriðarson, in early times was assumed when the mother outlived the father: it was never a mark of base blood; as amongst the Spaniards, where El Hijo de ruin padre, Toma el apelido de la madre.

In 1855, a curious official paper was published under the title " Um Mannaheiti á Íslandi." It shows that the island has only 63 native surnames, and 530 men's and 529 women's Christian names: no wonder that "nicknames" are common as amongst

---

[1] Of course the first sibilant, the sign of possession, is not used when the noun is otherwise declined. For instance, Jón Arason, often written by foreigners Aræson, is the son of Are, whose oblique case is Ara; yet there are popular exceptions, *e.g.*, Bjarnarson (pron. Bjatnarson), son of Björn, is vulgarly pronounced, and even written, Björnsson.

Moslems and Brazilians. Hence local cognomens are also much used, as Peter of Engey, and Jón of the "Strönd," *i.e.*, the coast from Hafnafjörð to Keblavik. The popular address would be Herra Bonde (Mr Farmer), Herra Hreppstjóri (Mr Constable), or "Good day, comrade!" sounding very republican, and accompanied by a resounding kiss.

Every fifth man appears to affect, in one of five forms, the fourth Evangelist. Jón (Johns, 4827), Jóhannes (498), Jóhann (494), Hannes (154), and Hans (80), making a total of 5053. On the other hand, whilst Odin has disappeared, Thór, in compounded shape, enters into 2010 male and 1875 female "Christian" names = 3885. Guðrún[1] numbers 4363; Marguerite, 1654; yet Marias, elsewhere so common,[2] are only 384; and Rosas decline to 269. Amongst historical names, we find 122 Sæmundr; of Biblical names, even the quaintest and the most Hebraical, such as Samson, Samuel, and Solomon, Jael, and Judith, are here common as in all Protestant countries: Catholics more wisely avoid them, leaving them to their original Jewish owners. The western counties affect the strangest terms, such as Petra, Petrea, Petrina, Petulína, and Tobía, a feminine. And throughout the island there is arising a new fashion of combining names almost as ingenious as that of the Latter-Day Saints. For instance, the daughter of Brynjólfur by Thórdís will be called Bryndís; the son of Sæmundr by Elina is named Elínmundr. Of course nothing can be more barbarous, but what does "fashion" care for barbarism?

In pagan times the wife was often assisted by Friðlas or supernumeraries, and, though she was liable to be exchanged or loaned, as was the case amongst the polished Hindús, the Greeks,

---

[1] Thus the islanders preserve the memory of a "beautiful fiend," one amongst many, who, after a very human fashion, began life as a coquette, and ended it as a *dévote*, being the first to learn psalm-singing, and to take the veil in the new convent. This hyperborean Ninon de L'Enclos deserves forgiveness for one of the cleverest sayings uttered by woman—a revelation of its kind. When asked which of her half-a-dozen lovers and husbands she preferred, her wise and witty answer was, "Theim var ek verst, er ek unnti mest"—"Whom I treated worst, him I loved most;" alluding to Kjartan Ólafsson, murdered by her behest. In old days, Gudrún and John answered to the "M. or N." of our Catechism, and to "those famous fictions of English law, John Doe and Richard Roe."

[2] This is probably a relic of early ages, when "Maria" was a name too much revered for general use.

and the Romans, she could put away her baron for so slight an offence as wearing a chemisette, or any other article of feminine attire. The simple process was to declare before witnesses that they twain ceased to be one flesh. The marriage tie sat almost as lightly upon Icelanders as upon Scandinavians generally, even in the Catholic days: since the introduction of Lutheranism, it has, as we might expect, been still less binding.[1] We may therefore conclude that a certain love of change is in such matters a characteristic of the race. At present every *peine infamante* allows divorce; and incompatibility of temper, shown by three years of separation, with the consent of the mayor, is a plea of sufficient force to claim from the Minister of Justice at Copenhagen freedom *a mensâ et thoro*. Both parties are able to remarry, and they may be reunited, unless they have misconducted themselves whilst living apart; in this case they must obtain a dispensation from the chancellerie of the empire.

## § 5. DISEASES.

It is calculated that the yearly deaths at Reykjavik average 59-60, and this figure, if correct, is high for the population, in 1870 only 2024, now at most 2500. For instance, the mean of London being 19 per 1000, and all England 20·8, to say nothing of Glastonbury, Reykjavik, with the most favourable calculations, would be 24.[2] With more attention to hygiene, the headquarter village should not show a death-rate exceeding 17 : 1000—the beau-ideal of the modern sanitarian.

The list of diseases is so extensive that little beyond the names can be mentioned. They result mainly from the utter absence of hygiene; from want of cleanliness; from bad living, hardship, and fatigue; and from exposure to cold, especially after living in close and heated rooms. The latter is a fertile source of ill-health: so at St Petersburgh the higher classes suffer from

---

[1] Yet the Polygamia Triumphatrix (Liseri) of Lund, A.D. 1682, was publicly burned at Stockholm.

[2] We may add, Paris, 23; Berlin, 25; Panama, 26; Bombay, 27; New York, 28; Glasgow, 34; Madras, 35; Vienna, 36; and Rome the same, if not more.

the maladies of Calcutta, hepatalgia, jaundice, and spleen-enlarg-
ments; and, after a certain number of "seasons," they must seek
health in the Crimea, or in Southern Europe. Hence the fondness of Icelanders for sour food which equals that of the acid-
loving citizens of Damascus. The pudding of the island is Skyr,
which the Dictionary wrongly translates "curdled milk, curds,"
and which Rafn derives from the Sanskrit Kshira (milk): it is
the Khir of Sind and Belochistan; the Laban of Arabia; the Dahin
of Hindostan; the Saure-milch of South Germany; the Kisalina
of Styria and Slavland, and the Hattelkit or Corstorphine Cream
of Scotland.[1] Icelanders eat it with sugar, which gives it a sickly
taste. Hence the use of acid butter; of Mysuost, or whey cheese,
brown, and not unlike guava cheese; of Valle, fermented whey,
somewhat like Koumiss; of Sýra, or sour whey, acting small beer,
and used in pickles like vinegar; of Súr mjólk, or sour milk; and
of Blanda, the favourite drink, half whey and half water, into
which blueberries, and black, crake, or crow berries (Icel. Kræk-
juber, *Empetrum baccis nigris*) are sometimes infused. And
hence, finally, the use of Korn-súra (*Polygonum viviparum*),
*Cochlearia* (*officinalis* and *Danica*), trefoil (*T. repens*), *Sedum
Acre* (house leek), and other social plants, which are considered
antiseptic and antibilious.

The skin diseases are alopecia, herpes, and psora inveterate
as on the Congo River. "St Anthony's fire" was cured by binding live earth-worms upon the part afflicted. Scurvy (Skyr-
bjúgr) results from "thinness of blood," induced by want of
proper nourishment, especially by the overuse of salt and dried
meat and fish: the increased growth of vegetables, not to speak
of medicines, has much modified its malignancy. Measles and
scarlatina are rare, but periodical attacks of smallpox, which
often appear in history,[2] still compel the capital to convert one

---

[1] Thus Skyr is a congener of the Persian "Shír" and of the Slav Sir (cheese).
The first stage is the "run-milk," the second is the "hung-milk" (because suspended in a bag) of the Shetland Islands. Everywhere it is differently turned;
by sour whey in Iceland, by buttermilk in Scotland, and by rennet and various
plants in Asia and Africa. No milk-drinking nation drinks, as a rule, fresh
milk. The Icelanders want the manifold preparations known to the Scoto-
Scandinavian islands.

[2] Dr (afterwards Sir Henry) Holland introduced, or rather first brought, the
vaccine virus.

of the best houses into an hospital. In 1872, it was occupied by French fishermen only; there was no case among the natives. The author did not see a single instance of the protean and the most cosmopolitan of diseases, whose various phases are known as Lepra Arabum, Leuce, and Mal Rouge; Leontasis, or Facies leonina; Elephantias, Elephantiasis, and Barbadoes Leg. It is known to old writers as " Icelandic scurvy," to the islanders as Lík-thrá-sótt, or corpse-pang, which Henderson translates, a rotten, rancid corpse;[1] Holdsveiki, or flesh-weakness, and Spital-ska ('Spital sickness), the latter being the biblical term. When the extremities drop off, the term generally applied was Limafall-siki.

In the ninth century, leprosy required some 19,000 hospitals in Europe; and it has perhaps lingered longest in the Færoes and in Iceland. Here, curious to observe, its very headquarters were about Skagi and Reykjanes, the best and mildest climates. A few cases still remain, but the establishments built in Catholic days have not been kept up by the Reformation, perhaps showing the want to be less urgent. The horrid malady is evidently dying a natural death, like others which have yielded their places to new comers, or which are gradually disappearing, without leaving issue. The best authorities explain the change by the use of bromide of potassium and the increase of vegetable diet. And to the question of Aretæus, " Sed quænam medela excogitari-poterit, quæ Elephantem, tam ingens malum, expugnari digna est?" Iceland answers, fearless of Cobbett, the potato. The latter has taken the place of the old-fashioned simples, the tops and berries of juniper (*J. communis*), of *Dryas octopelata*, of *Vaccinium myrtillus* (bilberries), of Sanguisorbs, and of similar sub-acid tonics.

It is impossible to enter into a subject which has filled many a volume, but it may briefly be stated that no cosmical cause of leprosy has ever been discovered; and that what seems to account for its origin in one place, completely fails in another. India, especially Malabar, attributes it to biliary derangements, caused by fish and milk diet. The Brazil, like the Jews, the

---

[1] From Lík, Germ. Leiche, Eng. Lych, as in lych-gate, and Thrá, a throe or pang. Hold is flesh.

Moslems, and other pig-haters, refers it to pork; Syria and Palestine, ignoring the "impure," declare it to result from atavism and inheritance. Iceland remarks that it was worst when men wore woollen garments; and similarly Sir George Staunton assigns the modern exemption of Europe to the general use of linen.

Peirce declares that syphilis (introduced, according to Uno Von Troil, about A.D. 1753), chlorosis, mania à potu, caries of the teeth and intermittent fevers are unknown, or almost unknown. He is certainly incorrect with respect to the latter complaint; typhus and various febrile affections are very common in the finest and warmest months, when many of the peasantry show signs of "malaria." Pleurisy is popularly supposed to be infectious. Rachitis, called in Norway the "English sickness," because it is supposed to have passed over in late years from Britain to France, Holland, and Germany; scrofula and consumption are ráre. Chiragra is attributed by old writers to "handling wet fishing tackle in cold weather."[1] The trismus infantium seu neonatorum, called "ginklofi" when opisthenous, and "klums" if emprosthonous, has raged like a plague, especially at Heimaey, one of the Vestmannaeyjar. The children, contrary to the practice of all wild peoples, were weaned after the first week, and were fed upon the flesh of the foul mollie, or fulmar-petrel: the same was once the case at St Kilda, with similár results. At Heimaey, 64 per cent. of babes have died between the fifth and the twelfth days after birth: since a medical man was stationed there, the tetanus has been arrested; and of 20 births, only a small proportion has been lost.

The other complaints are catarrhs, influenzas (where the stars have little "influence"), and chronic rheumatisms, the latter an especial plague; hysteria, gout, and arthrites, constipation and diarrhœas, very prevalent during spring. The endemic echinococcus and cysticercus, affecting one-seventh of the population, are subjects of remarkable interest, which have been treated at

---

[1] This, like other forms of gout, certainly depends much upon the popular beverage. In England we find it amongst the beer-drinking poorer classes : Padua, the author was informed by the celebrated Dr Pinalli, does not produce a single case even to lecture upon.

considerable length.    No less than seven species of hydatids have been detected in dogs.    An able analysis of writings upon these internal cysts, causing " liver-complaints " and " staggers," will be found in Schmidt's Jahrbücher der in-und Ausländischen Gesammten Medecin (No. V., Band 134 of 1867, and No. X., Band 152 of 1871).    The principal northern authorities quoted are Hjaltalín, Jón Finsen, Krabbe, Thorarensen, and Skaptason.

## SECTION VI.

### EDUCATION AND PROFESSIONS.

#### § 1. EDUCATION.

All Icelanders can read and write more or less, they learn the three R's to say nothing of the fourth R(evolution); but this alphabetic state of society may consist, as in the Paraguayan Republic under Dr Francia and the two Presidents Lopez, with a profound state of barbarism.    In Iceland, however, the press is not trammeled; and the newspaper, as will appear, holds its own.    During the last generation it was otherwise.    Education, a domestic growth, ignored modern science and especially mechanics; reading, indeed, was confined to Saga-history and theology, both equally detrimental to mental training and to intellectual progress.    It is still of home manufacture : the high school exists but not the school, and in so thinly populated a country we can hardly expect the latter.    At Reykjavik private tuition may be found; and throughout the country some clergymen prepare scholars.    But the pursuit of knowledge is evidently carried on under difficulties; " their learning is like bread in a besieged town, every man gets a mouthful, but no man a bellyful."

Christian III., the Reformer, ordered a school to be built near each cathedral church—a Moslem action which did him honour. Skálholt had forty, and Hólar thirty-four students when the high school, which, as in the United States, is called the "Latin school," was removed to Reykjavik in 1801; in 1805 it was transferred to Bessastaðir, and in 1846 it again returned to the capital. Bishop Pètursson (p. 365, et seq.) gives the fullest account of the establishment till 1840. In 1834 Dillon found the whole number reduced to forty, of whom some received stipends of \$33, and others of \$60 per annum. In 1872 the total of scholars was sixty-three; the maximum being eighty-eight and the minimum fifty-eight; of these forty are distributed amongst the dormitories, and board with different families in the town; twenty-three are day scholars residing with their families or friends. The lads matriculate after confirmation, if from the country; and the usual ages are fourteen to seventeen. They are separated into four classes (Icel. Bekkur; Dan. Classe), but No. 3 is subdivided into A and B; thus making the total five. No. 4 also demands similar treatment, but room is wanted and also money to fee extra professors. No. 1, which is the junior class, studies Icęlandic, Danish, Thýsku[1] (German), and Latin, as far as Cæsar and Phædrus; Bible history and theology, general history, geography, and zoology. No. 2 continues these items and introduces the student to mathematics, Greek, and English. No. 3 adds geology, mineralogy, and botany; and No. 4 French and general information. The course lasts six years, ending with the maximum age of twenty-three; after which the scholar is "demissus" and can become a "candidat" of theology, or devote himself to law or physic. The shorter holidays are from December 23 to January 3, and from Holy Wednesday to the Wednesday after Easter Sunday. The long vacation is that of our venerable universities, originally designed for allowing poor scholars to beg and to take part in the all-important labours of ingathering the harvest; between July 1 and October 1

---

[1] Thýðverjaland, or Thjóðverjaland, is Teuton-land, Germany, the adjectival forms being Thýðverskr, Thýzkr, and Thýeskr. Icelandic here has evidently borrowed from the Gothic Thjuth, the German Diutisc (Diutisch or Tiusch), the low Latin Theotiscus, and the modern Teutsch or Deutsch, through traders in the eleventh or twelfth century (Cleasby). But Rafn (Antiquités de l'Orient, p. xlix.) quotes the Roman de Rou of Robert Wace:

"Cosne sont en thioiz et en normant parler,"

to show that the two terms were applied to a single tongue. From the old root come the Italian Tedesco and the English "Dutch," which the vulgar in the United States still persistently apply to Germans. Schöning (p. 310, Copenhagen, 1777) and Laing (Heimskringla, iii. 349) confused Thýzkr with "Turkish!"

being the busy time at home: moreover, the lads have a long and a hard way to travel. The high school year is thus of nine months.

The students are known by their "signums," a lyre in circle borne upon the cap-band, but some appear to prefer the cross as a badge. In the college they rise at 6.30 A.M., and if not dressed and ready by 7 A.M. they are reprimanded. At that hour they drink coffee with sugar and milk, and fifty minutes afterwards they go to chapel, which lasts till 8 A.M. The morning lectures now begin, and at 10.45 A.M. they are dismissed to a breakfast of coffee, bread and butter, cold fish, and sometimes meat.[1] The pupils do not take their meals in the school building, but at the different houses where they board. No stimulants whatever are allowed, nor must the pupils smoke, snuff, nor chew in or about the buildings, but of course they can indulge outside it. The second lecture then continues from 11.15 to 2 P.M., after which two hours are given to recreation and dinner of hot fish or meat. Till 7 P.M. the studies for the next day are prepared; and supper, cold like the breakfast, leads to more private reading between 8 P.M. and 10 P.M., at which time all boarders must be in college. The day ends in the chapel, hymns accompanying the prayers; and all are in bed at 10.45, or 11 P.M. on Sundays and festivals. Thus there are five and a half hours of lectures; five of preparation for the next day, and seven hours thirty minutes for sleep. Punishments are confined to degradation in the class and, in extreme cases, to expulsion; of course there is no flogging, and the prison and unsalutary semi-starvation of the French college are equally unknown. Fasts are not kept, even after the fashion of Oxford, which, in the author's day, noted "abstinence" by the addition of fish.

Public examinations take place every year about mid-June; they are held in the first-floor front hall of the building where the Althing meets. They begin with writing, a professor walk-

---

[1] For a full account of the ancient dietary as prescribed by law in 1789, see Baring-Gould, p. 29. The items are meat and peas; sausages cold and warm; meat, broth, and soup; haddock and flounder; stock fish and butter ("the staff of life"); skyr (not curd) and cold milk; meal-grout, buckwheat-porridge, and barley-water grout with milk and butter.

ing about to prevent " cribbing," and they end in *vivâ voce*. These determine the students' claims to the stipendia, of which there are three grades. There are twenty-six Heil-Ölmusa [1] (whole scholarships), each of $100 per annum; twenty-four Hálf-Ölmusa of $50, and four Quarter-Ölmusa, the latter often not distributed. Moreover, those who proceed for study to the University of Copenhagen are entitled to $15 per mensem.

The Latin school (Latínuskóli i Reykjaviki) publishes yearly transactions, in a short yellow pamphlet, Icelandic and Danish (Skýrsla um hinn Lærðaskóla Reykj. Einar Thorðarson). In that of 1871 we find the following names:

The Rector is the only official who lives in the college, and he receives a salary of $1816 per annum. The actual tenant (1872) [2] is Hr Jens Sigurðsson, brother to Jón, the O'Connell of Iceland, and he has made himself eminent by his historical studies.

The Yfirkennari, or head-master, lectures the fourth, or highest class, in Greek, Latin, and French, with a salary of $1192. The present occupant is Hr Jón Thorkelsson.

Of the following professors (Skólakennari, Dan. Adjunct), three receive a total of $3756 per annum = $1192, including house-rent; the theological lecturer (Prestaskólakennari, Dan. Docent) about the same sum; while the two assistants receive something more than half ($612). Their names and duties are :

1. Haldór Kr. Friðriksson, who lectures all the classes in Icelandic, Danish, German, English, and geography.

2. Gísli Magnússon, in Latin, Greek, and Hebrew; the Hebrew, formerly so much affected, is now become almost obsolete; there are only eighteen pupils at the priests' seminary, and a single Oriental student on the island, Rev. Thorwaldr Björnsson, whom we shall presently meet. It is curious how those who hold to " the Bible and nothing but the Bible," neglect the Oriental text for translations, which are so far from being correct that the best often utterly pervert the meaning; and, stranger still, that the vast stores of exegetical and hermeneutical learning should

---

[1] Ölmusa or Almusa is the Greek Ἐλεημοσύνη, the German Almosen, and the English Alms (Cleasby).
[2] He died November 2, 1872.

still lie locked up in the forbidden Talmud,[1] and in the pages of Jewish commentators.

3. Jónas Guðmundsson, in Latin, Danish, and theology.

4. Haldór Guðmundsson, in arithmetic, physics, mathematics, and botany.

5. Hannes Árnason, in geology and minerology.

The three extra professors are:

1. Procurator P. Melsteð, in Danish history and geography; he is a Tímakennari (Dan. Timelærer) paid by the hour, 40 skillings.

2. Saungkennari (Dan. Musiklærer), the organist, P. Guðjónsson, who receives annually $250, without house-rent.

3. Kennari i leikfimi (Dan. Gymnastiklærer), C. P. Stunberg, said to be a retired officer in the Danish Army; his salary is the same as No. 3.

And, finally, there is the inspector with a pay of $220 per annum.

The only unequivocal success of an Iceland education appears to be the hand-writing; it is caligraphic as in the Brazil and Paraguay; probably for the same reason, namely, that time is not money. As will appear in the Journal, a smattering of modern languages has been allowed gradually to usurp the place of Latin, which few even of the priests now speak fluently—the traveller frequently regrets the change. The Rob Roy canoeist finds the classical tongue a meagre vehicle for intercourse; he would not do so if he knew the neo-Latin languages, and would give an hour per day for a few weeks to the colloquies of Erasmus, pronounced Italianistically, and to conversation with a foreign priest. Professor Blackie proposes Greek as the language of the future; we shall next expect to see Sanskrit or Chinese[2] advo-

---

[1] The author is aware that a student who reads Greek and Latin, Italian, Spanish, Portugese, French, German, and English, will find almost all the Talmud, certainly all the valuable parts, in translation at the library of the British Museum. But, unhappily, British Museums do not exist everywhere. Till the constitutional days of Italy the five Jewish Synagogues at Rome were not allowed to own copies of this vast repertory of Hebrew lore.

[2] If English, as appears likely, is to become the cosmopolitan language of commerce, it will have to borrow from Chinese as much monosyllable and as little inflection as possible. The Japanese have already commenced the systematic process of "pidgeoning," which for centuries has been used on the West African Coast, in Jamaica, and, in fact, throughout tropical England, Hindostan alone excepted.

cated: the difficulties of the ancient dialect, with its duals and middles, are enormous, and no such thing as modern Greek yet exists.[1]

The Icelandic pronunciation of the Latin vowels is Italian rather than French, *e.g.*, *Dominum* (like "room," not Dominom) and *náútá*, a sailor, not nota: *j*, after vernacular fashion, is equivalent to *y* (ejus = eyus); and *g* in *gener, regio*, and *gymnast* are hard (*get*, not *George*). The stranger must carefully conform to these peculiarities or he will not be understood.

Icelanders have two grievances connected with the Latin school, one not unreasonable, the other urgent. They complain that youths learn bad habits at the capital, and parents prefer the days of the "schola Bessestadensis." Moreover, they declare that the suppression of the northern school has caused loss of time and money—families being obliged to send their children from the eastern quarter almost round the island viâ the north to Reykjavik. The Danish Government could hardly do better than to restore the northern centre of learning, and, perhaps, transferring the southern to Thingvellir would improve the present state of things.

Art simply does not exist in Iceland, and, to judge from the little museum of Reykjavik, it was always rude as that of Central Africa: the only attempt appears to be on the part of the goldsmith. There is a single painter at Reykjavik, and his career has been cramped by inability to study in lands where the sun shines. The sculptor and the architect have no business here. Even music and dancing, especially the latter, which reminds us of that "accursed thing," the dancing-master lately denounced in Argyleshire, have hardly passed, except at Reykjavik, from the savage to the barbarous stage. We read of the Fidla or violin, and of a Lang Spil like that of the Scoto-Scandinavian islands, an oblong box about two feet three inches wide, and ending in a "fiddle-head;" the three steel wires were

---

[1] The dialects vary so much that we can hardly speak of modern Greek. The only approach to it is the bastard, half-classical jargon, almost confined to the professors and the λογιώτατοι of the capital and chief towns. Worse still, all the Romaic grammars and dictionaries are devoted to teaching a tongue which no illiterate person speaks, ever spoke, or ever, it is to be hoped, will speak. Except by actual travel it is hardly possible to learn the charmingly *naïve* dialects of the peasantry.

either scraped with a bow, or were scratched with the forefinger, the instrument being placed upon a table. But local colour has departed and we hear only that piano which civilised men just prefer to the guillotine, an occasional flute, and some form of "musical bellows," harmonium, or accordion. The traveller's ears are never regaled with the Norwegian Ranz des Vaches, nor the plaintive airs which have struck earlier visitors. And the people appear to be deficient both in time and tune; their lullabies are horrible; "Hieland Laddie" is painfully distorted, and the snatches of song are in the true "rum-ti-tiddy" style, grateful, perhaps, to Dan Dinmont, but assuredly to none but he.

A little volume of 180 pages published by the Icelandic Literary Society, at Copenhagen (Islenzk Sálmasaungs og Messu-bók), and costing $1, suggested that there might be some remnants of music handed down from the past. But it proved to be merely a collection of old German hymns well-known throughout the Lutheran world; and the only specimens worth reproducing were these.

*No. I. (82b in original).*

Túnga mín &c. (Sá krossfesti Kristur lifir).

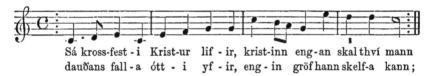

Sá kross-fest-i Krist-ur lif-ir, krist-inn eng-an skal thví mann
dauðans fall-a ótt-i yf-ir, eng-in gröf hann skelf-a kann;

theim, sem lú-inn threyr, upp-bú-in thæg er sæng, að hvíl-ist hann.

*No. II. (in Book No. 83).*

Um dauðann gef thú, drottinn, mèr.

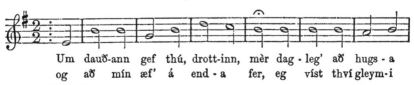

Um dauð-ann gef thú, drott-inn, mèr dag-leg' að hugs-a
og að mín æf' á end-a fer, eg víst thví gleym-i

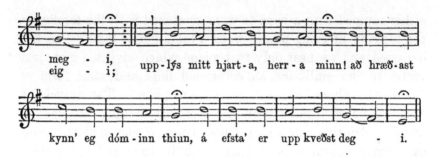

meg - i,    upp - lýs mitt hjart - a,   herr - a   minn! að hræð-ast
eig - i;

kynn' eg   dóm - inn   thiun,   á   efsta'   er   upp kveðst deg   -   i.

### No. III. (in Book No. 90).
### Thèr thakkir gjörum.

Ljós ljóm - ar   dag - ur,     lífs kæt-ist hag   -   ur, sjá, ljós sveit

vek - ur,     sól nótt burt hrek   -   ur. Enn föð - ur   ald -

a    ei - líf - um gjald   -   a thökk skal thre - fald - a.

### § 2. Professions.

The army and navy being unknown to Iceland, the liberal professions are confined to three—Church, Law, and Physic.

The Church is a favourite profession, and we shall soon see the reason why. "Magnam, quæ in templa eorumque ministros ante viguerat," says Bishop Pètursson, "munificentiam post Reformationem evanuisse et ex eo inde tempore conditionem sacerdotum Islandicorum miserrimam fuise constat." The ecclesiastical division was formerly into two bishoprics—Skálholt, established in A.D. 1057; and Hólar, in A.D. 1107.[1] The digni-

---

[1] The two cathedrals of Catholic days were burnt : their successors were humble buildings ; that of Skálholt was a wooden barn ; the building at Hólar was, like the Viðey church, of stone, a rare thing outside Reykjavik.

taries were originally under the jurisdiction of the Archbishop of Bremen-cum-Hamburg. In A.D. 1103-4 they became subject to Azerus (Aussur or Össur), first Archbishop of Lund; and, lastly, in A.D. 1152, they were made suffragans of the Bishop of Throndhjem. In A.D. 1797 the sees were united; a single bishop appointed by the Crown was stationed, as now, at Reykjavik; and the cathedral lacked, as it still lacks, a chapter. Since Norway was divided from Denmark, the chief dignitary was placed under the ecclesiastical jurisdiction of the Seeland Bishopric, but this authority is sometimes questioned. It was proposed by a pragmatical innovator of late years that the present bishop should be consecrated by the Archbishop of Canterbury, but the attempt failed before the indignation of the clergy and laity; it aimed, in fact, at yielding the question of apostolic succession. The machinator took refuge in England.

The clergy are also appointed by the bishop, subject to the confirmation of the Crown. They were divided into Hèraðs-prófastr (Dan. Stiftprovest), or archdeacons (now obsolete); Pró-fastur (præpositus), provosts or deacons, ranking between rector and bishop; Prestar, rectors or curés; and Aðstoðarprestur, alias Kapellán, corresponding with our curates. There is no expression equivalent to "vicar," and it must be coined for purposes of translating him of Wakefield.

In 1772 the island had 189 parishes (Presta-köll), namely, 127 under the see of Skálholt, and 62 under Hólar; in 1834 there were 194 livings or parochial churches; and in 1872 the number had fallen to 171. A yearly report, published at Copenhagen (Anglýsing um Endurskoðað brauðamat á Íslandi), gives a sufficiency of details. According to the last issue (1872), the island contained 171 ecclesiastics, or 1 : 456, a strong contrast with the 7000 priests at Rome; there were 301 churches and chapels (Annexja = Annexe) to 305 in 1818; consequently 130 were not filled, and service was confined to about once in three weeks.[1] The revenues, however, are appropriated to the incumbents of other livings.

---

[1] Bishop Pètursson (299-305) supplies a " Specification " of all the priesthoods and their revenues in the island.

There are twenty Profástdæmid (deaconries), viz. :

| Parishes. | | | Parishes. | | |
|---|---|---|---|---|---|
| Norðurmúla, | numbering | 9 | Brought forward, | | 86 |
| Suðurmúla, | ,, | 11 | Dala, | numbering | 5 |
| Austurskaptarfells, | ,, | 5 | Barðastrandar, | ,, | 8 |
| Vesturskaptarfells, | ,, | 7 | Vesturísafjarðar | ,, | 6 |
| 5. Rangárvalla, includ- | | | Norðurísafjarðar, | ,, | 7 |
| ing the Vestman- | | | 15. Stranda, | | 4 |
| naeyjar, | ,, | 12 | Húnavatns, | | 13 |
| Árnes, | ,, | 14 | Skagafjarðar, | ,, | 13 |
| Gullbringu[1] and Kjó- | | | Eyjafjarðar, | ,, | 13 |
| sar, | ,, | 8 | Suðurthingeyjar, in- | | |
| Borgarfjarðar, includ- | | | cluding Myvatn's | | |
| ing Reykholt, | ,, | 6 | Thing, | ,, | 11 |
| Mýra, | ,, | 7 | 20. Norðurthingeyjar, | ,, | 5 |
| 10. Snæfells, | ,, | 7 | | | |
| Carry forward, | | 86 | Total, | | 171 |

The smallest living is that of Sandfell í Öræfum = $111·89;
the highest that of Hof i Vopnafirði = $1545·33: in Dillon's
day, "Breiðabólstaðr" was the most lucrative benefice. The
bishop's salary is now $3416; and the rector of Reykjavik draws
$1524·77. Seven livings pass $1000 per annum; three, $900;
six, $800; six, $700; eleven, $600; twenty-four, $500; twenty-
seven, $400; thirty-three, $300 (below which sum pay is considered poor); thirty-nine, $200; and twelve, $100. Mr Vice-
Consul Crowe (Report, 1865-66) makes the priest's honorarium
average about 300 rixdollars annually, or £34. When Henderson travelled (1818), the richest living, if he be correct, which is
open to doubt, was of $200; many were of $36, and some of $5
per annum. Other old travellers speak of $33, and even $30.
They justly term these incomes "miserably limited," but they
neglect to add rent-free manse and glebe-land, often some of the
best in the county, besides various minor sources of gain. It
became the fashion to pity the Icelandic clergy, who were compelled to be farmers, fishermen, and craftsmen after the fashion
of St Dunstan. The latter in 1834 are represented to have been
especially numerous; but as every man in Iceland is more or
less a blacksmith and a carpenter, we may again suspect invol-

---

[1] Gullbringu is the Sýsla which contains Reykjavik; but the cathedral town is,
of course, under a separate jurisdiction.

untary misrepresentation. This life of labour is still the case with the Maronites, whose Church is far from being a *refugium peccatorum*. The " Prestr," who had an industrious wife, and no taste for fine wines and tobacco, was better placed than his kinsman the Bóndi,[1] who had to pay, instead of receiving, tithes. And considering the relative value of money, we may doubt if he was ever so severely pressed by the wolf Poverty as many an English ecclesiastic, a scandal which is only now being removed.[2] In 1810 the bishop received, with the contributions of the school-fund, $1800 per annum; this £200 was fully equal in those days to £2000 in modern England. The author, when in Iceland, never saw a parson shoe a horse or take money for his hospitality.

The bishoprics of Skálholt and Hólar at first followed the ecclesiastical regulations drawn up by St Ólafr of Norway. In A.D. 1097 they adopted the tithe laws, which Sæmund the Wise had compiled, which were sanctioned by Bishop Gizur Isleifsson, and which were proclaimed by the President of the Icelandic Republic (Lögsögumaður), Markus Skeggjason. An order of the Althing (A.D. 1100-1275) divided this Tíund into four quarters, paid respectively to the bishop (Biskups-tíund), the priest (Prests-tíund), the church (repairs, etc., Kirkju-tíund), and the poor (Fátækra-tíund); and this division still obtains in the case of tithes from properties exceeding a certain value. After April 16, 1556, the bishop's portion was appropriated by the sovereign under the name of " Crown tithes." This form of tax is obsolete in Europe, but it can hardly be altered for the better in a sparsely populated country like Iceland, attached to

---

[1] Bóndi (of old, Búandi and Bóandi), *plur.* Buéndr or Bóendr (Germ. Bauer, Eng. Hus-band) included all the owners of landed property and householders (Bú), from the petty freeholder to the franklin, especially the class represented by our yeomen and the "statesmen" of Cumberland and Westmoreland. It is still opposed in Iceland to the "klerkar" (clergy), to the knights, to the barons (Hersir-or Lendir-menn), and to the royal officers (hirð). In more despotic Norway and Denmark, "bóndi" became a word of contempt for the lower classes; and in modern Danish, Bönder means plebs, a boor. Bú, from að búa, to build, to inhabit, is the household and stores, opposed to Bær, the house (Cleasby).

[2] In 1873, no less than 4385 "livings" in the Church of England were under £200 per annum: of these, 1211 were under £100 ; 1596 ranged between £100 and £150 ; and 1578 from £150 to £200. Measures have lately been taken to abate this scandal, which pays less for the " cure of souls " than for the care of stables.

the *mos majorum*, where the state of society differs little from that which originated the impost.[1]

In 1810, the Tíund of twelve head of fish, or an equivalent of 27 skillings, then = 1 shilling, was required from every person possessing more than five hundreds,[2] and it increased in uniform ratio with property. The subject of tithes has become a mass of intricacies, and only the outlines of the system can find room. The Tíund (Teind of the Shetlands) is now an impost of one per cent. on the value of all assessable property, viz., on land, boats, horses, cows, and sheep. The tithes of properties not exceeding five "hundreds," or about $150, are applied undivided to supporting paupers; above that sum, they are quartered, as before mentioned.

Tithes may also be divided into two classes—the first, taken upon all the hundreds of immovable property, land, and houses; the second, levied after the fifth hundred, upon movable goods, money, horses, cattle, and fishing boats with their gear. Formerly every fisherman contributed one share of one day's fishing to the hospitals; now he pays ½ ell, or 12 skillings, of every 120 heads of fish, and 1 ell, or 24 skillings, for every barrel of shark liver oil (Law 12, Feb. 1872). Church and Crown estates are exempt. Hospital lands, like the property of the governor, the bishop, the amtmenn, and the priests, pay only the "few-taking," quarter-tithe or poor-tax.

The clergyman also adds to his temporalities by fees for baptisms, marriages, and burials. Each farmer is bound to feed an ecclesiastical mutton from mid-October to mid-May. This is a relic of Catholicism, when the "lamb of SS. Mary and Joseph" was intended as a feast, given by the priest to his parishioners

---

[1] The traveller cannot but think that our scientific political economists are apt, in outlying countries, to neglect the first rule of taxation, namely, to avoid imposing novelties, and to levy imposts with which the people are accustomed. Thus India willingly contributes salt and capitation taxes, and especially Nazaránah, or legacy duties, whilst she hates the name of income-tax. No one will deny that the two former are objectionable for a host of reasons, but the question is, whether they are less injurious than those which lead to the many evils engendered by chronic discontent.

[2] The system of hundreds will be discussed when treating of taxation. Suffice it here to say that in modern Iceland, as in England of former times, the value of land tenure was estimated not by extent, but by produce. Indeed, superficial land-measures, such as the "mark" of the Færoes (= 32,500 square English feet), are unknown to the island.

after they had communicated. Now the latter graze the mutton, but do not eat it. The Prestr can also command a *corvée* of the poorer peasantry for at least one day to get in his hay-crop. And what distinguish his position in Iceland are the high proportion and the comparative value of Church property.

In 1695 the distribution of the 4059 farms upon the island was as follows:

| | | |
|---|---|---|
| Crown lands, | . . | 718 ⎫ |
| Church lands, | . | 1494 ⎬ 2212 |
| Freehold lands, | . . . | 1847 ⎭ |

Uno Von Troil (1772), quoting the Liber Villarium, or Land-book of 1695, thus distributes the Church property:

| | | |
|---|---|---|
| Bishopric of Skálholt, | . . . . | 304 farms. |
| ,,       Hólar, | . . . . | 345 ,, |
| Church glebes, | . . . . . | 640 ,, |
| Clergy glebes, | . . . . . | 140 ,, |
| Glebes of superannuated clergymen, | . . | 45 ,, |
| For the poor, | . . . . . | 16 ,, |
| For hospitals, | . . . . . | 4 ,, |
| Total, | . | 1494 ,, |

Here, out of a total of 4059, the sovereign, the clergy, and the poor whom they represented, monopolised a total of 2212. And in the present day the whole number of farms being 4357,[1] the clergy still hold the ,best properties. The total of 87,860 hundreds may now be divided as follows:

| | | |
|---|---|---|
| Crown hundreds, | . | . 8,886⅓ |
| Priest hundreds, | . . | . 15,309 5⁄12 |
| Hospitals and poor hundreds, | . | . 1,099½ |
| Farmers' hundreds, | . . | . 62,363 |

The proportion has declined from half to little more than a third, but it is still abnormal.

The power of landed property, combined with superior education and the facility of evicting tenantry, makes the Iceland parson a " squarson " of purest type, as the witty compounder of

---

[1] It should be remembered that "Heimili" (households, families) are quite different from "Jarðir" (farms); and the two must not be confounded. The number of the former is 9306, of the latter 4357.

the word understood it. He inherits, moreover, not only the respect, but even the political power of the old pagan Goði. He commands elections as a rule,[1] and can return himself, as well as his friends, to the Althing. Indeed, nothing in Iceland struck the author more than the despotism of the Lutheran Church. It is like the state of Bavaria, where the priests manage the polling by threatening the well-known " Fire of Heaven."·

Nothing need be said of legal studies in Iceland, as the course is relegated to Copenhagen.

The island being divided into medical districts, gives a certain impulse to aspirants. The head physician, or surgeon-general (Land-physicus) of Iceland, who, after being passed by the Faculty of Copenhagen, lectures at Reykjavik, is Dr Jón Jóusson Hjáltalín: his publications are well known throughout Europe, and he will often be mentioned in the following pages. His salary is $1766 a year, and he supervises the eight, formerly seven, district Doctores Medicinæ. These at present are :

1. Dr Thorgrímr Ássmundsson Johnsen, stationed in the eastern part of the Southern Quarter.
2. Dr Thorsteinn Jónsson, in the Vestmannaeyjar, where his treatment has been most successful.
3. Dr Hjörtur Jónsson, in the southern part of the Western Quadrant.
4. Dr Thórvaldur Jóusson, in the northern part of do.
5. Dr Jósep Skaptason, in the Húnavatn and Skagafjörð Sýslas.
6. Dr Thórdur Tómásson, in the Eyjafjörð and Thíngey Sýslas.
7. Dr Fritz Zeuthen, in the eastern districts.
8. The Candid. Medic. Ólafr Stephánsson Thórarensen, in the north-east, Hofi and Eyjafjörð Sýslas.

These gentlemen must prescribe gratis, but they are allowed to sell drugs. Their salaries are about $900 per annum, and under

---

[1] In 1872 contested elections were almost unknown; at least only one was quoted, and the candidate had learned the practice in England. The position of Al-thíngis-maðr was also an object of scanty ambition except to those who required the small salary, or who had a political theory to work out. The assertion in the text is denied by Icelanders; but the author repeatedly heard it made by Danes and other foreigners settled in the island—at any rate, we may expect to see it realised by the new constitution. Knowledge is power in Iceland as elsewhere, and the numbers of the priesthood secure their influence, whilst the physicians and lawyers are too few to be of much account.

the most favourable circumstances their incomes do not exceed $1000 to $1200. The only apothecary on the island is M. Randrŭp, a Dane, who is also Consul de France. He distributes medicines without taking fees, and draws an annual salary of $350.

The number of midwives[1] (Icel. Yfirsetu-konur, oversitting wives) is about a score. That devotion to homœopathy recorded by travellers in the early nineteenth century, appears to be going the way of all systems, after a short but not a wholly useless career.

---

## SECTION VII.

ZOOLOGICAL NOTES (ANIMALS WILD AND TAME)— NOTES ON FLORA—AGRICULTURE AND CATTLE-BREEDING — FISHERIES AND FISHING — IN-DUSTRY AND EMIGRATION.

§ 1. ZOOLOGICAL NOTES AND SPORT.

Iceland, which is an exaggeration of Scotland, whilst Greenland exaggerates Iceland, is supposed to number seven families and thirty-four species of mammals, but of these twenty-four are "water creatures." Two quadrupeds have been considered indigenous, though evidently imported; the first is the mouse of many fables, the second is the fox. An old Iceland tradition asserts that Reynard was spitefully imported by a king of Norway, as magpies were sent to Ireland by the hated Saxon. Some are still floated over on the ice, but they seldom appear upon the east coast. A premium upon vulpecide dates from olden days, and increased demand for the robe has made the animals comparatively rare. Formerly they did immense damage amongst the newly-dropped lambs, and the farmers ignored the Scotch " dodge " of applying a streak of tar to the shoulder or

---

[1] The English Midwife means "with-wife," from the Icel. "Með," the German Mit.

to any part of the youngling. The people divide foxes into tame and wild: the latter grapple the sheep by their wool and never loose them till they fall exhausted.

Horrebow the Dane (Nat. Hist. of Ice.) mentions dark-red foxes, but Hooker neither saw nor heard of them. Kerguelen refers to red as well as to black,[1] blue, and white foxes. Uno Von Troil declares that some of the animals are called "Gras tóur" (or grass-eating tod);[2] usually two varieties are recognised, *C. lagopus* (Mel-rakki) and *C. fuliginosus;* but the *Isatis* or white Arctic and the sooty-brown are probably the same animal at several seasons. Some assert the former to be white all the year round, but no hunter ever pretends to have found a white cub. The blue fox, which haunts certain places, very seldom comes to market, because the chief chasseur is dead. The white coat is cheap, the fine brown is rare and dear. Iceland, of course, abounds in folk-lore and Æsopian tales of Skolli (the skulker), as well as of mice, gulls, and ravens; the string of foxes hanging over the cliffs, and the contrivance of the vixen to escape from the hounds, show ingenuity in the inventor.[3]

The history of the imported reindeer (*C. tarandus*) is well known. In 1770 Hr Sörensen, a merchant, embarked thirteen head from Norway; of these ten died on the passage, and three fawned before 1772. They were never used for sledges: as the mule is the familiar of the Latin family, and the camel of the nearer East, so the reindeer can be developed only by the Lapps, Finns, and Tungusians. Moreover, the reindeer is fitted only for a snowy country; the skin and hair do not readily throw off water, and the animals suffer severely from wet—hence Iceland proved anything but the expected paradise. The average life of the Havier (stag) is said to be sixteen years. The young horns were eaten by the old Norwegians, and, when hard, they were cut into cramp-ring like those of the elk (*Alce equicervus*)—a *curatio*

---

[1] So Styria and Istria boast of a "Kohl-fuchs," so termed from his coal-black waistcoat.

[2] May not the idea have arisen from a confusion of "Tó," a grass-tuft, with "Tóa," or "Tófa," a tod? The older name, Mel-rakki, is derived from burrowing in the sand.

[3] Uno Von Troil (p. 140) also mentions wild cats (Urðar-kettir, cats-o'-stone-heap) and rats.

*per contrarium.* Some of these attires are grand as those of the Canadian Wapiti. There are now only two known herds upon the island, and details concerning them will be given in the Journal.

The Fjárhundr or shepherd-dog (*C. Islandicus*), according to Mackenzie, is of the Greenland breed; the "prick-eared cur" certainly resembles the Eskimo, sometimes with a dash of our collie. Formerly they were far more numerous than men; and old authors mention several breeds—"lubbar" or shag-dogs; dýr-hundar, deer or fox hounds, and dverg-hundar, dwarf hounds or lapdogs. Foreign animals are now rare; the common sort is a little "pariah," not unlike the Pomeranian; stunted, short-backed, and sharp-snouted, with ruffed neck and bushy tail, or rather brush, curling and recurling. The colour is mostly brown-black, some are light-brown, deep-black, white, and piebald. Those brought to Reykjavik appear shy, savage, and snappish as foxes. Formerly they were trained to keep caravan-ponies on the path; now they guard the flocks, loiter about the farms, and keep cattle off the "tún."[1] Good specimens easily fetch $6; a horse may be exchanged for the most valuable, those which, they say, can search a sheep under nine ells of snow. They are accused of propagating amongst their masters, hydatic disease and intestinal worms (*Tœnia echinococcus*); and this considera-tion induced the Althing, in 1871, *magno cum risu* of the public, who asked why the cats were not assessed, to impose an annual dog-tax of $2 per head upon all exceeding a certain number on each farm—it will cause the premature death of many a promis-ing pup. Half of the amount is the perquisite of the Hreppstjórar, the other moiety goes to the Treasury. The danger would be less if the dogs were not so often allowed to lick the platters clean, and to perform other and similar domestic duties.

Cats are common, especially in the capital, showing that de-fence is necessary against rats and mice. Herds of swine are alluded to in the island Sagas; and Iceland, like the Færoes, is full of such names as Svina-fell, Svína-dalr, and Svina-vatn. Not a single head is now seen except at Reykjavik, where a few

---

[1] The Irish "town-land," *i.e.*, yard and meadow; Scotch "toun;" Cornish "town;" Dutch "tuyn," a garden; and Germ. "tzaun."

are annually imported for immediate slaughtering. The peasants cannot afford to rear such expensive animals, which, moreover, damage the "tún." A few goats are said to linger about the northern parts of the island; formerly they were common, but about 1770 they began to be proscribed for injuring the turf-roofs —where they can find no vines.

There are six families and some ninety species of birds, fifty-four of the latter being water-fowl. A valuable list of the air-fauna may be found in Appendix A. to Baring-Gould's volume, "Notes on the Ornithology of Iceland," by Alfred Newton, M.A. Almost every traveller has dipped into the subject, but Mr Newton has twice visited the island to study his specialty. His conclusion is thus stated: "The character of the avi-fauna of this country, as might have been expected from its geographical position, is essentially European, just as that of Greenland has American tendencies." Of course many are emigrants from the south, and, treating of this subject, we should not forget the poetical, and apparently practical, theory of Runeberg the Skáld of modern Sweden. He makes the object light, not merely warmth: "The bird of passage is of noble birth; he bears a motto, and his motto is 'Lux Mea Dux.'"

The most interesting of the game denizens is the ptarmigan (Tetrao lagopus). The people recognise only one species, but in these matters they are of no authority, and foreigners suspect the existence of two as in Norway. The small mountain-ptarmigan (Lagopus vulgaris) of the Continent is white in winter and grey speckled black at other times; its note is compared with the frog's croak, the sheep's cough, or the harsh cry of the missel-thrush. The Danish Skov or Dal-rype (wood or dale ptarmigan) is some seventeen inches long, white-plumed in winter, and during the rest of the year clad in warm yellow-brown, like the red grouse; the "cluck" can be heard a mile off. Metcalfe recognised in Iceland a modified cluck, while Faber and Yarrell believe the islander to be a new species. The cock is locally called Rjúp-karri, and the hen Rjúpa (Reb-huhn), evidently from the cry. It carries the young on the back, and is said to be stupid as the Touraco; this was not the author's experience. Mackenzie appears to be in error when he makes the Scotch ptarmigan haunt the hills, and the Icelander prefer the lowlands. The bird enters largely into folk-lore : the fox of fable blinds it by throwing the snow in its eyes; and when the ger-falcon pierces its heart, he screams for sorrow to find that he has slain a sister.

Flocks of geese, also mentioned by the Sagas, are now found, like swans, only in the wild state; yet there is little apparent reason for the change. The raven will be treated of in another place ; there are no crows except stragglers blown to sea by the southern gales. Poultry is still bred in small numbers about the farms, and, if the proportions were greater, they would be useful in clearing the ground of the injurious lumbrici. But the traveller observes that gallinaceous birds, originally natives of the tropics and of the lower temperates, though easily acclimated to the higher latitudes, will not thrive beyond the habitat of the civilised cereals. At any rate in Iceland their productiveness is limited.

It is generally known that there are no snakes in Iceland as in Ireland. Islands disconnected from continents by broad tracts of sea like Annobom and St Helena, notably lack venomous reptiles; the latter, however, have passed over the nineteen miles between Fernando Po and the Camarones main-land. Papilios and sphinxes, newts and lizards, frogs and toads, also shun the cold damp air. Mackenzie found a coccinella near the Geysir; and Madame Ida Pfeiffer secured two wild bees which she carried off in spirits of wine. The pests are gnats, midges, and fleas; the pediculus is well known, but the cimex, as in older England, has not yet become naturalised.

Mr J. Gwyn Jeffreys kindly obliged the author with the following note concerning a small collection forwarded to him.

" WARE PRIORY, HERTS,
5th October 1872.

" MY DEAR SIR,— . . . . The Iceland shells are as follows :
Marine—
    1. Littorina obtusata, Linné ; var. = L. palliata, Say. = L. limata, Lovén.

Land—
    2. Helix arbustorum, L.
    3. Succinea putris, L.; var. Groenlandica, Beck.

*Fresh-water—*
  4. Pisidium nitidum, Jenyns ; var. Steenbuchii, Müller.
  5. Limnæa peregra, Müller ; var. Vahlii, Beck.

" Most of the land shells of Iceland are usually thin, from a deficiency of lime or calcareous material. This is not the case with the succinea, or with the fresh-water shells, and much less with the marine.

" Nearly all your shells were broken.—Yours truly,
(Signed)    " J. GWYN JEFFREYS."

Baring-Gould (p. 114) found " fossil fresh-water shells on the sand formations between the trap-beds."

The sportsman must not expect to see in Iceland that " abundance of game," promised by old and even by writers of the last decade; he may content himself with No. 5 shot—No. 1, or swan shot, being now useless. Fur is hardly to be had; no foreigner has yet brought down a reindeer ; and the seals belong to the owner of the shore. The people kill Reynard with " fox-shot "—but vulpecide will scarcely commend itself to the Englishman. Feather is nearly as rare. Eider ducks are defended by law, and the author, after visiting the most likely places, can count the ptarmigan flushed; they are generally " potted " sitting in the snow when they approach the farms. Only four whoopers showed themselves *dulcibus in stagnis;* these singing swans, whose music is mentioned by every winter-traveller, are becoming strangers as in the Orkneys and Shetlands. The great auk is gone—for ever gone ; all his haunts have lately been ransacked in vain. Eight or nine years ago the lakes and ponds swarmed with duck; now their places know them no more. Sandpipers, common and purple; malingering golden plover,[1] oyster-catchers, curlew, and whimbrel, and the characteristic whimbrel (*Numenius phæopus,* Icel. Spói), all of them detestable eating, with an occasional snippet or snipe, especially the Hrossa-gaukr[2] (" horse-snipe," *Gallinago media*), so called from

---

[1] This bird (*Charadrius pluvialis,* Icel. Hey-ló and Hey-lóa, the fem. Hey-láa commonly used, the hay-sandpiper), "quite the commonest in Iceland" (Baring-Gould, p. 411)—the snow-bunting being perhaps the commonest of the small birds—is black breasted in the breeding season, and afterwards becomes "golden."

[2] Gaukr (mod. gickr) is a congener of the A. Sax. Gacc ; the Irish Cuach (hence Mo-chuachin, "my little cuckoo !") ; the Scotch Gowk ; the German Gauch ; the Danish Gick, and the Slav. Keuk or Kukavitsa : the Serbian legend makes it a sister calling upon a lost brother. The Index Vocum, etc. (Land-námabók, p. 486), explains it Cuculus.

its neighing cry, and, perhaps, from the popular idea of its throwing somersaults in the air, can hardly be called inducements—except to a Cockney gun. The one sufficient reason for this disappearance of birds is the systematic robbery of their nests; an ever-increasing population with decreasing means must eat up everything eatable.

## § 2. Notes on the Flora.

The vegetation of Iceland, like Greenland, is that of Scandinavia, which Dr Hooker has shown to be one of the oldest on the globe. The popularly adopted computation gives 407 species of Phanerogams, of which one-eighth are grain-bearing; one-eighth leguminous; one-ninth cyperaceæ; one-seventeenth composite, and about one-eighteenth crucifers.

That the present poverty of bread-stuffs is comparatively modern, may be proved by such names as Akrey, Akureyri, Akranes, Akra-hverar, and a host of others, all derived from Akr, a corn-field; the Aker of Lappland (ἀγρός, ager, acker, acre). We have also the distinct testimony of ancient literature. The Landnámabók (p. 15) mentions the Arðr [1] (aratrum) and ploughing with cattle. The Njála says, "Bleikir akrar en slegin tún" —the corn-fields are bleached (to harvest) and the tún is mown. Though the island is now placed north of the barley-limit, crops of barley and rye have apparently been grown.

Forbes and other writers attempt to explain away the significance of "akr," by suggesting that the {indigenous wild oat might have been cultivated in former days, and hence the traces of tilled and furrowed fields which have been allowed to relapse into the savage state. This grain of many names (*Avena arenaria*, *Elymus arenarius*, *Granum spicatum*, *secalinum maritimum spicâ longiooe*, and *arundo foliorum lateribus convolutis acumine*

---

[1] This is a lineal descendant from the ancient and venerable root which named the Aryan race, Ἄριοι, *i.e.*, ploughers not pastors, and which produced Ar-atron, Ar-atrum; Bohemian, Or-adlo; Lithuanian, Ar-klas; Cornish, Ar-adar, and Welsh, Ar-ad, and which survives in our word to "ear." The Arðr of the Sagas was probably heavier and bulkier than the Plógr, a late word of foreign stamp, which "our American cousins" will degrade to "plow."

*pungente)* is popularly called Melr;[1] and old authors divide the
"sea-lyme grass" of Iceland into two species—(1.) *Avena arenaria,*
and (2.) *Avena foliorum lateribus convolutis.* The opinion is un-
tenable for two reasons. Firstly, the cereal is a local growth,
flourishing chiefly in the Skaptarfells Sýsla and in the Mýrdals
and Skeiðarár Sandur; it exists in the north-east of the island;
but it does not yield food. Secondly, transplantation has often
been tried during the last few years, for instance, to the Borgarfjörð, and other highly favourable spots, with one effect—like Kan-
garoo grass in Australia, the grain refused to ripen. Finally, we
may observe, Ólafsson and Pállsson on their journey through
Iceland, nearly a century ago, mention wheat growing in the
southern districts.

The cause of the change, sometimes attributed to oscillations
of temperature, is simply disforesting, which has promoted the
growth of bog and heath now covering half the island, which
allows storm-winds to sweep unopposed over the surface, and
which, since the Saga times, has necessarily rendered the cold
less endurable to cereals. A number of local names, beginning
with Reynir, the sorb apple (*Sorbus edulis*),[2] proves that groves
of the wild fruit-tree, whose pomaceous berries, rich in malic
acid, were munched by the outlaw, once flourished where there
is now not a trace of them. The Landnámabók (chap. i., p. 7)
expressly declares that Iceland was wooded from the sea to the
mountains, or inner plateau (var thá skógr milom fjalls og fjöru);
and tells us how, as in Madeira Island, the woods were destroyed by fire. Vain attempts have been made to remedy an
evil which is now all but irreparable; without nurseries and
walls, the young plants are always wind-wrung. As in the
Orkneys and Shetlands, the only trees now growing wild are
rowans; birches (*Betula alba, nana,* and *fruticosa*), and ground-

---

[1] This word, Melr (*plur.* Melar), wild oats or bent, also Mel-gras (whence
Mel-rakki, the fox), must be distinguished from what the Dictionary, erroneously
I think, makes its secondary sense, a sand-hill, dune, dene or link, overgrown
with such grass, and a sandbank generally, even when bare. The question is,
was the oat called from its sand-bed or *vice versâ?* For a description of this
feature, see Chapter IX.

Etymologically, Reynir is applied to a cousin, the rowan tree, or mountain
ash (*Pyrus aucuparia*), especially sacred to Thor. Hence the Vikings were
called ash-men, because they sat under the sacred ash, which defended them
from the evil eye.

juniper (*J. communis*, Icel. Einir); the dwarf red, grey, and green-grey willows (*Salix Lapponum*, etc., Icel. Grá-Víðir), of which sixteen species have been collected, hardly ever exceed the size of sage, which, indeed, the Selja (*S. caprea*) greatly resembles. The twiggy birch-thickets seldom surpass six feet in height, the northern part of Iceland being the extreme limit of the growth; and a tree whose topmost leaves rise fifteen feet excites general admiration. The verdant patches labelled Skógr (forest), and scattered in the map, especially about the Lagarfljót, the Thjórsá, and the Hvítá, denote this scrub. Yet the bogs supply tree stumps a foot and more in diameter.

The wild flora of Iceland is small and delicate, with bright bloom, the heaths being especially admired; and the traveller is at first surprised to find no difference in the vegetation of the uplands and the lowlands.

Baring-Gould (Appendix C.) gives of Dicotyledons, Ranunculaceæ (14 species), Papaveraceæ (2), Cruciferæ (22), Violaceæ (4), Drosereæ (2), Polygalaceæ (1), Caryophyllaceæ (25), Linaceæ (1), Hypericaceæ (1), Geraniaceæ (3), Leguminosæ (8), Rosaceæ (20),[1] Pomeæ (2), Onagraceæ (9), Haloragaceæ (2), Portulacaceæ (1), Crassulaceæ (17), Saxifragaceæ (19), Umbelliferæ (7), Araliaceæ (1), Cornaceæ (1), Rubiaceæ (10), Valerianaceæ (1), Dipsacaceæ (2), Compositæ (26), Campanulaceæ (2), Vacciniaceæ (4), Ericaceæ (7), Pyrolaceæ (3), Gentianaceæ (15), Polemoniaceæ (1), Boraginaceæ (6), Scrophulariaceæ (18), Labiatæ (8), Lentibulariaceæ (2), Primulaceæ (3), Plumbaginiæ (2), Plantaginaceæ (6), Chenopodiaceæ (3), Sceleranthaceæ (1), Polygonaceæ (13), Empetraceæ (1), Callithrichaceæ (2), Ceratophyllaceæ (1), Urticeæ (2), Betulaceæ (3), Salicaceæ (17), and Coniferæ, only one J. Communis.

The Monocotyledons are Orchidaceæ (13), Trilliaceæ (1), Liliaceæ (1), Melanthaceæ (3), Juncaceæ (11), Juncaginaceæ (2), Typhaceæ (1), Naidaceæ (7), Cyperaceæ (47), and Gramineæ (50). The Acotyledons are Polypodiaceæ (13), Ophioglossaceæ (2), Lycopodiaceæ (8), and Equisetaceæ (6).

---

[1] Hooker (ii. 325) found a true rose, the *Rosa hibernica*, growing in the Seljaland, but only there. Thus it is not wholly wanting, as in the southern hemisphere.

The traveller refers for details to his own pages, to Hooker's Journal (1813), to Zoega's "Flora Islandica," to Preyer and Zirkel's "Reise nach Island," to Dr W. L. Lindsay's "Flora of Iceland" (Edinburgh New Philosophical Journal, July 1861), and to Dr Hjaltalín's "Grasafræði" (Handbook of Icelandic Botany, 8vo, 1830).

Building-wood is wholly imported. Fuel, here used only for the kitchen, is supplied by the Argul of the Tartar, "chips" (*fimo bubulo pro lignis utuntur*); by peat, which varies in depth from two to twenty-seven yards; and by driftwood, which adds considerable value to the shores receiving it. There are two chief deposits, the northern supplied by Septentrional Europe, and the western by the New World; the latter has of late years so much diminished that the islanders expect soon to see it cease.

Concerning the origin of that miocene growth, Surtar-brand,[1] or Iceland lignite, there are two conflicting opinions. Older writers believe it to be a local production, a growth like that which created the coal of the carboniferous period. The more modern support the theory that it is accumulated driftwood, semi-fossilised like Zanzibar copal, by heat and pressure. The question is still open to new light; but as fossil leaves of plants were brought from Disco by Sir Edward Belcher's Expedition; as we have convincing proofs that those latitudes were once inhabited by forests presenting fifty to sixty species of arborescent trees, elm, oak, pine, maple, and plane; and, what is more remarkable, by apparently evergreen trees and quasi-tropical flora, showing that these regions must have had perennial light; we must incline to the old opinion. Early in this century, the Danish Government promised rewards to "persons who shall find out

---

[1] Further notices will occur in the Journal (Chap. V.) about this Surtar-brand (not "Surtur-brand"). Etymologically, it is from Surtr (a congener of "swarthy") "the Black," a fire-giant, who, coming from the south, will destroy the Odin-world, and Brandr, a firebrand. After the change of faith, this northern Ahriman or Set (Typhon) was ready to hand, and at once became the Semitico-Scandinavian "Devil." Upon the same principle, the latter is known in Scotland as "Auld Sootie," since the classical gamins gave horns and tail to Pluto, and the face of the great god Pan was blackened by the monks. The Surtshellir tunnel in western Iceland, famed for the atrocious "Cave-men" (outlaws), is also derived from the Surtr of Scandinavian mythology. The author did not visit it, but the descriptions and illustrations suggested the Umm Níran in the lava formations of the Safá, near Damascus, noticed in "Unexplored Syria."

easier methods of breaking and using Surtar-brand from the rocks" (Hooker), but we do not hear that any one has deserved such generosity.

The greatest deposits of Swart-brand are on the north-western Fjörŏs, where it has been mined to a small extent, and whence specimens have been sent to England. It is mostly found bedded in layers three or four inches thick, alternating with trap. The surface is usually black and shiny, flaking, and otherwise behaving like lignite; burning with a weak flame and a sour smell like wet wood. The smiths formerly preferred it to sea-coal, "because it did not waste the iron;" when powdered, it preserved clothes from the moth, and, being an antiseptic, it was used internally against colics. The author was shown a specimen of true pitch-coal from the Hvítá valley; it is mentioned by Mackenzie (p. 368), who describes it as highly combustible, but not existing in large quantities. This source of wealth, as well as Iceland spar, Iceland moss, cryolite, and especially the sulphur fields, will be noticed in future pages; further details about the interesting Surtar-brand will also be given in the Journal.

## § 3. AGRICULTURE.

At present the grass lands are the wealth of the island, as they pasture the flocks and herds, which form the chief means of subsistence, and the most important articles of industry and commerce. The meadows are grassed over by nature, not ploughed nor harrowed, such implements being rarely used. Nor are they seeded, although Dillon (p. 125) speaks of the weedy grass crop being *sown* in May, growing about June in weedy pastures where, shortly before, no vegetation had been, and being fit for mowing in later August, when the snow is off the hills,[1] and when garden-stuff is ripe. The grass is soft and thick, much like our red-top, and about six inches high; only in rare places the ponies wade up to their knees in through the rich meads. The hay is carefully "sheared," and is exceedingly

---

[1] In Switzerland, also, the minimum of snow coincides with the last of July and early August.

sweet. White clover (*Trifolium repens*, Icel. Smári) flourishes; and on the streams it is found growing spontaneously with carraway (*Carum carui*); the red species wants, they say, the fructifying insect.

Mackenzie, and other old travellers, assure us that the island requires nothing but active and intelligent men, able to combat the prejudices and to stimulate the exertions of the peasantry. The latter complain of the neglect of the Danish Government, and call upon Hercules, but will not help themselves. It is conceded that draining, ploughing, and manuring would improve the soil. But the question still remains, Is the short summer sufficient to ripen grain? Late experiments with seed-corn have proved failures, one quarter of a barrel yielded only half a barrel; this suggests that in the older day seed was imported. Moreover, the taxes and the tenure of land militate against improvement; whilst the excessive labour and expense required for the first steps, such as levelling the soil, place the preliminary operations beyond the reach of most Bændr. Governor Thodal (1772) sowed barley, which grew very briskly: a short time before it was to be reaped, a violent storm scattered the grains from the ears (U. v. Troil, p. 47). Governor Finsen tried oats in his compound, but they stubbornly refused to ripen. Many a summer will pass before an island poet will again sing the "Georgics of Iceland," and before the island can bear the motto, "Cruce et Aratro."

At the close of the eighteenth century the Crown of Denmark established, in the northern district of the Húnavatn, model farms, chiefly directed by foreigners. The grains experimented upon were mostly oats, barley, and rye, autumnal and vernal (*Secale cereale, hybernum et æstivum*). When protected by walls, the rye almost ripened, but the ears were seldom fecund. Still remain for trial various German ryes (*Johanniskorn* or *Studentenkorn*); spelt (*Triticum spelta*); the buckwheat of Tartary (*Polygonum Tataricum*); the *Triticum monococum*, and sundry kinds of barley, the square autumnal (*Hordeum vulgare hybernum*); the square vernal, so useful to middle Europe (*H. v. æstivum*); and, above all, the Lapland barley, which Linnæus says may be planted at the end of May, and reaped on July 28. Abyssinia and the Western Hemisphere will supply the island with edible meadow-grasses and millet-grasses, Poas, and Festucæ (*Ovina* and others),[1] and especially with the Quinoa (*Chenopodium quinoa*) of the Peruvian Andes, which ripens where no other corn grows. And let us hope that the indigenous cereals have not yet had a fair chance.

In the last century Hr Haldorsen introduced the potato, which has now extended over the island. Dillon calls it a pigmy, and compares it with a tennis ball; but it has improved since his day. Turnips would flourish, especially upon the warmer coasts, where the sub-soil is palagonitic sand, and where manure of sea-weed abounds. Radishes, as now cultivated, are hard, coarse, and woody : spinach is a success, and much might be done to fatten the indigenous sorrel. The Stranda Sýsla to the north-west has attempted with various fortunes, sundry kinds of caules; the broccoli, which grows quickly; the turnip-cabbage (*Brassica oleracea gangloides*), eaten in summer; the curled cole-wort (*B. o. sabellica*), kept for winter use; the red cabbage, strong to resist cold; the large growing white variety (*B. o. capitata alba*), and the cauliflower, which hardly exceeds the size of a man's fist—it is found, however, that the two latter refuse to seed. The other pottage-plants are lettuces, common in gardens ; beetroot, red and yellow; carrots; onions, garlic, and shalots (*Al. asculonicum*); chervil (*Scandix cerefolium*); black mustard, which, considering the climate, attains unusual dimensions; water cress; radishes; horse radish (*Raphanus niger*); and parsley, the latter taking six to seven weeks before it rises above ground. In 1865, there were about 7000 garden plots.

The tenure of land is either by lease from the Crown and the Church, or held in fee simple; the latter is the old Óðal,[2] pre-served in modern Norway. Since ancient times, there has been a fourfold division of estates : (1.) King's land, bearing a succes-sion duty of 1 per cent., and assigned to a family as long as it pays its rent; (2.) Church land; (3.) Freehold, held by contribut-

---

[1] The indigenous Poas number twelve, and the Festucæ three.

[2] Óðal is a congener of the German Edel and Adel, noble, as the "chiefs" of Scandinavian and Teutonic communities were the land-holders. Hence the mid. Lat. Allodium ; and (Cleasby) "feudal" is fee-odal, odal held as a fee (Germ. *vieh;* Dutch, *vee;* pecunia, capitale) from the king : Dr Sullivan prefers *Feodum* from Fuidhir, fugitives. Popularly, Udal, Allodium, prædium hereditarium, is opposed to feudal.

ing land-tax; and (4.) Land charitably bequeathed to the poor. Crown property may be granted either by the Sýslumaðr, whose income is often eked out by a temporary tenure gratis; or by the Umboðsmenn,[1] of whom there is generally one for every two Sýslas. They are also paid by grants of Government farms; they receive a percentage upon those they lease, and they report to the Land-fógeti (treasurer). Church property is under the Amtmaðr, controlled by the bishop, but, as a rule, it is sub-leased by the parish priest in whose living it is. A large proportion of farms is thus held. The poor lands are let by the rector and the Hreppstjórar, superintended by the Sýslumenn. The tenant, besides agreeing to support one or more paupers, pays ground-rent for all buildings upon the farm, and he can underlet it in parts, the sub-tenant paying, perhaps, a barrel of rye per annum.

Mackenzie compares the tenure of land leased to the farmer with the Scotch "steel-bow;" the rent is paid in two ways:

1. Landskuld, lease-money or rent owed by the tenant to the Crown, the Church, or the landowner. It is taken in specie or in kind, at the rate of $2 to $3 per $100. The latter is supposed to be fixed by ancient valuation; practically, it is very unsettled; and in Iceland, as elsewhere, the landlord will strive to obtain the terms most favourable to himself.

2. Lausa-fè, the rent on movable property, especially kine and sheep, opposed to land, or even land with its cattle. It is generally levied in butter, one of the articles of currency. Each tenant is bound to take over from his predecessor the permanent stock on certain conditions, and to leave the same number when he quits.

Property cannot be entailed. The estates of those dying intestate are distributed amongst the children; formerly, whole shares fell to sons, half shares to daughters—all now share equally. This process justifies De Tocqueville, who, expressing his surprise that ancient and modern publicists had paid so little attention to succession laws, regarded them as the most important of political institutions.

---

[1] The Icelandic Umboð are our Umboth-lands, formerly belonging to the bishop, and afterwards transferred to the Crown. Etymologically, the word means a charge or stewardship.

Dufferin seems to think (pp. 141, 142) that almost perpetual leases are the rule in Iceland: the contrary is the case; and the small proportion of freehold is a crying evil. Many farms are let to tenants at will from year to year, with six months' notice: evictions are allowed by law for neglect or misconduct, easily proved by the rich against the poor; and the ejected farmer's only remedy is to disprove the charges by a survey of the Hreppstjórar, and of two respectable neighbours. The instability of landed tenure, the undefined state of the tenant-right, and the certainty of rents being raised by the parson or the Umboth-superintendent, if profits increase, for instance if minerals be discovered, are potent obstacles to regular and energetic improvement. The remedy evidently lies in the sale of Crown property, and in the secularisation of Church lands, with due compensation to the actual holders.

The farms are all named, mostly from natural features. There are, however, not a few which have borrowed from the outer world, for instance a Hamburg in the Fljótsdalr: even "Jerusalem" is not unknown—the result of Crusading days. The best are on the north side of the island; yet the three most generally cited as models are Viðey off the west coast, and Hólmar and Möðrudalr, to the east. The south-western (not the southern) shore supports a fishing rather than a pastoral or agricultural population. The non-maritime people live in scattered homesteads, which nowhere form the humblest village: this is the unit of the constitutional machinery of Iceland, as the township was amongst the Anglo-Saxons. The only settlements are the trading-places on the sea-shore.

Drainage and fencing are not wholly neglected. In 1856 there were 40,202 fathoms of ditching, and 44,671 fathoms of railing, these improvements being all modern work. Each farm has, besides the "tún," a bit of lowland upon which grass is grown, and a large extent of barren hill and moorland, where the sheep graze during the fine season; this is always assumed to belong to the property. Hence the Shetland phrase, "fra the heist off the hill to the lawest off the ebbe" (milli fjalls og fjöru). The "Bær" is divided from its neighbours by Vörður ("warders"), or landmarks, natural and artificial; the latter are stone heaps, the former some marked limit, as a hill, a rock, or a stream. The boundaries are a perpetual cause of dispute, and some of the most complicated lawsuits have thus arisen. Not a few of the wilder peasantry live in a chronic state of land-feud; they "make it up" over their cups, and they return to the natural belligerent condition when sober.

The tenants of an Iceland farm usually number six classes.

1. Bonders (Bændr),[1] the Shetland Boonds, franklins, farmers, or yeomen; the "upper ten."

2. Húsmenn, or tómthúsmenn, who have houses upon the farm, but are not allowed pasturage or haymaking. They have been confounded by travellers with—

3. Kaupamenn, labourers working for hire.

4. Hjáleigumenn (crofters), those who occupy the hjáleiga, or a small farm, an appendage to the larger establishments.

5. Servants (Icel. Vinnumenn).

6. Paupers (Icel. Ómagar or Niðursetningr).

Much harm is done by the multitude of lazy loons that gathers round the farmer, a practice dating from ancient days, all striving to live upon the best of the land, with the least amount of work.

Thus we see that "agriculture," being absolutely confined to haymaking, is a mere misnomer in Iceland, nearly three-quarters of whose population is pastoral, though not nomad. The wealth of the country consists of sheep, horses, and black cattle; goats are spoken of in the north, but the author did not see a single head.

Since the first third of the nineteenth century, Iceland has witnessed a gradual and regular increase of population, and a proportionate decrease of live stock.[2] The following are the numbers of animals given by Mackenzie for 1804:

---

[1] See Section VI.

[2] The author's statement made in the *Standard* found objectors. Hr E. Magnússon impudently contradicted what he termed a *contradictio in adjecto*, apparently ignorant of the simple truth that neither logic nor Latin can affect facts and figures. It is amply confirmed by the Consular Report of 1870-71 : "The stocks of domestic animals have shown a steady tendency to decrease, especially as regards the sheep flocks, which at times have been cruelly decimated by scab epidemics ; the occasional failure of the grass crops exercises also a destructive influence on their herds and flocks generally, as they have no means at hand of substituting other fodder for the excellent wild pastures with which in ordinary years Nature supplies them so bounteously. These occasional epidemics and

| Cows, | . | . | . | 15,595 | Milch ewes, | . | . | 102,305 |
|---|---|---|---|---|---|---|---|---|
| Heifers, | . | . | . | 1,556 | Rams and wethers, | . | | 49,527 |
| Bulls and oxen, | | . | | 1,132 | Lambs, | . | . | 66,986 |
| Calves, | . | . | . | 2,042 | Total of sheep, | | | 218,818 |
| | Total of cattle, | | | 20,325 | Total of horses, | | | 26,524 |

In 1834-35, according to Mr John Barrow, jun., repeated in 1854 by Mr Pliny Miles, the total of sheep, the chief staple of the land, was 500,000. M. Eugène Robert gives 617,401 for 1845. But in 1855 appeared the disease (*scabies*) which, according to the "Oxonian" (p. 389), in two years killed off 200,000 head: in many parts of the island it still rages.

In 1863 Paijkull assigned 350,000 sheep and 22,000 head of black cattle to 68,000 souls. In 1871 the official numbers are:

| | |
|---|---|
| Milch ewes and lambs, . . . . . . | 173,562 |
| Barren ewes, . . . . . . . . | 18,615 |
| Wethers and rams above one year old, . . . . | 55,710 |
| Yearlings, . . . . . . . . | 118,243 |
| Total, | 366,130 |

or a falling off of 134,000, where the population has gained since 1834-35 upwards of 13,700.

The next source of profit in Iceland is breeding black cattle. According to the same traveller, the total in 1834 was 36,000 to 40,000 head. The official tables for 1871 give:

| | |
|---|---|
| Cows and calves, . . . . . . . . | 15,634 |
| Bulls and bullocks above one year old, . . . . | 828 |
| Yearlings, . . . . . . . . . | 2,649 |
| Total, | 19,111 |

or a falling off of nearly half, when the population has increased about one-fifth.

The following table shows the comparative numbers:

| | | | | | | | |
|---|---|---|---|---|---|---|---|
| 1855 | there were of sheep, | 489,132 | of horned cattle, | (?) | of horses, | (?) |
| 1860 | ,, | 309,177 | ,, | (?) | ,, | (?) |
| 1866 | | 393,295 | ,, | 20,357 | ,, | 35,241 |
| 1867 | | 368,591 | ,, | 19,003 | ,, | 33,768 |
| 1868 | | 351,167 | ,, | 17,968 | ,, | 31,796 |
| 1869 | | 356,701 | ,, | 18,342 | ,, | 30,835 |
| 1870 | ,, | 352,443 | ,, | 18,189 | ,, | 30,078 |
| 1871 | ,, | 366,130 | ,, | 19,111 | ,, | 29,688 |

grass failures are bewailed by the Icelander as national calamities; but it is a question whether they may not prove to be the reverse, by opening his eyes to the necessity of devoting his energies and small capital to the better and more regular prosecution of the fisheries, which are boundless in extent, and less dependent on vicissitudes and seasons."

Thus, not including 1871, the number of horses since 1855 has decreased upwards of 25 per cent., horned cattle 23 per cent., and sheep a little more than 31 per cent.

Black cattle, according to Mackenzie, resemble the largest Highland breed; the author thought them far more like our short-horns in general, and especially Alderneys. Dillon makes them generally hornless,[1] and the breed has remained unchanged. The cows yield an abundance of milk, sometimes ten to twelve quarts a day. There has been no disease amongst the " slaughter-creatures," as Icelanders call black cattle, but the gold of California and Australia has affected even Ultima Thule. In 1830-40 the price of a cow, $4, had increased to $28 in 1870; in 1872 it had risen to $50-$80, and the animal often cost $100 to $120 in rearing. Twenty years ago the pound of beef fetched eight to ten skillings (farthings); now it averages one mark (fourpence) to one mark three skillings. Few householders own more than eight head of cattle, and probably half that number would be a high average. The community lives chiefly upon milk and fish; hence the sale of a cow is to the children the death of a friend, causing tears and lamentations.

The large but scattered flocks of sheep are the chief support of the islandry. The peasants pay rent and debts in June and July by the wool which is then washed and ready for sale; and in September and October by wether-mutton smoked and cured; by grease and tallow, and by sheep-skins and lamb-skins with the coat on. They reserve the butter and cheese mostly for bargains and for household use. In 1770 the wether sold for $1; in 1810 it had risen to $2, and even $5, and in 1872 to $9. Besides supplying food, the animals yield material for local industries—coarse cloth, clothes, frocks and jackets, mittens, stockings and socks, made by the women, and used or exported. The fleece, which may average two to four pounds,[2] is not sheared,

---

[1] " Perhaps," says Peirce (p. 29), "this is why the official statistics, with a sort of grim humour, number the 'horned cattle' at 23,713, while other authorities say there are 40,000 'cattle.'" He also quotes Dillon (p. 291) about four-horned and six-horned sheep—"quadricorns" are exceptional in Iceland as in most countries.

[2] More exactly the average yield of a one-year old is $1\frac{1}{4}$ lb.; of a two-year, $2\frac{1}{2}$ lbs.; and of a three-year old, 3 lbs.

but "roo'd," or plucked when loose, with little pain to the wearer. Though coarse it is long, while under the hard outer coat (Icel. Tog or Thel) there is a fine soft tog, not a little resembling the "Pashm" of Persia, Afghanistan, and Northern India. The price varies considerably, the usual limits being tenpence to a shilling. Of course it depends greatly upon the export, which in some years has reached 1,750,000 lbs.; in 1868 about 625,000 lbs. were shipped to England. The "scraggy," long-legged animal suggests, on the whole, the old Scotch breed. Intermixture of merino and other blood has been partially tried, but it is a disputed point whether improved form and quality of wool have or have not brought increased liability to disease. The surest way to improve the island-sheep is to feed it better, but the peasant is too lazy to shear the hills for hay not absolutely necessary.

The exportation of live stock unaccompanied by proportional emigration may end in a calamity. Fatal famines deform the island annals, and in any year another may result from an inclement summer, producing scarcity of grass. It would be justifiable to part with necessaries if the profits were laid out upon improvements; but this is far from being the case. The peasant sells his cattle and sheep to buy for himself vile tobacco; "bogus" cognac; brennivín or kornschnaps, and perhaps even "port" and "sherry;" and for his wife chignon and crinolines, silks and calicoes, instead of the homely but lasting frieze cloth. His grandfather infused Iceland moss; he must drink coffee, while raisins or cassonade are replaced by candied or loaf sugar. Figs boiled with rice and milk were then offered to guests, and angelica root was a *boccon ghiotto*. And so with other matters. The Althing has attempted to curb the crying evil of ever increasing drunkenness, the worst disease of the island because the most general, by a tax which will be described under the head of cesses; and sensible men would see it increased.

During the last forty years the number of horses has gradually fallen to half; in 1871 the total was only 3164 over the 26,324 which Mackenzie gave for A.D. 1804. In 1834, according to John Barrow, jun., a careful observer, though apparently his figures do not come from official sources, the census varied from 50,000 to 60,000; and the same is given for 1835 by Mr Pliny

Miles (1854), who may have copied his predecessor. In 1845 the census numbered 34,584. In 1862 the late Professor Paijkull counted 37,000, or 0'5 per head of population; during that year 828 (?) were exported to Scotland viâ Belgium. The last census, for June 6, 1871, shows:

| | | | |
|---|---|---|---:|
| Horses and mares, four years old and upwards, | . | . | 23,059 |
| ,, | ,, | under three years, . . . . | 6,629 |
| | | Total, | 29,688 |

The following figures denote only the exportation from the capital; though many animals are bought in other parts of the island, they are usually driven to Reykjavik, and the people complain that the west, where horse-flesh is scarcest, sends out the most. Those embarked at the chief port, sometimes in troops of 400, were either two-year olds or upwards of ten-year old, and many appeared to the author fit only for the knacker's yard.

In 1861 (Consular Reports, 1865) were imported into Great Britain, 444 head.
,, 1862 total export (Paijkull) 828 head ; Parl. Rep. give      856 ,,
,, 1863 Consular Report                  ,,      345 ,,
,, 1864     ,,      and official figures on island ,,      470[1] ,,
,, 1869 official figures                 ,,      507 ,,
,, 1870     ,,                            906 ,,
,, 1871     ,,                  ,,      1018 ,,
,, 1872 a conjecture perhaps understated       ,,      2000[2] ,,

For three years Dr Hjaltalín advised the Althing to impose a heavy tax on exported horses, and to expend the income upon road-making: the plan was too sensible to suit the majority. The theorists, who are not a few in Iceland and Denmark, object to unfree trade, and look only at present profits—when will nations learn that to imitate one another often produces not a copy but a caricature? Upon the subject of horse-flesh, further details will be found in the Journal.

To resume: Mr Consul Crowe (Report, 1870-71) gives the following value-tables of farm-produce:

---

[1] Valued at a total of £2468, or about £5, 5s. a head. The prices will be considered in the course of the Journal.
[2] The steamer "Queen" in 1872 embarked 1030 head and the "Yarrow" 1414; these figures are given from the *Scotsman*. In 1873 the price had risen to £10 to £14, and the hire was a Danish dollar a day; thus the peasant was deprived of transport for himself and his goods.

|  | 1864. | 1865. | 1866. | 1867. | 1868. | 1869. |
|---|---|---|---|---|---|---|
| Salt meat, brls. | 1,902 | 716 | 2,206 | 2,985 | 2,003 | 2,758 |
| Tallow, lbs. . | 453,279 | 461,193 | 452,261 | 556,254 | 530,798 | 451,655 |
| Salted sheep-skins, pieces, | 8,438 | 2,870 | 11,552 | 14,592 | 8,861 | 14,746 |
| Sheep-skins, do. | 8,411 | 31,649 | 30,729 | 26,886 | 12,393 | 15,862 |
| White wool, lbs. | 1,215,162 | 1,393,161 | 1,547,169 | 1,223,580 | 1,423,392 | 1,218,067 |
| Black ,, ,, | 15,893 | 21,858 | 25,886 | 8,303 | 7,779 | 7,942 |
| Mixed ,, ,, | 109,538 | 116,241 | 132,394 | 96,881 | 122,456 | 97,618 |

Of which the annual exported value is—

|  | S. AMT. | W. AMT. | N. & E. AMT. | WHOLE ISLAND. | |
|---|---|---|---|---|---|
|  | Value Rix dols. | Value Rix dols. | Value Rix dols. | Quantities. | Value Rix dols. |
| Salt meat, . . . | 3,150 | 2,185 | 35,910 | 2,095 brls. | 41,245 |
| Tallow, . . . | 15,334 | 5,813 | 61,394 | 484,240 lbs. | 82,541 |
| Salted sheep-skins, . | 826 | 112 | 8,602 | 10,176 pcs. | 9,540 |
| Sheep-skins, . . | 525 | 331 | 893 | 20,988 ,, | 1,749 |
| White wool, . . . | 121,218 | 65,847 | 205,354 | 1,336,755 lbs. | 392,419 |
| Black ,, . . . | 2,253 | 835 | 1,201 | 14,610 ,, | 4,289 |
| Mixed ,, . . . | 6,922 | 4,126 | 12,394 | 112,521 ,, | 23,442 |
| Total, | 150,228 | 79,249 | 325,748 | ... | $555,225 |

## § 4. FISHERIES.

Faber mentions forty-five species of fish, seven of them being inhabitants of fresh waters; but the list is evidently incomplete. Of Cetaceæ alone the Iceland seas produce thirteen varieties : we shall visit the headquarters of whale-catching on the eastern coast. The Hákall, or edible shark, is also an animal of importance far surpassing the seal. The halibut (Spraka) is rare in the south, but it is found in abundance in the north-west; the sole is wanting, and the herring (Sild) is unaccountably absent, except in the north and east; the latter sometimes enters the bays and gives a little work about Seyðisfjörð and Akureyri, but it does not pay.[1] Mackerel, lobsters and oysters, shrimps and

---

[1] This is not the case with Norway, situated in the latitude of Iceland and Greenland, as the old rhyme shows:

prawns, are unknown; there are crabs which contain little meat, and a variety of limpets (*Patella*), and mussels (*Mytilus edulis*), eaten and used for bait. The principal fish upon the coast are the true cod (*Gades morrhua*); the ling (*Lota morrhua*), with the long dorsal fin; the hake (*G. merlucius*); the haddock (*G. æglefinnus*); the coal-fish (Icel. Isa; *G. carbonarius*); the skate (*Raia;* Icel. Skata), and the stinging-ray (*R. trygon;* Icel. Graŏ-skata or Tindabikkja). The rivers teem with salmon (*S. salar*); the lakes and ponds with trout (Silungr) and char (*Salmo Alpinus*).[1]

Ichthyological study is everywhere in its infancy, and awaits its full development, when the greatly increased density of earth's population will enhance the difficulty of supplying it with a sufficiency of food. The late Professor Agassiz ably vindicated the superiority of fish-diet for brain-workers, as well as for the poor classes of society,—it abounds in phosphorus and "ohne Phosphor keine Gedanken." The noble fisheries of Iceland are still in the most primitive style of development; the appliances are of the poorest, and the people display neither energy nor intelligence, which must be aroused by an impulse from without. The returns, as we shall see, are considerable, but they might be indefinitely augmented if modern improvements and commercial enterprise were enlisted to make the best of this generous source of wealth.

For the ocean is emphatically the poor man's larder. With equal capital and labour it is made far more productive than the earth, and the ratio is ever increasing in its favour. Whilst land-animals give birth to one or two young at a time, fish produce their millions, and the bulk far exceeds anything that walks the earth. Whilst, at most, one-eighth of Iceland is capable of yielding food in any appreciable quantities, the circumpolar

---

" Sidst i Torri og först i Gio,
   Skal Sild og Hval være i Sio."

" At the last of Torri (first moon after Christmas) and first of Gio (the second moon),
   The sillock (herring, *Clupea harengus*) and whale in the sea will show."

Yet in Coxe's time (late eighteenth century) the herring had disappeared from the shore, being found only in deep water; and Fortia (Travels in Sweden) tells us, that firing of guns was not allowed for fear of frightening the fickle fish.

[1] Concerning the fresh-water fishes, details will be found in the Journal.

seas swarm with profuse life, tier upon tier extending thousands of feet deep. "In hot latitudes the deep-sea temperature diminishes till the mercury stands at 40° (F.); in the parallel of 70° the ocean, many degrees warmer than the land-surface, is of the same temperature at all depths."[1] And as the voyager advances toward the poles, the diffusion of animal life increases prodigiously. The waters around Iceland, as about Greenland, produce endless forage for their tenants, such as the squids (*Sepiadæ*), and the *Clio Borealis*, the favourite pasture of the whale; whilst fine and nutritious grasses occupying the shore and the shallows yield pasture for the seals.[2] The rivers rolling glacier-water, and the white streams tinged by *detritus*, are, it is true, barren; but they bear down the alluvium of cultivated lands, and the drainage serves to augment the supply of food.

The abundant sea-harvests, especially of cod, soon attracted the attention of foreign nations; and as early as A.D. 1412, thirty European ships or crafts frequented the coasts of Iceland. Until 1872, the maritime territorial limits of four Danish, or nearly twenty English, miles, laid down by the law of 1787, were preserved with all its wholesome provisions, pains, and penalties. The new retains the old ordinance in case of necessity, but annuls certain objectionable parts; for instance, it allows the necessary landing and warehousing of fishermen's stores on the payment of a moderate and conditional charge to the local poor-box.

It has been shown that the fisheries of Iceland are worked by 3500 boats, manned by upwards of 5000 souls, only one-tenth of those employed upon the farms. But this would give a false idea of the important industry which, depending upon the peculiar character of the people, has determined more than anything else the modes and the inspiration of national life. Especially between February and May, the "fishing peasants" flock to the shore; the seaboard farms and factories become populous, and the whole

---

[1] R. J. Walker, quoted by Peirce. Dr Carpenter and Professor Wyville Thomson, in the "Lightning," made the remarkable discovery that sea-water at different depths, is of different temperatures—the older theory being that the sea was of a uniform temperature of 39° (F.).

[2] In intertropical and temperate latitudes *Phocæ* and *Manatis* devour the fetid marine vegetation which collects on river bars, chokes the mouths, and causes "Yellow Jack" to prevail from Florida to Rio de Janeiro.

energy and interests of the island are turned to its characteristic occupation. Off the south-western county there is perennial fishery—salmon in spring, and cod nearly all the year.[1]

Cod fishing is carried on along the coast generally, sometimes even in the inner harbours. The western shores are peculiarly rich; and that most favoured is the southern coast between Keflavík and Hafnafjörð. Desolate in appearance beyond all other regions, excepting the giant Jökulls to the south-east, the south-western peninsula has deserved the name Gullbríngu Sýsla, "gold-bearing county," from its sulphur diggings and magnificent fisheries.[2] And a glance at the map will show the admirable spawning-grounds off the western coast.

A royal decree, dated A.D. 1292, forbids the sale of dried cod to foreigners on the ground of an expected famine. Before the Reformation, England fished for herself; and as late as James I. the Iceland waters, where few are now seen, employed 150 vessels. Little by little, France, with patient and strenuous action, established a hold on, and afterwards a monopoly of, the Iceland deep-sea fishery; thus securing, as in Newfoundland, not only a source of national wealth, but a powerful reserve of experienced seamen. Certainly, no better school for sailors can be imagined than the dangerous and intricate navigation of the Iceland Fjörðs. In 1859, there were 269 French smacks and ships, varying from forty to eighty tons burden, and manned by 7000 fishermen; in 1872, even after the Prussian-French war, these figures were 250, averaging ninety tonneaux, and 3000 hands (*Revue Maritime et Coloniale*). They are protected by two, formerly three, men-of-war, which cruise about, repressing disorders, and aiding their compatriots with spars, provisions, and medical comforts. Collisions between natives and foreigners

---

[1] Of course the "finny brood" is not without its folk-lore. There is a variety of "troll-fish" which, being ominous and unlucky, are thrown overboard by their captors. The same takes place farther south, as we learn from Lucas Dobes (Færoe Reseratar, Copenhagen, 1673).

[2] "Gullbringusýsla (literally, Goldbreast county) derives its name from some hills called Gullbringur (Goldbreasts), about twelve English miles distant from Reykjavik. They were so called because tradition says that the old Víking Egill Skallagrímsson there buried the treasure given him by King Athelstan for his assistance at the battle of Brunenburgh" (Jón A. Hjaltalín). This derivation is far more probable than the popular version given in the text: for a third interpretation see the Journal, chap. ii.

take place when the latter are driven, by the weather, the currents, and the movements of the fish, within the prohibited limits, now one league (= three miles) from the coast: also entanglement of gear often ends in a free fight. Forbes (Commander, R.N.) tells us (p. 208) that no such powerful reserve of trained seamen exists, except those engaged in the same occupation, and under similar regulations, on the cod-banks of New-foundland.

Mr Consul Crowe (1865-66 and 1870-71), whose exhaustive Reports must be consulted for details which cannot find room in these pages, divides the Iceland "fisheries of the present day into three kinds, viz., the cod-fishery, shark-fishery, and whale-fishery."

According to him (p. 30), the large cod, here not a migratory fish, remain during the winter near the island, and from February to March approach the south and west coasts to spawn, their course being from the west and south. The earliest and best fishings begin with early spring in the more temperate waters, and farther northwards about latter June or early July, ending with August. The fish, where it keeps close to the bottom, is landed by small drift-nets; it is "more squat and plump, with smaller head," than those caught on the hook. Fishing with the ordinary long lines, and deep-sea or hand lines, opens about mid April; the little extension given to it arises from the poverty of the people. From one to four lengths of a strong thick line, each measuring sixty fathoms, are spliced together; and hanging lines six feet long are fastened at distances of from six to nine feet: the French can afford to use lines measuring 1500 to 2000 fathoms. The hook is the ordinary tinned English (No. 5), baited with mussels. "In order to obtain a white flesh, the first operation is to rip up the belly, the head is cut off, and the body is gutted, the liver and roe being separated and carefully kept. The backbone (blód-dalkr) is next extracted, as far as the third joint below the navel, after which the carcase is washed in salt water, and salted, one barrel (about 224 lbs.) being used to 352 lbs. After lying in salt for three or four days, the fish is washed and laid out singly on the rocks to dry; it is protected from dust and damp, and is frequently turned by the women, that both sides may be alike." For home consumption, the cod is split and hung up unsalted in the "wind-house." It is known by its shrivelled appearance, and, like the refuse heads, it is eaten uncooked. Although Hamburg pays 12s. 6d. per cwt. for fish guano, Iceland neglects this exportation. Finally, the cod-fish is sent in great part to Northern Europe (Denmark and Hamburg), and at least one-half to Spain and the Mediterranean; in fact, wherever the old world keeps Lent, and eats "baccalá." The French, although great consumers, of course supply themselves.

Details concerning the whale and the shark will be found in the Journal (chap. xiii.). The supply of salmon from the northern and western coasts has been pronounced "literally inexhaustible;" yet mismanagement of rivers shows that they can greatly be damaged. The Laxá, near Reykjavik, in Mackenzie's day (1810), yielded from 2000 to 3000 lbs. per annum; in 1872, the catch was nearly nil, although in the summer of 1873 it somewhat improved. Salmon was exported as early as 1624, but in small and irregular quantities, till taken up by Messrs Ritchie of Peterhead and Akranes. The house still employs nine Scotch hands to preserve the fish caught in the Borgarfjörð, the embouchure of the great Hvítá. But, although salmon began to appear in the returns as a regular article of export, the 22,000 lbs. of 1858 fell to 4000 in 1868, on account of the river being overworked. During the early season of 1872, the take was small, but it afterwards so increased that tins were wanting for preserves: the superintendent at Akranes pays thirteen skillings (3¼d.) per lb. to the Borgarfjörð fishermen.

Iceland lacks the *Otaria* or eared seals, sea lions, elephants, and wolves, of which one species, the *O. Falklandia*, supplies such valuable pelts; all its Phocæ are inauriculate. Naturalists give six species, viz.:

1. *Phoca fœtida.*

2. *Callocephalus vitulinus* or *Phoca littorea*, the common land-seal.

3. *Phoca barbata*, the great seal.

4. *Phoca Grœnlandica* or *oceanica*, the harp-seal.

5. *Cystophora cristata* or *leonica*, hooded or hood-cap seal (*Stemmatopus*).

6. *Phocula leporina*, haaf-fish or open-sea seal.

Old authors mention four kinds, viz., Rostungr (walrus), Vööruselr, Blööruselr, and Gránselr. Modern Icelanders preserve, like the Scotch,[1] three great divisions : 1. The land-seal, which keeps near the shore, and breeds there in spring; 2. The open-sea seal, that affects the distant rocks and reefs; and 3. The Greenland seal, which, during winter, haunts the Fjörðs. Further details will be found in the Journal.

The Iceland waters show four porpoises, viz. :

1. *Delphinus phocæna*, the common porpoise, smallest of the Cetaceæ.

2. *Delphinus bidens* or *bidentatus*, Baleine à bec, the bottle-head or bottle-nosed whale; the " ca'ing whale " of the Scoto-Scandinavian islands.

3. *Delphinus orca*, the grampus.

4. *Albicans* or white Beluga.

The following are approximate returns for fish and their products exported from Iceland in—

|  | 1806 | 1849 | 1870 |
|---|---|---|---|
| Fish, . . | . 650,000 lbs. (Danish) | ... | ... |
| Dried fish, . | . 750,000 lbs. | 938,080 lbs. | 527,040 lbs. |
| Salt cod, . . | 150 barrels | 5,248,000 lbs. | 7,507,840 lbs. |
| Cod oil, . . | 807 ,, | | |
| Shark oil, . . | 1,663 ,, | 3,259 barrels | 9,424 barrels |
| Seal oil, . . | 24 ,, | | |
| Fish liver, . . | 12 ,, | ... | ... |
| Salted salmon, . | 28 ,, | 5,810 lbs. | 245,392 lbs. |
| Salted shark skins, | 1,568 | ... | ... |

The subjoined table shows what has been the export of cod and oil during the last six years.

---

[1] The three species on the west coast of Scotland are :

1. The Rawn, or Common Seal (*Phoca vitulina*), from five to six feet long; coat, tawny-white, spotted brownish-black on back and sides, with darker haslets and dusky-grey belly. The skin is of short bristly hair, but no fur.

2. The Tapraist, or Grey Seal (*Halichœrus griseus*), somewhat larger than the former ; the muzzle is black, and the coat dirty brown, looking silver-grey only when the sun strikes the recurved hair.

3. The Bodach, or Old Man (Halket, *Halichœrus ?*), somewhat smaller than No. 1, and very easily tamed.

| | 1864. | 1865. | 1866. | 1867. | 1868. | 1869. |
|---|---|---|---|---|---|---|
| Salt-fish, lbs. | 6,296,224 | 2,917,024 | 3,855,104 | 8,026,656 | 3,916,000 | 5,243,744 |
| Dried do. . | 139,040 | 13,728 | 79,904 | 335,280 | 266,464 | 442,816 |
| Salt-roe, brls. | 2,390 | 452 | 770 | 1,962 | 578 | 977 |
| Liver oil, . | 6,572 | 9,520 | 8,952 | 13,083 | 8,757 | 7,744 |

The noteworthy point is the falling off of the salt-fish : perhaps the reason may be the expense of imported salt. During the last century the State established a saltern at Ísafjörð, but it was soon closed for want of patronage—Mr Consul Crowe remarks, " The very high temperature of the numerous hot springs which are quite accessible, would give an ever ready heat applicable for evaporation, and, I believe, a fresh attempt to utilise them would repay itself." But salting is ever difficult.

It must be observed, of this table, that no account is kept of the quantity reserved for home consumption, which is doubtless large—the daily bread of some 70,000 souls. The general belief, however, is that the greater proportion of the catch is exported. Mr Consul Crowe thus calculates, according to the prices current during their respective years, the value of the average year's export.

| | S. Amt. | W. Amt. | N. & E. Amt. | Whole Island. | |
|---|---|---|---|---|---|
| | Value Rds. | Value Rds. | Value Rds. | Quantities. | Value in Rds. |
| Salt-fish, . | 215,229 | 87,171 | 609 | 5,078,898 lbs. | 303,009 |
| Dried do. . | 12,120 | 5,370 | 720 | 213,664 ,, | 18,210 |
| Salt-roe, . | 5,910 | 30 | ... | 1,188 brls. | 5,940 |
| Liver oil, . | 33,352 | 65,890 | 101,068 | 9,105 ,, | 200,310 |
| Total, | 266,611 | 158,461 | 102,397 | ... | Rds. 527,469 |

The following figures show the export of cod from the beginning of the seventeenth century when the system of monopolies was introduced.

| | | | | | | |
|---|---|---|---|---|---|---|
| In A.D. 1624 it was of lbs. 2,273,440 | | | In A.D. 1806 it was of lbs. 1,440,400 | | | |
| ,, 1743 ,, 2,057,680 | | | ,, 1840 ,, 5,375,040 | | | |
| ,, 1772 ,, 3,091,200 | | | ,, 1855 ,, 7,705,280 | | | |
| ,, 1784 ,, 2,845,920 | | | ,, 1868 ,, 4,202,240 | | | |

The peculiarity of this table is the immense irregularity of the figures.

A few model establishments, like the Newfoundland, scattered round the island would teach the best and cheapest way of curing fish—now a barbarous process of turning, scraping, splitting, and housing, without "stages," "platforms," or other necessaries. The substitution of improved decked and half-decked smacks for the open row-boats actually in use, would save the time and toil at present wilfully wasted: improvement of the fishing lines is also urgently wanted. But the initiative must come from Denmark or, at least, from abroad; Iceland has remained so hopelessly in the background that she has not the means, even if she has the will, to help herself.

Piscator in Iceland will do somewhat better than Venator: he will find the lakes, lakelets, and rivers which do not issue directly from snow-mountains, rich in fish. The salmon ascends the streams as far as their cataracts; it is finer for the table than that supplied by our home market. The trout, speckled and white-fleshed, is not worth eating: the Forelle,[1] or red char (*Salmo Alpinus*), called "sea-trout" in the Scoto-Scandinavian islands, and elsewhere "salmon-trout," is coarse and rank—too trouty, as the red mullet of the Levant is too mullety. Some travellers limit the weight to four pounds; others increase it to ten and even fifteen. At the outlet of the Thingvalla Lake the maximum of twenty-five, brought to bank in a few hours, was seven pounds, and only two were under six pounds; but the char does not give such good sport as the white-fleshed. Fishing may be had within a few hours of Reykjavik, and a day shadowed with dense clouds after a burst of sun will soon fill the basket. But the sport is uncivilised like the land. The fish either rush at the bait, "snapping at flies," as Icelanders say, and swallowing the food before it touches water, or they lie sulking and will not be persuaded to rise. Some travellers curiously assert that in

---

[1] Forelle is German and Danish; the general Icelandic name of trout is Silungr, but, as might be expected, the nomenclature is rich. Hooker notices this char (i. 97). The "suburtingur" of Baring-Gould (Appendix, 423), a fresh-water fish with pink-coloured flesh and sometimes weighing twenty pounds, does not appear in the Dictionary.

a region full of gnats and midges, the fish, and especially the
trout, are " unaccustomed to flies." The contrary is the case,
but the preference greatly varies; some find the only rule that
darker colours are usually bit at most greedily; while others
declare the fish fondest of artificial minnows, spoon-bait, or flies
with any kind of tinsel, when not to be tempted by the ordinary
loch fly. The author's friends tried in turns the black midge;
the grilse; the black hackle, with silver wing; the Hofland's
fancy, red body and partridge wing; the common cow-dung; the
marsh brown; the red fly, with jay's wing; and the woodcock
wing, with body banded red and orange. The fisherman should
bring out the ordinary trout-hook and salmon-bait which he uses
at home, always remembering that the spring in Iceland is a
month to six weeks later than that of Scotland. He must not
neglect to provide himself with gloves and face-veil to keep out
the "midges" which, under that humble name, sting as severely
as the mosquitoes of the tropics.

## § 5. Industry.

The principal occupation of the women is spinning yarn
during the summer, and knitting and weaving in winter. A
rude loom fixed and upstanding, not a little like that of ancient
Egypt and of modern Central Africa, and worked, as in negro-
land, by both sexes, stands in every farm.[1] A good hand can
weave three yards a day. The Vaðmál[2] is the Danish Vadmel,
and the Wadmaal, Wadmal, or Shetland Claith of the Scoto-Scandinavian archipelago; it much resembles the tweeled cloth or
frieze worn by the Leith fishermen and the Media-lana of
Northern Italy.

There is only one kind of Wadmal generally worn, but in
most parts of the island, and especially in the east, there are finer
qualities used for " store-clothes " and woman's attire. The

---

[1] A description and plate are found in Ólafsson.
[2] The word Vaðmál (pron. *Vathmowl*) is derived from Váð, Vóð, or Voð, stuff,
cloth, weeds (*e.g.*, widows' "weeds"); and Mál, a measure—"stuff-measure,"
because it was the standard of all value and payment before a coinage came into
use (Cleasby). The form "Wadmal" will here be preserved, although England
prefers "Wadmill," *e.g.*, in "Wadmill-till" for waggons.

Ormadúkr is worked like drill, the Einskepta like twill. It is sold by the ell, or two Danish feet (= $2\frac{2}{3}$ English feet), at the following rates—the breadths being 2 to 2·5 feet and the length indefinite:

| | | | | |
|---|---|---|---|---|
| Coarse or common, . . . | $0 3 0 to $0 3 | 8 per ell. |
| Middling, . . . . . | 0 4 8 ,, 0 5 | 0 ,, |
| Fine and thin (skarlat), . . | 0 5 0 ,, 1 0 | 0 ,, |

The manufacture varies in the several Quarters. The usual colours are grey, black, light-blue, and murret (Icel. Mórautt), the moret or russet-brown of the undyed wool; white is sometimes seen, but not the red—now confined to tradition. It is excellent stuff, durable, and, after a fashion, waterproof. The moderns prefer to this home-made article the cheap broad-cloths and long-cloths of European machinery; and so in West Africa we find the admirable "native" *pagnes* becoming too expensive for everyday work.

Details concerning the goldsmith's trade will be found in the Journal. The principal is silver filagree, which will compare with that of Norway, but poorly with the work of Genoa, Malta, Delhi, and Trichinopoly.

A few hands find employment as pilots.[1] They are licensed

---

[1] The following is the translation of the "Advertisement to mariners who enter the harbour of Reykjavik:"

"In pursuance of the laws, and under the punishment fixed by law, the following rules are to be attended to by the masters and crews of vessels that touch at the port of Reykjavik.

"1. As suspected, with regard to health, are considered all vessels (*a*) coming from countries or places where pestilential or epidemic diseases are found; (*b*) having merchandises on board, which are brought from such countries or places, or there packed up; (*c*) having had during the voyage, or having at the arrival, any sick person on board, whose disease can be considered as ill-natured or contagious; (*d*) having had, on the sea or near the land, communication with any vessel from suspected or infected places. Such vessels are bound, at the arrival to the harbour, to hoist a green flag, or, in default of such a one, their national flag on the maintop, with which they remain lying, until further order is given.

"As to other vessels, against whom there is no reason for suspicion of this kind, the masters thereof are peremptorily enjoined to land first at the bridge of Quarantine (distinguished by a green flag), to be submitted to the legal examination of the state of health of their crew, and to produce their bill of health, if they have any. Before this is done, nobody from the vessel is permitted to go on shore. The landing can take place from 8 o'clock A.M. to 8 o'clock P.M.

"2. It is the duty of the master, when arrived on shore, instantly to present himself in the Police Office for showing there his ship's documents and clearances. Loading or unloading is not permitted before this is performed, and Icelandic maritime pass redeemed. Commerce on board with the inhabitants ('speculant-

without fee by the Sýslumenn; and in the district of a professional pilot, men cannot ply the trade without this permission.
Found at all the commercial establishments, they are generally
farmers; he of Vopnafjörð is a cooper : a flag hoisted at the
fore is the usual signal. The pay is not settled; upon the
eastern coast they demand $2 per mast; the "Queen" paid $6,
her funnel, it is presumed, being counted as a mast. The Reykjavik pilot may make £10 per annum. All these gentry come
or stay away as they please, even when the Danish steamer
heaves in sight.

The post office, that best of standards for taking the measure
of civilisation, also employs a few hands. The postmaster-
general resides at Copenhagen; the departmental-chief at Reykjavik is Hr O. Finsen, an Icelander, brother to the Amtmand
of the Færoe Islands. He keeps a book-store, and sells station-
ery, plain and fancy, in the Parson's Gréen, opposite the French
Consul's; he speaks English, and nothing can exceed his civility
to strangers. The tariff which he gave the author was as follows :
Ship letters weighing three Danish kvints, or half-an-ounce Eng-

---

trade') is not permitted, except after a previous information thereof to the Policemaster.

"3. When any of the crew commits disorders on shore, it will be examined
how far the master himself can be considered as responsible for such offences committed by his crew, especially when he has permitted them to remain on shore
till late in the evening or night.

"4. In order that the breeding of the Eider ducks in the islands in the neighbourhood of the harbour (Viðey, Engey, etc.) shall not be disturbed, no firing of
cannons, except in cases of distress, or as to men-of-war, in what the service ex-
acts, is permitted within half-a-mile Danish (about two and a half miles English),
or of guns within a quarter of a mile Danish (one and a quarter English) from the
said islands. Nor is it permitted to go on shore on the uninhabited islands surrounding or near the harbour (Effersey, Akurey), without a special permission
from the owner; hunting or disturbances of the breeding of the birds in these
places are, accordingly to the laws concerned, punished with peculiar severity.

"5. It is prohibited to take ballast on the ground or beach belonging to the
town, except in places pointed out by the Policemaster. Throwing overboard
of the ballast may not at all take place on the harbour, and not in other places
than such as will be pointed out by the police.

"6. Water to the use of mariners may only be taken in places pointed out by
the police. As water money every vessel of the burthen of above forty tons pays
for each voyage one rixdollar Danish; of less burthen, half a rixdollar.

"Given in the Police Office of Reykjavik, July 4, 1870,
"(Signed)  A. THORSTEINSON.

"N.B.—This advertisement, which is delivered by the pilot, and from the
Police Office, is made for the use of sailors. Wanting notion of it does not exempt
from liability to punishment for offences, mentioned or not mentioned here, that
are committed by mariners."

lish, pay 14 skillings for three postage stamps, one of 8, and two. of 3 skillings, a total of 3½d., which is exorbitant. A similar sum is charged for every three additional kvints, or 8d. an ounce. Newspapers pay 3½d. for eight kvints; parcels 1s. 6d., and larger packages 9d. per cubic foot.

"Postal delivery" is of course unknown, even at the capital; the same was the case at New York fifteen years ago. The inland post was very poorly managed, but something was done in 1872 to remedy the main grievance. At Copenhagen the ship-postage could be paid, not the land transit; consequently the letters for the out-stations, unless re-posted by a friend, lay for an indefinite time at the Reykjavik office. It was common to see despatches written in January received on the eastern coast in July. The Althing has now established branches at the several stations where the steamers stop; and the sum of $30 per annum is paid for an immense amount of work; perhaps Iceland is not singular in this matter. There is a northern courier-road which takes five days viâ Reykholt and Arnarvatns-heiði to Akureyri, but in winter it is impassable. No regular overland communication connects the western with the eastern coast, which the postman visits a few times during the year; and if there be any duly prepaid letters for the dangerous southern shore, the same courier will run that way.

A favourite occupation in Iceland is gathering the eider down (Æðar-dún)—the Édredon so celebrated as a non-conductor of heat. It is best in the coldest climates, like Greenland; here it is good, especially after a wet season, when the birds lay most. In the Færoe Islands, and off the Northumberland coast, it is not worth collecting for sale; and the same is the case in the Orkneys and Shetlands. For instance, the people of Rousay, an island of some thirty square miles, do not preserve their "dunters" (Somateria dispar?); they eat the bird after the breeding season, in August or September, and they pickle the eggs for winter use. The eider is found in the Pacific, but only on the northern coasts of Asia and America.

The first lay of eggs, beginning in May and ending six or seven weeks afterwards, is from four to six; the second from two to four, and the third from two to three; if not carried off, they will accumulate from ten to sixteen. The duck gives about an ounce of down each time the house is robbed, or three nests yield a total of half-a-pound. After the third *ponte*, the drake contributes an ounce and a half of whiter material, easily distinguished; and if further outrage be offered, the unhappy couple quit the bereaved home. Older authors speak only of eggs (egg-ver), never of the down; and it is believed that the English trade in the fifteenth and sixteenth centuries brought the name and the article into foreign markets. Jón í Brokey (born A.D. 1584), who learned the art and mystery of cleaning in England, introduced it here; and the rude process is still preserved. An open sieve is made of yarn stretched over a hoop, and the feathers are stirred with a pointed stick. Thus the finer material (gras-dún) remains above, the coarser stuff (thang-dún, or seaweed down) and the heterogeneous matter fall through—this operation reduces the yield to about half. The work is done by men and women, in autumn and winter. The *Édredon* taken from the dead fowl loses elasticity, and is of little value.

The annual supply of Iceland was 2000 lbs. in 1806; it gradually rose to 5000 or 6000, valued at about £5000 ; and in 1870 it was 7909 lbs. The two islets, Viðey and Engey, off Reykjavik, have produced as much as 300 lbs. in a year. About 1½ lbs. are required for an average coverlet. The clean lb. in 1809 cost $3; in 1854 (Pliny Miles), 50 cents = 2s. 2d.; in 1860 (Preyer and Zirkel), from $2·66 to $4·53; in 1862 (Shepherd), 12s. to 15s.; and in 1872, $7 to $8. As the cleaned material sells in England for 18s. to 19s. per lb., and the uncleaned for 8s., little profit can be made out of it. In "Some Notes on Greenland, etc." (Alpine Journal, Aug. 1873), Mr Edward Whymper says still more: "At Copenhagen, eider down is worth 20s. per lb., yet in London, quilts weighing 4½ lbs. are sold for 36s. How much chopped straw and old feathers has the British tradesman to insert in order to realise his honest profit ?"

Eider down is the *haute volée* of its kind. Most of the sea-fowl, especially the Lundi or puffin (*Fratercula Mormon*), when purified of its peculiar pediculus, supply feathers for exportation. Since 1866, this branch of industry sent annually some 18,000 or 19,000 lbs.; and in 1870 it was 32,081 lbs. Almost every bed has its feather quilt; and the Devonshire superstition that no one can die comfortable on a mattress stuffed with goose feathers is quite unknown.

Iceland moss (*Lichen Islandicus, Cetraria Islandica*), by the people called Fjalla-grös (neut. plur.), is still an article of export. As the native name shows, it is the gift of the hills. We find it on the Brocken, in the Carpathians, the dolomites of Tyrol and Italy (where it is called "Lichene"), and in other parts of Europe. The brown-green leaf, with deeply palmated edges, much resembles sunburnt and withered dandelion. It must be washed in several waters, to remove the bitter astringent taste, before it is eaten with cream and sugar. Of late years, it has been partially superseded by the amylaceous "Carrigeen Moss," grown on the green terraces of the Ardmore Cliffs. This succedaneum, after being sun-dried, and allowed to receive one or two showers, is again dried, packed in bags, prepared for sale, and used to make tea or blancmange. Uno Von Troil (p. 108), or rather Eggert Ólafsson, gives a list of five lichens, each with its Icelandic name; and Baring-Gould (p. 438) names eight lycopods. Peirce (p. 82) distinguishes this "Fell-grass" from a "sort of fjall-grass, which is used for making gruel."

A small quantity of wild Angelica (*Archangelica;* Icel. Hvönn), though held to be poisonous in the United States, is exported for comfitures; in Iceland, it no longer, as of old, flavours ale, nor is it used as a vegetable. The warm root is chewed, or put into soup; and when cut into pieces, it is stored in bottles of brandy and schnaps, giving an aromatic taste. The Umbellifer, grown near houses, is less valued than the hill plant; animals seem to despise both. The Færoese "Quonn" has a stem thick as a man's wrist; the bitter, astringent rind is removed before the plant flowers and becomes woody, and the stalk, preserved in sugar, is eaten like the leaves, with sweetened milk.

The simples collected for use are the Holta-rót (*Silene acaulis*, or moss campion); the Alchemilla or Burnet, a sanguisorb; the Geldinga-rót (*Statice armeria*); the Speedwell (*Veronica officinalis*); and various gentians. The "ptarmigan-leaf," or mountain avens (*Dryas octopetala*, the Holta-Sóley of older travellers, and the modern Rjúpa-lyng) makes a tea good for jaundice; the root also is eaten. The half-digested flowers of the blaeberry (*Vaccinium myrtillus*) and the bog-whortle (*V. uliginosum*) are taken from the ptarmigan's crop to make ptisane. The reindeer moss (*Cenomyce rangiferina*), a small pale-green species, with hollow stem, is gathered for sheep-feeding. The wild geranium also produces a blue tint, of old called Odin's dye.

Of late years, a little business has been done in women's hair for the European market. First three Jews came out, then two, and lastly one was found sufficient to manage the trade—we shall meet him in the Journal. They cleared about £300, exaggerated to £3000, especially by the *blond cendré*, the most expensive item of the £300,000 annually imported by England. As a rule, Iceland demands, instead of supplying, false hair; in 1871 about 200 lbs. were introduced in the shape of chignons and braids.

Another produce of the island is Iceland spar, which is mentioned in Fortia's "Sweden" as "calcareous spar which doubles the object." This "Silfr" or "Silbr-berg," the "Calcite" of Dana, is crystallised carbonate of lime, useful for polarising-instruments. The main axis being disposed at a different angle from the minor or bi-axis, causes it to be doubly refracting; moreover, the former expands, whilst the latter contracts. Thus all blood-crystals, to specify no other rhombs and hexagons, show two parallel lines where only one exists: the white spaces receiving the light transmit it to the retina.

Calcite is produced chiefly on the eastern coast, but its existence is reported in many places where the peculiar tenure of ground deters the farmer from attempting to better his property. The author heard of it on the slopes of the Esja and at Berufjörð. The principal mine is at Reyðarfjörð—not at Seyðisfjörð as generally asserted. The present contractor is a certain Hr Tullenius, who, by private arrangement, pays one-fourth to the Crown and three-fourths of the lease to the Church in the person of his father-in-law, pastor of the Hofs parish. His establishment is at Eskifjörð to the north-west of Reyðarfjörð, and he transports the material in winter by sledges to the coast where it is shipped direct for England.

The spar is taken from calcined basalt, apparently infiltrated there in small veins alternating with a green mineral supposed to be the plutonic stone transformed; the surface is often rough with a zeolitic or calcareous coat. Large pieces have been found: Paijkull mentions one in the Copenhagen museum which was bought for $400 and weighed 176 pounds. Till late years it was rare and expensive; the geological museum in Jermyn Street contained (1872) only a shabby little bit, and a certain professor bought for £6 what was worth £60. In these days Mr T. Tennant (naturalist, the Strand) and Mr J. Browning (optician, Strand and Minories) can produce hundreds of pounds lying useless. The smaller pieces now cost one shilling to one shilling and sixpence per pound. The best and most valuable specimens are the large prisms; the worst when cut show spotted surfaces or prove full of flaws running right through; some, like amber, contain red clay, drops of water, and other heterogeneous substances. They can be tested only by the electric light, and even that sometimes fails to detect faults which appear after working. A friend commissioned the author to bring home a large specimen, purchaseable after trial—he knew little of the islandry. It is dearer, as usual, in Iceland than in London: the people think that all the world wants their one popular mineral.

The following branches of industry still await development:

Iron-ore certainly exists, but it is hard to see, with the present scarcity of coal and wood, what use can be made of it: should peat companies prove a success, it may still appear in the market. Copper has been reported to occur in the jasper formation, and cupriferous specimens have, it is said, been brought to Reykjavik from the great Hrauns of the Skaptárjökull, the centre of supply being at the Blængr mountain in the Vestr Skaptár Sýsla. Professor Winkler of Munich found, on dit, quicksilver at Mőðru-vellir on the way to Akureyri. The Tindastóll Range, west of the Skagafjörð, has yielded galena embedded in amethyst-quartz: and we shall see silver glance. The cryolite, so abundant in Greenland,[1] is found here and in Norway: the late Mr Ander-

---

[1] The "Napoleon book" (p. 364), gives a sketch of a "mine de criolithe:" one of the veins embedded in granite is eighty feet thick. Mr Walker (Peirce's Report, p. 3) is mistaken in asserting that cryolite is found only in Greenland,

son met with large blocks, they say, at Vestdalr; and the Abbé Baudoin assured the author that he had seen it on the Seyðisfjörð, which opens to the north-east, near a stream north of, and about twenty minutes' walk from, Vestdalr. There are large supplies of fine obsidian, jasper, zeolites, and chalcedonies.

Mr Consul Crowe (Report, 1870-71) supplies the following statistics of " domestic industry," which, however, is confined to woollen articles:

| | 1864. | 1865. | 1866. | 1867. | 1868. | 1869. |
|---|---|---|---|---|---|---|
| Two - threaded guernseys, pieces, | 85 | 143 | 50 | 134 | 185 | 85 |
| One-threaded do. do. | 22 | ... | ... | ... | .. | 59 |
| Two-threaded stockings, prs. | 41,561 | 34,347 | 37,422 | 41,025 | 60,976 | 76,816 |
| One-threaded ,, ,, | 1,008 | 298 | 412 | 884 | 908 | 1,092 |
| Socks, ,, | 13,254 | 37,101 | 10,930 | 7,673 | 5,247 | 28,431 |
| Mittens (one-fingered), | 14,672 | 14,736 | 26,904 | 53,267 | 29,873 | 55,601 |
| ,, (full-fingered), | 1,623 | 1,325 | 744 | 825 | 976 | 69 |
| Wadmal, yards, | 176 | 549 | 249 | 805 | 569 | 280 |

but doubtless the largest known supplies are there, the development being due in great part to American (U.S.) enterprise. The natives used it only in the pulverised state—like quartz—to " lengthen out " their snuff; and similarly the " Red Indians " of the Brazil utilised their diamonds as counters. This double fluoride of sodium and aluminium, popularly called natural soda, is a mineral of ever increasing value ; it is employed in the manufacture of soda and soda-salts, hydrofluoric acid, fine glass, and earthenware almost infrangible ; the residue makes a flux ("Steven's flux," etc.) capital for the treatment of difficult metallic ores. Perhaps the chief use is in the manufacture of aluminium and its alloys, a noble metal which can be carried to white heat before it oxidises, and whose brilliancy is unaltered by sulphuretted hydrogen, water, acids, salts, and organic matter. The price till lately was about one-third that of silver, but increased cheapness has extended the use, especially in coinage and jewellery. Tenacious as silver, sonorous, easily melted and moulded, about as hard as soft iron, and one-third the weight of zinc ; it is valuable for watch-cases, mirrors, spectacleframes, opera and field glasses, hand-bells, pendulum-rods, small weights and balances, chemical apparatus, instruments of precision, and articles where lightness is required. It has also been converted into dinner services and cooking apparatus, in which, unlike tin and copper, it is absolutely harmless. The common form is *bronze d'aluminium*, with one of that metal to ten parts of copper ; the tenacity of the alloy is about that of steel.

Of which the annual exported value is:

| | S. Amt. | W. Amt. | N. & E. Amt. | Whole Island. | |
|---|---|---|---|---|---|
| | Value Rds. | Value Rds. | Value Rds. | Quantities. | Value. |
| Two-threaded guernseys, | ... | ... | $95 | 114 pieces | $95 |
| One-threaded    ,, | $6 | $3 | ... | 14 ,, | 9 |
| Two-threaded stockings, | 57 | 120 | 14,024 | 48,691 pairs | 14,201 |
| One-threaded    ,, | ... | 32 | 112 | 767 ,, | 144 |
| Socks, . . . . | ... | 9 | 3,554 | 17,106 ,, | 3,563 |
| Mittens (one-fingered), . | 93 | 497 | 2,119 | 32,509 ,, | 2,709 |
| ,, (full-fingered), . | ... | 23 | 286 | 927 ,, | 309 |
| Wadmal, yards, . . | 15 | 9 | 188 | 657 yards | 212 |
| Total, | 171 | 693 | 20,378 | ... | $21,242 |

The same Report shows:

" Total value of collective exports, . . . Rds. 1,103,936
    Equal to, for each individual, . . .   ,,     15·88

"The value, therefore, of an average year's export of fish, farm-produce, and domestic industry was in 1870 $1,103,936; to this may be added the other known articles of export, such as"—

Eider-down, . . . . . . . . Rds. 38,064
Feathers, . . . . . . . . ,,  9,848
Horses, . . . . . . . . ,, 10,472
Salmon and other fish, swan-down, fox-skins, etc., ,, 96,064

Making the total exports from the island, . . $1,200,000

              Or, sterling, . . £133,333
Equal to about £1, 18s. 4d. per head of population.

The conclusion to which the reporter arrives from these tables is, that "nearly all the cod and roe is fished and exported from the western districts, and that the shark fishery and export of liver-oil takes place from the north side.

"On the other hand, the cattle and sheep-rearing, whose produce is greater than that of the fisheries, centres in the northern and eastern parts of the island, where the excellent natural grass pastures are formed in abundance."

## § 6. EMIGRATION.

Modern emigration was not attempted till fourteen years ago, and the islanders chose the worst destination they could find—the Brazil. In 1862, the trial was renewed by some eighty head, with the same want of success, except in two or three instances; and ten years later, about fifty left to "plant man" in the tropical empire. The report is, that they were decimated by cholera at Hamburg. A far more auspicious movement was made to Minnesota, Milwaukee, and Wisconsin: the head was a retired trader, Einar Björnsson, who bought an island in Lake Superior. Shortly before the author's arrival at Reykjavik, a small party of fourteen or seventeen had sailed, not 714, as asserted by certain English papers. The later emigrants sent home glowing reports of the country and, although those in the towns were not so successful, the rural settlers did remarkably well. And the movement will be beneficial to the islander, who, instead of dawdling away life at home, will learn to labour and to wait upon a more progressive race.

In the summer of 1873, these pioneers were followed by 200 to 220 recruits, of whom a portion preferred Canada, and is said to be doing well. The autumn of 1874 sent out 340; the men were employed on the Toronto railway, and some 40 women went into service. As yet, emigration has not had a fair trial; and Icelanders, a pastoral and fishing race, are wholly unaccustomed to agriculture and manufacturing. At the same time, they have the advantage of being to a certain extent mechanics as well as labourers. The Norwegian papers, which are translated and spread over the island, strongly recommended the movement; consequently the authorities at Reykjavik, and the official class in general, as strongly opposed it; but, it need hardly be said, their prejudices are not shared by the distinguished Dr Hjaltalín. If this be, as we apprehend, the movement of a people seeking, like the Irish and the Basques, a new "racial baptism," it may assume important dimensions. It might well be worth while for the Dominion to secure a number of these sturdy and strong-brained

Northerners, who would form admirable advanced posts along the valley of the Sasketchawan. The author's companion in travel, Mr Chapman, had the acuteness at once to see the use that might be made of the movement, and proposed recommending the Government of New Zealand to take advantage of it. The common order of Icelanders show the greatest interest in America, and strangers are always subjected to cross-examination on the subject. If the current be allowed to set that way, efforts to arrest it will not be easily checked: for many years the author has wondered how and why a poor man ever lives in Europe, or a rich man in America.

## SECTION VIII.

### TAXATION—COINS, WEIGHTS, AND MEASURES —PRICES AND IMPORTS—COMMUNICATION AND COMMERCE—VISIT TO THE STORE.

#### § 1. TAXATION.

The system has the serious drawback of being complicated and troublesome; on the other hand, it dates from olden days, and is familiar to the people. The island is not, and of late years never has been, self-supporting. The whole revenue does not exceed $44,000, and the expenditure for official salaries, ecclesiastical and legal establishments, and education, being about one-third more ($62,000), the Home Government must supply the deficiency.[1]

It has before been observed that property in Iceland, as in older England, is measured not by extent, but by produce, the area in fact never being ascertained. The basis of calculation is the ell of Wadmal, or its equivalent, two heads of fish and a

---

[1] This again is the popular assertion which has been strongly opposed by Mr Jón A. Hjaltalín (see note at end of Section III.). The reader, however, will observe that the patriotic Icelander confesses to the figures in the text, as matters now stand.

fraction bringing it up to nearly 2·50. The hundred [1] was either tísætt hundrað (the decimal hundred, 10 × 10), introduced with Christianity, and now chiefly used in ecclesiastic and scholastic matters, or tólfrætt hundrað (duodecimal, 12 × 10), the latter being the root of the English system, which has hitherto successfully resisted foreign innovations. Hence our farmers long retained in selling cheese the great hundred (120 lbs.) and the little hundred (112 lbs.). The old adage says—

> " Six score of men, money, and pins,
> Five score of all other things."

And the " shock," or half (60), is preserved in the German threat, "Shock schweren noth" (You want five dozen)!

In old times, there was a double standard: (1.) The hundrað talið, hundred (of wool, etc.) by tale = 120 ells; and (2.) The hundrað vegið (weight) or sifrs (of silver), in rings, coin, and so forth, the latter = 2½ marks = 20 ounces = 60 örtugar, the half örtug being probably the unit. The phrase, "Six ells to an ounce" (*i.e.*, 120 ells = 20 ounces), refers to silver and Wadmal at par; but, as the coinage was debased, the 6 became successively 9, 10, 11, and 12.

In 1810, the absolute value of the hundrað represented :

One milch cow or two horses (each = 60 ells).

A proportionate number of sheep (= six to eight) and lambs (= eighteen); each milch ewe = 20 ells in spring, and each wether = 10 ells.

One fishing-boat, with six oars, nets, and lines.

$46 in specie.

In 1872, the proportion was:

One bull, bullock, ox, or cow, calf-bearing or not.

Two horses or three mares, four years old or upwards; riding-horses = two-thirds of the hundred.

Six milch or eight milkless ewes; six wethers, three years old, and older; ten wethers, two years old; or eighteen sheep, one or two years old.

---

[1] The political sense of 120 franklins, several of which composed the English shire, is unknown to Iceland.

All boats, large and small:[1] the oars are not counted, but the nets and lines which follow the boat are reckoned at half-a-hundred. The half-decked vessel, with nets and lines, ranges from 100 to 1·50.

$40 in specie: $20 represent the half hundred, and nothing below it is cessible.

240 head of fish, which must weigh 2 lbs. In 1770, 48 head were = $1 (specie); the value often changes, but the modern rate of the Fiskvirði (worth) may be assumed at about 12⅜ skillings (or in round numbers, 3d.).

In 1770, 24 ells of Wadmal = $1: now the ell may represent 24¾ skillings.

Former travellers represented the direct taxes to be tithes, church and poor rates, with the Sýslumenn's stipends ($1·50 specie, according to Hooker). They also divided the items of taxation into five, viz.:

1. Skattr, Scat, or tribute,[2] originally the poll-tax levied by the king on the franklins (Skattbændr), and afterwards more generally applied. This cess is paid when movable property in hundreds (cows, sheep, etc.) exceeds the number of individuals composing the household, or to be maintained upon the form. De Kerguelen describes it as a "tax of twelve francs contributed by heads of houses whose income surpasses sixty francs." In 1810 it was represented by 4·50 skillings per ell of Wadmal, converted into specie, or so many fishes, twenty-four to thirty head being = $4 to $5. In 1872 it is neither more nor less than forty; for instance, a household of seven souls and eight hundreds pays forty fishes, and the same sum would be levied upon seven souls and ten hundreds. All officials, priests, and candidates of theology, are exempt from this tax.

2. Gjaf-tollr (gift toll) was so called because at first it was supposed to be, or rather it was, a voluntary payment to the Sýslumaðr and Prófastr for overlooking or winking at small offences punishable by a fine. It is said to have been paid as

---

[1] The "Sharker," moreover, pays a variable sum (say 24 skillings) per barrel of oil as an hospital tax, and this is now appropriated to the district physician.

[2] Compare the German Schatze and our Scot in Scot-free, Scot and Shot; Róma-skattr would be Peter's Pence.

early as 1380. The French traveller, who held it to be a voluntary contribution for supporting legal establishments, lays it down
at sixty centimes to six francs. The rate of Gjaf-tollr, which
also is levied only on movable property, now represents :

| | | | |
|---|---|---|---|
| 1 fish per . . 50 | 5 fish per . 400 |
| 2 ,, . . 100 | 10 ,, . . 500 to 900 |
| 3 , . . 200 | 12 ,, . . 1000 to 1200 |
| 4 , . . 300 | 20 ,, . . 1200 |

And above 1200 nothing more is taken.

3. Lögmannstollr dates from the days of Icelandic independence, and, representing the salaries of the Presidents of Things
(assemblies), was preserved in memory of the ancient grandeur
of the island. Formerly, it was thirty-five centimes per head of
house. It is independent of hundreds, and paid in money at the
rate of 6¾ skillings per farm. In case of sub-letting, it increases; for instance, if a proprietor leases half his land to another man, both pay 4½ skillings. The Sýslumaðr receives one-
sixth for the trouble of collecting it, and the rest is paid into
the public Treasury of Reykjavik under the Landfógeti.

4. Althingistollr was a property tax paid, according to
Cadastre, for the support of the Diet. Each deputy formerly
received nine francs per diem, and now $3, besides his travelling
expenses coming and returning home.

5. Tíund, or tithe, paid to the Crown: these have been discussed in the ecclesiastical section.

The present complicated system will best be explained by a
copy of the Thinggjaldskvittunarbók or Receipt Book for the
Thinggjald, the general taxes. Each large farmer keeps one,
and the forms are printed either at Reykjavik or at Akureyri.
The following will be filled up as the specimen of cesses levied
upon a large merchant who hires a farm from the Church:

| Ár (year) 1868. | Fólkstala (number of household), 22. | Jarðarhundrað (landed property), none. | Lausafjarhundrað (movable property), 27 hundreds. | | |
|---|---|---|---|---|---|
| | | Fiskar (fishes). | Rixdollars. $ | Skilling (estimated at 96 : $1). | |
| Skattur, | | 40 | | | |
| Gjaftollr, | | 20 | | | |
| Tíund (royal tithe), | | 16·2 | | | |
| Til Samans (total), | | 76·2 | 9 | 50½ | |
| Lögmannstollr, | | ... | ... | 4½ | |
| Thinghústollr, | | ... | ... | 4 | |
| Jafnaðarsjóðsgjald, | | ... | 2 | 24 | |
| Althingisgjald, | | ... | 0 | 0 | |
| Allt gjaldið samlagt (grand total), | | | 11 | 83 | |

The Skattur forms the chief item of the income of the Sýslumaðr.

The Lögmannstollr is still devoted to paying law taxes.

The Thinghústollr, or charges for provincial assemblies, is always four skillings; the householder where the meetings take place pays the same sum, and receives it back as part of the hire of the room. It directly derives from the old Thingfarar-kaup (fee for travelling to the Parliament, as judges, jurors, witnesses, etc.) levied upon every franklin; and those who did not pay it could neither sit as arbiter nor as "neighbour." The Thingheyjandi (Thing-performer) received a sum proportioned to the number of days' journeys he and his retinue had to travel.

The Jafnaðarsjóðsgjald is also called Sakamálatollr, i.e., a repartition fund paid to the Amt or Quarter for public purposes, posts, roads, criminal prosecutions, and other unforeseen expenses. All who have one and a half hundreds in movable property must contribute, and the Amtmenn settle every year the sum required, and the proportion appertaining to individuals.

The merchant contributes no Althing-money, because he is not a landed proprietor. This tax is taken from all landed property in the country, except that belonging to the Crown and the Church; three-fourths are paid upon immovable, and the remaining one-fourth upon all movable possessions. Every year, the Hreppstjórar, aided by two landowners of the parish, estimates how much Landskyld (rent) is paid either by the owner of the farm or by his tenants and sub-tenants. The Stiftamtmaðr (governor) having decided upon the sum required, the amount is duly reparted on landed property.

In addition to these taxes the Iceland farmer pays three other tithes—viź., to the priest, the Church, and the poor (16·2·ells, or $4 each)—besides a ljóstoll or light-tax = 4 lbs. of tallow, to illuminate the church: its equivalent being seventy-two skillings. He feeds one lamb for the priest (lambsfóður, or heytollur—hay-tax), or pays its forage = $1, 48sk. Those who own property, movable or immovable, to the amount of twenty hundreds, must also make offur (offertory) to the priest, amounting to not less than $3. Those who own less property than five hundréds, work one day for the priest during the hay-making season, or pay an equivalent of $1, 4sk. By the law of 12th February 1872 an annual tax is levied on landed property, 1½sk. per hundred. For the money thus raised model farms are to be established and young men taught farming. By far the heaviest item of taxation is, however, the poor-rate (fátækra útsvar), over and above the poor tithes, for it is nowhere less than equal in amount to all the other taxes put together, and in some parishes it is even double the amount of all the other taxes. This tax is levied by the Hreppstjóri at the autumnal parish meeting. The pauperism is an evil fraught with imminent danger to the island, and requires the immediate attention of the legislature. It need hardly be suggested that emigration is the perfect cure for the sturdy vagrants who infest the land, and that free passages to America, or elsewhere, would be well laid out.

The taxes in kind (Wadmal, yarn, woollen stuffs, fish, butter, hay, oil, cattle, sheep, tallow, hides, skins, and all vendibles) are estimated by the Hreppstjóri, who transmits his account to the Sýslumaðr, and the latter checks the report by referring to the mean value of the parish. He then commutes what is paid to him into money, through some trading firm; and, as he is liable to loss by the fluctuations of the market, he is allowed to retain one-third by way of remuneration. A " crack collector," to use an Anglo-Indian term, may make as much as $3000 per annum

—though less than half that sum would probably be a high average.

The Sýslumaðr again reports to the Amtmaðr, who checks his accounts by reference to the mean amount of previous revenue, whence results the Kapitulstaxti verðlagsskrá, or chapter value. The specie is then remitted to the Bæarfógeti,[1] or assistant treasurers. These officers are three in number; at Reykjavik, where the holder is also the Sýslumaðr, at Ísafjörð (west), and at Akureyri (north). Thence the total revenue finds its way into the hands of the Landfógeti, or chief treasurer.

The taxes on movable property are considered just and equal. Those on land are not, because the meanest soil pays as much as the best. Another grievance is the unequal distribution of the poor-tax, which is managed differently in different Quarters. For instance, a clerk with a salary of $300 per annum will be charged $10, whilst the priest of the same parish with treble the revenue pays only $20.

## § 2. Coins, Weights, and Measures.

Accounts in Iceland are kept in skillings, marks, and dollars (rigsbankdaler or rixdollars, and specie). The following table shows the comparative English value in

| 1809. | | 1872. |
|---|---|---|
| 1 Skilling = 1 halfpenny | = | { 1 farthing and one-eighth, in round numbers a farthing. |
| 16 Skillings or 1 mark = 8 pence, the local shilling | = | { 4 pence and four-fifths, say fourpence halfpenny. |
| 6 Marks or 1 Rigsbankdaler[2] = 4 shillings | = | { 2 shillings and 3 pence, or 60 cents (U.S.), the local half-crown. |
| 2 Rigsbankdalers = 1 specie dollar = 4 shillings and 6 pence | = | { 4 shillings and 6 pence (the crown). |

The silver mark originally was worth eight ounces (eyrir)[3]

---

[1] The Icelandic word is Fógeti (low Lat. Vocatus, Germ. Vogtie, a bailiwick, hence "Landvogt" Gessler), which dates from the fourteenth century (Cleasby). It corresponds with the Fowd and Grand Fowd, chief magistrate of the Scoto-Scandinavian islands.

[2] In these pages "$" always refers to the rixdollar, which, like the Brazilian milreis, is half the milreis of Portugal or the dollar of the United States.

[3] In the plur. Aurar is supposed to be corrupted from Aurum, as the coins first known to Scandinavia were Roman and Byzantine, Saxon and English. It was

of pure silver; and the eyrir = 6 peningar = 3 ertog. Each of the eight parts represented six ells of Wadmal, and thus the total was = 48 ells. In old times we read of the Örtug, a coin worth one-third of an ounce (eyrir) or twenty peningar (pence). In these days the Ort is worth only one-fifth of the specie dollar, and, being a Norwegian coin, it does not circulate in Iceland. The traveller must beware of Norwegian money, especially paper, which may be offered him by the Leith agent of the Danish steamer—it is perfectly useless, and Hr Salvesen must know it.

The following is the coinage current on the island:

*Copper.*—One skilling and a few old two-skilling bits.

*Base metal.*—Two (the penny), three, four, and eight skillings, the latter being half a mark. Of half-marks there are three or four issues. The old is inscribed " 2½ Skillings Schleswig-Holstein's Courent;" the second bears only " 8 skillings," and the third, or newest, has the figure 8 above and 2 below.

*Silver.*—One mark: of this coin also there are three issues; two old, marked respectively 5 and 6 skillings, and one new, marked 16 skillings. Two marks: now rarely seen. Three marks, or half the rixdollar: very common and very useful. Four marks: an old coin almost obsolete, and generally called " one-third specie," because equal to eight rigsbank skillings. One specie dollar: presenting our crown, and very cumbrous.

According to a royal proclamation of 25th September and 29th December 1873, a new coinage is to take the place of the old one next year. It will consist of

### SILVER MONEY.

| New Coin (Crowns). | | Old Icel. | | | | English Equivalent. | | | |
|---|---|---|---|---|---|---|---|---|---|
| 1 Króna (100 aurar) | = | $4 | 3 | 0 | | £0 | 1 | 1½ | |
| 1 Eyrir | = | 0 | 0 | 0½ | | 0 | 0 | 0 ½ farthing. |
| 4 Krónur | = | 2 | 0 | 0 | | 0 | 4 | 6 | |
| 2 ,, | = | 1 | 0 | 0 | | 0 | 2 | 3 | |
| 50 Aurar | = | 0 | 1 | 8 | | 0 | 0 | 6½ | |
| 25 ,, | = | 0 | 0 | 12 | | 0 | 0 | 3½ | |
| 8 ,, | = | 0 | 0 | 4 | | 0 | 0 | 1¼ | |

applied to coinage opposed to baugr, gold or silver rings. Hence the phrase "Aurar ok óðal," money and land. Ær or Ör was probably the name of a small coin; so the modern Swedish Öre is a coin worth less than a farthing, and the Norsk Ort (contracted from Örttog, Örtug, Ærtog, or Ertog) is the fifth part of a specie dollar (Cleasby). Upon the ancient money of Iceland the reader will consult Dr Dasent's Burnt Njal, ii. 397.

GOLD COIN.[1]

| NEW COIN (Crowns). | | OLD ICEL. | ENGLISH EQUIVALENT. |
|---|---|---|---|
| 20 Króna peningur (20 crown-piece) | = | $10  0  0 | £1  2  3 |
| 10      ,, | = | 5  0  0 | 0  11  1½ |

In travelling through the island it is advisable to carry a few dollars (specie), many half-dollars, and an abundance of marks and half-marks, with smaller pieces useful to pay minor charges. And it is useless to burden one's self with a huge bag on board ship: silver can generally be bought at Reykjavik, with a loss of some five per cent. The Danish bank-notes with Icelandic words on the back are to be avoided, as the peasants distrust an article which a wetting may reduce to a rag. In Denmark there are $5 notes (grey paper, with blue border); $10 (yellow paper, with brown border); $20 (light-green); $50 (brown paper, with straight lines in the ground); and $100 (light-brown paper, with wavy lines). For Iceland there are no bank-notes, but when Paraguay manages to raise a loan, she need not despair of civilising her currency.

In July 1810, according to Mackenzie, the war had made the English sovereign worth 15 paper rixdollars on 'Change; and in 1812 it further rose to $25 paper. The rixdollar at par was then worth four shillings English; as has been seen, like all the smaller coins, it has fallen to a little more than half. In 1872 the metallic value of the English sovereign in Denmark was = $8, 5m. 0sk.; but at Copenhagen it was readily exchanged for $9 to $9, 0m. 4sk. The pound sterling in English silver was worth only $8, 1m. 11sk. At Reykjavik the merchants will not hesitate to offer $8, 4m. 0sk., and some will even attempt $8, 2m. 0sk. The author was once assured by one of the principal tradesmen that the Exchange at Copenhagen was $8, 5m. 0sk; but on consulting the newspaper it was found that this was the price of bills. Thus money-changing becomes a profitable business, realising from five to ten per cent., and strangers will call upon the traveller with the object of " turning " a quasi-honest penny. Yet the simplest way is to take from England sovereigns and ten-pound notes. The foreigner can hardly expect to have

---

[1] In 1872 it was not a legal tender.

a cheque honoured after what has lately happened. The last
blow to the English traveller's credit was dealt in October 1871,
when two yachtsmen "did a little bill" with Hr Thomsen, converted their dollars into sovereigns, and went their way. The
names of the delinquents are well known, but that is no reason
for quoting them.

Weights and measures in Iceland are simply Danish:

| | |
|---|---|
| 3 Kvints | = 1 Lod[1] (half-ounce avoird.). |
| 32 Lods | = 1 Pund (= 1 lb. 1 oz.' 8½ grs.). |
| 16 Punds | = 1 Lispund[2] (roughly our stone). |

Sometimes the Norwegian weights are used, viz.:

| | |
|---|---|
| 2 Lods | = 1 Unze. |
| 8 Unzes | = 1 Mark. |
| 2 Marks | = 1 Skaalpund (10 per cent. more than the English pound avoird.). |
| 12 Skaalpunds | = 1 Bismerpund. |
| 3 Bismerpunds | = 1 Vog (36 lbs.). |
| 16 Skaalpunds | = 1 Lispund. |
| 100 Skaalpunds | = 1 Centner (the hundredweight of Germany, Austria, etc.). |
| 20 Lispunds | = 1 Skippund (320 lbs.). |

Of the length measures:

| | |
|---|---|
| 12 Danish inches | = 1 Foot (= Eng. meas. 12·356 in. or about 67 : 69 ft.). |
| 2 Feet | = 1 Ell (Alen). |
| 24,000 Feet | = { 1 Mile[3] (or 4 = 1° = 4½ English statute miles in round numbers). |

The Norsk measures are the same, but the foot is = 1·029
English, and the mile is of 36,960 feet (= 13,320 English yards
= 7½ English statute miles). The only Icelandic measure of
length is the Thingmanna-leið, or journey of the Thingman,
about twenty English statute miles.

The Danish Pot is = 0·300 gallons; the Kanne is about three
quarts, and the barrel of oil contains between twenty-five and
twenty-six English gallons.

---

[1] The German Loth and the corrupted Italian Lotto.

[2] Uno Von Troil (1770) makes the Lispund = 20 lbs. English, and adds the
Vaett = 5 Lispunds, and the Kapal 12 to 15 Lispunds. Both Lispund and
Bismer are now falling out of use in Iceland, where only the Danish pound is
preserved. She should follow the example of Austria, and introduce the metrical
system.

[3] The Danish mile is the long league; 15 being = 1° of latitude.

## § 3. COMMUNICATION AND COMMERCE.

Export trade began in Iceland from the date of its official colonisation. Long before the Norman Conquest, the Norwegian kings and jarls trafficked with the island. Snorri Sturluson mentions that King Ólaf Haraldsson (Helgi, or the Holy) made much profit by his transactions with Hallur Thorarinsson of Haukdal; and an edict of King Magnús Erlingsson (A.D. 1174) alludes to the annual cargoes of flour and other merchandise sent by the Archbishop of Nidarós. Already in the thirteenth century we find Iceland in commercial relations with England, and a little later with Germany. This "free trade," which was on a considerable scale, presently fell before protection, and it did not recover itself till about the middle of the present century.

In a historical sketch of the island trade, published in 1772, an Icelandic author makes the following deductions:

I. The native trade was most advantageous to the island.

II. The Norwegian was honest.

III. The British was matchless ; of every foreign trade it was the most complete and the most advantageous to the island.

IV. The German trade was unjust ; it was, however, more tolerable than the

V. Danish trade, which took its place.

The union of Calmar (A.D. 1397) made it a royal monopoly, carried on only in vessels belonging to, or licensed by, the Crown. This system lasted till A.D. 1776, and, practically closing the country to all but a few privileged Danes, it was injurious as unjust. The island was thus threatened with the fate of Greenland, whose utter desolation probably resulted from want of home-supplies rather than from Eskimo attacks. English merchants were the principal interlopers, receiving fish in barter for meal and clothes: and in A.D. 1413 one of the first acts of Henry V. was to send five ships to Iceland with letters proposing that the harbours be opened to British hulls.

In A.D. 1602, and again in 1609, Christian IV. prohibited intercourse with the Hanse Towns, the powerful confederacy which had taken the commerce from the hands of the Norwegians and Danes; and in 1620 he bestowed it upon the guilds of Copenhagen, Malmoe, and other ports. They established the first Iceland company, which lasted from A.D. 1620 to 1662. The concession was granted on condition of its paying a small sum for the use of each haven, $2 to the governor for every ship that broke bulk, and contributing to the royal magazines in the Vestmannaeyjar. But when the great piratical irruptions in A.D. 1627 to 1630 proved them unable to provide for, and to protect, the island, as they had undertaken to do, the resentment of the Crown caused the shares of $1000 each to sink to half-price and eventually they fell to nothing.

After A.D. 1662 the trade of each haven was sold to the highest bidder once in every six years. In A.D. 1734 arose the second Iceland company, which paid an annual sum of $6000 to the Crown, and sent twenty-four to thirty ships, frequenting twenty-two havens. This monopoly again was a great grievance; it was injured by smugglers and interlopers, and, by its working, the island fell to its lowest condition. In A.D. 1776 arose the third Iceland company, nominally headed by the Crown, which directed a fund of $4,000,000, provided by the country. At the end of ten years, when the ships and stock were sold, the loss proved to be $600,000; the residue was placed under commissioners, and the latter had the power of lending money to those who embarked in the trade at the rate of 4 per cent.; 10 per cent. being then the legal limit. In A.D. 1787 the commerce, averaging $45,000 per annum, was exempted from all imposts for a period of twenty years, afterwards prolonged for five (A.D. 1812). As has been said, during the Danish war with Great Britain, a humane order in Council (1810) saved the island from absolute starvation. At length, after 250 years of a grinding monopoly, not, however, confined to Denmark, Iceland was finally reopened to free trade by the law which came into action in April 1854. At present there are no restrictions beyond taking out a licence or maritime passport at a cost of two shillings and threepence per ton of the ship's burden. There are, or rather till 1872 there were, no duties on merchandise outwards or inwards, and foreigners now enjoy the same rights of trade, residence, and holding property as the natives.

After April 1854 the imports rose within ten years to a million and a half of rixdollars. Yet something remains to be done in facilitating trade, and especially in the matter of communication, seven mails a year being now utterly inadequate to local requirements.

Sea-passes are usually taken out by foreign ships from Copenhagen, after submitting to medical examination if not provided with clean bill of health, and paying all the legal shipping dues before bulk can be broken, otherwise they must be bought at one of the six following places:[1]

1. Reykjavik, in the south-west.
2. Vestmannaeyjar, south.
3. Stykkishólm, west.
4. Ísafjörð, north-west.
5. Eyjafjörð (Akureyri), north.
6. Eskifjörð, east.

Thus the "Queen" steamer, sent in 1872 for ponies to Berufjörð, could not land cargo without going to Eskifjörð, and returning to her destination—a useless or rather an injurious restriction. She had to pay the Sýslumaðr $1 per ton register, for transmission to the Danish treasury. This compensation for admitting goods duty-free, is a severe tax upon a small charter, and it would certainly be better and fairer to the merchant if the equivalent were levied upon the freight not upon the bottom. Where trade is so poor, every form of nursing should be attended to, and the minimum of protection is here the maximum of benefit.

The whole system of Iceland trade, like that of Shetland and the Færoes, is the "Trust" of the West African oil rivers, so troublesome to consuls and cruisers. The storekeeper must advance goods to the farmer, and the latter refunds him when he can, especially in June and July, September and October, when wool is pulled and wethers are killed. A few of the farmers have money at the merchants, who do not, however, pay interest; many are in debt, and the two classes hardly balance each other. Prices are generally high, but the prohibition category is unknown.

Formerly it was the practice to hold fairs or markets at the

---

[1] Formerly there were only four—viz., Nos. 1, 3, 5, and 6—established by law of April 15, 1854, regulating the trade and navigation with Iceland.

chief comptoirs upon the coast;[1] these "Markaðr" lasted for a week or ten days in early July, a period known as Höndlunartíð (Dan. Handelstid). The peasants came, often after a week or more of riding, with their goods carried in crates and panniers by pack-horses; pitched their tents, and began the year's business, which was enlivened by not a little gross debauchery. The canniest of their canny calling, each party sent forward some noted "knowing hand" to find out which merchant gave the largest price, and all went to him *en masse*. Consequently the traders were obliged to defend themselves by a counterunion, all conforming to a certain tariff; and now, if one store pay a skilling less than any comptoir within reach, the purchaser will claim to be refunded.

The fair system is becoming obsolete; many merchants have opened new trading stations, and even the most secluded bays are visited by market-ships. These "Spekulants," however, are not allowed to visit the out-havens where there is no comptoir—another scrap of protection to the storekeeper which calls for abolition. They are limited, reasonably enough, to four or five weeks of yearly trade at each place, but they may divide the time at several bays. Moreover, they must sell and buy only from the ships, and they cannot set up shops on shore.

---

[1] The following Danised names of the thirty-one privileged factories and trading places are given by Mr Vice-Consul Crowe (Report, 1865-66):

SOUTH QUADRANT.

| | |
|---|---|
| 1. Reykjavik (capital). | 5. Vestmanns Islands. |
| 2. Havnefjord. | 6. Papö. |
| 3. Keflavik. | 7. Landhussund. |
| 4. Örebakke. | |

NORTH QUADRANT.

| | |
|---|---|
| 8. Oefjord (called "a town"). | 12. Husavik. |
| 9. Skagerstrand. | 13. Ramforhavn. |
| 10. Hofsós. | 14. Thorshavn. |
| 11. Seydafjord. | 15. Sandarok. |

EAST QUADRANT.

| | |
|---|---|
| 16. Vapnafjord. | 18. Eskifjord. |
| 17. Seydisfjord. | 19. Berufjord. |

WEST QUADRANT.

| | |
|---|---|
| 20. Isafjord (called "a town"). | 26. Patriksfjord. |
| 21. Stykkisholm. | 27. Flatey (island). |
| 22. Olafsvik. | 28. Reykjafjord. |
| 23. Búdenstad. | 29. Bordöre. |
| 24. Bildal. | 30. Straûmfjord. |
| 25. Dyrefjord. | 31. Skeljavik. |

Regular postal communication is perhaps the first want of the island; there is hardly any for the three and a half months between November 29 and February 15. A steamer would take very few passengers at such seasons, but a stout and ably handled schooner-rigged craft of 120 tons (minimum), with a crew of seven men, should find no difficulty in carrying the mails. Yet the history of such attempts is not encouraging. The first postal packet, the " Sölöwen," went down, "man and mouse," off Snæfellsnes, a dead horse cast ashore giving notice of the calamity: about the same time another ship was lost with all on board. The first steamer was the " old Arcturus," Clyde-built, 280 tons register, and eighty horse-power; the captain (Andresen) and crew were Danes, and the engineers were Scotch. Messrs Henderson of Glasgow, who hazarded the speculation, obtained from Denmark a subvention of $6000 per annum for six years, besides an advance of $30,000 purchase money, at 4 per cent. interest for outlay. This " cockle-shell" made four, then six, annual voyages, the first in March, the last in October; and she touched at Grangemouth when outward and homeward bound. Her charges were cheap—£2, 2s. for eight days, board, wine, and whiskey included. She is now, they say, trading for the United Steam Company between Copenhagen and the Baltic.

But private companies, though receiving a grant of $15,000 per annum, did not thrive. The " Arcturus " was succeeded by the Danish " Póst-skip " " Diana," which was put upon the line in 1870. She is a converted man-of-war, formerly stationed at the island, with flush decks for guns. A " slow coach " and a fast roller, she formerly made five trips a year, now increased to seven; and the Appendix (No. I.) will give all necessary information about her movements. She offers the advantage of touching at the Færoes, and at Berufjörð, but it has been proposed to give up the latter station. On the other hand, she is exceedingly inexact, often lagging behind her time at Granton, and other places. During the season she is painfully crowded; "a state-room may be had against payment for all the berths therein;" but unless the kind and hospitable Mr Berry,[1] Consul-

---

[1] This gentleman is most obliging in giving all information about the steamer. No passport is required for Iceland.

General for Denmark at Leith, or the civil Vice-Consul, Hr
Jacobsen, telegraph to Copenhagen, none will be vacant. The
food is greasy, and soaked in fat. As long as Captain Haalme
and Lieutenant Loitved commanded the "Diana," there was little
official interference with passengers. Afterwards she fell into
the hands of a martinet, and matters changed for the worse.
She seems cheap, but she is really dear, as these figures show:

| | | |
|---|---:|---|
| First-class cabin from Granton to Iceland, . | £4 | 0 0 |
| Table, without wines (at 3s. 9d. per day), . | 1 | 13 9 |
| Wines, etc., . . . . . | 1 | 0 0 |
| Baggage, only 100 lbs. free; overweight (say 100 | | |
| lbs.), at 9d. per 10 lbs., . . . | 0 | 8 0 |
| Fees, etc., . . . . . | 0 | 8 0 |
| | £7 | 9 9 |

She does not pay, and no wonder, when the Reykjavik traders
sail their own ships. But these gentry have also determined so
to monopolise the traffic, that often the smallest parcel, even of
medium size, is refused, under the pretext of there being no
room. In fact, they have made the "Diana" peculiarly unpopular.
" It is difficult," says a friend, " to find any reason for such conduct, but that the Copenhagen merchants who furnish the stores
of Reykjavik with their poisonous liquors, which they pass off
for genuine, take every means to prevent anything like com-
petition."

In 1872, when the author visited Iceland, the export of ponies,
sheep, and meat cattle had caused a rapid development of communication. Already the " Yarrow " of Granton had been run for
three years by her owner Mr Slimon, who had bought and floated
her after she had been wrecked off Burntisland. She at first refused, but afterwards consented, to carry mails. With as many
as 450 head of horses on board, and towing a sloop with fifty
more, she was terribly down in the stern; and a pooping sea
would have been no joke for her solitary passenger. The " Jón
Sigurðsson" was also sent in May by her owners, a private Norwegian company, and she was followed by the " Queen." Concerning these two, ample details will be found in the Journal.

## § 4. The Store.

The present is an age of "manufactures and diffused wealth," which calls for as many observations on trade and business as the traveller can make. Before visiting the stores, however, a few words must be bestowed upon an interesting detail.

Foreigners are apt to complain that Icelanders are uncommonly "sharp practitioners;" sleuth-hounds after money, and bull-dogs in holding it, like Yorkshiremen. It has become the fashion to say that the islanders are kind and hospitable at first, but succeed in jewing the stranger at last; and, like most of such generalisations, it contains a partial truth. Upon this subject an Englishman who knows the island well, wrote, "So far as my experience goes, I have never met with an Icelander who was a rascal; there are, however, men in Iceland, and especially at Reykjavik, who are pretty specimens of that form of animal life. . . . I have heard some travellers regard it as a swindle that horses are dear when wanted to purchase, and cheap when sold; but they forget that in early summer there is plenty of work for beasts, and the demand raises their price by the natural law. At the approach of winter there is no work for them and scanty food, consequently the value falls."

The traveller, as a rule, will meet but little imposition, except in two notorious cases, alluded to in many a page. One is the rapacious Rev. Mr Bech, now Prófastur (archdeacon) of Thingvellir, who charged Prince Napoleon 220 francs for camping ground, and who is said to have demanded $47 from Lord Dufferin. The other is Pétur Jóusson, the farmer at Mý-vatn, who has fleeced generations of tourists; he was made by nature to keep an inn at Palermo, or lodgings at Dover. Against these and a few other instances, may be set off many a small farmer who will declare that he has been paid too much; and often the boatman seems surprised at being paid at all. The people appear eminently honest in the country parts. About the capital this can hardly be expected: a revolver and a silver snuff-box if dropped will not be recovered.

In business the foreigner will fall into the hands of the Danish

storekeepers, who certainly have more than a "theoretical knowledge of the value of money;" and he will be fortunate if he
escape unscathed. One of these gentry, attempting to extort 500
francs from the Capitaine Le Timbre for throwing a seine, without taking a fish, into an unpreserved part of his river, failed,
as he deserved. The bad example has to a certain extent infected the Iceland trader. Messrs Henderson & Anderson were
ruined by their agent. An English storekeeper came out in
1872, with the object of recovering certain debts from the present owner of the "Glasgow House." He had spent some years
on the island, he knew Danish well, and he was accustomed to
treat with the people; yet he wholly failed, and the worst part
of his failure was, that no Procurator (lawyer) would undertake
the foreigner's case against a brother islander.[1] But if these
two were disappointed, Messrs Ritchie and Messrs Hogarth have
been successful. And many of our countrymen who land in
Iceland for trade should certainly not throw stones at the
islanders. One of these clerks, a decidedly "sharp" young
man, not to use the comparative form of the adjective, attempted
to make himself richer and the author poorer by £25, on the
pretext that he had bought ponies, for which the hirer should
be responsible.

The storekeepers at Reykjavik are called merchants (kaup-
maðr = chapman), and their establishments, which lack signs and
names, are the conspicuous buildings fronting the sea. Mostly,
they are paid employés of Copenhagen firms, who receive fixed
salaries. The following is a list, beginning from the west:

1. Hr Egill Egilsson (Icelander), of the Glasgow House, and
agent of the "Jón Sigurðsson" steamer.

2. Hr Fischer, a Dane, married to an Icelandic wife, settled at

---

[1] Upon these remarks Mr Jón A. Hjaltalín observes, "The case referred to is
as follows: The Scotchman's claim may have been good in point of Scotch law,
but it was not in point of Icelandic law. That is the reason why the Procurators
would not undertake it. He has therefore to blame the law, not the men. I
know, as a fact, that both the Procurators of Reykjavik have conducted cases for
foreigners, e.g., Messrs Henderson & Anderson against Icelanders. It would
have been more questionable practice, although perhaps more lawyer-like, if they
had induced the plaintiff to go on with the case, although they were sure that he
would lose it. Foreigners often think they are wronged if a case, which is clear
according to their own laws, breaks down according to foreign laws: Icelanders
have gone through that experience in Scotland."

Copenhagen, and occasionally visiting the island. He occupies the corner tenement to the right of the Bridge House; and he has large stores fronting his shop.

3. Hr Havstein (Dane), who has not long been established; his private dwelling is attached to his store at the west end of Harbour Street, but he usually lives at Copenhagen. This house charters two or three ships a year to carry its goods.

4. Hr Hannes Jónsson, an Icelander, son of the former Bishop Steingrimur Jónsson. His stock is furnished by Hr Jonsen of Copenhagen, who has also establishments at Hafnafjörð, Papós, and Seyðisfjörð.

5. Hr Robb, the son of an English merchant, who settled at and was naturalised in Iceland.[1] He speaks German, but not a word of English. It is the smallest of all the establishments, and seems to do business only in lollipops.

6. Hr P. C. Knutzen, a Dane, whose agent is Hr Sivertsen. He trades on his own account, without a company; and, being young and wealthy, he prefers Copenhagen to Reykjavik. At Hafnafjörð he has another establishment, and an agent (Hr Zimsen).

7. Hr Möller. The Club is held at his house.

8. Hr Schmidt (Danish), who hires a house at Reykjavik, and passes the winter at Copenhagen. He is Consul for Holland.

9. Hr Th. A. Thomsen, a Dane of Flensburg, born in Iceland. He passes the winter at Copenhagen; and, besides being one of the principal traders, he is well-known for his civility and kindness to strangers.

10. Hr Edward Siemsen, at the east end of the town. He is agent for his brother and their nephew, and he also acts Consul for Denmark.

Including M. Randrŭp, Consul de France, the Consular Corps, none of them belonging to *la carrière*, consists of three, England, of course, being unrepresented, though she does the largest business in coal and salt. Thus the tricolor is the only foreign flag seen in the island, the other two staves bear Danish colours. As has been shown, most of the traders pass only the summer in

---

[1] Naturalisation is wisely made easy in Iceland. The foreigner swears allegiance, pays $2, and straightway becomes a citizen.

Iceland, and they solace themselves with frequent rides and pic-nics at the Laxá River.

Kerguelen has left us an excellent description of the Iceland trade in A.D. 1767. It was managed by a Danish company (No. 2, before alluded to), which had bought an exclusive privilege from the king, and which kept factors and warehouses at the several stations. The only money was fish and butter,[1] whilst one ell of pig-tail (tobacco) = one fish. The fisheries were very extensive, and would require four frigates thoroughly to protect them. Exports were included under salt meat, beef, and mutton; tallow; butter, close packed; wool in the grease; skins of sheep, foxes, and seals; feathers, especially eider down; oil of whales, sharks, and seals; fine and coarse jackets of Wadmal, woollen stockings, and mitts; stock-fish and sulphur. The imports were fishing-tackle, horse-shoes, carpenters' woods, coffee and sugar, tobacco and snuff, beer, brandy, and wine, dry goods (calicoes, etc.), flour (wheat and rye), bread and biscuit.

The imports of the present day, to mention only those of chief importance, are timber, salt, coals, grain, coffee, spices, tobacco, and liquor. The timber consists of pine and fir, mostly the latter; the forms are beams for roofing and framing, twenty-two to twenty-four feet long, one-inch boards for side-lining of houses, three-inch planks, and finer woods for the joiner. Salt comes chiefly from Liverpool, which is ousting the Spanish trade, and the average price may be $2 per barrel = 176 pots = 44 gallons. The people declare that they cannot afford the expense of salt-pans, and that the sun is hardly hot enough for evaporation: this was not the case a few years ago, but Iceland, like Africa, finds it cheaper to import the condiment. English coals are carried in British bottoms, either direct or viâ Copen-hagen; from the latter only small quantities come; birch wood, sawn and split for fuel, is introduced for private use, not for the general market; and there is no charcoal at Reykjavik, although birch "braise" is found inland. The cereals, whose consumption ranges from twenty-four to thirty bushels a head, are wheat and rye, in grain, flour, and biscuit; baking-ovens are found only at

---

[1] In the secluded parts of the island fish and butter still form a currency of exceedingly variable value.

the capital. The rice is more often cheap " Rangoon," than fine " Carolina;" the people, who are fond of rice-milk, do not appear to know the difference, and the import quintupled between 1864-70. The spices are chiefly cinnamon, generally mixed with black pepper; pepper,[1] cloves, and nutmegs. Coffee,[2] whose consumption is 6·7 pounds per head, is chiefly the Brazilian growth; tea is very rare, and a little chocolate is brought from Copenhagen. In hard times, for instance after 1855, the consumption of these luxuries notably falls off. The tobaccos are usually the common Danish article; foreign growths are represented by twist, for chewing as well as smoking; by shag, bird's-eye, and some specimens of the thousand mixtures which have become so popular of late. As may be expected, the cigars are dear and bad; the best, or at least the most expensive, are the Hamburg " Havannahs," which are pretentiously wrapped up in a plaintain-leaf, veritable " cabbage." Perhaps the favourite form is snuff (= about $3 per pound), which is loved by males of all classes and ages. There are few men who "take nothing between their fingers;" the consumption of this Tupi article is about two pounds per head of males.[3]

The list of wet goods in a general store is extensive, including port and sherry, claret and champagne, rum and cognac, with liqueurs like cherry-brandy. These are mostly dear and bad; the beer imported for tavern use, and the Brennivín, Kornschnapps, or rye-spirits, are too cheap to be adulterated, except for the peasantry. Not a few country merchants can sell per annum of this liquor twenty barrels, each containing thirty gallons. The Althing imposed an import tax, to come into force on July 1, 1872, of $0, 0m. 8sk. (about 2½d.) per pot or quart, upon every bottle of wine and spirits, beer only being excepted.[4]

---

[1] No Cayenne is procurable, and those who ask for it will probably be served with curry powder in bottles, that do not suffice for a single dish, but cost one shilling.

[2] Coffee did not come into general use before the end of the eighteenth century; tea and tobacco are mentioned in the satirical poem, "Thagnarmál," 1728, by Eggert Ólafsson, who died in 1768 (Cleasby).

[3] The Consular Report says, "1 lb. per annum for every man, woman, and child."

[4] The Report has it that the duty of eight skillings per pot or quart has been laid upon ale, wine, and spirituous liquors, when imported in casks or hogsheads,

But the law unhappily said "drinkable spirits," and the merchants were able to exempt pure and methylated alcohols from the impost. Consequently "brandies" were made at Reykjavik and at other trading stations, greatly to the detriment of public health as well as of morality, and despite the exertions of sensible men like Dr Hjaltalín, the "Land-physicus." The duty upon twenty barrels would be $200; it is paid into the Treasury under the charge of the Landfógeti, superintended by the Stiftamtmaðr. The sooner an "Adulterations Act" is passed the better, but in Iceland as elsewhere *magna est pecunia et prevalebit*. The island is not cursed with a Manchester school and its moral mildew, but commercial interests are amply sufficient for more than self-protection.

It may be useful to compare the prices in 1810 by Stephensen (History of Iceland), with those of 1872, on the western and eastern coasts:

| | In 1810. | In 1872. | On East Coast. |
|---|---|---|---|
| 1 pair trade mitts, . . . | $0　0　4—6 | $0　2　0 | $0　0　14—20 |
| 1 pair stockings, . . . . | $0　0　12—18 | $0　4　0 | $0　2　0 |
| 1 pair fine socks, . . . | $0　0　64 to $1 | $1　0　0 | |
| 1 common Wadmal jacket, | $0　0　40—60 | $3 to $4 | none made for sale. |
| 1 fine Wadmal jacket, . . | $2 to $3 | $6　0　0 | |
| 1 lb. (Dan.) wool, . . . | $0　0　12—20 | $0　3　4 | $0　2 to $0　4 |
| 1 lb. eider down, . . . | $2　3　0 to $3 | $7　3　0 | $7　0　0 |
| 1 lb. feathers, . . . . | $0　0　17—20 | $0　2　0 | $0　2　0 |
| 1 lb. tallow, . . . . . | $0　0　16—22 | $0　1　4 | $0　1　0 |
| 1 lb. butter,[1] . . . . . . | $0　0　10—28 | $0　2　0 | $0　1　0 |
| 1 Skippund (320 lbs.) "flat fish,"[2] . . . . . . | $12 to $20 | $26　0　0 | $20　0　0 |
| 1 Skippund klip-fish,[3] . . | $15 to $30 | $30 to $40 | none. |

and a duty of equal amount per one and a half pint, when imported in bottles, jars, or kegs.

[1] Iceland home-made butter is poor, white, full of hairs, and made in a way peculiarly unclean. It is mostly of ewes' milk, that of the cow not sufficing. Travellers of course prefer the imported, but it is not always to be had at the shops. The favourite native form is "sour butter," which, like the Ghi of Hindostan, lasts twenty years, though if salted it becomes rancid : it takes the place of salt and seasoning ; it is considered to assist digestion, and it "diffuses an agreeable warmth over the stomach." The climate demands such carbon-producing food, and "Fat have I never refused!" is a saying with the islanders.

[2] Flat fish, not being flat, is a misnomer for the sun-dried preparation which is unknown abroad, and unfit for European markets.

[3] This salt fish on the eastern coast is chiefly for home use, the catch being too late for curing, and dry weather being mostly wanting at that season.

|   | In 1810. | In 1872. | On East Coast. |
|---|---|---|---|
| 1 barrel sharks' liver oil, . | $12 to $20 | $30  0  0 | $25  0  0 |
| 1 skin, white or Arctic fox (*C. lagopus*), . . . . | $3  0  0 | $1  4  6 | none on East Coast. |
| 1 skin, blue (*i.e.*, deep iron grey) fox, . . . . . | $3  0  0 | $8  0  0 | |
| 1 brown (*C. fuliginosus*), . | $5  0  0 | $8  0  0 | |
| 1 Rein-deer skin,[1] . . . | $5  0  0 | $5  3  0 | |
| 100 Swan-quills, . . . . | $2 to $3 | $8  0  0 | very rare. |
| A horse, . . . . . . | $6 to $40 | according to demand, | £3 to £10 |
| A cow, . . . . . . . | $16 to $24 | $50 to $80 | and upwards. |
| A wether,[2] . . . . . . | $2 to $5 | $9  0  0 | $9  0  0 |
| 1 ewe and lamb, . . . . | $2 to $2½ | $12  0  0 | $9  0  0 |
| A lamb, . . . . . . | $1  2  0 | $3  0  0 | not for sale. |

Details of imports for 1865, occupying nearly a page and a half, will be found in the Consular Report of that year; the total importations represented £21,468. The kind, weight, and value of the primary items are thus tabled in 1870-71 : the account applies to the whole island, but only the principal articles are mentioned :

|   | 1864. | 1865. | 1866. | 1867. | 1868. | 1869. | Average Yearly Value in £. |
|---|---|---|---|---|---|---|---|
| Rye and rye-flour, barrels, . . . . | 35,620 | 41,596 | 37,968 | 29,426 | 27,973 | 28,905 | 40,044 |
| Barley, . . . . | 17,490 | 19,960 | 16,708 | 12,992 | 10,463 | 10,455 | 24,463 |
| Pease, . . . . | 4,524 | 4,177 | 4,481 | 3,158 | 3,173 | 2,775 | 4,953 |
| Wheaten bread, lbs., | 317,216 | 339,511 | 252,511 | 244,754 | 182,783 | 196,068 | 3,494 |
| Rye bread, lbs. . | 18,033 | 26,869 | 21,389 | 18,844 | 13,754 | 20,714 | 210 |
| Spirits, quarts, . | 567,675 | 608,864 | 529,426 | 479,285 | 385,273 | 351,752 | 12,402 |
| Coffee, lbs., . . | 393,164 | 462,227 | 483,852 | 403,840 | 403,707 | 389,544 | 12,011 |
| Chicory, lbs., . . | 87,864 | 120,602 | 108,753 | 102,089 | 102,762 | 133,909 | 9,488 |
| Sugar candy, lbs., | 347,745 | 429,467 | 385,942 | 410,558 | 335,501 | 344,842 | 9,487 |
| Loaf sugar, lbs., . | 101,918 | 152,840 | 135,350 | 118,229 | 113,960 | 111,229 | 3,087 |
| Brown sugar, lbs., | 27,751 | 47,020 | 41,602 | 36,456 | 34,268 | 32,043 | 786 |
| Treacle, lbs., . . | 16,199 | 19,257 | 14,289 | 12,100 | 9,972 | 12,807 | 208 |
| Rice, lbs., . . . | 80,946 | 127,304 | 251,201 | 230,338 | 236,965 | 388,938 | 2,535 |
| Snuff, lbs., . . . | 72,422 | 69,172 | 83,625 | 69,402 | 45,651 | 61,492 | 1,691 |
| Leaf tobacco, lbs., | 5,449 | 11,619 | 8,448 | 3,665 | 4,496 | 2,234 | 176 |
| Chew tobacco, lbs., | 35,011 | 39,908 | 37,081 | 34,727 | 30,617 | 34,527 | 2,972 |
| Tobacco, lbs., . . | 9,953 | 14,854 | 14,865 | 10,730 | 10,531 | 11,459 | 254 |
| Cigars (pieces), . | 274,000 | 236,100 | 262,800 | 191,900 | 170,000 | 301,000 | 266 |

The peculiarity of this table is that while the consumption of

---

[1] Only two pelts were sent in 1872.

[2] The merchant weighs the carcase when cold, melts the tallow, and pays a price varying according to the market, from fourteen skillings to a mark. The people have a strange idea that sheep falling into snow crevasses, and found a year or two afterwards, are naturally salted—a curious appendage to the " freezing upwards " theory.

colonial goods remains at the usual average, and while rice has
nearly quintupled, there has been a decrease in the import of rye,
barley, pease, and wheaten bread, a circumstance not easy to
account for, with a growing population in an island which produces no cereals.

The collective value of these imports is somewhat over
$1,100,000 = £122,222, which is but $100,000 less than the
total value of the exports of 1869 ($1,200,000 = £133,333);
and, as only the most important items have been mentioned,[1]
we may conclude that the two totals almost balance each other.
The consumption of brandy, coffee, sugar, and tobacco is alone
equal to about $418,000, or one-third of the whole value of the
exports.

In 1869, the number of foreign vessels that visited the trading
stations was

|  |  |  |
|---|---|---|
| From Denmark direct, | 99 vessels, with | 9,358 tons. |
| ,, other countries, | 50 ,, | 4,555 ,, |
| ,, other island stations, 137 | ,, | 13,913 ,, |

Of the 149 direct foreign arrivals

|  |  |  |  |
|---|---|---|---|
| Cleared in to | Reykjavik, | 31·1 | per cent. |
| ,, | Akureyri, | 9·3 | ,, |
| ,, | Seyðisfjörð, | 9·3 | ,, |
| ,, | Ísafjörð, | 8·2 | ,, |
| ,, | Berufjörð, | 6·4 | ,, |
| ,, | Hafnarfjörð, | 51·0 | ,, |

We will now enter the establishment, and see the stock-in-
trade of a general "merchant." The usual dwarf entrance-hall,
after the outer door is passed, opens upon two rooms to the right
and left: one is the public shop, filled at the "fair season" with

---

[1] The other imports not accounted for are alum, drugs, ashes, ink, brushmakers'
work, cocoa, chocolate, ale in bottle and in cask (the latter, 11,776 lbs. in 1865),
wine in bottle and cask (the latter, 23,137 lbs.), vinegar, essences, catechu and
galls, indigo, dyestuffs and varnish, playing-cards, "galanterie wares," glass
ware, resin and gums, caps, stone china, pork and hams (2,480 lbs.), méat
(2,279 lbs.), cork, buckwheat meal (880 lbs.), oatmeal (319 lbs.), spices (1,016
lbs.), coals (157 tons), cotton goods (62,484 lbs.), silk (11 lbs.), woollen goods
(686 lbs.), block metal (786 lbs.), bar and hoop iron (63,486 lbs.), nails (23,441
lbs.), iron chain (404 lbs.), iron wares (33,770 lbs.), zinc in plates, hardware
sundries (6,981 lbs.), cheese (1,736 lbs.), paper (6,210 lbs.), soap (12,225 lbs.),
sago, etc. (811 lbs.), saltpetre (297 lbs.), prepared hides, and skins (4,508 lbs.),
acids (309 lbs.), tea (918 lbs.), ropemakers' work (22,770 lbs.), wood goods
(14,294 cubic feet), worked woods (42,993 lbs.), vitriol (4,519 lbs.), and bar steel
(1,441 lbs.).

jostling boors and drunken loafers; the other is the private store, mostly provided with railed pen for the benefit of the clerk and account-keeper. Besides the mainstays of commerce before mentioned, the rooms will contain the following articles: Dry goods, broad cloths and long cloths, woollen comforters, threads, and a few silks and satins. Hardwares of every description; iron for the blacksmith's use; hoop-iron and bar-iron (no pig), the metal being preferably Swedish, for the best of reasons; a little steel and brass wire, but neither copper nor zinc; farriers' and carpenters' tools; cooking utensils; spades and scythes; sewing machines; and fish-hooks, the smaller sort for long lines, the cod-hooks large and of tinned iron. The arms and ammunition, especially old military muskets and muzzle-loaders, are fit only for the Gold Coast: Copenhagen weapons are cheap and good, £2, 5s. being the average price of a breech-loading single-barrelled rifle. Pistols are not seen, and there is a tradition of the barrels being cut for alpenstock rings. Besides cereals, the stores supply sugars, brown, candy, and white, refined at Copenhagen; hams (rare, and no potted meats, so much wanted by travellers); sausages and sardines; butter (foreign sometimes); figs, raisins, prunes, and olive oil. The Quincaillerie consists of pots and pans, boxes, funnels, kettles and watering-pots, lamps and lanterns. The walls are hung with leather for saddles, thongs, straps, and raw hides for shoes. There is an abundance of cheap crockery and glass ware. Paraffin and petroleum have lately come into general fashion; stearine candles are kept mostly for private use, and the peasants make their own farthing dips.

A narrow back passage, often connecting the public and the private shop, will have a ladder leading to the usual cock-loft, scattered with boxes and bales. Here a few skins and birds stuffed for sale, some of them sadly damaged by rats, hang from the beams; and the following are the chief items:

The falcon[1] (*F. islandicus*, Icel. Fálki, a foreign word, or Veiði-fálki); a good white, stuffed specimen costs $10. This bird, so much valued during the Middle Ages, and considered the elder

---

[1] Here and there an eagle skin may be bought; and in country parts the quills of the royal bird are used as pens. The only species is the white-tailed Haliaetus (*H. albicilla* or *F. leucocephalus*).

brother of the gerfalcon (*F. gyrfalco*) or peregrine, was protected by kings and bishops, who claimed the right of exporting it. A royal mews was established at Reykjavik. In 1770, the falconers paid $7 for the grey bird, $10 for the dark-grey, and $15 for the white, which was considered the most beautiful and docile. Many were sent to England as late as the seventeenth century: in 1871, a few birds were bought for the Hindostan market. This falcon is very destructive to ducks, and ranges far, making upwards of 1300 miles per diem.

Whoopers, hoopers, or wild swans (*Cycnus ferus*, Icel. Álpt or Svanr in poetry, the Fær. Svener), are now, from the rarity of the skins, sold at fancy prices.

The Iceland golden-eye (*Clangula islandica*, Icel. Húsönd) fetches, according to quality, $0, 5m. to $1, 2m.

The gulls (*L. glaucus*, Icel. Hvít-máfur or Hvít-fugl) and the great black-backed *L. marinus* (Svartbakur) are cheap, and good specimens may be bought for $0, 2m.

The great northern diver (*Colymbus arcticus seu glacialis*, Icel. Himbrimi or Brúsi), if good, costs $1, 4m.; usually it is sold when the coat is changing from winter to summer wear, and is not worth buying.

The red-throated diver (*Colymbus ruficollinus seu septentrionalis*, Icel. Lómr or Therrikráka) is worth $1, 2m. when in good condition, with red around the throat and about the breast.

The other skins are the whimbrel or curlew-knot (*Numenius phaeopus*, Fær. Spogvi, Icel. Nefvoginn-Spói); the pretty redheaded pochard (*Fuligula ferina*), extending from the Himalayas to North America, from Italy to Greenland; the beautifully painted harlequin, or stone duck (*Histrionicus torquatus seu Anas histrionica*, Icel. Straum-önd or stream-duck); the white-breasted and crooked-bill'd goosander (*Mergus castor*, Icel. Stóra-toppönd or Gulönd), so different of robe in male and female; the red-breasted mergander (*Mergus serrator*, Icel. Lilla Toppönd), whose brick-hued bill, ending in a white horny nail, has various serrations, according to sex; the shag, scarf, or cormorant (*Phalacrocorax carbo*, *Carbo cormoranus* or *Pelicanus carbo*, Icel. Skarfur, Toppskarfur, and Dílaskarfur), never taught in Europe to fish; the gannet (*Sula bassana* or *Pelicanus bassanus*, Icel.

Súla or Hafsúla); the various'skuas or Arctic gulls (*Stercorarius* Icel. Kjói); the Iceland gull (*L. leucopterus*, Icel. Hvít-máfur), white, with ash-blue back; the guillemot (*Uria troile*, Icel. Svartlag, Langnefia, or Langvia), whose flesh is eaten, and whose feathers sell for twenty-eight skillings per lb.; the black guillemot (*Uria grylle*, Icel. Tejsti); the grey-lag goose (*Anser ferus*); the scaup-duck (*Fuligula marila*); the black scoter (*Oedemia nigra*); the long-tail duck (*Harelda glacialis*); the pin-tail duck (*A. acuta*); the red-necked phalarope (Icel. Óðin's-hani, *Phalaropus hyperboreus seu tringa borea*); the gadwall (*A. strepera*); the wigeon (*A. Penelope*); the mallard (*A. boschas*); the teal (*A. crecca*).

---

## SECTION IX.

## CATALOGUE-RAISONNÉ OF MODERN TRAVELS IN ICELAND—PREPARATIONS FOR TRAVEL.

### § 1. Catalogue.

And first a few words concerning Icelandic literature.

Iceland has been loudly proclaimed to be the "home of the Eddas,"[1] which is emphatically not the case. The Elder or poetical Edda is distinctly Continental; it abounds in un-insular ideas and similes: the sun-stag, the high-antler'd deer, the

---

[1] Mr Jón A. Hjaltalín observes : " If by ' home ' is meant the place where the songs were first made, this is undoubtedly correct, according to accepted theories; but then Norway would not then be their home any more than Iceland. On the other hand, it is indisputable that their last and only home was in Iceland, when they were nowhere else to be found. The allusions in the songs give no clue to their birthplace. You may find an Icelander of the present day singing of lions and elephants. And if they can do so now, why not in former times also?" The author would remark that the Elder Edda has evidently been preserved by memory from earlier ages, and that its origin must have been in Continental Scandinavia. It is rather the spirit of the poetry than the scattered allusions which suggests that much of it was not addressed to islanders. A comparison of the Völuspá with any Icelandic composition will explain what is here meant; and Mr Benjamin Thorpe seems to have been struck by the same idea.

wolf,[1] the strong-venom'd snake, the mew-field's bison or path of ship over the sea, the lily and the pine forest, are poetical imagery, wholly unfamiliar to the untravelled Icelander.

The authentic historical literature of Scandinavia opens about the middle of the ninth century; that of Iceland with its Norwegian discovery, when the copiously and irregularly inflected tongue, the "delight of philologists and the traveller's despair," was apparently in its highest form. The learned Bishop of Skálholt (Hist. Eccl. Isl.) assigns four distinct ages to the classical productions of his native island:

I. Infancy: from the first colonisation (A.D. 874), when every man appears to have been a Skáld[2] or bard, ending with the introduction of Christianity in A.D. 1000. The Sturlunga (i. 107) asserts that all the Sagas of that date were committed to writing before the death of Bishop Brandr (A.D. 1201).

II. Youth: when colleges and schools were introduced, ending with A.D. 1110.

III. Manhood and zenith of splendour: from that time till A.D. 1350.

IV. Decline and fall between the mid-fourteenth century and the Reformation.

Thus the Augustan age endured for the unusually long period of some two and a half centuries.

The island, though scantily peopled, enjoyed immense advantages for study. It had taken the first great step in civilisation, SLAVERY, and while carl and thrall tilled the field, Jarl, clerk, and franklin found ample leisure for literature. The long rigorous winters, when neither farming, fishing, fighting, nor sea-

---

[1] We find an Ulf's-vatn in Iceland, but probably the name was given in memory of the old home, or as Ulfr was a proper name like Vuk in Slav, the first settler may have so christened it.

[2] Skáldr (Germ. Schalte) means a pole; and inasmuch as the Scald-pole (Skáld-stöng or Níð-stöng) was scored with charms and imprecations—as Martin Capella (fifth century) writes:

"Barbara fraxineis sculpatur runa tabellis;"—

so "pole" came to signify a libel. Hence Skáld may be akin to the Germ. Schelten, and the familiar English "Scold." Afterwards it took the meaning of poetry in a good sense, and Skáldskapr (Skaldship) was applied to the form of verse, metre, flow, and diction (Cleasby). It is hardly necessary to observe that the word is of disputed origin, the five general derivations being Skalla (depilare), Skiael (wisdom = our "skill"), Skjall (narratic), Skal (sources), and Gala (to sing). "Hirðskáld" corresponds with our poet-laureate.

faring was possible, proved highly favourable for reading, writing, and reciting; and hence the phenomenon that the history of mediæval Iceland is more complete than that of any European country. The extensive piratical wanderings of the race gave, moreover, a cosmopolitan complexion to its compositions. Some modern writers wonder to see such display of literary activity, especially during the last fifty or sixty years of the Commonwealth, when society was convulsed by sanguinary feuds, and when every man slept weaponed. As we often find in history, it was this very turbulence which gave the spur; after the union with Norway, the island became peaceful, and her poets and historians found their occupation going or gone. The noble Icelandic prose, which in terse, picturesque, and crystal-clear expression, vied with Latin, and which equalled Greek in distinctness and combination of words, was no longer written; and between the fifteenth and the mid-sixteenth centuries men of letters contented themselves with transcribing and annotating their classics.

The poetry of the Augustan age was, at first, simple and sufficient as the prose—it reminds us of Firdausi's Shah-nameh. But presently, as is ever the case with a decaying literature, came the Skáld, whose highest merit was that of calling nothing by the right name, of saying common things in an uncommon or rather in an unintelligible way. Space forbids even an outline of his system, the vast variety of quaint conceits, the abuse of metaphor, of " Kenningar " (circumlocution), of simile, and of allegory, and the prodigious complication of metres, which formed his stock-in-trade; suffice it to say that he used 150 synonyms for an island, fifty for a wave,[1] and à greater number for gold. Thus Rask remarks that with a half-a-hundred terms for a ship there is no word for "benevolence." The Skáld's vocabulary added to the copiousness of Arabic, the polysynthesis of Sanskrit; his inversions and transpositions of speech are so complicated, that modern commentators after quoting the lines, mostly number the words or subjoin the construction.

It is interesting to observe the family likeness between the

---

[1] Von Hammer counts 5744 Arabic terms for a camel.

two distant cousins, Persian and Icelandic. Hafiz, for instance, from Alif to Ya, is one long example of Skáldic poetry; he sings the praises of wine when he means, or is understood to mean, heavenly love, and his verse, like that of Ultima Thule, requires for every line a dictionary—not of words, but of the *double entendres* which lurk under words. Grimm, when pronouncing Icelandic to be the "true source of all the Teutonic languages," cannot but remark its Oriental turn. It is in fact after the Slav, the purest type of the Indo-European, which has been so modestly called the "Indo-Germanic" family.

The Reformation stirred up the popular mind, and the result, as usual, was a revival of literary energy. But the produce—theology with poetry religious and ethical; history, or rather continuations of the old annals; criticism, exegesis, and grammatical studies—showed decline in matter as well as in manner. The originality, the strong individuality of the old pagan, was succeeded by the mechanical industry of the copier, who had other models to work from. This modern period still continues. The love of letters, inspired by soil and climate, even now characterises the Icelander despite his poverty and isolation. During the last century abundant good work has been done in editing and publishing the classical literature, and some excursions have been made into the regions of science, mechanics, and political economy.

The list given by Uno Von Troil contains the names of 120 works; and the Reports of the Icelandic Literary Society between 1852 and 1871 show, besides its yearly transactions (Skirnir), the titles of fifty-one publications, some old but mostly modern. Bishop Pètursson (Hist. Eccl. 330) gives a list of six folio pages, containing the titles of Libri Biblici, Catechetici, de Evangeliis, Precum, Conciones, et alii piis usibus Libri. It is interesting, again, to compare this hyperborean literature with that of the little Istrian peninsula. The latter, despite such drawbacks as poverty and political excitement, and the torments of plagues, droughts, famines, invasions, and intestine strife, can point to a roll numbering about 3000 names:[1] England herself is hardly richer in local literature.

---

[1] The total is 3060, but this would include the classics who have treated of Istria.

Amongst the subjects which Icelandic has treated, we may number proverbs, the "marrow of the language." The first collection (Orðskviðasafn) was made by Guðmundur Jónsson, and printed in octavo by the Literary Society (Report of 1872). The Cleasby-Vigfusson Dictionary also contains a considerable number which deserve separate publication, for the benefit of those who appreciate this highly ethnological form of literature. Even the Færoe Islands possess their *répertoire* (Description, etc., by the Rev. J. Lundt: London, Longmans, 1810), and some of them are *naïve* in the extreme. For instance, " Calumny never dies," and " Seldom are pigeons hatched from a raven's egg." Some five years ago Mr Jón A. Hjaltalín translated into English a collection of Icelandic proverbs, adding to it those of the late Dr Scheving. His plan was: (1.) to give the text; (2.) a literal translation; and (3.) a common translation, *e.g.* :

> Berr er hverr á baki nema bróður eigi ;
> Bare is every on back unless brother have ;
> Bare is back where brother is not.

Thus the Advocates' Library has the largest and the most complete collection of Icelandic proverbs ever made, whilst, *mirabile dictu*, it is in MS., being unable to find a publisher.

Finally, the days are past since Sir Joseph Banks could collect the three hundred rare and valuable MSS. which were deposited in the British Museum. At present not a single article of literary worth is to be bought on the island.[1]

We will now proceed to Icelandic travellers, and more especially to the English travellers of the present century.[2]

---

[1] Mr Lidderdale of the British Museum has lately catalogued its Icelandic books, and by another list of all those printed, shows what is wanted to perfect the national collection. The latter possesses some rare volumes which are not in the National Library of Copenhagen.

[2] The most noted of the old writers are the following: Arngrímr Jóusson published a variety of books on local subjects, Brevis Commentarius (1592), Anatome Blefkeniana (1612), Epistola Defensoria (1618), Apotribe Calumniæ (1622), Chrymogæa (1609-1630), Specimen Islandiæ (1643). In 1607 appeared the "Islandia, etc." of Difmar Blefkens (Blefkenius). The author lived a year at "Haffnefiordt," and then passed on to Greenland. He greatly scandalised the islanders by making them purify their skins and strengthen their gums like the Celtiberi of Strabo and Catullus, and the coquettes of rural France. In 1608, Iour Boty printed his "Treatise of the Course from Iceland to Greenland" (Purchas, iii. 520). In 1644, La Peyrère wrote an "Account of Iceland" (Churchill, ii. 432), from which an extract has been made. In 1746, John Andersson, after-

1. Mr (afterwards Sir) William Jackson Hooker, F.R.S., L.S., and F. Wern. Soc. Edin., produced his "Journal of a Tour in Iceland in the Summer of 1809," 2 vols. 8vo, London, Longmans

wards Burgomaster of Hamburgh, there published his "Nachrichten von Island," which was translated into Danish and French. His statements were contradicted in 1750 by the Dane Niels Horrebow, "Tilforladeliga Eftèrretningar om Island med ett nytt Landkort, og 2 Aars Meteorologiska Observationer," also translated into German and English.

The marking book of the last century was the "Introduction à l'Histoire de Dannemark," par M. Mallet, à Copenh. 1755, 2 vols. 4to. It was reproduced in English and German. This pioneer of northern literature was ·born at Geneva, became French Professor at Copenhagen (1752), travelled in Norway and Sweden (1755), returned home and died (1762). The work is obsolete, but Mallet's "Northern Antiquities," edited by Bishop Percy, and supplemented by Mr I. A. Blackwell, would form a valuable item of Bohu's Library (London, 1859), were it provided with a decent index, and purged of the blemishes which now dishonour it. Imagine the effect of such a note as this (p. 42): "The Himalaya, or Heavenly mountains; the Sanskrit, himala, corresponding to the M. Gothic himins; Alem. himil. . . . Engl., heaven."

In 1766-67, M. de Kerguelen Tremarec voyaged over the North Sea, and published in 1772 his "Relation d'un Voyage dans la Mer du Nord." In 1772, Uno Von Troil accompanied Sir J. Banks to Iceland, and wrote a most valuable series of twenty-five letters. They have been reproduced in many collections: the edition always referred to in these pages is the 4to of Robson, London, 1780, kindly given to the author by Mr Bernhard Quaritch. Another important book is that of Eggert Ólafsson and Biarní Pállsson (usually Danised to Olafsen and Povelsen), "Reise igienem Island, with Zoega's Botanical Observations," 2 vols., Soroe, 1772, 4to; it was translated into German and into French, and a compendium of it, given in English, was largely quoted by Henderson. In 1772, Bishop Finn Jóusson (Finnus Johannæus), the learned author of the "Historia Ecclesiastica Islandiæ (vols. 3, Hafn., now very rare), treated of the "depopulation of Iceland by cold, volcanic eruptions, and famine." Guðbrandus Thorlacius, Bishop of Hólar, also wrote a "Letter concerning the Ancient State of the Island." In 1789, Mr (afterwards Sir) John Stanley addressed two "Letters" to Dr Black, which were printed in the "Transactions of the Royal Society of Edinburgh."

The various collections of "Voyages and Travels" contain many interesting notices of Iceland. The "Scoprimento dell' Isole Frislanda, Eslanda, Engroenlanda, Estotilanda, and Icarea, fatto per due fratelli, M. Nicolò il Caualiere et M. Antonio, Libro Vno, col disegno di dette Isole," appears in Ramusio, vol. ii.; in Purchas, iii.; and in Hakluyt, iii. Hakluyt, i., gives "King Arthur's Voyage to Iceland" (A.D. 517), and King Malgo's conquest (A.D. 580), by "Galfridus Monumentensis." Also "A Briefe Commentary of the True State of Island" (or Iseland, both used indiscriminately), by Jonas Arngrim. Volume iii. reprints "A Voyage of the ships 'Sunshine' and 'North Starre' (of the fleet of Mr John Davis), to discover a Passage between Groenland and Iseland" (A.D. 1586). J. Harris (Navigantium atque Itinerantium Bibliotheca; or, a Compleat Collection of Voyages and Travels, 1705 and 1748), in book ii., chap. ii., sec. 30, p. 489, et seq. (edition 1748), offers "A Voyage to the North, containing an Account of the Sea Coasts and Rivers of Norway . . . and Iceland, etc." (circa 1605), "extracted from the Journal of a Gentleman employed by the North Sea Company at Copenhagen." "A Collection of Modern and Contemporary Voyages and Travels," published by Sir R. Phillips (London, 1805), reprints (vol. ii.) "Travels in Iceland, performed by order of His Danish Majesty, etc., by Messrs Olafsen and Povelsen" (the Ólafsson and Pállsson before alluded to), translated from the Danish, map and four plates. Kerr ("A General History and Collection of Voyages and Travels, etc.," 1811-24) has a chapter (vol. i., sec. 1, p. 4, et seq.)

and Murray, 1811. 2d edition, 1813. The author had lost his notes with the ship which carried him, and wrote much from memory, hence the extreme cacography of the Icelandic words. Henderson (ii. 136, note) finds the work "intolerably free-thinking"—times have changed. The botanical notes are valuable, and the volumes will, despite all their disadvantages, take rank as "classics.".

2. Sir George Steuart Mackenzie, Bart., President of the Physical Class of the Royal Society, etc., published his "Travels in the Island of Iceland during the Summer of the year 1810," Constable, Edinburgh, 4to; and the book reached a second edition in 1812. He took charge of the geological and mineralogical departments, whilst Dr (the late Sir Henry) Holland and Dr Bright (of Bright's disease) studied the history and literature, the zoology and botany. The illustrations and statistical tables are highly valuable; and although the Geysir theory is now utterly obsolete, literary Icelanders still consider the volume an. authority upon scientific matters.

3. "Iceland, or the Journal of a Residence in that Island during the years 1814 and 1815." By Ebenezer Henderson, Ph.D., M.R.S. Gottenburgh, Hon. M. Lit. Soc. of Fuhnen, and Corr. M. Scan. Lit. Soc. of Copenhagen. 1st edition, 2 vols. 8vo, Oliphant, Edinburgh, 1818. 2d edition, 1819. A notice of his book will conclude this Section.

4. " Statistisk Udsigt over den danske Stat i Begyndelsen af Aaret, 1825, af Frederik Thaarup, Etatsraad," 8vo, Kjöbenhavn, 1825, with Atlas. Valuable for tables of figures.

5. F. Paully. "Topographie von Dänmark einschliesslich Islands," etc., Altona, 1828.

6. Björnus Gunnlaugi, filius. " De Mensurâ et Delineatione Islandiæ interioris," etc. In Monasterio Videyensi, 1834.

7. John Barrow, jun. " A Visit to Iceland" (in 1834), published in 1835 : the volumes are highly useful, as affording an excellent comparison of the past with the present.

---

on the Discovery of Iceland by the Norwegians in the ninth century about A.D. 861. J. Laharpe (vol. xvi.) quotes Horrebow (1750), Anderson (1746), Jonas Arngrim, and "Flocco, a Norwegian pirate." The "Allgemeine Historie der Reisen zu Wasser und zu Lande," etc., Leipzig, 1769 (pp. 1-63, map and plate), contains "Besondere Geschichte von Island."

8. The Hon. Arthur Dillon published "A Winter (1834) in Iceland and Lapland." 2 vols. Colburn, London, 1840. The season happened to be especially rigorous, of course preventing long travels into the interior: the studies of agriculture and fisheries have especial interest. Mr Dillon has visited Iceland more than once.

9. "Lettres sur l'Islande," par X. Marmier, 8vo, Paris, 1837.[1]

10. "Voyage en Islande et au Groenlande, exécuté pendant les années 1855 et 1856 sur la Corvette 'La Recherche,' commandée par M. Tréhouart, Lieutenant de Vaisseau dans le but de découvrir les traces de la Lilloise. Publié par ordre du Roi, sous la direction de M. Paul Gaimard, Président de la Commission Scientifique d'Islande et de Groënland." 8 vols. 8vo.

Tome 1. Histoire de Voyage, par M. P. Gaimard, 8vo, Paris, 1838.

„　2. Histoire de Voyage, par M. Eugène Robert, 8vo, Paris, 1850.

„　3. Journal de Voyage, par M. Eugène Mequet, 8vo, Paris, 1852.

„　4. Zoologie et Médicine, par M. Eugène Robert,[2] 8vo, Paris, 1851.

---

[1] In 1837 appeared the first southern attempt at a novel upon hyperborean subjects—"Han d'Islande," which Jules Janin (Les Catacombes, i. 102) described as "Cette vive, passionée et grossière ébauche d'un homme qui avait Notre Dame de Paris dans la tête et les Orientales dans le cœur." The great author's mind must have been very young when he wrote it. This silly and childish farrago bears the same relation to "Notre Dame" as "Titus Andronicus" to the "Tempest" or to "Othello." Han is an impossible savage, ever with a *tempête sous un crâne*. Ordener is a ridiculous Timon, and the sudden conversion of Schuhmacher to absurd benevolence is worthy of caricature-loving Dickens. With the exception of a few striking remarks, it shows more of fury and frenzy than of fine wit. It forcibly calls to mind the late Prosper Merimée's harsh judgment of M. Victor Hugo as a poet: "He is all imagery. There is neither matter, nor solidity, nor common sense in his verse; he is a man who gets drunk on his own words, and who no longer takes the trouble of thinking." And Han d'Islande explains how the austere old littérateur detected a vein of insanity in the greatest poet of the French Revival, the Romantic School which dates from 1830.

Nor amongst travellers can we reckon M. Jules Verne's "Voyage au Centre de la Terre," the least meritorious of the "terribly thrilling" and marvellously impossible series ; its scene is chiefly below "Sneffles" (Snæfelljökull), a sniffling disguise, which seems to have been, but is not, invented in jest.

[2] M. Robert was the mineralogist, geologist, and botanist of the expedition; he received special directions from M. Adolphe Brogniart (Professor of Botany in the Museum of Natural History, Paris) ; he traversed the greater part of the island in 1835-36, and at his request Hr Vahl, a Danish botanist, who had lived long in

Tome 5. Minéralogie et Géologie, par M. Eugène Robert, 8vo, Paris, 1840.

„ 6. Physique, par M. Victor Lottin, 8vo, Paris, 1838.

„ 7. Histoire d'Islande, par M. Xavier Marmier, 8vo, Paris, 1840.

„ 8. Littérature Islandaise, par M. Xavier Marmier, 8vo, Paris, 1843.

This expedition was determined upon in the year 1835, and was followed by another in 1836. The government of Louis Philippe, claiming to be in the van of civilisation, resolved to give the voyage a scientific aspect, and to publish it regardless of expense— the cost is about £21. It is admirably got up, with every *luxe* of printing; there is Gallic discipline in the strict editorial control; and each contributor is allowed full advantage of space and illustrations — what a contrast to the shabby article which ultra-economical England would have produced! But, though semi-official, it is an immense mass of undigested information, greatly varying in value; and the President, who had accompanied Captain Freycinet in the circumnavigating frigate "Uranie," is not generally over-appreciated in Iceland. His illustrations are so exaggerated as to be simply ridiculous, and unfortunately they have been transferred to the pages of succeeding authors. Thus Dufferin borrows the two Needles off Snæfell and the Icelandic girl, and Paijkull takes Hekla, whilst the cave of Surtshellir and the domestic interior are reproduced by Forbes, who gives additional horrors to the Bruará.

11. "Historia Ecclesiastica Islandiæ ab anno 1740 ad annum 1840," auctore P. Pètursson. Havniæ: Bianco Luno, 1841. A continuation of the learned Hannes Finsson's well-known book, written in Danish and Latin by the present Bishop of Iceland.

12. Lieutenant-Colonel North Ludlow Beamish, "Discovery of America by the Northmen in the Tenth Century, with Notices of the Early Settlements of the Irish in the Western Hemisphere" (1841).

---

Greenland, revised the published lists, especially Hooker's, and drew up a fresh list, corrected to 1840. Since that time, Iceland has been visited by Mr Babington of Cambridge (1846), who also made collections. For others, see Section VII.

13. Vol. 28 of the Edinburgh Cabinet Library. Edinburgh, 1840. A compilation.

14. "Physisch-geographische Skizze von Island mit besondere Rücksicht auf Vulcanische Erscheinungen." Von W. Sartorius von Waltershausen. Göttingen Studien, 1847. Erste Abtheilung Seiten 321-460, Göttingen, 1847. The author visited the island in 1846; his scientific reputation attracts readers, but he writes with a prodigious exaggeration on general subjects, and especially on scenery.

Amongst books of Icelandic travel, again, we cannot include the "Letters of Columbus," edited by Mr R. H. Major, Hakluyt Society, 1847, and recording the remarkable visit of the explorer in A.D. 1477 to the country which in mediæval times discovered the New World. The fact had already been established by Finn Magnússon in his "Nordisk Tidsskrift for Old-Kyndighed." This was followed by the even more interesting "Voyages of the Venetian brothers Nicolò and Antonio Zeno to the Northern Seas in the Fourteenth Century" (written out by Antonio Zeno, and first edited in 1558 by their descendant Nicolò Zeno, junior. Mr Major has identified "Frislanda" with Færöisland of the Danes; "Estlanda" on the map, and "Estlanda," "Eslanda," and "Islande" in the text, with the Shetlands; "Porlanda" with the Orkneys; "Engronelanda" with Greenland; "Estotilanda" and "Drogeo" with parts of North America; and the mysterious "Zichmni" with Henry Sinclair, Earl of Orkney and Caithness. He has also "rehabilitated" Ivar Bardsen and the lost Gunnbjarnarsker, the Skerries of Gunnbjörn, son of Ulf Kraka, who reached them in A.D. 877.

15. Professor Robert Wilhelm Bunsen of Heidelberg (nat. 1811) visited Iceland with M. Descloiseaux in 1846, spent eleven days at the Geysir, and published two papers: (1.) Memoir on the intimate connection existing between the pseudo-volcanic phenomena of Iceland (works of the Cavendish Society, "Chemical Reports and Memoirs, edited by Thomas Graham, V.P.R.S., London, Harrison, 1848); and (2.) On the processes which have taken place during the formation of the volcanic rocks of Iceland (from Poggendorff's "Annalen," part i., Nov. 1851, "Scientific Memoirs, selected from the Transactions of Foreign

Academies of Science, and from Foreign Journals," London, Taylor & Francis). The great chemist's article on Palagonite in the "Annalen der Chimie und Pharmacie" (vol. lxi.) won for him the Copley medal of the Royal Society of London; and his studies on Iceland are the basis of modern scientific knowledge. It is to be regretted that his two admirable papers are buried in bad translation amongst the voluminous transactions of obscure societies, and their reproduction in a popular form would be a boon to travellers not only in the island, but also throughout the volcanic world. Mr B. Quaritch kindly allowed the author to make manuscript copies of these two articles: they have afforded material to the able lecture "On some of the Eruptive Phenomena of Iceland," by Dr John Tyndall, F.R.S. (Royal Institution of Great Britain, June 3, 1853).

16. P. A. Schleisner. "Island undersögt fra et lægevidenskabeligt Synspunkt," Copenhagen, 1849. The author, an employé of the Danish Government, resided some time on the island, and made useful physiological observations—one of them has before been alluded to.

17. Madame Ida Pfeiffer ("Reise nach dem skand Norden," 1845), after travelling in Syria and "the East," visited Iceland in 1844, hoping "there to find Nature in a garb such as she wears nowhere else." She laughs at the "dreadful dizzy abysses;" but the "dignified coldness" of the popular manners and the selfishness, only too apparent to an undistinguished foreigner, made her write what Mr Pliny Miles ungallantly calls a snarling, ill-tempered journal. The American traveller, also, is too severe when he says, "Where she does not knowingly tell direct falsehoods, the guesses she makes about those regions that she does not visit—while stating that she does[1]—show her to be bad at guess-work." Her translated volume, "A Visit to Iceland," etc. (London, Ingram, 1854) has been analysed in the "Cyclopædia of Modern Travel" (Bayard Taylor, 1856).

---

[1] The writer could have learned this only from Iceland information, and he should have been more cautious in listening to the islanders, especially when they were criticising what they consider a hostile book. On the other hand, Madame Pfeiffer has left an impression upon the reader that the clergy take money from travellers—which is certainly not the case now, and probably never was general.

18. "Bidrag til Islands geognostiske Fremstilling efter Opteg-nelser fra Sommeren, 1850" (Contribution to the Geognosy of Iceland, from Observations made in the Summer of 1850), by Theodor Kjerulf. Published in the "Nyt Magazin for Naturvi-denskaberne," vol. vii., part 1, Christiania, 1853 (New Magazine of the Natural Sciences, which records the transactions of the Physiographical Society of Christiania), an excellent equivalent of our "Annals of Natural History." The author differs from Von Waltershausen and Bunsen upon the genesis of Iceland (Dr W. Lauder Lindsay).

19. "Norðurfari, or Rambles in Iceland," by Pliny Miles, 12mo, New York, 1854. The author was the first American tourist who visited the island (1852), and he attempts little more than an entertaining narrative of his adventures. There is a fair amount of "spread eagle," and the tone is "England for ever, and America one day longer." An officer nearly cuts a shark in two with a sword. The whales can be heard from one to two miles off, and spout every one or five minutes, throwing up water from thirty to fifty feet—they must blow like himself!

20. "Tracings of Iceland and the Färoe Islands," by Robert Chambers, London, 1856. The author visited the island in 1855, voyaging on board the Danish cruiser "Thór," the first steamer—before his time the dangers of the northern seas were faced by sailing craft. The little book was translated into Danish, but the islanders affect to despise it.

21. "Voyage dans les Mers du Nord à bord de la corvette 'La Reine Hortense,'" par M. Charles Edmund. Paris: Levy, 1857. The author describes Prince Napoleon's tour in a volume which has all the characteristic merits and faults of the average French traveller. In the following pages it will be called the "Napoleon book."

22. Messrs Wolley and Newton confined themselves, with an especial object in view, to one particular parish in the south-western corner of Iceland. An "Abstract of (the late) Mr J. Wolley's Researches in Iceland, 1847, 1851, and 1852, respect-ing the Gare Fowl, or Great Auk;" by Alfred Newton, M.A., F.L.S., appeared in the "Ibis" of October 1861. The author's name is sufficient warrant for the value of this excellent paper.

In Baring-Gould (Appendix, p. 400), Mr Newton quotes numerous works upon the avi-fauna of Iceland.

23. " Letters from High Latitudes," by Lord Dufferin, London, 1858. The amiable author visited the island at the same time as Prince Napoleon, and proposed to cross the unknown tract between Hekla and the north-eastern coast; unfortunately the yacht " Foam " was carried away by the attractions of Jan Mayen and Spitzbergen. The adoption of a quasi-dramatic form has caused the book to be pronounced "most entertaining and perhaps a little extravagant;" it is written in the best of humours and in the most genial style, but it has failed to please the islanders who do not understand *plaisanterie.*

24. J. Dayman. " Deep Sea Soundings between Iceland and Newfoundland," etc. (1858).

25. " A Hand-book for Travellers in Denmark, Norway, Sweden, and Iceland," with maps and plans. London: John Murray, 1858, and republished in 1871. The island is dismissed in barely three pages, which contain a vast variety of errors; for instance, the population is preserved at 60,000; we are taught to write " Almannia Gja;" and we are told that Henderson wrote before 1825—*connu!* The recondite blunders may almost compare with the four pages on Istria in the "Handbook for South Germany." Happily for the traveller, Baedecker's excellent series is speedily consigning the cumbrous and tedious " Murrays " to well-merited oblivion.

26. J. Hogg. " On the History of Iceland " (1859).

27. D. Streye. " Beskrivelse over den $\phi$ Islandia," etc. Kjöbenhavn, 1859.

28. G. Thomsen. " The Northmen in Iceland," etc. (1859).

29. " Iceland: its Volcanoes, Geysers, and Glaciers." By Charles S. Forbes, Commander Royal Navy (Murray, London, 1860). The volume was kindly lent to the author by Captain Bedford Pim, M.P.; and its merit has been acknowledged by the general regret that there is not "more of it.".

30. C. Irminger. " Strömninger og Isdrift ved Island." Kjöbenhavn, 1861.

31. " Reise nach Island im Sommer 1860." Mit wissenschaftlichen. Abhängen von William Preyer und Dr Ferdi-

nand Zirkel. 8vo, Leipzig, 1862. The statistical part is exceedingly valuable. The work also contains the most complete notice of the birds that has been published after the "Prodromus der isländischen Ornithologie," by Friedrich Faber, better known as "Fugl Faber;" but it is judged that "the writer has not shown sufficient discrimination in its compilation."

32. "A Tour in Iceland in the Summer of 1861." By Edward Thurstan Holland, A.M. Chap. i., vol. i., 2d series: "Peaks, Passes, and Glaciers; being Excursions by Members of the Alpine Club." Edited by Edward Shirley Kennedy, M.A., F.R.G.S. London, 1862. The author attempted in 1861 to ascend the southern side of the Öræfa Jökull, but the mists prevented his enjoying the good fortune of Swend Paulsson and of Henderson.

33. "The Oxonian in Iceland; or Notes of Travel in that Island in the Summer of 1860." By Rev. Frederick Metcalfe, A.M. 12mo, Hotten, London, 1861. This traveller crossed a bit of new country north-east of the Sprengisandur, and thus deviated from the common line. He has preserved the traditional exaggeration which characterises Icelandic travellers, and the dangers which he faces on Mount Hekla must have been simply a dream. His map, purporting to be reduced from Ólsen's, is peculiarly bad.

34. W. Lauder Lindsay, M.D., F.L.S. "On the Flora of Iceland," New Philosophical Journal; and "On the Eruption, in May 1860, of the Kötlu-gjá Volcano, Iceland." Neill & Co., Edinburgh, 1861 — valuable papers which should accompany the traveller. They were kindly lent to the author by Mr William Longman.

35. G. G. Winkler. "Island seine Bewohner," etc. Bravansch, 1861.

36. M. Barbatier de Mas. "Instructions nautiques sur les Côtes d'Islande." Paris, 1862.

37. A. J. Symington. "Pen and Pencil Sketches of Färoe and Iceland." Longmans, London, 1862. Unpretending.

38. "Iceland: its Scenes and Sagas," by Sabine Baring-Gould, M.A. London: Smith & Elder, 1863. This handsome volume of 447 pages is written with an object, to illustrate the Sagas and to represent their *Mise en Scène*. The author sees the

Icelander as he is; the topography is that of a geographical traveller; and the book contains an immense amount of useful information. Taking the realistic view, this excellent work is not a favourite in Iceland; my only complaint is that it lacks an index.

39. C. Irminger. "Notice sur les Pêches, etc., de l'Islande." Paris, 1863.

40. Carl Vogt. "Nordenfahrt von Dr Berna" (1863).

41. "Notes on a Trip to Iceland in 1862." By Alexander Bryson. Edinburgh: Grant, 1864. The object of the livret (56 pages) was to gauge and to determine the heat of the Geysir tube, by means of deversing thermometers; and the author has sensibly questioned the " central-heat " theory.

42. M. Thoyon. "Renseignements sur quelques Mouillages sur la Côte d'Islande." Paris, 1865.

43. "Travels by ' Umbra ' " (Clifford). Edmonstone & Douglas, Edinburgh, 1865. The author, by ascending the Jökull of Eyrikr, that northern Cacus, reached eternal winter's drear domain. He justly derides the horrors and terrors of Búlandshöfði.

44. "The North-Western Peninsula of Iceland," by C. W. Shepheard. London: Longmans, 1867. This was the author's second excursion, and he ascended the Dránga Jökull in the north, where the mountains are lower and accessible.[1]

45. W. C. Paijkull. "Bidrag till Kännedomen om Islands Bergsbyggnad." Stockholm, 1867. Translated by the Rev. M. R. Barnard, M.A. London: Chapman & Hall, 1868. The author, now dead, was a Swede, and professed geology at the University of Upsala; he travelled in 1865, and unfortunately neglected to supply his volume with an index and a decent map. Its merits are much debated, and, as a rule, its tone is

---

[1] Amongst Icelandic travels we cannot include the valuable commercial papers, often alluded to in these pages—(1.) by Mr Vice-Consul Crowe, " Report on the Fisheries, Trade, and General Features of Iceland, for the years 1865-66 ;" and (2.) by Mr Consul Crowe, " On the Trade and Fisheries of Iceland, for the years 1870-71." It is evident that the able author has not been in Iceland or he would not say "the *schools* are excellent and well attended," when there are absolutely no schools. It is to be regretted that the Foreign Office does not enable writers to correct their proof-sheets ; we should then not have in a single page such blemishes as Skrid Sökler (Jöklar) ; Oræfa Tokull (Jökull) ; Odada-hrann (Ódáða Hraun); and Kekjavik-cum-Keykjavik (for Reykjavik) repeated throughout the paper.

greatly disliked by the islanders. An excellent authority, Dr Hjaltalín of Reykjavik, who has published several important studies of his native land,[1] considers it of scant value; on the other hand, Mr Jón A. Hjaltalín recommends it for its moderation to English travellers.

46. H. Mohn of the Institut Météorologique de Norvège. " Temperature de la Mer entre l'Islande et l'Ecosse." Christiania, 1870.

47. "A Report on the Resources of Iceland and Greenland." Compiled by Benjamin Mills Peirce, U.S. State Department, Washington Government Printing Office. The author was charged by Mr Secretary Seward to inspect the sulphur mines, 1868. He personally visited the island and produced a useful paper, collating the accounts and the figures published by his predecessors; but, like such compilations generally, it abounds in errors, and it makes scanty attempt to discriminate the various value of the information which it gleans.

48. " Six Weeks in the Saddle: a Painter's Journal in Iceland." By S. G. Waller. London: Macmillan, 1874. An unpretending volume which has held its ground at Mudie's, and which carefully avoids disputed points and exaggerated statements. The illustrations are very poor compared with the charming studies of scenery and animals made by the author, and it wants index and map, without which the home-reader will hardly follow the line over the now rarely visited southern shore.

49. The *Alpine Journal*, No. 45 (Longmans, London, 1874), contains " Interesting Notes on Mountain Climbing in Iceland," by Dr James Bryce, who also during the same year published his " Impressions of Iceland " in the *Cornhill Magazine*. He justly remarks that the difficulty is not so much to climb the peaks as to traverse the inhospitable desert separating them from the inhabited parts.

Mr S. Baring-Gould (Intr., pp. xxxiv., xxxv.) gives a catalogue of the fifteen books and manuscripts usually found amongst the priests and farmers; and in Appendix D. a list of Icelandic

---

[1] Dr Hjaltalín has written many articles on sanitary matters and the natural history of Iceland, which have appeared in various periodicals, Icelandic, Danish, and English. He has also published for several years the " Heilbrigðistíðindi " (Sanitary News).

published Sagas (thirty-five), local histories (sixty-six), annals of bishops (twelve), annals of Norway, etc. (sixty-nine), and romances translated into Icelandic (nineteen), a total of 201; besides law-books, Bible stories, and tracts on poetry, geography, astronomy, etc. The various editions of the Bible and of the Testament, as well as the newspaper press, will be noticed in future pages.

Miscellaneous general information concerning Iceland is found in the following works: The *Foreign Quarterly Review* (vol. ix., Jan.-May 1832) contains an excellent paper on the "Literature and Literary Societies of Iceland." The "Mémoires de la Société Royale des Antiquaires du Nord" are a mine of information to the student. Mrs Somerville's "Physical Geography." The "Progress of the Nation," by G. R. Porter, Esq., F.R.S. ("Institute of Natural Science," Paris correspondence. London, 1851). "Meddelelser fra det statistiske Bureau," vols. i.-vi. Kjöbenhavn, 1852-1861. In the fourth volume of the "Description of the Coast of Iceland" ("Fierde Hefte af Beskrivelsen over den islandske Kyst") by P. de Löwenörn, is a paper which was strongly recommended for translation to the author of these pages by Captain Tvede of Djúpivogr. The various numbers of the "Mittheilungen aus Justus Perthes," etc. Herschel's "Physical Geography," 2d edition, Edinburgh, 1862. Lippencott's "Complete Pronouncing Gazetteer, or Geographical Dictionary of the World," 8vo, Philadelphia, 1866. Chambers' and other Cyclopædias. Bayard Taylor's "Cyclopædia of Modern Travel," New York, 1856. "Cyclopædia Britannica," vol. xii., 1856. Knight's "English Encyclopædia" (pp. 1333-1345) of 1873, has printed an admirably condensed paper on Icelandic language and literature, by Mr Jón A. Hjaltalín.[1]

As the "marking book" of the last century was M. Mallet's "Antiquities," so there are three which distinguish the present age. The late Mr Benjamin Thorpe's "Edda of Sæmund the Learned"[2] (London: Trübner, 1866) is a text-book of Scandi-

---

[1] Near the end of the paper we read, "Iceland was now (after union with Norway) governed as a colony;" this assertion, it is said, belongs not to the author but to the editor.

[2] Laing's "Heimskringla" is a work of a very different kind, not translated from the original.

navian mythology delighting Icelanders by the literal rendering of their classical poem; it must be familiar to the student before he can attack the difficulties of Skjáldic song. The second is the " Story of Burnt Njal," etc., by George Webbe Dasent, D.C.L. (2 vols., Edmonstone & Douglas, Edinburgh, 1861). The introduction is the work of a scholar; the translation rivals Lane's " Arabian Nights," in fidelity, picturesqueness, and, withal, sound old English style, and the maps and plans well illustrate the topography. It has sent one, it will send many an English tourist to gaze upon the Lithe-end; and it will serve as an example how such books should be treated. But the *magnum opus* of the day, the greatest boon to students yet known, is the " Icelandic-English Dictionary " (3 vols. fol., Macmillan & Co., 1869, 1870, and 1874).[1] Based upon the MS. notes of the late Richard Cleasby, under whose name, as is his due, it is referred to in these pages, the work was enlarged and completed by the first of Icelandic philologers, Mr Guðbrand Vigfússon, M.A., formerly one of the stipendiaries of the Arna-Magnæan Library at Copenhagen. The herculean task has been completed after the patient toil of nine years (1864-1873), and all credit is due to the delegates of the Clarendon Press, who " generously fostered this Icelandic Dictionary and made it a child of their famous university." The introduction, by Mr Dasent, awards high praise to the work, but nothing that he can say is too high.

Iceland is not in want of maps; almost every traveller has contributed his own, and hence the atlases have borrowed a variety of blunders. The most interesting of the older sort are those of Hendries (Jodocuf, A.D. 1563-1611), which shows a curious acquaintance with certain *fodinæ sulphureæ;* and of Pontanus (A.D. 1631) Auctore Giorgio Carolo Flandre. The latter displays Hekla, the towering cone of our childish fancies, vomiting a huge bouquet of smoke, while it ignores all other volcanoes.

---

[1] The author can practically answer for its value. When travelling in 1872 he had only the first volume, and thus whilst tolerably acquainted with the words between A and the first half of H, he found it impossible, within given limits, to master the rest. In the "Days of Ignorance" it was necessary to learn Danish in order to use the Icelandic Dictionary. It is only to be hoped that the English-Icelandic half of the work will follow in due season, and doubtless some enterprising publisher, like Mr Trübner, will presently give us portable editions of both.

The islands are especially incorrect: the "Westmanna seu Pistilia (for Papyli ?) Eijar," fronted on the main by "Corvi Albi," [1] are out of form and measure; the archipelago called I. Gouberman (Gunnbjörn Skerries ?) off the north-western coast, does not exist; and Grimsey has dimensions which are strange to it. As in all of them; the north is placed too high; the Arctic circle traverses nearly the centre of the island, the furthest septentrional point being N. lat. 68° 15'. The eastern shore is also laid down too far west (E. long. Ferro, 10°) : hence, as Barrow shows, Arrowsmith's map of 1808 was sixty-seven miles wrong in the longitude. Henderson supplies Krísuvík with a non-existing inlet upon which foreigners have counted for embarking their sulphur, and reduces the vast Mýrdals Jökull to the Kötlu-gjá fissure.

Shortly before the time when Henderson travelled, several Danish officers, detained in Iceland by the war with Great Britain, began an exact trigonometrical survey, not only of the coast, but of the interior; and their bench-marks still crown many a conspicuous point. Their names, well remembered by all Danes upon the island, were the "Herr Officeerer," Major Scheel, Lieutenant Westlesen, and Landmaler (surveyor) Aschlund. After 1820, the work was carried on by Captain Born, Lieutenant (afterwards Captain) W. A. Graah,[2] R.N., an adventurous sailor, and a scientific officer, who died about a dozen years ago. Between 1820 and 1826 the following five sheets were published:

---

[1] Possibly a confusion with the pied crow (*C. Leucophœus*) of the Færoes. In Scandinavian mythology the raven was white, but, like the Hajar el Aswad of Mecca, it turned black in consequence of babbling and tale-bearing.

[2] He made an expedition to East Greenland in 1828-29; and his volume was translated by the late E. Gordon Macdougall, and published (London, Parker, 1837) by the Royal Geographical Society of Great Britain—a most sensible step. His determination that the East Bygð was on the west coast has of late been successfully questioned by Mr R. H. Major (Ocean Highways) through the 1507 edition of Ptolemy, the map of Van Keulen (circ. A.D. 1700), and the "Chorography" of the old Greenland colony, with sailing directions for reaching it from Iceland by Ivar Bardsen, steward of the colonial bishop. Captain Graah had denied the existence of Gunnbjörn's Skerries, and so forfeited the guidance of Ivar Bardsen. His book, however, is a valuable study of hyperborean regions generally, and especially useful as a standard of comparison between Iceland and Greenland. In the latter we find the hot springs of Önnartok depositing silicious sinter, like the Geysir and Strokkr, whilst the unfinished church of Kakortok reminds us of Færoese Kirkjubæ.

1. Snæfellsjökull to Cap Nord, in 1820, by Frisch, Westlesen, Smith, Scheel, Born, and Aschlund.

2. North Coast, in 1821, by Majors Ridder and Scheel, and Captains Frisch and Born.

3 and 4. South Coast, in 1823, by Scheel, Born, Graah, and Aschlund.

5. East Coast, in 1824, by Olsen, Born,· Graah, and Aschlund.

The general chart of 1826, uniting these "trigonometrical, geographical, and hydrographical surveys," is, according to Mr Alexander Findlay, F.R.G.S., carefully executed, and became the basis of all subsequent issues.

Unfortunately, it is the local fashion to ignore these scientific preliminary labours,[1] in favour of Professor Björn Gunnlaugsson's large map, which was executed after a comparatively running survey, during the twenty years from 1823 to 1843, and which, after being drawn up by the late Major Olsen, was printed at Copenhagen in 1844. The title is Updráttr Íslands á fjórum blöðum (in four sheets) gjörðr að fyrirsögn (executed under the direction of) Olafs Nikolas Olsen, gefinn út af enu (published by the) Islenzka Bókmentafèlgi. The scale is $\frac{1}{480000}$, about six or eight miles to the inch. The four-sheet edition has three different tintings—one physico-geographical, the second administrative, and the third hydrographical, giving soundings, etc. In London it costs £2, 2s.; at Reykjavik, $9 (= £1). There is a portable edition, a single sheet ($\frac{1}{960000}$), of two kinds, physico-geographical and administrative, costing six or seven shillings. The third or smallest size, prefixed, with sundry alterations, to these pages, costs one shilling at Reykjavik.

Of miscellaneous cartography we have the following: Dr Heinrich Berghaus's "Physikalisher Atlas;" Verlag von Justus Perthes,

---

[1] The fact is, it has become a party question. Hence strangers who, like Dr W. Lauder Lindsay (p. 7, "On the Eruption, in May 1860, of the Kötlu-gjá Volcano, Iceland"), are otherwise employed than in making general inquiries, ignore the basis. When this great *opus* was printed (1844), few countries in Europe had charts on such a scale, so accurately detailed, and so well engraved. Even at present it wants only the names of places being made more legible; it is still the standard work, for which seamen and landsmen have reason to be grateful, and it forms a solid foundation for future addition to all time. Mr Thorne (Ramsdale, Thorne, & Co.) kindly lent his copy to the author, who ungratefully kept it nearly three years.

Gotha, 1852; Colton's "Atlas of the World," New York, 1855; Hr Kiepert's "Allgemeiner Hand-Atlas der Ganzgen. Erde," Weimar, in Verlage des Geographischen Atlas, 1873; and the excellent "National Atlas" of Keith Johnston (sen.). The latest charts are English, French, and Danish—the latter being also used by the Norwegians, who have none of their own.

(a.) The English Admiralty chart, "Iceland Island," was based upon the Danish survey (1845; corrected, 1872).

The nomenclature of our hydrographic works greatly wants reform; even the exact Raper adheres to "Reikiavig" and to "Sneefeldsyökell."

(b.) The Danish charts principally used are:

1. Kaart over Pollen i Skutilsfjord, Isefjords Dybet, opmaalt fra Skrueskonnerten Fylla, Junii, 1865-67.
2. Islands Vestkyst, Stykkishólmr med Grunder og Kolgrafa-Fjörðr, 1869.
3. Kaart over Island, med omgivende Dybder, 1871.

(c.) The French, as we might expect from their commercial activity, had published before 1868 about a score more of charts and harbour plans than all other nations. The principal are:

1. Carte réduite des Côtes Septentrionales d'Islande depuis le Cap Nord jusqu' à l'île Malmey, 1822.
2. Carte réduite des Côtes Occidentales d'Islande, depuis Sneefields-Jokel jusqu' au Cap Nord, 1822 (Cartes danoises de Löwenörn).
3. Carte réduite des Côtes Occidentales d'Islande, depuis Fugle-Skiærene jusqu' à Huam Fiord, 1822 (Cartes danoises de Löwenörn).
4. Carte réduite des Côtes Septentrionales d'Islande, depuis l'île Malmey jusqu' au Cap Langanaes, 1823 (Cartes danoises Löwenörn).
5. Carte réduite des Côtes Meridionales d'Islande, depuis le Cap Ingolfs-Höfde jusqu' au Cap Riekienaes, 1832 (Cartes danoises de Löwenörn).
6. Carte réduite des Côtes Orientales d'Islande, depuis Vopna-Fiord jusqu' au Cap Ingolfs-Höfde, 1832 (Cartes danoises de Löwenörn).

7. Carte réduite d'Islande et des îles Feroës, 1836. D'après les Cartes danoises de Löwenörn et de Born.

8. Plan de la baie de Reikiavik, 1842 (MM. West; De la Roche, ingénieur-hydrographe; R. de Saint-Vulfran, et autres officiers de la Marine, 1840).

9. Plan du Mouillage d'Onondar Fiord; Plàn du Mouillage de Patrix-Fiord (Islande), 1845; corr. 1862 (MM. Brosset et Soyer, officiers de la Marine).

10. Plan de l'entrée du Hyal-Fiord, 1855 (MM. Caraguel, Borius, et Rapatel).

11. Plan du Mouillage d'Eské-Fiord. Croquis des Mouillages du Spath et de Svartas-Kiær, 1855 (MM. Duval, H. Lavigne, et Delville).

12. Carte de Dyre-Fiord, 1856 (MM. de Rochebrunne, Mathieu, et Ternier).

13. Plan des Mouillages de Dyre-Fiords, 1856 (MM. Mathieu et Ternier, 1855).

14. Plan du havre de Gröne-Fiord, 1855; corr. 1858 (Veron et autres officiers de là Marine, 1857).

15. Plan de Faskrud-Fiord, 1858 (MM. Barlatier, De Mas et Pottier, 1856).

16. Plan des passes de Rode-Fiord, 1858 (MM. Veron, Pottier, etc., 1857).

17. Carte des atterages de Reikiavik (Faxe Bugt) 1859. Houzé de l'Aulnoit d'après les travaux exécutés de 1853 à 1857.

18. Plan-croquis du havre de Nord-Fiord, 1860 (MM. Veron, Launay, etc., 1858).

19. Plan du havre de Kolgraver-Fiord, 1860 (Veron et autres officiers de la Marine, 1858).

20. Plan de la partie de la Côte Sud du Brede-Bugt (Côte Occidentale d'Islande) 1861.

21. Croquis du Mouillage de Hogdal dans Dyre-Fiord, 1861 (MM. West, lieutenant du vaisseau, et De Sédières, aspirant).

22. Carte de l'entrée du Golfe de Berú-Fiord et de la baie de Hammard-Fiord. Carte du Breidals Bugt, 1862.

23. Plan du mouillage d'Akureyré (Oë-Fiord), 1864 (Butter, lieutenant de vaisseau).

24. Plan de Skutils-Fiord et du port de Pollen, 1867 (MM. Guérard et Petit de Baroncourt).

25. Croquis du mouillage de Bildal dans Arnar-Fiord, 1867 (MM. Guérard et Petit de Baroncourt).

This section can hardly end more appropriately than with a notice of Dr Ebenezer Henderson's two volumes which, though published in 1818, and although we no longer land in Iceland as in Africa (i. 9), are still useful in 1874. The author died in 1829, but he is remembered by the islanders; and his name, cut in Hebrew letters upon the " soft yellow tufa" (Palagonite), the nafna-klettar (Wady el Mukattab) of Hýtardal, nearly sixty years ago, is, and long will be, shown to travellers. Lacking scientific training, and, probably, one of the *seri studiorum*, for his learning, especially his Hebrew, reads like an excrescence upon the simple journal, this writer has solid merits, and he enjoyed unusual advantages. His style is respectable; he has an exceptional eye for country, rare in the traveller as catching the likeness is in the portrait-painter; his powers of observation are remarkable, as shown by the observations upon the Skriðjöklar; he received every attention and much information from the clergy, in those days even more powerful than now; his employment as a colporteur of the " Sacred Oracles," which, by the by, were so faultily translated that they did not deserve to supersede Bishop Guðbrand's version, threw him much amongst the people; and his extensive travels during three years enabled him to publish the best, because the most general, book on Iceland known to the English tongue.

On the other hand, his pious expressions are so obsolete, that in these days we look upon them as almost irreverent. He has all the narrow-mindedness of the early nineteenth century—the Georgian era and the golden age of the evangelical middle classes. His credulity is astounding; he has a bulimia of faith; he eagerly records every ridiculous tale he hears—if you disbelieve him, you are a sceptic with a sub-flavour of atheism. He quotes without surprise the igneous vapours attaching themselves to the persons of the inhabitants; the under garments of a farmer being consumed when the outer suit was uninjured; and the lightning which burned in the pores of a woman's body, singeing the clothes she wore (i. 311, 316), a tale frequently copied by others. He borrows his natural history from Horrebow, and from Ólafsson and Pállsson, who wrote in A.D. 1755. The weakest fox manages to secure all the food (ii. 98). The silly bear deluded by the mitten, a fable so well known to children's books, is his. Upon the authority of a parson and an old woman, he supplies the *Mus sylvaticus* not only with a cow-chip canoe, but also with a mushroom carpet-bag (ii. 185): it excels the *animantia plaustra* of Polignac's Anti-Lucretius. His terrific descriptions of the road and the ford, dangers mostly fanciful, and his exaggerated horrors, must not be set down to want of manliness. An earnest and pious man, he yearns in every page to pull off his hat, to fall upon his knees, and to thank protecting and preserving Providence for some imaginary hair-breadth escape. The French travellers made observations for temperature and other matters in the floods which he describes as the most dangerous; and his eight-miles-an-hour current (i. 181) is simply a delusion.

The book has one great element of success, and the string of initials appended to the author's name prove that it has been successful. To use a popular phrase, all his " geese are swans " —a view highly flattering and very agreeable to the good geese, but a process hardly likely to leave a truthful impress upon the unprejudiced reader's brain. He complains that there *are* free-thinking priests, but every clerk he meets is a model of orthodox piety. He vaunts the hospitality of the land, and only casually lets fall the remark that, although he was employed on a highly popular mission, a single peasant refused to take money from him. Critics are agreed upon his estimate of " J. Milton's Paradisar Missir," by Jón Thorlakson.[1] " The translation not only rises superior to any other translation of Milton, but rivals, and in many instances in which the Eddaic phraseology is introduced almost seems to surpass, the original. . . . Thorlakson has

---

[1] Every serious Icelandic traveller of the nineteenth century has alluded more or less to the career of the Rev. Jón Thorláksson, parish priest of Backa, who

not only supported its prevailing character, but has nicely imitated his (author's) peculiar terms and more refined modifications." . . . And "although Thorlakson has found it impossible to give the effect of certain sounds, yet this defect is more than compensated by the multiplicity of happy combinations where none exist in the original" (vol. i., 98). All good judges declare that the Icelander has recast Milton in Scandinavian mould, and has produced a beautiful Icelandic poem upon the English groundwork. The narrow bounds of the narrative measure (Fornyrðalag [1]) could never contain the now sweet now sonorous Miltonic verse; and the last sentence quoted from Mr Henderson, as well as his own specimens of the work, clearly show his ignorance of what a translation should be.

Mr William Longman, Vice-President of the Alpine Club, has done good service to the Icelandic traveller by digesting Mr Henderson's Itineraries (Suggestions for the Exploration of Iceland. London: Longmans, 1861), and by adding many useful

---

lived as best becomes a poet, in poverty, and who died in poverty, æt. seventy-five, in 1819. He thus laments his hard fate:

> " Yes; Penury hath been my bride
> Since e'er I saw the world of men;
> And clasped me to her rugged breast
> These seventy winters all but twain:
> And if we separate here below,
> He only knows who made it so."

His "living," besides glebe and parish gifts, was £6 per annum, of which half was paid to an assistant (Henderson and Barrow); and he did not live to receive the £20 collected for him in England. He translated Pope's Essay on Man, Klopstock's Messiah, and Paradise Lost. The three first books of the latter were printed by the Islenzka Lærdómslista-fèlag (Icel. Lit. Society) before it was dissolved in 1796. The original MS. is deposited in the rooms of the Literary Fund, London.

[1] Forn-yrði, an old word, an archaism; hence Eddaic verse. We may illustrate its alliteration by Peirce Plowman:

> " I *looked* on my *left* half
> As the *Lady* me taught,
> And was *ware* of a *woman*
> *Worthlyith* clothed."

Finn Magnússon and Rask thus converted Virgil into narrative verse:

> " Arma virumque
> Cano, Trojæ
> Qui primus ab oris
> Italiam,
> Fato profugus,
> Lavinaque venit
> Littora," etc.

items of information. But the reader, however capable, must not expect to carry out the programme. In page 30 the author seems to think ten days sufficient to attempt the ascent or exploration of Kötlu-gjá, Kálfafell, Skeiðarárjökull, Öræfa, and Breiðamerkr Jökull. Each of these " congealed Pandemonia," with the inevitable delays in travelling from one to the other, would probably consume a fortnight. Iceland is no place for *dilettanti grimpeurs;* it has neither comfortable inns nor Bureaux des Guides—these Alps are not to be passed over *summâ diligentiâ;* and M. Jules Verne's balloon has not yet found its way there.

## § 2. PREPARATIONS FOR TRAVEL.

Icelandic travel is of two kinds—the simple tour and the exploration. Most men content themselves with landing at Reykjavik, and with making the Cockney trip to Thingvellir, the Geysir and Hekla, perhaps visiting the Laxá, Laugarnes Bessastaðir, Hafnarfjörð, Krísuvík, and Reykir. Others add to this a run to the local Staffa, Stappa, a more or less complete ascent of Snæfellsjökull, and a visit to Reykholt, Surts-hellir, Baula, and Eldborg. If more adventurously disposed, they cross the Arnarvatnsheiði and the Stórisandur to Akureyri, the northern " capital;" they push from Hekla across the Sprengisandur and the centre of the island; or they land at Vopnafjörð, and traverse the north-east corner viâ the Mý-vatn to Húsavik.

For these and other beaten paths very scanty preparations are necessary. Tourists usually exceed in their *impedimenta.* One party brought out butter where " smjör " is a drug; a second imported the Peter Halkett air-boat and wooden paddles, for crossing rivers three feet deep;[1] a third carried a medicine-chest, where air and water are perfection; a fourth indulged himself with a fine patent reading-lamp, where diamond type is legible at the " noon of night "—a new edition of warming-pans to Calcutta, skates to Brazilian Bahia, and soldiers' pokers for stirring

---

[1] As will appear in the Journal, all the principal streams have ferries or some *succedanea*, and no Iceland guide is in the habit of exposing himself recklessly.

wooden fires in Ashanti-land. The " Oxonian in Iceland" his advice was taken by another tourist party, who invested £20 in presents for the clergy and clergywomen, books, razors and pen-knives, scissors and needles, ribbons and silk kerchiefs: on return to Reykjavik these inutilities fetched a dollar per pound. The only gifts required are silver specie; if you make a present, you are a *richard*, and your bill, as all the world over, will be doubled. To the usual travelling-dress add fishermen's kit,[1] not the dandy Mackintosh, which sops at once in the pelting and penetrating rain. The boots should meet the waterproof: Mr Metcalfe objects that with such gear you cannot walk, and that if your pony fall in one of the " giddy rapid rivers," you will be pounded to death by stones and water—but possibly you were not " born to be drowned." Perhaps the best wear for the nether man would be long waterproof stockings, not the wretched stuff of West-End shops, nor Iceland oilskins, which are never imper-meable, but Leith articles made for wear, drawn over common boots and overalls, fastened round the waist, and ready to be cast off in hot and sunny weather, or when preparing for a walk over lava. Horses and horse-gear, as well as tents and mattresses, will be described in another place. A common canteen, with iron plates and cups, lamp and methylated spirits, suffices for the cooking department. Cigars, tobacco and snuff, must be carried by those who are not likely to relish the island supply; also tea and cognac, if coffee and Danish " brandy-wine " are not good enough. Sundry tins of potted meat and soup and a few pounds of biscuit are the only other necessaries, to which the traveller may add superfluities *ad infinitum*. The fishing-rods and nets, the battery, instruments and materials for writing and sketching, must depend upon the tourist. It is as well for him to bear in mind that he will suffer from stinging gnats and midges near the water as much as from thirst, the effect of ab-normal evaporation, upon the hills, and from dust and sand upon the paths called roads.

Exploration in Iceland is a very different affair. In these

---

[1] Hunter & M'Donald of Leith sell sou'-westers for 2s. ; outer and inner hose, at 3s. 6d. and 2s. 6d.; sailors' trousers, for 10s.; stout oil coats, at 18s. 6d.; and fisher-men's mitts, at 1s. 3d. Foreman, also of Leith, supplies excellent boots for £2, 10s.

days when a country, apparently accessible, has not been opened, we may safely determine *à priori* that its difficulties and dangers have deterred travellers. Here the only parts worth the risk, the expense, and the hardships, are the masses of snowy highland thrown into one under the names of Vatnajökull and Klofajökull, and the great desert, Ódáða Hraun, subtending their northern face. To investigate these "awfully romantic" haunts is a work of expenditure; and tourists arriving in Iceland know nothing of what is wanted. A party of less than four, one being a Swiss or Færoese mountaineer, would not be able to separate when necessary; and each must have ten horses,[1] as food, forage, and fuel have all to be carried. In the snow and the lava they will find nothing, and the tent will be the only home. Provisions would be represented by barrels of biscuits, bread, beef, and pork, with compressed vegetables, the maximum weight of each keg being 40 lbs. For drink, whisky or other spirits, the forbidden oil of whisky to be preferred if procurable. Patent fuel and pressed hay can travel in Iceland crates. At least one of the party should be able to shoe horses, so as not to rely upon the guide, who may perhaps prick two hoofs in one day. A change, or better still two changes, of irons for each nag, and four times the number of nails, must be the minimum: the lava tears off everything in the shape of shoes, and three hours without them lame the animal. The party might set out about early June in a schooner hired at Copenhagen, and land their impediments at Djúpivogr. After buying ponies and engaging native servants, they would ascend the Fossárdalr, strike the lakelets called Axarvatn and Líkarvatn, ford the Jökullsá near its head, and penetrate into the great snow-fields. Or they might make the Lagarfljót at Hallorm-staðir, ferry over the river, establish a depot at Valthjófstaðir, or Egilstaðir, the highest farm up the valley, and march south.

For the snowy range, the explorer needs all the "implements

---

[1] A very young traveller, Mr John Milne, F.G.S., has thus taken the author to task: "Fancy yourself with forty horses, riding over snow bridges by the dozen." Is it then necessary to explain that the ponies are intended for the Ódáða Hraun, a tract about the size of Devonshire? When Mr Watts started on his second expedition, he declared it was "essential that the party should not be less than six," and he preferred eight, calculating that the expenses would not exceed £50 per man.

of Alpine warfare," with the addition of a pair of inflatable boats, each carrying two—the reason will appear in the Journal. Ice-axe and spikes can be bought from Moseley, Henrietta Street, Covent Garden; and ropes from Buckingham, Broad Street, Bloomsbury: all these articles are also sold by J. S. Carter, 295 Oxford Street, "under the patronage of the Alpine Club." Mr Whymper prefers the Manilla rope, though somewhat heavier than Italian hemp; the former being 103, and the latter 93, oz. per 100 feet. They should not break with a lighter weight than 2 tons, or 196 lbs. falling 8 feet, or 168 lbs. falling 10. At least four 100-feet lengths[1] should be taken; and the tyro, who had better stay at home, should learn from "Scrambles among the Alps" (London: Murray, 1871), the way to tie and not to tie. The knapsack and alpenstock must be light; Mr R. Glover, Honorary Secretary of the Wanderers' Club, kindly assisted the author in applying to the War Office, Pall Mall, for one of the "male bamboos," now used as cavalry lances: it proved, however, somewhat heavy. A cousin, Edward Burton, was also good enough to send for a pair of *truviers*, or Canadian snow-shoes; but these rackets are not so useful as those of country make.[2] Boots for riding, for walking, and for wading, are absolutely necessary. Binoculars, French grey spectacles, and sun-veils must not be forgotten, and when they come to grief, the face, especially the orbits, can be blackened, after the fashion of the Cascade

---

[1] "Ropeing" is not a new thing, as many Alpine travellers seem to think. Pállson, when ascending Öræfa Jökull (1794), used "a rope about ten fathoms in length," and "left a distance of two fathoms" between himself and his two companions. The latter is the modern average, the extremes being nine and fifteen. The author never heard of Icelanders objecting to this precaution, but "G. H. C.," who in August 1, 1874, inspected the Kötlu-gjá (*Field*, October 10, 1874), says that his two guides "apparently regarded such proceeding in the light of a capital joke, and, connecting the idea with that of horses (*i taumi*) at a sale, declared 'they had never heard of a horse-fair on a Yokull.'"

[2] Every kind of snow requires its own shoe. Thus the Norwegian "skies" are very different from the Iceland skí, which resembles the Finn "öudrar," or "andrar." These articles are six, seven, and even twelve feet long, by five inches wide, in fact like large cask-staves. The front ends are a little bent up, and the sides are garnished with iron (saddlers') D's, through which leather thongs, or bands of willow-withes, are passed to secure the feet. Sometimes for facility of turning, one is made longer than the other, and the Lapps sole the right foot with hairy skin, so as to hold the snow in the back stroke. The alpenstock in Iceland is a bone handled staff, with a stout spike: the author never saw the stick shod with a wheel three inches broad, and safe against sinking, which is used on the Continent.

Range Indians, with soot and grease—the explorer will look like an Ethiopian serenader, but there will be no one to see him. Watches and instruments must be in duplicate, or, better still, in triplicate. The map should be in four sections, guarded from the wet with copal varnish; and skeleton pocket-maps save trouble. Mr Longman (Suggestions, etc.) supplies a copious list of explorer-tools : the author travelled with two pocket aneroids, a larger one left behind for comparison; three B. P. thermometers; Saussure's hygrometer; a portable clinometer; an *aréometre selon Cartier;* three thermometers (max. and min.); two hygrometers, the usual wet and dry bulbs;[1] a prismatic compass; and Captain George's double pocket-sextant—almost all supplied by Mr Casella. A six-pocket waistcoat, with an inner pouch for money, is the handiest way to dispose of the aneroid, small field thermometer, compass, clinometer, silver-sheathed pencil, penknife, and strong magnifying glass. Mr Watts, a young law-student, of whom more presently, suggested for crevasse crossing a ladder twelve feet long, which, turned up at one end, might serve as a sledge : it reminded me of Mr Whymper's troubles. This, together with the bamboo alpenstock, the snow-shoes, lamp, spirits of wine, kegs, and other small necessaries, were left at Djúpivogr for the benefit of future travellers.

For the Ódáða Hraun, besides food, forage, and fuel, the explorer will require to carry water. The sun's heat is intense even after Syria; and dust-storms, when not laid by sullen, murky sheets of mist, or the torrrents discharged by angry, inky clouds, are bad as in Sind and the Panjáb. Native attendants must be carefully rationed : they will live, at their own expense, on bread and butter, or rather on butter and bread; but they will eat the best part of a sheep at the employer's, and they will drink, as the saying is, " any given quantity." On the Hraun, Rigby's " Express Rifle " may be useful in case of meeting a reindeer, and pistols and bowie-knifes will encourage the guide to defy the Útilegumenn, *les hommes hors de la loi,* with whom

---

[1] One of the thermometers was broken on the way to Edinburgh, and, curious to say, it could not be repaired in the capital of Scotland. Professor C. Vogt prefers to the Alpine Sympiesometer, the *Barometre Compensée Metallique* of M. Richard, Rue Fontaine du Roi, Paris : he used it in Iceland, and found it answer admirably.

their superstitions people these solitudes. It is as well to carry glycerine for chafes and sunburns, poor man's plaister, and materials indispensable in case of accidents. The holsters should contain lucifers, and the coat-pockets metallic note-book and measuring tape, insect bottle with bran, and an old magazine for carrying plants to camp.

The Reykjavik guides will assuredly refuse to accompany such an expedition, and will declare that no Icelander can be persuaded to say yes. This, as will be seen, is not the fact. But raw men who take scanty interest in exploration, can hardly be expected to incur great risks. About the end of July, somewhat late in the year, students *en vacance*, speaking good Danish, a few words of English, French, and German, and perhaps a little " dog Latin," would be persuaded by three or four rixdollars per diem to become "vacation tourists," and something more. They must not be treated like common guides, and they also should be furnished with strong boots and bedding, for nights on the lava and in the snow.

This long Introduction may conclude with a pleasant quotation from Prof. C. Vogt: " Plus je reporte mes souvenirs vers nôtre voyage accompli cet été, plus je me sens attiré vers l'Islande, dont la nature, eminemment sauvage, porte un cachet tout à fait particulier, et dont le sol volcanique offre encore tant de questions à resoudre." And the traveller's memory will in future days dwell curiously upon the past, when

> " The double twilights rose and fell
> About a land where nothing seemed the same,
> At noon or eve, as in the days gone by."

THE DWARFIE STONE, HOY, ORKNEY.

# ULTIMA THULE;

# A SUMMER IN ICELAND.

## CHAPTER I.

THE STEAM-SHIP " QUEEN "—THE ORKNEYS AND MAES HOWE—THE
SHETLANDS AND THE FÆROE ISLANDS.

ADIEU, O Edinburgh! whether thou prefer to be titled Edina,
Dun-Edin, Quebec of the Old World, the Grand Chartreuse of
Presbyterianism, Modern Athens—a trifle too classical—or Auld
Reekie, good Norsk but foul, fuliginous, and over familiar.
Many thanks for the civilities lavished, with one " base exception," upon the traveller, who returns them in a host of good
wishes. *E.g.*, May the little lads and lasses that play ball and
hop-scotch upon thy broad *trottoirs* presently rise, like the
infantry of Ireland and the Cici of Istria, to the dignity of shoes
and stockings! May the odious paving-stones, which, under
gigantic " busses," make thee the noisiest as thou art the most
picturesque city in the empire, disappear before the steam-
roller and the invention of thine own son Macadam: the former,
after having long been used in the virgin forest of the Brazil,
has at length found its way to London, and why should it not
travel north? May unclean wynd and impure close, worse than
the Ghetto of Damascus, perish with krames and lucken-booths,
and revive in broad way and long square! May the railroad
cars put in an appearance amongst the open hackneys, whose
reckless driving, like that of the Trieste jarvey, seems to be connected in business with the undertaker; and may the stands no

longer be wholly deserted on the Scoto-Judaic Sabbath! May there
be some abatement and mitigation of the rule, "Let us all be unhappy on Sunday"—when man may drink "whusky," but "manna
whustle"—that earthly and transitory equivalent, as the facetious
Roman Catholic remarked, for the more durable, but haply the
not more unendurable, Purgatory! May thy beef lose its pestilent
flavour of oil-cake, thy dames look less *renfrognées*, and thy
sons unlearn the stock phrase which begins every answer " Eh!
nae!" And lastly, St Giles grant that so hospitable a city may
condescend to set on foot a club where the passing stranger, not
only the "general commanding," can see his name enrolled for
a month or two of membership, and no longer suffer from the
outer darkness of utter clublessness!

The spring of 1872 was tardy and dreary, and though I had
left London *en route* for Iceland shortly after mid-May, June
began before the normal severity of a septentrional summer
justified departure northwards. Travellers of the last generation
were still subject to the sailing ship. Mr Chambers and his
party are the first (1855) who had the chance of a "smoky
Argosy," and the wild island-fishermen flocked to save a ship
which appeared to be on fire, whilst the country people fled from
the monster to their lava fastnesses. So in 1832 the first steamer
passing the Shetlands coast, greatly excited the unsophisticated
peasantry by suggesting witchcraft—I am not sure that some did
not expect Thor to be on board. So, finally, Captain Trevithick's
"puffing devil" was held by Cornishmen to be the gentleman
in black; and French peasants shot at balloons, holding them
to be monstrous birds.

During the summer of 1872 there was embarrassment in the
wealth of conveyance. The royal mail steamship (Danish
Government) "Diana" touches at Granton[1] and Lerwick once a
month between March and November. The Norwegian steamer,
"Jón Sigurðsson," visited the chief port of the Shetlands with a
certain irregularity, but the electric telegraph could always give
timely warning. The "Yarrow" of Glasgow, belonging to Mr
Slimon, ran during the season; and Mr Robert Buist of Edin-

---

[1] The *Saturday Review* (December 14, 1872) informs its readers that the Danish
mail packet runs from Leith—which it does not.

burgh chartered the "Queen" from the Aberdeen, Leith, and Clyde Shipping Company. We shall see them all in due time.

Accompanied by my brother Stisted, I ran down to Granton betimes on June 4, along a road whose sides are coped walls, not rails and hedges, through a country still showing early spring, although some six weeks more advanced than Iceland. A couple of hours' delay gave us time to inspect Granton, and we owe it a debt of gratitude for saving us the mortification of ancient Grangemouth. Scotch tourists in Iceland compare its regularity with the irregularity of Reykjavik: it is regular as a skeleton, this sketch-town, this prospectus, this programme-city with its three piers—the Mineral, the Middle, and the Break-water; and with its square composed of two sides, the gaunt, grim hotel forming half the whole. The staple trade appears limited to blue-green barrels of the old "petreol," which now seem to travel all round the world.[1] The central quay—whose promenaders, though no longer fined threepence, may not smoke —is remarkably good; and wind-bound ships affect the harbour, because its bottom is soft mud, and because they are charged for shelter only one penny per ton during the whole stay, dis-charging cargo for sixpence instead of a shilling at Leith. The place is the property of the bold Buccleuch, who, bolder this time than even at the British Association, expended, ὡς λέγουσι, £1,200,000 for an annual consideration of £15,000. Despite its stout-hearted progenitor, it is a dull, young Jack of a settlement, all work and no play; but we shall find it perfect civilisation, a little Paris in fact, on landing from Reykjavik.

At 1.30 P.M. we cast loose, or, to put it more poetically with a modern author, we assisted at the "chorus of sailors," who are supposed to sing—

> "The windlass ply, the cable haul
> With a stamp and go, and a yeo-heave-oh!"

The little knot of friends—T. Wright of the 93d and D. Herbert of the *Courant*—wave farewell hats from the pier. It is an

---

[1] From most parts of the world, too, even from Hungary and Fiume, the casks are sent back to the United States, not broken up, but in bulk, because the heavy freight pays well where labour cannot be bought.

exceptional day. The German Ocean wearing an imitation azure and gold robe, with the false air of a southern sea, treacherously promises a yachting trip. The smoke of many steamers forms a thin buff canopy, far-stretching over the waste of pale sky-blue waters striped here and there with long bands of yet milkier hue—*placidi pellacia ponti*. The Firth of Forth somewhat reminded me of the fair entrance to Tagus; only here, instead of obsolete windmills and huge palaces, we see red-tiled roofs and tall stacks, artificial fumaroles vomiting pitchy vapours —the various symbols of a very busy race. Along the populous shores of the Fifeish "kingdom" whose *riant* hills are loved by foxes that love lambs, where the Lomonds give a *faux-air* of resemblance to the Bay of Bombay, rise successively Burntisland, Kinghorn, Kirkcaldy, Wemyss, and Leven with gables facing the sea and fringing the main, "as lace embroiders the edges of a lady's petticoat." After yet a little time there will be a single line of habitation along what the late M. Alexandre Dumas, the inventor of the "Lapin Gaulois," called the "Fifth of the Fourth, or sea arm running up to Edinburgh," and its limits will be Dunbar and St Andrews. In the rear rises the lumpy blue sofa that formed Arthur's Seat, a local Cader Idris, very like, under certain aspects, the Istrian Monte Maggiore; here the husband of Queen Guenevere is what Wallace and Auld Michael are to the rest of Scotland, 'Antar to Syria, the Devil or Julius Cæsar to Brittany, and Sæmund-the-Learned-cum-Gretti-the-Strong to Iceland. The volcanic outcrop, famed by Huttonians, is flanked to the north by the basaltic Salisbury Crags, whose billows of stone I had last seen in the limestone cliffs of Marmarún or Dinhá (*vide* Unexplored Syria); and a thin white thread at the base denotes the "Radical Road" (to Ruin), round which the ragged ruffians and rascals run.

And so we steam past Inchkeith; here a tall lighthouse is flanked seawards by a pile of buildings which would have been better sheltered on the other side, and which ought to be a mass of batteries like Gibraltar. We cannot but remark the utterly defenceless state of the northern capital, which lies literally at the mercy of a single ironclad, commanded by any Paul Jones. But happily in these days we battle with gold not with steel;

we arbitrate instead of fighting. Otherwise we might be tempted to propose torpedo stations, iron-rivetted turrets, and other appliances of an art which the policy of the last five years has made utterly antiquated, not to say barbarous. The Westminster players of 1872 grumble—

> " Ah ! minimè refert quid sentiat Anglia ! Totam
> Mutandis sese mercibus illa dedit.
> Pacis amans quovis pretio, maris arbitra quondam
> Nunc ipsa externo pendet ab arbitrio—"

and grumble in vain.[1] However, " we have heard about that before." We have also heard of yon quaint pyramid on the starboard bow, concerning which Mr Henderson says (i. 36), "The term 'Law' is still applied to many hills in Scotland, as 'Largo-Law,' and so forth." But the verbal resemblance to the natural Lögbergs (law-mounts) of Iceland,[2] Orkneys, and Shetlands, corresponding with the artificial moot-hills of Scotland, is a trivial accident which has caused a philological stumble. "Law" is simply the Anglo-Saxon Hlæw or Hlaw, primarily a low hill, secondarily a tumulus, cairn, or sepulchral burrow (Bearw or Bearo), heaped over the dead, as Lud-low the Low of Lude. Berwick-Law, though shaped very like a Lögberg, means only Berwick Hill. Farther east is the Bass, "sea-rock immense," northwards steep-to apparently the rule of the northern coast and the Orkneys, a broad-shouldered and misshapen stack rising, like Ailsa Craig, sheer from the sea, and now very far from being the "terror of navigators."

During dinner, at the primitive and Viennese hour of four P.M., we had passed Fifeness, alias the East Neuk of Fife, not our "nook," an indention, but the Norsk Hnjúkr or Hnúkr, a knoll; the high, lone hill, like Arthur's Seat, occupies a long, blue tongue, which projects a perilous reef some ten miles out to sea. The Firth of Tay—"firth," from Fjörð, is right; "frith," from Fretum,

---

[1] I need hardly remark that this was written before the glorious days of February 1874, when the English nation, centuries ahead of Ireland, Scotland, and Wales, by one of the noblest constitutional revolutions known to its history, buried that *felo-de-se*, the Radical Cabinet, and pulled down its programme Disestablishment, Retrenchment, and Non-intervention, the latest modification of Liberté, Égalité, Fraternité, and—Death.

[2] We have seen that in Iceland the Lögberg, or Hill of Laws, was confined to the Althing.

is wrong—with its many brethren, are foretastes of Iceland and Norway; the huge gapes of dwarfish bodies, embouchures whose breadth promises a length of many hundred miles, which the shortness of the watershed reduces to scores. Such are the estuaries and giant mouths of the Gaboon, and, indeed, of all the South African rivers save five—the Congo and Zambezi, the Rufiji, the Limpopo, and the Orange; and we need hardly go so far to study the feature, as the Mersey of Mercia is a first-rate specimen. We peer from a distance at the "Geneva of the North" (*proh pudor!*), the Faridon dé, the Donum Dei, famed in the days of terror as the abode of the "reverend citizen Douglas," where of late the mob-caps have had a famous bout of "clapper-clawing" with the bonnets of bonnie Dundee; and where, according to its own *Advertiser*, "there are heathens who read newspapers during the Christmas holidays."

Broad daylight blazed till ten P.M.; but fog, probably born of smoke, and marring the effect of the pretty sail, obscured the outlines of Fowls' Heugh, in Kincardineshire. These are cliffs some 300 to 400 feet high, where adventurous cragsmen still risk broken necks to plunder birds' nests. The Færoese hold that the unfortunates falling from great heights burst in mid air; and it has been remarked by those who have had ample opportunities of induction, that the many who have thrown themselves off the London monument wear placid countenances, showing none of the horrors of agonising death. It is possible, then, that the sudden shock may cause asphyxia and apoplexy—we will hope that it does.

Before "turning in," as the wheezing of the wind and the pelting showers of blacks suggest, let us shortly survey the ship and our shipmates, a process which travellers apparently despise as unworthy of their high-mightinesses. The " Queen," Captain William Reid, is a crowded little thing of 280 tons register; a startling contrast to Messrs Papayanni's large and comfortable "Arkadia," Captain Peter Blacklock, in which I last sailed as *the* passenger from Bayrút. She is licensed to carry forty-seven miserables; her old-fashioned engines half-consume twenty-three tons of coal in twenty-four hours; and her horse-power (230) makes her bore through the water at the maximum rate of nine knots.

She has no bath; washing is at a discount amongst these northerners; her offices are truly awful; and the berths are apparently
built for Arctic exploration, or for the accommodation of General
Tom Thumb and Commodore Nutt: the close vapours would gener-
ate nightmare, but, happily, only the stewards sleep in the main
cabin. The food is profuse but primitive—giant tureens of oleagin-
ous soup; fish which cannot be kept quite fresh; huge junks of meat,
of course carved at table; mutton chops—not cutlets—all fat, or
rather tallow; vast slices of "polonies," lard-speckled, and very like
the puddings of sheep's blood farther north; marbled potatoes;
graveolent cabbages; parsnips and carrots, hateful to Banting; poor
bread; good hard biscuit; excellent butter, much enjoyed by Icelanders; rice puddings, and huge pies of rhubarb, locally called
overring or southern wood; tea which resembles nothing that
fancy can suggest; coffee much resembling a watery decoction of
senna; excellent whisky; the usual brandy, *not* right " Nantz,"
and gin clean forgotten.

The passengers are all first-class, and those who should be
seconds pay somewhat less than the usual return fare, £6—board
not included. In these lands, the three R's are the great levellers;
and for a certain roughness, moral as well as physical, we need
hardly visit Canada or the Far West; our Lowlander, emphatically opposed to the Highlander, supplies us with an admirable
specimen. Many of the travellers are bound northwards on
business, and their "Gentlemen, who says feesh?" reminds us
of Mr *Punch* and his "pudden." There is a laird of the parts
about Aberdeen, accompanied by an intelligent Scotch bailiff;
an army man, Major B., and his brother-in-law, Mr S.; a navy
man, Captain H., much addicted to fishing; another Piscator,
popularly known as Johnny B.; and a missionary, who will not
walk the quarter-deck on "the Sabbath." He offers a tract to
our parson—we can longer quote amongst British proverbs,
"Coals to Newcastle"—the Rev. R. M. Spence, originally of
Kirkwall, Orkneys, and now holding the manse of Arbuthnott.
I must name him; his local knowledge was most valuable to all
on board; it was given freely and without stint, and after his
"parson's week," he was kind enough to correspond with me
during my stay in Iceland. Kirkwall has produced much "good

company," but none better than the Reverend Spence. There is
a stewardess, who stoutly cleared for herself the ladies' saloon.
The steward and his mate are of the type often seen on board
the "leather-breeches mob of steamers"—an epithet, mind, which
I do not apply to the "Queen." They are fond of bumping you,
of spilling the soup, of putting unclean towels upon your open
books, of carrying a host of articles in one hand, of charging the
smallest and meanest items, and of being peculiarly civil on the
last day. The captain soon merits the general description of a
"regular brick;" he has no pilot who knows coast or course,
not a soul on board has ever been in Iceland, yet he accepts all
responsibility like a man and a seaman; and he will spend on
deck two successive nights of fog and wet. Finally, although
the "Queen" is not one of the floating coffins which have roused
Mr Plimsoll's just indignation, she was sent out in a peculiarly.
reckless way,[1] and without so good a sailor as Captain Reid, she
—and we—ran the very best chances of coming to a bad end.

*June 5.*

During the few dark, or rather chiaro-oscuro, hours, we ran
along the coast north-east and by east, turning the great shoulder
north of Aberdeen. As the raw and rainy morning dawned,
high loomed on the port bows Duncansby, popularly written
Duncansbay, Head, whose castellated and ruin-shaped rocks of
yellow-brown sandstone, streaked with white layers of guano,
were new features to us; much resembling in form, though not
in formation, what Iceland will show. The steep and frowning
headland, sentinelled by needles, the Shetland "drongs," the

---

[1] After many years of the "*quousque tandem?*" state of mind, my astonishment at
the amount of legal murder authorised and sanctioned by authority in England,
and my wonder that abuses so hideous did not become a public scandal, have been
explained away by the sacrifices which the patriotic Mr Plimsoll found necessary
before he could obtain a hearing. The manner in which his small inaccuracies of
detail have been made to obscure the whole "palpitant question," the counter-
charges of sensationalism and ultra-philanthropy which have been brought to
refute the main charge, and the notable worship of Mammon and vested abuses,
are hardly encouraging to the optimist's view of "progress." But the day is now
done, let us hope, when crews of "murdered men" can be sent to sea in floating
coffins insured at thrice their value. The simplest preventive would be an order
that every consul should report all flagrant cases, with the express understanding,
however, that he should not be punished nor be made to suffer for doing his "unpleasant duty."

Færoese "drengr," and the Icelandic "drangar," bluff to the sea, and sloping backwards in long brown-green dorsa, is lit up by a sickly, pallid sun, which picks out of the dark curtain the snowy wings of myriad sea-fowl. The parallel strata supply the celebrated flags of Caithness, and the softer parts are readily hollowed into " Devil's nostrils," Helyers,[1] or sea-washed caverns, with pyramidal entrances which cause frequent cliff-falls.

Beyond this point the coast is fretted into shallow bays of good soil, fronted by sandy beaches of dwarf proportions, and here and there by a small scaur; the chord is also pierced by long winding passages, incipient Fjörðs, whose vistas end in yellow shingle. These pasture-lands of Caithness are scattered with cots, "infield" and "outfield," but we look in vain for copse, wood, or forest. As a northern writer said some hundred years ago, "A single tree does not appear that may afford shelter to friendship and innocence" (why innocence?), and fuel must be supplied by wreck-wood and drift-wood, by peat and wrack, by cattle chips and bones. The cause is one from the Prairies and the Pampas to the Carso of Trieste, and the rich uplands of Spain, Syria, and the Haurán. Be the soil ever so fertile, its growth, without the protection of walls or depressions in the level, is soon blasted by the furious cutting winds. The experiment of planting pitch-pines (*Pinus picea* and *Pinus abies*) was tried by Governor Thodal of Iceland, but the trunks never rose above two feet from the ground, and, like Dean Swift, they died at the head. The scene already suggests Thule without its Jökulls; scattered byes, greenish *túns* ("towns," or home-fields), brown distances, low stone walls, and big bistre-coloured cliffs, black below where bathed by the flowing tide.

Behind Duncansbay Ness[2] we are shown the site of John o' Groat's House; there is no need to walk there, as a stage coach now runs along the fine broad road from the "(ex-) Herring Capital

---

[1] Found in St Helier, and written "Helyer" in the Scoto-Scandinavian islands. Evidently the Icelandic Hellir (*plur.* Hellar), a cave, common in local words, *e.g.*, Hellis-menn, the cave-men; it is akin to Hallr, a slope, a boulder, much used for proper names of men and women, as Hall-dór (Hall thor) and Hall-dóra (Cleasby).

[2] John Brand (A Brief Description of Orkney, etc., Edinburgh, 1701, Pinkerton, iii. 731) writes Dungisbie Head, and Duncan's Bay. The Scandinavian form of Duncansbay Head is Dungalsnýpa.

of the North" (Wick). The old "Norwegian," as some miscall him, left Holland with Malcolm Cavin, and brought to Caithness a Latin letter from James II. of Scotland recommending him to the northern lieges. It is still a disputed point whether the Grotes of the Orkneys are the original stock, or drifted there through Scotland. Strangers are taken to the semi-historical ruin, a one-storied octagon, with its eight windows, which appeased fraternal wrath—if, at least, there were eight, and not two brothers. It is supposed to. be a banqueting-hall, as there are no bedrooms, and only the photograph for sale at Wick, probably taken from some apocryphal sketch, caps it with a small look-out. A dull grey barn is here fronted by a dwarf sand-streak, up which fisher boats are drawn, whilst others, with stained sails, scud and toss over the unquiet waters. The colouring matter is peat. In the Bahia de S. Salvador (Brazil) the Piaçaba palm supplies the tannin-dye, while Venice and Dalmatia assert superior claims to art by rough pictures in coloured earths and oil. The object is everywhere the same—to make the canvas last.

And now with the rock ledges called "Pentland Skerries" on our right, we dance over the tide-rip of the terrible "Pightland Firth,"[1] which has become classical in the north, like Pharaoh's Ford in the Gulf of Suez. Mýsing, the sea-king, according to the Elder Edda, ended the "Peace of Fróði," by slaying Fróði, king of Denmark; he also captured the clattering hand-quern Grótti, and the two prescient damsels Fenia and Menia. The victor ground white salt in the vanquished ships until they sank in Pentland Firth, causing the main to become briny: there has ever since been a vortex where the sea falls into the "well" or mill's eye, and the roar of the ocean is the grinding of the quern.[2] And all this folk-lore because at times storm-wind meets tide running some five to seven knots an hour with "waws" and "swelchies," causing sore grief to many a gallant ship. Yet there are men still young—Colonel Burroughs of the 93d (Sutherland) Highlanders is one—who habitually crossed this firth in open boats.

---

[1] Pettlands Fjörð in Icelandic from Pight-land or Pict-land.
[2] For other interesting details see the Gróttasöngr, or Lay of Grótti.

We had now turned the north-eastern end of Scotland, where Ben Dorrery, a blue saddleback somewhat crater-shaped, rose supreme; and where Foss or cascade water, anciently Fors, draining Lake Lunnery, suggested Scandinavia. We presently passed the Paps of Caithness, and admired the grand profile of classical Dunnet Head,[1] whose flanks are horizontally streaked with broad golden patches, whilst a Cockney gun of our party brought out a swarming colony of birds from their cliffy homes. Behind it lay Thurso (Thjórsá, or Bull water), built with the dull grey stone of Bath, not the picturesque red of Edinburgh, nestling in the usual fertile bight, shallow withal and open to the northern ocean. We halted for the first and last time off Holburn Head to take in and deal out letters. Beyond it the picturesque Sutherland Highlands ended in a long line of bluffs remarkably quoin-shaped. Dim in the slaty and stormy sky rose Farout Head, not unlike the Elephant Mountain, the classical Mons Felix that outlies the murderous Somali Coast. Ten miles west of it rose

---

[1] The old Cape Orcas, derived, as has been said, from Latin Orca, Gaelic Orcc or Orc, and Icelandic Orkn—"*Delphinus orca,*" a dog-seal—the addition of -*ey,* an isle, makes Orkney. This point is the Ptolemeian Tarbetum or "Taruedum, quod et Orcas promontorium, finis Scotiæ dicitur," and unduly placed in N. lat. 60° 15', and long. 31° 20' (lib. i., cap. 3). The word derives from the Gaelic Tarbet, a drag, a portage, a haul-over, common names in Scoto-Scandinavia, and equivalent to the Icelandic Eið (aith). It lies only six miles from the nearest of the archipelago, which Pomponius Mela called Orcades, evidently a Roman corruption of the indigenous "Orkneyjar," the Irish Innsi Orcc, and the Inis Torc of Ossian. Fordun's "Scotichronicon" (ii. 2) calls the Orkneys "Insulæ Pomoniæ;" and Buchanan says, "Orcadum maxima multis veterum Pomona vocatur." As *poma* are not abundant there, the name has caused considerable argumentation. In the "Société Royale des Antiquaires du Nord" (1845-49), and in the "Proceedings of the Society of Antiquaries of Scotland" (Edinburgh, Neill, 1852), Professor A. Munch, of Christiania, contributes an able paper, "Why is the Mainland of Orkney called Pomona?" Before his time Dr (D.D.) George Barry, in an excellent book, "History of the Orkney Islands" (London, Longmans, 1805) had derived Pomona from "pou," small (query, "Bú," a settlement, or "bol," corrupted to "bull," a house?), and Mon, Patria; also from the Norsk terms signifying "Great-land." Professor Munch quotes Torfæus (Orcad., p. 5), "Pomona . . . a Julio polyhistore Diutina appellatur." Solinus Polyhistor, facetiously known as Plinii Simius, says of Thule (chap. xxv.), "Ab Orcadibus Thyle usque quinque dierum et noctium navigatio. Sed Thule larga et diutina pomona copiosa est" (Thule is a fertile country, and plentifully productive of long-lasting corn). He would read the evidently mutilated text, "Sed Thule larga et Diutina pomona copiosa est," or "Sed Thule larga et diutina, Pomona copiosa est,",and he finds that "Diutina *ergò* Pomona—ab esse ad posse valet consequentia." But it is over ingenious to account by the error of a text for a popular term four hundred years old, *e.g.,*

"Our rare Pomonia, which the natives style
The Mainland."

the north-western Land's End of Scotland, a mere hummock low down upon the horizon. This was Cape Wrath, which some understand literally, whilst others derive it from "Rath," a conical hill, or a fortified place : it is evidently Cape Hvarf, a common name, as Hvarven, near Bergen, for a sudden turn of coast. "You should see it in December," said the steward, when we were disposed to deride its anger: he had doubled it in a casual vessel from Liverpool to Dundee carrying sugar and palm oil.

And now it is time to cast a look starboardways from Duncansbay Head. The first feature is Stroma Island (Straumsey, corrupted to Stromey), bluff to the north-west, and sloping gradually to the south-eastern sea; the inner sound is a narrow channel, lately rendered safe by a red beacon. The scrap of land— a small item of the two hundred inhabited which form the British archipelago—is politically included in Caithness, but, popularly speaking, it belongs to the Scoto-Scandinavian race, the fourth great family of Great Britain, utterly dissimilar from the Norman of the Channel Islands, the Kelt, and the Anglo-Kelt. Their neighbours talk of the "poor sneaks of Stroma," and these retort by the opprobrious term "ferrie-loupers." The memory of many a broken head and bloody fray in bygone day is preserved in the couplet—

> "Caithness cabes (*i.e.*, ticks), lift up your heads,
> And let the Orkney sheep go by!"

How soon will telegrams and steamers—there is a daily mail between Thurso and Stromness—cause these local differences to share the fate of the national garb ?

Behind Stroma, and towering over it in the purple grey cloud, is South Ronaldshaw, or Ronaldsha, in whose corrupted and degraded name we can hardly trace the pure and classical Norsk termination.[1] Properly Ronansey, from St Ronan, Ringan, or

---

[1] To quote the Dean's English, "it is part of a (Radical?) movement to help forward the obliteration of all trace of the derivation and history of words:" as such it may be highly recommended to the "Japs." The Icelandic or pure Scandinavian form, simple and compound, is *ey* (gen. and plur. *eyjar*); each vowel being pronounced distinct, and not confounded, as some foreigners do, with the German ö or the French *eu*. *Ey* is the Keltic "hy," as found in the classical Hy Brazile, the mysterious island west of Galway, and so called during centuries before the real Brazil was discovered. Again the form appears in "Ireland's Eye," which Cockneys pronounce Ireland's H'eye; the pure Irish form is *I* (O'Brien's Irish-English Dictionary, sub voce), or *aoi*, an island or region, which that learned

Ninian, it still preserves an old-world flavour. Till the last thirty years wreckers were rife: it was held "best to let saut water gang its gate;" in other words, uncanny, as we find in "The Pirate," to save a drowning sailor. Mariners lost all their rights when keel once touched sand; whatever was cast ashore became the lawful property of the people; Earl Patrick, who now is cursed at Scalloway because "he hung the Shetlanders," was blessed for his wise laws against all that would help ships amongst the breakers; a wreck was a sight to "wile the parson out of his pulpit in the middle of his preaching," and the blessing upon the shore was coupled with a wish that the Lord would send "mair wrecks ere winter." Men still remember the old Orcadian minister's prayer: "O Lord, I wish not ill to my neighbours, but if wrecks be going, remember Thy poor island of Sandey!"[1] The clergy feared to offend those sturdy pagans, their "little ones," by denouncing from the pulpit what the devoutest held to be a "dispensation of Providence." A pious fraud began by excommunicating all who broke the Sabbath in such Satan's work, and the course of time did the rest.

But old ideas do not readily die. Lately a farmer in Orphir parish (Ör-fjara, or Ör-fyri, "a reef covered by high tide"), having lost many head of cattle by "witching," applied to the "spae-wife," who prescribed the sacrifice of a bull-calf, probably by cremation, to Baal. The practice is, of course, kept secret, yet the best possible authority at Kirkwall told me he had reason to suspect that such offerings to the sun-god are by no means singular. The late pugnacious Sir James Simpson (Archæological Essays) also heard of a cow being buried alive as a sacrifice to the spirit of murrain. The Yule bonfires and the games of ball at that season were also in honour of the greater light.

Beyond South Ronaldshaw we had a fair profile view of Hoy (= Há-ey, high isle), a three-hilled, long, narrow parallelogram

---

writer derives (?) from the Hebrew "ai," insula, regio, provincia. "The Norwegian öy, the Danish öe, the Swedish ö, the Anglo-Saxon êg (-land), and the German aue, are found in ey-ot and Leas-ow, Chels-ea and Batters-ea; and whilst the Orkneys corrupt it wofully, we retain it pure in Cherts-ey, Aldern-ey, and Orkn-ey" (Cleasby). Munch (Ant. du Nord) has corrected the error of Webster, who derives "island" from ea or ey, water (!), and land. It is simply ey-land, "terra insularis."

[1] Properly Sand-eið, or Sand-aith, a sand-isthmus connecting two headlands.

which took us some five hours to pass. The fierce south-westers which scoop and scallop western Scotland, like western Iceland and the occidental coasts of north Europe generally, render cultivation impossible except on the leeward side, where the "links" are.[1]  *En passant*, it may be observed that the island capitals between Caithness and Iceland, as Stornoway of the Hebrides, Kirkwall of the Orkneys, Lerwick of the Shetlands, and Thorshaven of the Færoes, are all built upon the eastern shore.  We strained eyes in vain to sight the position of Walter Scott's "Dwarfie Stones," so called *per antiphrasin*, says Brand; and equally vain was the "search for the great carbuncle" of Ward Hill, now invisible as the gem of the Diamond Rock, and probably never seen save by the eyes of faith.  I heard of the same mysterious light in the far Gaboon River.  We were more fortunate with the Hill of Hoy, the tallest part of the dorsum (1500 feet), whose "Old Man," which farther north would be called a "witch finger," appeared first a dot, then a column, and lastly a dome upon the summit of a huge cathedral. It is of the "Old Red," a pale, unfossiliferous sandstone, the normal material of the western mainland, though some describe it as a slaty formation supported by a base of granite, which also crops out near Stromness.  According to Bleau, the midnight sun can be seen from it in midsummer; Dr Wallace qualifies the statement by opining that the true solar body cannot be visible, but only its image refracted through some watery cloud upon the horizon.  The last glimpse of Hoy was Ronay Head, a glorious bluff at least 1000 feet high, and beyond it lay nought save *pontus et aer*.

I will here step out of the order of my journey, which would more wisely have been reversed.  To begin with Iceland is to begin at the end, neglecting the various steps and stages of Orkneys, Shetlands, and Færoes, whilst to describe the climax and its anti-climax, would be utterly uninteresting and bathetic. My three days (Sept. 10, 11, and 12) at the Church-bay (Kirkju-vágr, vogr, vad, waw, wall) produced some results, and these shall be briefly recorded.

---

[1] "Links," from Lykkur, locked or closed fields.

The good ship "St Magnus" ran up "the String" to Kirkwall Roads, and landed me after a ten hours' passage from Lerwick. My first care was to send my introductory letter, the gift of Mr Gatherer, to Mr George Petrie, well known in the anthropological world. He kindly led me to the little museum, which, like that of Lerwick, is far behind the order and neatness of Reykjavik. The collection contains good specimens of netting needles, cut out of rein and red deer bone: the former animal extended to the Orkneys, as broken bones have been found in the burghs, and suggest that they were continental. There were natural stone knives, looking as if shaped by art—the Brazil shows heaps of celts equally deceptive—pots of micaceous schist and steatite from Shetland; combs conjectured to have been used for ornamenting pottery; a two-handed scraper of whale's bone; specimens of "bysmers" and "pundlers," wooden bars used as steelyards, the former three, and the latter seven, feet long: they carried the Norwegian weights, "bysmars" and "lispunds,"[1] which took root in the Shetlands. I noticed the huge Varangian[2] fibulæ and torques; the querns still common amongst the islandry; red "keel" or pigment of silicious hæmatite, showing that even the artless dames did not ignore the art of rouge; rude beads of bone and clay; and a human skull with four rabbit teeth, possibly bevelled by the "bursten bigg,". coarse roasted bere or barley, even as the Guanches of Tenerife ground down their molars with parched grain. My guide showed me his ingenious plan for "squeezes," and making casts of spearheads and similar articles by means of warmed gutta-percha applied to the stone, and lastly cooled in water.

Scapa (Skálpeið) Brock, the highly interesting ruin discovered by Mr Petrie in 1870, was of course visited. At the Earl's

---

[1] "Bismari" in Icelandic is a steelyard, and "bismara-pund" a kind of lb. The Norwegian Bismerpund is = 12 Skaalpunds (100 : 110 Eng. avoird.), and the Lispund is = 16 Skaalpunds. The Icelandic word is Lífspund, from Lífl, and = 18 lbs. Scots (Cleasby).

[2] Varangian, Icel. Væringi, from Várar, a pledge (al. Wehr, Vær, ware or active defence): the Væringjar of the Sagas, the Russian Varæger, the Βαράγγοι of Byzantine historians, and our Warings, popularly known through Gibbon and "Count Robert of Paris," formed the Scandinavian bodyguard of the Eastern empire. These battle-axe men were at first Northmen from Kiew in A.D. 902, under the Emperor Alexis, and successively Danes, Norwegians, and Icelanders (Cleasby and Mallet: Mr Blackwall, note ‡, p. 193, attempts and fails to correct Gibbon). What possessed Mr A. Mounsey (Journal through the Caucasus and Persia) to derive "Feringi" (Frank) from Varangian?

Castle, whose approach is choked with trees like that of
Baalbek, I remarked that the kitchen and the banqueting-room
had false and shouldered arches, which might have been borrowed from the Haurán.   We pitied poor St Magnus the Martyr
for the insult lately offered to him in the shape of a wretched
court-house—a similar affront has been inflicted upon York
Minster.   The old cathedral, grand in its rude and ponderous
Norman-Gothic, is made remarkable by the red sandstone mixed
with whitey-grey *calcaires:* it shares with St Mungo the honour
of being the finest remains of Catholicism in the north, and it is
unduly neglected by strangers.   The view from that eye-sore, the
stunted spire, is charming.   North-west stretches the Bay of
Firth, famed for oysters, backed by the dark heights of Rousay
(Hrólfsey); while north-east lies Shapinshay (Hjápandisey),[1]
smiling with corn and white houses, with the dark hillocks of
low-lying Edey in the distance.   Amongst the smaller islets
may be mentioned castled Damsey (Daminsey); the Holm
of Quanterness; Thieves' Holm (Thjófaholmr), where robbers,
who were supposed not to swim, found a safe prison, and often,
too, a long home; and the whale-back of Gairsey (Gáreksey),
with the stronghold of that Sveinn (Sweyn), who lost his pirate
life when attacking Dublin—the Vikings seem ever to have
preferred these fragments of earth where the sea, their favourite
element, was never far distant.   Nearer and rising from the
reniform "Mainland," *alias* Pomona, by the Sagas called Hrossey
or Horse Island, is Wideford (Hvitfjörð) Hill, backed by the
Oyce or Peerie Sea.   The ground-wave is dark with bloomless
gorse, and ruddy with fading heáth, whilst higher still

> " Earth clad in russet scorns the lively green."

It is a progressive country : middle-aged men have shot grouse
in the mosses near Kirkwall where now the fields bear corn.
The peasant's father despaired of growing grass : the son ploughs
the bog, builds dry walls with the larger stones that cumber the
surface, cuts deep drains, and top-dresses with sand and lime.
Hands, however, are wanting; the fisheries bring more money

---

[1] Popularly but erroneously derived from Kolbeinsey or Kaupmannsey, "Chapman's Isle."

From a Photo.

Mc Farlane & Erskine Lith.rs Edin.r

Sᵀ MAGNUS CATHEDRAL & EARL'S PALACE, KIRKWALL.

than agriculture; and the good landlord will not part with his slow old tenantry, because he cannot replace it.

Two monuments in the cathedral are peculiarly interesting, and partly relieve the desert and dismal appearance of all Catholic places of worship converted to a " purer creed." The first is that of the Irving family, true Orcadians, who never changed their name since A.D. 1361, and one lies murdered in A.D. 1614. Mr Petrie, the discoverer, communicated with the great Washington of that ilk, who replied courteously, forwarding at the same time a presentation copy of his works. Mr Pliny Miles (Norðurfari) and others of his class are fond of claiming all distinguished names for their own country; for instance, Snorri Thorfinnsson, "the first Yankee[1] on record," is the fore-father of Finn Magnússon and Thorvaldsen, whilst Captain Ericsson is the descendant of Eric the Red. It would be easier far to trace all American celebrities directly to Europe, and many of them would not be sorry to see the process thus inverted.

The second tomb, much more interesting to me than those of King Hakon and Maid Margaret, is the cenotaph of Dr Baikie, R.N., designed and inscribed, I believe, by Sir Henry Dryden: certainly both design and inscription deserve scanty credit. Not a word about the original profession of poor " Hammie," as he was called by a host of friends. And why should it be a cenotaph ? Why bequeath the explorer's bones to the ignoble " European's grave," S'a Leone ? Worse still, the journals, once so interesting, have been allowed to lie in obscurity for want of an editor, and a decade in these days takes away almost all the value of an African traveller's diary. Dr Baikie is supposed also to have left a valuable collection of Nigerian vocabularies—these, at least, might be forwarded to the Anthropological Institute. I can only express a hope that the bereaved family will bestir itself before the cold shade of oblivion obscures the memory of a heroic name.

After a long spell of cloudy, misty, and rainy weather, Thursday, the 12th September, broke fine, with a clear sun and a high rollicking wind which swept the rolling surface-water like a

---

[1] Mr Blackwall (p. 257) more modestly says the "first European."

broom. In these islands, July, August, and September are
frequently wet; in October the " peerie simmer " [1] of St Martin,
the Indian summer of the United States, sets in and gladdens
the eye of man before the glooms of winter round off the year.
Mr Petrie proposed himself as guide to Wideford Hill, Ingis-
howe (Howe of Inga), Maes Howe, Stennis, Borgar (Brúargarðr),
and Stromness—I need hardly tell the pleasure with which his
kind offer was accepted. He has not only admirably described
these and other antiquities (especially in his " Notice of the
Brochs, or Large Round Towers of Orkney," etc., read before the
S.N.A., June 11, 1866): he has done far more important work
by converting popular *insouciance*, and even ridicule, into a
something of his own enthusiasm. Nor should I forget to say
that in this great task he has been ably and efficiently supported
by the landlord-class, amongst whom Colonel Balfour of Balfour
Castle and Ternaby (Tjarnabær), the owner of Maes Howe, has
especially distinguished himself. We shall now hope to have
heard the last of such barbarism as breaking up the venerable
" Odin's Stone " into building material. These acts are like the
state of Uriconium, a national disgrace; we only wish that Jarl
Hakon had Mr M——'s leg. in the " Cashidawis," or " Warm
Hose "—a fitting reward for those who justify the sneer—

> " Quod non fecerunt Gothi
> Hoc fecerunt Scoti."

It is also to be desired that the liberal proprietor of Maes Howe
would take active steps to defend the highly interesting central
chamber from the inclemency of the weather; the barrow was
opened in July 1861, and already the interior has suffered from
exposure.

The most interesting event of the day was the inspection of
Maes Howe, which some one has lately suggested to be " simply
a Norse fort." It would be mere impertinence to offer a general

---

[1] " Peerie - folk " means the fairies, both words evidently congeners of the
Persian Pari or Peri. Grimm, an excellent authority, derives the French Fée,
the Provençal Fada, the Spanish Hada, and the Italian Fata, from the Latin
Fatum—remarking that Fata and Fée have the same analogy as *nata* and *née*,
*amata* and *aimée*. In connection with " Simmer " or " Sea," " Peerie," meaning little, is by some deduced from the French " petit;" in the Shetlands it is
further emphasised to Peerie-weerie-winkie (of a foal, etc.).

description of this unique barrow after the studies of Mr Farrer ("Notice of Runic Inscriptions discovered during Recent Excavations in the Orkneys," made by James Farrer, M.P.; printed for private circulation, 1862); lately popularised by Mr Fergusson in "Rude Stone Monuments." The three mortarless *loculi* of huge slabs and their closing stones reminded me so strongly of the miscalled "Tombs of the Kings," north of Jerusalem, that I felt once more in the "Holy Land." It is a glorious monument of the great tomb-building race, or races whose animistic creed, the essence of fetichism, expresses itself in tent-tombs (chambered cairns) and cave-tombs (rock-cut chambers) upon the Siberian steppes, the Algerian plains, the Wiltshire downs, and the Scoto-Scandinavian islands. At Maes Howe we find all its characteristics—the stone circle which drove away the profane; the long passage which keeps warm the cave or hut; the vestibule for the funeral feast, and the various rooms for the dead to live in. And at the first sight of the Branch Runes,[1] otherwise called Palm Runes, I remembered having seen a similar alphabet in northern Syria.

A ride to Hums, of old Emesa (February 27, 1871), and a visit to my old friend the Nestorian Matrán (Metropolitan) Butrus, introduced me to the alphabet known as El Mushajjar, or the branched, one of the many cyphers formerly and, for aught I know, still current amongst Semitic races. Returning to England, I sent a copy of it to the Anthropological Institute, intending to illustrate a paper which was reprinted in "Unexplored Syria" (vol. ii., Appendix, p. 241): unfortunately the copy was lost.

According to the Matrán's MS. there are two forms of El Mushajjar, one applied to Arabic, and the other to Pehlevi. Both are read from right to left, and the following is the Arabic form:

---

[1] The ordinary runes, I need hardly say, have been shown by Rafn to be derived from archaic Greek; and probably from coins which found their way north during the first centuries of our era.

## No. I.

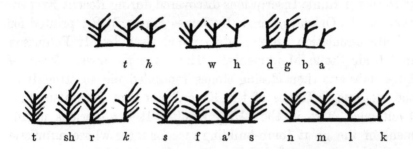

The adjoined is the Pehlevi.

## No. II.

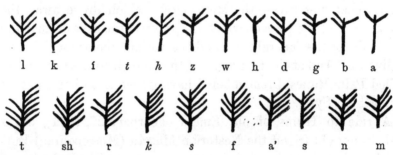

No. III. is the Norsk-Runic alphabet, read from left to right, as classified by Mr George Petrie, to decipher the palm-runes in Maes Howe.

## No. III.

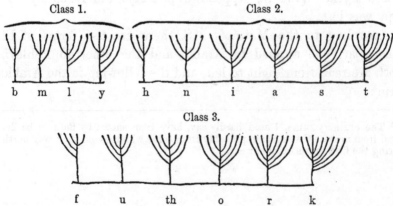

And the following are the inscriptions on the walls of Maes Howe:

## No. IV.

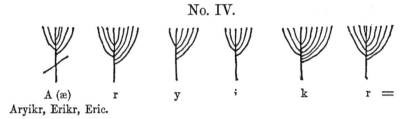

A (æ)      r      y      ;      k      r =

Aryikr, Erikr, Eric.

The key to the cypher is here shown by the tranverse stroke on the stem of the first letter to the left (A or æ).

## No. V.

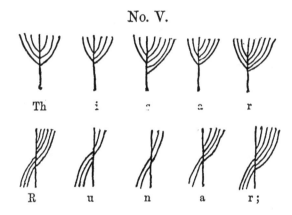

Th      :      ᷎      ᷎      r

R      u      n      a      r;

forming an inceptive—" these runes." In the word " Runar," the left-hand branches are turned down by way of variety; of course the number is the same. Finally, it is interesting to compare this " Mushajjar " with a similar system, the Irish letters, which bear the names of trees. They are:

h      d      t

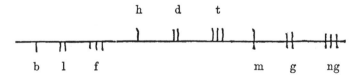

b      l      f      m      g      ng

And even in the common runes, we may observe that there is only one (R) which is not composed of a rune-staff, supporting offsets disposed at various angles.

No. I., the Arabic form connected by horizontal base-lines, contains two sets of three, and four sets of four letters, read as usual in Semitic alphabets; beginning with Alpha and ending with Tau: it is in fact the Aleph-Tav of the Hebrews and of the older Arabs, as preserved in the numeral and chronological syllabarium "El Abjad." I need hardly note that this was characteristic of the world-conquering Phœnician, that glorious gift to Greece, usually attributed to Cadmus (El Kadim, or the Ancient), and by us incongruously applied to our Aryan speech; a comparison of the sequences *a, b, c,* and *d* (Abjad), and *k, l, m,* and *n* (Kalaman) with any other system at once proves direct derivation. In the Pehlevi Mushajjar the letters, it will be seen, are not joined at the base, and sundry branches are formed in a different way.

Mr Farrer, who first "established the important fact of Runic inscriptions existing in Orkney, where none had hitherto been found," gives both sets of palm-runes (Plates VIII. and IX.). He borrows the following information (p. 29, referring to Plate VIII.) from Professor Stephens, a good Norsk scholar: "The six crypt runes or secret staves represent the letters A, Æ, R, L, I, K, R, and signify Aalikr or Erling, a proper name, or perhaps the beginning of some sentence." Professor Munch observes, "The other characters in the third line are known as 'Limouna,[1] or Bough-Runes.' They were used during the later times of the Runic period in the same manner as the Irish Ogham, but are not here intelligible. The writer probably intended to represent the chief vowels—A, E, I, O, U, Y. The Runic alphabet was divided into two classes: the strokes on the left of the vertical line indicating the class, and those on the right the rune itself." And Professor Rafn declares, "The palm-runes underneath cannot be read in the usual manner; the first, third, and fourth of the runes being *a, o,* and *i;* the writer probably intended to give all the vowels, but some of the letters have been obviously miscarried, and have perhaps been altered and defaced at a later period by other persons. In the first of these a cross line has been added to show that the letter *a* is intended." Of No. XVIII. (Plate X.), Mr Farrer notes, "The palm-runes are rarely capable of being deciphered." Professor Munch similarly declares, "The bough-

---

[1] Gen. Lim-rûnar (lim or limr being the limb of a tree opposed to the bole), which Cleasby explains as "a kind of magical runes."

runes are not easy to decipher;" whilst Professor Stephens asserts, "The palm-runes on the first line indicate Thisar Runar—'these runes.'" They are mentioned in the Elder Edda (Sigrdrífumál, stanza 11):

> " Lim-runes thou must ken,
> An thou a leech wouldst be,
> And know to heal hurts."

The crytogram, "El Mushajjar," was forwarded to Mr Petrie, who replied as follows: "I attempted by means of your tree-branched alphabet to read the palm-runes of Maes Howe, but failed. It then occurred to me that they might correspond with the Futhork, or Icelandic alphabet, and, obtaining the key of the cipher, I completely succeeded after a few hours' trial. On referring to Mr Farrer's copies of the translations given by the Scandinavian professors, I find that Professor Stephens appears to have put five runes in each of the first two classes, which makes the third palm-rune (inscription No. I.) to be L instead of Y; moreover, he does not give the key. My first attempt at classifying the runes by means of the cipher turned out correct, and I have therefore retained that classification in reading the second inscription. It is evident that the classification could be altered at will of the person using it, and this uncertainty of arrangement must constitute the difficulty of interpreting such runes."

In Nos. XIX. and XX. (Plate X.) we read "Iorsafarar Brutu Orkhröugh"—the Jórsalafarar (Jerusalem-farers, *i.e.*, pilgrim-visitors of Jerusalem) broke open Orkhow (shelter-mound), probably in search of treasure: the latter is an object especially Eastern. There are seven crosses, and one inscription (No. XIII.) must be read from right to left. We may therefore believe that certain old *Coquillards*, and possibly Crusaders, returning from Palestine, whence they brought the "hubby,"[1] violated the tombs, and left a single name and an unfinished inscription to record their propensity[2] for grave-plundering.

---

[1] "Hubby" is a loose robe, erroneously derived, like the Scotch Joop, the German Giup, the Italian Giubba and Giubbone, the French Jupe and Jupon, and the Slav Japungia, from the Norsk Hwipu. All these are simply corruptions of the Arabic "Jubbeh."

[2] These Northmen left their handiwork even on the "Stones of Venice."

We visited the museum at Stromness, the amorpholites or "Standing Stones," and that "Mediterranean in miniature," the Stennis Lake, whose flora is partly marine and partly lacustrine. Hereabouts, the plain shows distinct remnants of the two great epochs—Bruna-öld, the Age of Burning; and Hauga-öld, the Age of Burial. We have no reason to believe the tradition that Odin introduced cremation; doubtless, the "crematee" was chiefly of the wealthy classes, while the poor were inhumed—they were both synchronous in the days of the Twelve Tables: "Hominem mortuum in urbe ne sepelito, neve urito." Hence a valuable rule for tracing the exact limits of old Roman cities, even of Rome herself: the cemetery was always outside the city settlement, and, if possible, to the south.

The day ended happily, as it began, in meeting Colonel Burroughs of Rousay, and Dr Rea of Arctic fame. My memories of Kirkwall are pleasant in the extreme. It wants only a good modern hotel to deserve the patronage of tourists, who, in these days, are told to "try Lapland," when they have ample inducement to pass a summer in the "storm-swept Orcades," and in other sections of the Scoto-Scandinavian archipelago.

On Friday, September 6, the "Jón Sigurðsson," Captain Müller of whom more presently, made with some difficulty the Shetland Mainland. Many derivations are offered for the latter word, but, as the island is larger than all the rest put together, the obvious signification suffices.[1] A dark, thick fog had kept us drifting all

---

Readers may not be unwilling to see the legend upon the maneless and melancholy lion, the statue of Pentelic marble, ten feet high, once at the harbour mouth of the Piræus (Porto Leone), where the pedestal still stands, now fronting the arsenal, Venice, where, after the retreat from Greece, the Doge Morosini carried it in 1687. The hardly legible inscription on the right side of the animal is supposed to be, "Asmundr graved these runes united with Asgeir, Thorlief, Thórd, and Ívar, at the request of Haraldr Háfi (the Tall); although the Greeks, taking thought, forbade it." It is supposed that this Harold was the same who had the promise of seven feet in English ground. The left flank and shoulder are less uncertain, and the legend reads as follows: "Hakun, united with Ulfr (Wolf) and Ásmundr and Aurn (Örn), conquered this port. These men and Haraldr Háfi, on account of the uprising of the Greek people, imposed considerable fines. Dálkr remained (prisoner?) in remote regions. Egill fared with Ragnar to Rumania . . . and Armenia."

The inscriptions were first published in 1800 by Åkerblad, a Swedish savant; they have been frequently revised, and the last study is the "Inscription Runique du Pirée, interpretée par C. C. Rafn; et publiée par la Société Royale des Antiquaires du Nord," Copenhagen, 1856.

[1] The old Norsk Megin-land, land of might, or mainland, is evidently, like the

night close to the dangerous rocks called Hivda Grind, Havre de Grind, or Hardegrind, originally Nafargrind, from Grind (a hedge-gate or sea-way), and, perhaps, Höfða (a head or bluff). Our position, some seven miles E.S.E. of Foula (Fugley) Island, ex-plained the noise of the surf and the shallowing of water to thirty-two fathoms—it is far easier in these latitudes to hear than to see the land! The raw mist obscured the bold, grand scenery of the western coast till noon, when a sickly sun sublimed the vapours, reminding me of the Malabar coast after the Nilgherry Hills. Very mild was the Roost[1] or Race of Sumburgh, a Euri-pus, where nine currents are said to meet. We could distinctly sight Fitful[2] Head, and

> " We saw the tide
> Break thundering on the rugged side
> Of Sumburgh's awful steep."

Its flank of clay-slate showed vast rivas (clefts) and stone-slips, while beyond it lay the skeleton of Jarlshof (Earl's house), names now world-known. It is curious to trace how the practised eye and the wonderful memory which created our modern historical novel skimmed the very cream of Hjaltland peculiarities during a few days' visit in August 1814, the year in which he published the Eyrbyggja Saga;[3] and it is fortunate for writing travel-lers that Sir Walter Scott did not visit the Færoes and Ice-land. See what he did for the " Waverley Line" of Railway!

---

Scotch Mickle, connected with the Persian Mih or Mihin, great, power-ful, but not, as Mr Blackwall conceives, with "miracle." The classical name of the Orkney group, then numbering only seven, is Acmodæ in Pliny, iv. 16, and Hæmodæ in Mela, iii. 6. The Icelandic term is Hjaltland (pronounced *Zhatland*), hence Zetland, Hetland, and Shetland. Thus it still preserves the fame of old Hjalti, the Viking of the ninth century, who also survives in the modern "Sholto." Munch suggests that Hjaltland, hilt-land, may have been given from a weapon dropped in it; so trivial were the names of olden Scandinavia : he also mentions the legend of Swordland, a great country now submerged, between Norway and Hjaltland, its hilt.

[1] In Scandinavian, Dynröst, "thundering roost," from "að dynja," to din; hence the Tyne and Dvina Rivers. The Icelandic Röst, or current, is the French Raz ; that of " Petlandsfjörð" is especially celebrated. In the Orkneys " Roust" is a stormy sea caused by the meeting of tides; " Skail" (Icel. Skellr) is the dash-ing of surf upon the shore; " Skelder," the washing of waves, is a common name for farm-houses near the beach; and " Swelchie," which explains its own meaning, is the Icelandic Svelgr.

[2] Fit Fiall, *i.e.*, "planities pinguis," or, better still, Fitfulglahöfði, sea-fowl cape.

[3] An abstract printed in " Illustrations of Northern Antiquities," one vol. 4to, Edinburgh, 1814; reprinted verbatim in " Northern Antiquities," edited by Mr J. A. Blackwall, London, Bohn, 1859. In it we may note the origin of Norna the sibyl's " improvisatory and enigmatical poetry."

Amongst the islanders he is a household word, but though the Troils of Papa Westræ do not object to Magnus Troil, they are still incensed by the portraiture of that "fiddling, rhyming fool," poor Claud Halcro.

The approach to Bressey Sound, one of the finest ports in Great Britain, is unusually picturesque. On the right is the "Wart of Bressey"[1]—verrucose features are here common as in the Orkneys, but the word is the Icelandic "Varða," and the German "Warte," a watch-house. Its flanks are gashed for turf; and a goodly lighthouse is as much wanted on the dangerous western coast as on the Mediterranean shores of Africa. The island was lately sold, they say, for £20,000. On the left is the historic Knap or Knab (Hnapp meaning a button) of quartzose slate, backed by the quarries and the spreading town of Lerwick—mud bay. The (Arthur) Anderson Institute and the Widows' Asylum reminded me of a Shetlander who began life as a clerk, became M.P. in 1847-52, and died the chairman of the great "P. & O."—it is a pity that these fine establishments were not better endowed. The capital stands with its feet in the water; the houses, with their crow-stepped gables, being so built for convenience of smuggling, and its sons fondly compare it with cities on the Rhine. Half a dozen Dutch busses, riding in couples, now represent the hundreds of bygone days, when the British fisheries were called the "gold mine of Holland." Certain features suggested modern Tiberias, but the disproportionate number of the churches soon weighed down that flight of fancy.

On the day after arrival, I set out with Captain Henry T. Ellis, R.N. (of "Hong-Kong to Manilla"), to do the tour *de rigueur*—Scalloway[2] Castle and Moseyaburgum, the Mousa (Mósey) Broch[3]

---

[1] Originally Brúsey, from Brúsi, a proper name.

[2] Skála-vegr, the way of the court-house.

[3] Also written Brough, meaning a round tower. The word is usually derived from the Gothic "berga," to defend, but it has a far nobler origin. It is the Chaldee "burgadh," the Arabic "burj," the Armenian "pourc," the Greek "πύργος," and the Latin "burgus;" the Gothic "baurg," the Mæso-Gothic "bairg," and "borg," a mountain; the Scandinavian "borg," a fortress; the Armoric, Irish, and Welsh "burg," also found in Teutonic and Saxon; the Anglo-Saxon "beorh" and "beorg," a rampart, and "burh" or "burcg," a castle; the Belgian "burg," the Gaelic "burg," the French "bourg," the Italian "borgo," the North British "burgh" and "burg," as Edinburgh and Corrensburg; the Scoto-Scandinavian "brogh" or "broch," with the guttural uncompounded, and

or Pecht House. We took the excellent northern road, begun during the famine, and finished some four years ago (1870) : formerly when a picnic was intended, gillies were sent on to smooth the way for riders. After a few yards, we left the fertile seaboard, whose skirts and smooths are, as in Iceland, the only sites for agriculture, and entered the normal type of country, which begins in Scotland and Ireland. There can be no better description of bog and moor, of hill-land or commonty, and of " moss, mount, and wilderness, quhairin are divers great waters," than that which opens the first chapter of " Lord Kilgobbin," the last work of that most amiable and sympathetic writer, whose unworthy successor I now am : " Some one has said that almost all that Ireland possesses of picturesque beauty is to be found on or in the immediate neighbourhood of the seaboard ; and if we except some brief patches of river scenery on the ' Nore' and the ' Blackwater,' and a part of Lough Erne, the assertion is not devoid of truth. The dreary expanse called the Bog of Allen, which occupies a high table-land in the centre of the island, stretches away for miles, flat, sad-coloured, and monotonous, fissured in every direction by channels of dark-tinted water, in which the very fish take the same sad colour." Similarly we read of Scotland : " The inland, the upland, the moor, the mountain, were really not occupied at all for agricultural purposes, or served only to keep the poor and their cattle from starving."

The surface of this Irish Sliabh and Icelandic Heiði, a true " black country," natural not artificial, rolls in low warty moors revetted with moss, spangled with Fifa, or cotton-grass (*Epilobium*, or *Eriophorum epistachion*), and gashed with deep black earth-cracks, showing the substrata of peat; the tarns and flowing waters are inky as the many Brazilian " Unas " (Blackwaters), and though strongly peat-flavoured, they are not unwholesome. I could not find that they had been used for tanning, nor have the people yet found out the value of the " peat-coal," macerated condensed[1] peat, so long appreciated by the Grand Trunk of

---

even " borve," as in Sianborve, and " burr," as in Burraness; and, finally, the English " burg" and " burgh," " borough" and " burrow." Such are a few of its titles to antiquity and extent of domain.

[1] I am well aware of the difficulties, and especially of the expense, objected to

Canada and the railways of New England and Bavaria; even in
the Brazil a patent for the manufactory was taken out some
years ago, and Bahia now exports the article. Yet in Lyell's
" Principles of Geology " (11th edit., vol. ii., p. 504) we meet the
strange assertion, " No peat found in Brazil." The supply of the
bog factories near Montreal costs nine shillings to ten shillings
per ton, or about one-fourth the value of pit coal. The Torbite
of Horwich (Lancashire) is even cheaper, and experts have said
that it gets up steam to 10 lbs. pressure in one hour ten minutes,
and to 25 lbs. in one hour thirty-two minutes—the figures of
Lancashire coal being two hours twenty-five minutes and three
hours—at any rate, we may believe that when water is excluded,
its heating power is about half way between wood and coal.
Thus it becomes an article of general value to brewers, distillers,
and manufacturers; and the Swedish iron, equal to Low Moor,
as well as the yield of the Bavarian, the Wurtemberg, and the
Bohemian mines, are all treated with condensed peat. It is now
time to utilise the vast bogs of the finest deep black fuel, in
which Ireland and the Hebrides, the Shetlands and the Orkneys
abound, especially when perpetual colliery strikes, causing coal
famines and the immense rise in the value of the combustible,
have made steamers lie idle in our ports. Truly Torf-Einarr
Jarl, who first taught the art and mystery of " yarpha "-burning,
deserves a memorial statue on the Torf-nes.

In such " sea-girdled peat-mosses " as these, agriculture is a
farce, and only sheep can pay. The foundation of the rocks,
snowy quartz veining grey and chloritic slate, is that of Minas
Geraes, and yet crushing for gold has not, we were assured, been
attempted. Dr Cowie informed me that copper and iron are
now successfully worked near Sandwich; and I hope soon to
hear of prospecting for the nobler metal. At present our

---

condensing peat. But peat *au naturel* can be burnt as the *mottes* in France and
Holland have been used for generations. And I am also aware of the immense
interests wielded by the Coal League—surely these must sooner or later succumb
to the public good. Lands without coal leagues find no difficulty in the operation.
The two companies lately established at Oldenburg use a large flat-bottomed
steamer, which opens a canal 20 feet broad and 6 deep at the rate of 10 to 12 feet
per hour : the soil is heaped up on the banks, and is cut into brick-shape, after
which mere drying makes it fit for fuel.

African California, the Gold Coast itself, is not more thoroughly neglected.[1]

Shetland life is concentrated near the sounds and voes (the Vogr of Iceland), where the dykes of Galway and Roscommon, dry or mortared walls, enclose yellow fields of oats, barley, and potatoes black with frost. Churches, and manses bigger than the churches; kilns burning kelp and lime; substantial houses, thatched with barley-straw, upon "pones," or slabs of dried turf, the whole kept in place by "simmins" (straw ropes), stones, and logs, dotted the lowlands. Here and there stood a few willows and maple-planes, erroneously called sycamores,[2] under the shelter of walls; and uncommonly pleasant after Iceland was the twitter of the birdies. Many broken and unroofed cottages, some of them leper-houses in bygone days, reminded us that the disease lingered longer in Scotland than in England; in the Scoto-Scandinavian islands than in Scotland; and in Iceland than in the "Eyjar." The frequent ruined home-steads of small tenantry, compelled, when their land was "laid down to grazing," to seek their fortunes elsewhere, are the salient features. The "murid" (murret) coloured Shetland sheep have now made way for Scotch intruders; the cattle are from Ayrshire; and English horses, not "cussers from Lanarkshire," have taken the place of shelties. Ducks and geese are everywhere; skarfs and gulls are more numerous than the speckled cocks and hens; and salt-fish, which here is not sun-dried, lies piled, as in Iceland, upon the sands.

Much has been said in books[3] about the physical beauty of the Shetlanders, but neither of us could see it. There is a greater

---

[1] After Australian diggers had asserted for years that gold would be found in Bute, a specimen was lately (1874) extracted from a vein of quartz which runs out into the sea below the Skeoch plantation.

[2] Jerome Cardan, travelling in Scotland (1552), remarked the popular fondness for the *Platanus*, and explains it thus: "I think they take a special delight in that tree, because its foliage is so like vine leaves. . . . 'Tis like lovers, who delight in portraits when they can't have the original." Colonel Yule (Geograph. Mag., Sept. 1, 1874) asks whether these trees were the real plane (*P. Orientalis*) or the maple (*Acer pseudo-platanus*), commonly but erroneously so called in Scotland, and still more erroneously in England, "Sycamore." Hence also, he observes, by propagation of error Eastern travellers translate the Persian "Chínár" (*Platanus*) by Sycamore.

[3] Especially "Shetland," etc., by Robert Cowie, M.A., M.D. Edinburgh: Menzies, 1871. Will the author allow me to suggest that in his next edition of this valu-

variety of race than in the islands farther north, but less, as
might be expected, than in the Orkneys and Caithness. The
blue eyes are milder than in Iceland, the long bright locks are
the same, but the complexion is by no means so "pearl and
pink"—perhaps its muddiness may result from peat-water.
The blondes, as a rule, wear that faded and colourless aspect
which especially distinguishes the Slav race. The look is shy
and reserved, and the voice is almost a whisper, as if the speaker
were continually nervous: strangers notice this peculiarity even
in society. *En revanche*, the women appear to be peculiarly industrious. They crowd Commercial Street during the Monday
markets, and even when carrying their heavy " cassies," " cassie-
cazzies," or crates of peat, which serve for " Ronin the Bee,"
they spin yarn and knit " tree-ply stockings," apparently not
intended for their own naked feet. The Wadmel, or Wadmaal,
the North of England Woadmel, here better known as " Shetland
claith," cannot, however, compare with that of Iceland; the texture is loose, and the stuff in the shops is evidently meant to
sell, not to last.

After seeing the humble wonders of Scalloway Castle, we
struck southwards and across the Mainland, where we could hire
a boat for the Whalesback of Mousa. The leek-shaped Broch
has a pair of romantic legends attached to it, but they are too
modern for interest. This most perfect specimen of the seventy
round towers [1] has been often described, but no one seems to
have noticed the similarity of the double walls of the vaulted
and many-storied bee-hive chambers, and of the other peculiarities, with those of the pre-historic Sardinian Nurhágghi.
The " stepped domes " of dry stone, and the " concealments,"

---

able work—an exceptional guide-book, amusing as well as instructing—the medical
part from page 56 to page 88, and especially Chapter XIV., should be placed in
an appendix ? At present it reminds me of a volume which I read with the liveliest interest, " The Luck of Roaring Camp," regretting only that the order of the
tales had not been systematically reversed. Dr Cowie has been kind enough, at
my request, to draw up an account of the pre-historic collection at Lerwick,
which will be found in the note at the end of this chapter.

Since these lines were written, the papers have informed me that Dr Cowie,
after printing a second edition of his admirable guide-book, has passed from this
world when in the prime of manhood.

[1] The number of these places of refuge shows the Shetlands in proto-historical
times to have been densely peopled. I have made the same remark about the
Istrian Castellieri.

also reminded me much of similar features in outlying Syria. Some ill-conditioned party of " cheap-trippers," or " devil's-dust tourists," has lately fired the secular moss which clothed the south-western wall. On the way back to Lerwick there is another ruin in Clickamin (also written Chickhamin) Lake: interesting as the means of comparison, it has an addition evidently more modern of extensive outworks, which Mousa Castle wholly wants.

Unfortunately for myself, I had not time to call upon the late Mr Thomas Edmonston of Buness, whose philological labours are so valuable to northern students;[1] and to tell unpleasant truth, I was somewhat surprised by the success of the nineteenth century in abolishing all the old hospitality. We inspected the contents of the dark little room, the anthropological collection of the Shetlands, which deserves a catalogue, and other comforts of civilised life. Many Hjaltlanders have never heard of it. The most interesting articles are the steatite pots from Unst, and the ceramic remains, guiltless of wheel, collected in the Brochs. There are also some rough " thunderbolts "—here the stone celt is considered, as by the ancient Greeks, to be an ἀστροπελέκυς. Hence Claudian (fifth century) sings:

" Pyrenæisque sub antris
Ignea flumineæ legere ceraunia nymphæ. "

We ran into Thorshafn (Færoes) on September 4, when a shower of rain had laid the fog. The " Isles of Sheep," others say of " Feathers," are evidently built like Iceland, with submarine trap; and the deep narrow " grips " between them, passages free from any danger except the " vortices,"[2] which can be seen, suggest that they have parted into long narrow fragments under the influence of subaërial cooling and contraction. The deep black strata appear peculiarly regular, as those of the western Fjörðs of Thule, streaked with lines of red ochre, spotted with white guano, and not showing, in this part at least, any signs of Palagonite or sea-sand. The leaf-shaped valleys,

---

[1] Etymological Glossary of the Shetland and Orkney Dialects, by Thomas Edmonston. Edinburgh, 1866.
[2] Hence the name of Malestrom or Moskoestrom.

the water-falls, and the natural arches, are familiar to us after "Snowland;" the shallow turf lies upon the steepest inclines, and not unfrequently it is torn off by the frantic wind with as much ease as a rug is rolled up.

The course lay abreast of Mygganaes (Midge Naze),[1] with its head to the south, and projecting a long low tail cut by a "coupé," like that of Sark. We then opened Waagoe (voe islet), so called because imbedded in the greater Stromoe. At the southern end, where once whales abounded, as may be seen in prints of 1844, many "Battles of the Summer Islands" were fiercely waged. We pass Gaasholm, Tind-holm, or Peak Island, a slice of rock with jagged uplifted edge, here a common feature, the Koltar (Coulter), which passably represents its name, and Hestoe the horse-eyot. The latter is a common Scandinavian name for a feature with a long straight dorsum, ready as it were for the saddle—witness the Horse of "Copinshay" (Kolbeins-ey): the hunchbacks are mostly called "hogs," and the smaller out-liers "calves." The normal shape is a quoin, bluff to north or east, and sloping with a regular green incline to the water. There is no snow; the hay crop has been got in, and the settle-ments are villages, not Bærs or detached farms. We ran within easy sight of Kirkjubæ, which stands well out from its adjacent hovels; it is the last Roman Catholic building in the islands, and the "Reformation" left its sturdy walls unroofed. Visitors speak of an iron plate imbedded in its masonry, and supposed to denote treasure, which is not likely. The old Church still keeps up a mission-house and chapel at Thorshafn, but we found the building void of priests.

Whilst the "haaf," or outer sea, was calm as a lake, a cold and furious southerly wind, the gift of the funnel between Sandoe and Stromoe, blew in our faces, and when we had turned the southern point of the latter, it again met us from the north-east.

---

[1] "Lappmark's land-plague," says Mr Shairp, author of "Up in North" (London: Chapman & Hall, 1872), is of three kinds:

    1. Mygg, or long nose (*Culex pipiens*), the wretch of stinging bite and blas-phemous song.

    2. Knott (*C. reptans*), a villain that keeps close to the ground, and avoids horses.

    3. Hya or Gnadd (*C. pulicaris*), the smallest of the family, but when it "sticks," as the Swedes say, violent itching is the result.

From a Photo.

McFarlane & Erskine, Lith.rs Edin.r

KIRKJUBÆ RUINS IN FÆROE ISLANDS.

The capital Thorshafn is a small heap of houses, or rather boxes strewed "promiscuous" on the ground, and a large white church, whose belfry is adorned with a gilt ball and a profusion of crosses. It has, however, a literary dean, and, better still, a library. The site of the settlement is a spit of rock dividing the harbour into a northern and a southern "hop"—the latter being generally preferred. A green flag floating over a shed near the fort denotes the quarantine station; planked boat-houses figure conspicuously, and the roofs are more grassy even than in Iceland. Willows, elder-trees, and currant-bushes, looking gigantic after the stunted vegetation farther north, flourish in sheltered spots, especially near the well-bridged brook in the southern part of the city. Along the dorsum of the spit runs an upper road with a small central square, looking as if a single house had been pulled down to make room. Huge boulders have not disappeared from the thoroughfares, and the latter are the most crooked and irregular of any that claim to be in Europe; narrow, steep, and steppy—narrower than Malta, steeper than ramps at "Gib," and steppy like Dalmatian towns, for instance Curzola and Lésina: in places they are supplied with hand-rails.

The people are remarkably English in appearance, and perhaps an easy reason may be found for the resemblance. They appear rather shy than the reverse, and they notably lack Hazlitt's "Scotch stare." The women show the bloom of infinite delicacy that characterises the complexion of Iceland. The men, who unwisely shave their faces, still affect the picturesque island-dress, a peculiar-shaped cap of dark colour with thin blue or red stripes, long brown jacket, knee breeches of Wadmal, long stockings, and untanned spartelles, or "chumpers," the wooden-soled clogs of "Lankyshire."

We called on Hr Sysselmand Müller, and we left the Færoes with a conviction that its capital is one of the "slowest" places now in existence: the only possible excitement would be to buy a 560-fathom "fowl-rope,"[1] and to dangle like the samphire-gatherer of dreadful trade over the bird-precipices. "In a rope's

---

[1] The fowl rope contained sixteen ox hides, and the seven pieces each measured eighty fathoms. Early in the present century it cost only $10.

end between earth and heaven, with the blue sky above you, and below you the still bluer sea tumbling, between which two you swing to and fro like a pendulum," one might secure a novel sensation to take the place of many an *illusion perdue*. A St Bartholomew's Day of a hundred and fifty whales, a massacre headed, by the parson and the schoolmaster, must also have its charms, but these events are unhappily waxing rare.

---

## NOTE ON STONE IMPLEMENTS AND OTHER PRE-HISTORIC REMAINS FOUND IN THE SHETLAND ISLANDS. By the late Robert Cowie, M.A., M.D.

Of the pre-historic weapons of warfare, or implements of domestic economy, which have been found in the Shetland Islands, by far the most numerous and important are the stone implements. These naturally divide themselves into two classes, viz., the *polished* and the *rude*. First let us speak of the polished stone implement, celt, steinbarte, battle-axe head, or " thunderbolt." This implement has, for centuries, been an object of search, not only for the antiquary and the collector of curiosities, but for the native peasantry—the latter class regarding it with superstitious awe, as a sort of household god, who brings luck to the family that is fortunate enough to possess it. They term it the " thunderbolt," from a belief—everywhere found and dating from all times—that the weapon has come down from the sky during a thunderstorm. These " celts," or steinbartes, as they are generally termed in scientific language, again divide themselves into two varieties, viz. (1.) the single-edged steinbarte and (2.) the double-edged steinbarte.

1. The single-edged steinbarte, which is by far the most common, is thus very accurately described by Dr Hibbert, in his excellent work on Shetland: "This variety of blade has one cutting edge, generally of a semilunar outline, and tapering from opposite points to a blunted extremity or heel. In some specimens both sides are convex; in others one side only, the

other being flattened. All the edges except the broad sharpened margin are bluntly rounded off. The single-edged stone-axes of Shetland vary much in their dimensions, being from four to eight or ten inches in length; their breadth proportionately differing. When the Shetland steinbarte was used in war, its blunt tapering extremity may be supposed to have been introduced within the perforation made into some wooden or bone haft, and afterwards secured by overlapping cords, formed of thongs of leather, or the entrails of some animal; twine of hemp not being then in use."

From considerable personal observation, I can testify to the accuracy of the above description, except that there appears to be in these instruments greater variety in size than that indicated by the learned Doctor; the largest single-headed steinbarte in the Lerwick Museum being $14\frac{1}{2}$ inches long by $4\frac{1}{2}$ inches at the broadest point, and the smallest $4\frac{1}{2}$ inches long by $2\frac{1}{2}$ inches at the broadest point.

Continuing the paragraph just quoted, Dr Hibbert says: " Another kind of steinbarte has been said to occur in Shetland, the sharp edge of which describes the segment of a circle, whilst the chord of the outline is thickened like the back of a knife. Probably its blunt edge was fixed within the groove of a wooden or bone handle, so as to form a single-edged cutting instrument." This peculiar variety must have been very rare indeed, for no one appears to have seen it since the days of the Rev. Mr Low of Orkney, who wrote exactly a century ago.

2. The double-edged steinbarte is described as follows by Dr Hibbert: " The blade of this instrument is a stone completely flattened on each of its sides, and not more than the tenth of an inch thick; it is of an oblong shape, having one blunted margin perfectly straight, and, with the stone in such a position that the dull edge is the uppermost, we have the form of a blade presented, in which the two narrow edges are irregularly rounded off at their angles, so that one edge is much broader than the other. Every part of the margin but that which constitutes the summit of the outline is sharpened; by which means there is a great addition made to the extent of the cutting edge. The blade is $5\frac{1}{2}$ inches long, and from 3 to 4 broad." This descrip-

tion does not correspond with the specimens I have been able to examine. If they are to be considered fair specimens, I would describe the so-called double-edged steinbarte thus: An oblong flat piece of porphyry, serpentine, or some similar stone, 5 or 6 inches long by 4 or 5 broad, and about a third or a fourth of an inch thick, with a thin sharp edge all round.

These instruments, many of which are very beautiful both as regards form and polish, are generally formed of a peculiarly compact green porphyry or of serpentine. They have been found in most of the districts of Shetland, particularly in the parishes of Unst, Delting, Wells, and Sandsting. The situations and numbers in which they have been found, also present great variety. Some have been taken out of ancient stone coffins, others found inside of or near to old " burghs," while many have been dug up in the common—some near the surface and others several feet beneath it.[1]   Most of them have been found singly, but in many instances large collections of such weapons have been discovered.   Thus, in one instance, twenty-four of them were found in one spot, in another eight, and in a third seven, the last-mentioned series being arranged in the form of a circle.

Polished stones having the shape of spear-heads have also been found in Shetland, but very rarely. They are said to be about four inches long, having a groove apparently for receiving a wooden shaft.

Flint arrow-heads, although frequently dug up in Orkney, have not yet, as far as I can learn, been found in Shetland.

## 2. The Rude Stone Implements.

While the polished archaic stone implements have been known during a long period of modern history, the rude or unpolished have only very recently been discovered, or at all events recognised; and for this discovery we are chiefly indebted to the late Dr James Hunt, London; Dr Arthur Mitchell, Edinburgh; and Mr George Petrie, Kirkwall, who conducted archæo-

---

[1] One of those in the Lerwick Museum was taken out of the peat-moss six feet beneath the surface.

logical explorations in Shetland in the summer of 1865. Vast quantities of such articles must from time to time have been turned up by the peasantry; but it is only about this period they appear to have been recognised—a circumstance somewhat curious considering the many searches during a long series of years, made for relics of pre-historic times, by various accomplished antiquaries. These rough instruments present great variety both as to shape and size. Let us endeavour to indicate the chief types.

1. We have the club-like form, which is well illustrated by the accompanying copies of Dr Mitchell's excellent paper on

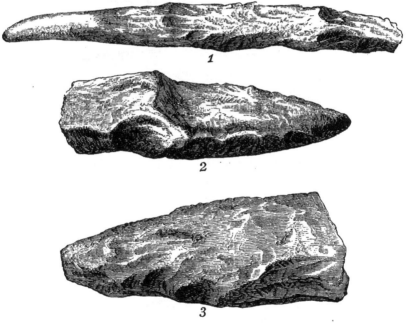

Fig. 1.—Stone Implements found in Shetland.

the subject.[1] This implement is generally of large size; one specimen measuring 21 inches by $2\frac{1}{2}$ inches at the greatest breadth, and weighing $6\frac{3}{4}$ lbs.; another is 20 inches long, 5 or 6 in diameter, but attains the great weight of 14 lbs. Many of

---

[1] On some Remarkable Discoveries of Rude Stone Implements in Shetland, by Arthur Mitchell, F.S.A., from Proceedings of the Society of Antiquaries of Scotland, vol. vii., 1866-67.

the small forms found in the collections to be described appear
to be fragments of this larger implement.

2. Next in importance comes a long, narrow, flattish stone—
" from 11 inches by 3 inches, to 6 inches by 1½—thinned and

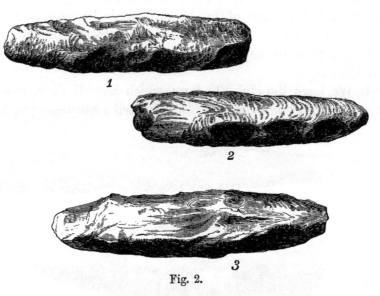

Fig. 2.

somewhat rounded at each end." Stones of this variety, which
are very numerous in the collections already made, present a
remarkable similarity. (See Fig. 2.)

(3.) The third type, which is illustrated by Fig. 3, is " a broad,

Fig. 3.

flat stone, showing a tendency to be pointed at one end." Dr
Mitchell considers most of these stones fragments of larger

implements; but two entire specimens of this type are to be found in a good collection made by Mr Umphray, of Raewick Shetland. The great majority of the rude stone implements found in Shetland belong to one or other of the types above briefly noticed; but we have still one or two less common varieties.

(4.) The fourth type, of which I have not been able to see a specimen, is described by Dr Mitchell as "a water-worn stone,

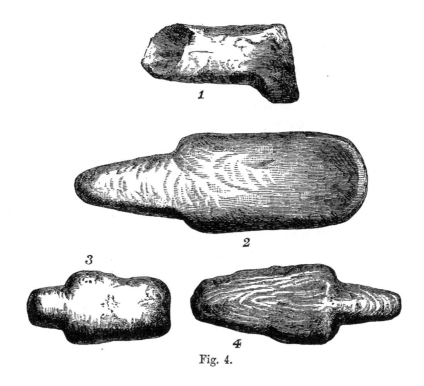

Fig. 4.

10 to 12 inches long, more or less cylindrical, but tapering at the ends."

(5.) The fifth variety, illustrated by Fig. 4, is a curious and very interesting spud-like instrument, of which only a few specimens have been yet found.

We next have three or four very rare and exceptionable varieties. The first of these is a cylindrical and apparently water-shaped stone, well worn at each end, as if it had been used as a pestle in crushing corn, or for some such domestic purpose (Fig. 5); the second a "flat, four-sided stone, 5 inches long, 3 inches wide, and 1½ inches thick," with a groove on each

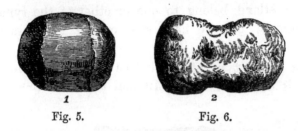

*1*　　　　　　　　　　*2*

Fig. 5.　　　　　　　　　　Fig. 6.

of the long sides, so as to give it a constricted appearance; and the third a piece of sandstone, or some such stone, with an oval cup-like hollow in it.

These curious implements, thus briefly enumerated, have been found in various districts of Shetland, notably in the parishes of Sandsting, Walls, Dunrossness, and Unst. It is interesting to note the different positions in which they have been found—*e.g.,* (1.) On the surface of the ground; (2.) in curious subterranean structures; (3.) in the heart of a large tumulus; (4.) on the outside of stone coffins with urns in them; and (5.) in the inside of a Kistvaen with a skeleton and a well-polished celt.[1]

Most of them are composed of sandstone, but a few of clay slate, or of micaceous schist. They apparently have been shaped chiefly by flaking, but in some instances also by picking.

In connection with these archaic implements, three questions naturally arise: By *whom, when,* and *for what purpose* were they formed? Were I able, this is not the place to discuss such difficult and important questions. On excavating "burghs" and opening tumuli, such pre-historic remains as fragments of rude pottery, pieces of charred wood, and teeth and broken pieces of bones of animals, are frequently discovered.

LERWICK, ZETLAND, *24th March* 1873.

---

[1] Dr Mitchell, paper supra cit.

# CHAPTER II.

### THE LANDFALL—FISHING FLEET—TO REYKJAVIK.

AFTER this interlude of Hysteron-proteron, we return to the
steamer " Queen," which has pertinaceously bored through

> " The Pentland, where the furious tide,
> Runs white for many a mile. "

After sighting Cape Wrath, she bade adieu to "Earth's proudest
Isle,"and dashed north-west intothe Deucalidian or Deucalidonian
Ocean, the Mare Pigrum of the classics, the sea which Adam of
Bremen terms *jecoreum et pulmoneum*, because it has a heavy
motion like those troubled with asthma, in the same sense as
Plautus speaks of asthmatic legs—"pedibus pulmoneis mihi
advenisti." The Germans called it Libersê (Adam Bremensis)
and complained that the abnormal quantity of salt made it a
Mare Mortuum. Hence Hoffman von Fallersleben sings :

> " De lebirmere
> Ein mere ist giliberot
> In demo wentilmere westerot
> Sô der starche Wint
> Giwirffit die Skef in den Sint, " etc.

The portentous waves remarked by old Icelandic sailors between
Iceland and America, are termed by them Haf-girðingar, or Sea-
fens, and the Polar wastes between Norway and Greenland
were known as Haf-botnar (deep-sea bay) and Trölla-botnar,
because here was the abode of Tröll-carl and Titan. The mighty
breakers of the North Atlantic are known to picturesque and
poetical tourists, not to seamen, as " Spanish waves." The sky,
before clear, was all cirrus and cirro-cumulus, and the slaty green
seas made the too lively " Queen" dance and reel with excitement. The cabin table was put into its straightest waistcoat,

and men avoided the deck—on shipboard, as in maritime Iceland, once wet, you cannot dry again. Our numbers shrank at mess, and the passengers seemed to become like the royal and feminine Legs of Spain. Ghostly sounds issued from the cabin; one "Caledonian stern and wild," attached to a black dog, big as a donkey and hairy as a bear, made fierce attempts to violate the toilette tables and glared hideously at expostulation. Our only consorts were spirting whales and audacious troops of numerous gulls—these escorted us with sundry reliefs of guard as far as Iceland.

Presently we sighted the "Stack," a split rock with a bald white head, and further to starboard the Bird Skerry, a low dome wholly unprovided with lighthouse—how many a good ship, densely be-fogged, has run her bows upon this Rock of Death, and melted away in the yeasty waves! At 6.30 P.M., we passed the "two solitary islands," Ronan and Barra, *alias* Sulisker, of old Sulnasker, north-easternmost outliers of the Hebrides. The former appears in hay-cock shape, the latter is a long flat-backed "horse," bluff as usual to the north, with a precipice 300 feet high. Both are uninhabited, and might serve for fancy eremites. To starboard rises Fair Isle, half-way between the Orkneys and the Shetlands, once belonging to the former, now to the latter. This rock supplies the shops of Lerwick and Kirkwall with its peculiar hosiery; and the primary colours, blue, red, and yellow, of the Etruscan tombs, and the Temple of Ephesian Diana,[1] are those which Algiers, Morocco, and the East, still know so well to blend. Mixed in the most daring way they are never inharmonious, glaring, and grotesque. It is well worth the artist's time and trouble to investigate and deter-mine the delicate differences of proportion which can make the "Devil's livery" so brilliant and pleasing to the eye. "Ye Yle of Fare," I need hardly note, is supposed to have derived its art from the shipwrecked seamen of the Spanish Armada. "Insula Bella," says Buchanan; of which Brand remarks, "I neither did

---

[1] At Ephesus blue formed the background of enrichments and sculpture in relief, whilst brilliant reds and yellows were applied to the parts requiring greater prominence. The idea that red, green, and blue, are primitives, with yellow, sea-green, and pink for complements, is very modern and rather startling.

see, nor was I informed of anything that affords us any reason
why this isle should be so appellatively taken and denominated
*bella* or fair." The Scandinavian name is Friðarey; otherwise we
might believe Fair Isle to be a congener of "Færoes," from Fier,
feathers, or from Fær, a sheep, because *plena innumerabilibus
ovibus*" (Dicuil).

June 6.

Still, as the weather waxed fouler, the aneroids rose higher
and higher. We had exchanged an angry Auster, which filled
the raw air with damp, for a wrathier Boreas that tore the clouds
to tatters. All the northerly winds, which rarely outlast the
fortnight in this capricious and treacherous climate, are cold and
dry, consequently heavy, whilst those from the rain-bringing
south notably want pressure. We are now approaching the
region of paradoxes, a practical joke of Nature, where the Rule
of Reverse seems generally to apply. Travellers tell us that
presently we shall see nine suns, which do not give the light and
warmth of one; sub-glacial volcanoes; fire issuing from icebergs
—is this not a dream of old Uno Von Troil?[1]—a summer without
thunder which is confined to winter; stone crumbling soft under
the touch; stalactites and stalagmites of lava, not of lime, Pluto
doing Neptune's work; rivers now bone-dry, then raging floods;
forests sans trees; fuel thrown up by the furious sea; deep
swamps clothing the high hill-slopes; lakes supplying ocean cod;
and wild ducks swimming the almost boiling springs; a land
where the men draw and carry water, and a population which,
thriving in the worst weather, sickens and dies of malignant
catarrh (the Kruym of the Færoes) when the heavens deign to
bestow a rare smile.

Our only *passe-temps* is that of calculating successive positions
on the chart. There to starboard lies Foula, which some write
Fowla and Foulah, and is evidently Fogla- or Fugla-ey,[2] fowl's

---

[1] He attributes (p. 49) the fire to crushed driftwood, but Adam of Bremen
declares the ice to be so dry that it can burn.

[2] The Icelandic "fugl" is especially applied to the gull. "Fowl-isle" amongst
the Scandinavians meant an isolated rock lying far out to sea, and supposed to
represent a bird swimming.

or gull's eyot. The claims of the "stately headland" to represent

"Thule, the period of cosmographie,"

have been discussed in another place. It belongs to Dr Scott (R.N.) of Melby; it numbers about two hundred souls, and it rejoices in a revenue of some £200 per annum—when fishing and crops are favourable. Like other islands, it has its magic carbuncle. Beyond it lies Papa Stour; Papey, the eyot of Culdees and anchorites: its natural arch will appear familiar after Iceland. About noon we found ourselves off the Færoes, and the rest of the day was spent upon the Ferry of the Northern Sea. We steam all unconscious over the "Sunken Land of Bus," in N. lat. 58° 2′ and long. 29° 55′; "Arctis," a continent which has lately been revived, and whose fragments are supposed to be Iceland, the Færoes, Greenland, Spitzbergen, and Franz-Josef's Land. This is a restoration, or rehabilitation, of Unger's Miocene Atlantis, which imitates Bailly's "in having taught us everything but its own name and existence." Older hydrographic books assure us that the western coast once "occupied many leagues of extent, but that after being overflowed, it is now not more than a league round when the sea is high. There was some years ago a large island named Finsland here, which was full a hundred leagues in circumference, and on which were many villages." Similarly, Brasil Rock ("Hy Brazile") was placed in N. lat. 57° 10′ and long. 16°: we have also the submerged land of Lionnesse (Leonnais) extending to the Scilly group and the drowned city of Ys, for which mass was recited till the beginning of the present century; the island of St Brandan, the Masculine and Feminine Islands, the island Scoria with its archbishop, and the island Antillia with the "Septem Cidade," mythical features, spawns of the old "Atlantis." Hr Thorsteinnsson of Reykjavik showed me the origin of Finsland, more generally called Friesland, upon a fragment of vellum chart, dating from the sixteenth or seventeenth century, almost "rotten with age," and ignobly converted into a book-cover. Evidently the "Isola Frislanda" of Messer Antonio Zeno, in A.D. 1380, is a mere clerical or cartographic error for the Færoes appearing in the shape of a large tract of ground close to and southwest of Iceland. Every map of the period supports its existence.

*June* 7.

As we approach Snow-land the north wind seems to fall, or rather, to judge from the cirrous sky, it blows high overhead. Sailors in these northern seas believe that after passing beyond the " roaring Sixties " they begin to sail " under the wind." In other words, they hold that the Polar current, rushing to supply the ascending atmosphere established by solar action at the equator, and forming the upper trades, describes an arc which touches the earth about lat. 60°; whilst in the higher latitudes of both hemispheres, the greatest force of the draught is high overhead. So, on the summit of Tenerife, we stand in a perpetual gale of upper trades, which farther north sinks to the sea surface and overflows Europe.

Our situation was none of the most pleasant. An English vessel, also unprovided with pilot and skilful crew, has lately been wrecked upon the dangerous and inhospitable southern coast of Iceland. The clammy fog enwrapping us like a wet blanket, made altitudes hopeless; the magnet is here bewitched, seeming as if it forgot the pole; the old English hydrographic charts used on board our ships are poor compared with the French and the Danish; and we might have been drifted eastward or westward under the influence of unstudied currents. We crossed the bows of a big-sterned brig, but as she could not exchange a word with us, we " Queens" could only say bitterly,

" Barbarus hic ego sum, quia non intelligor illis !"

Under the circumstances we envied Víkingr Floki his consecrated ravens, birds which, since the days of Genesis, are always supposed to make for the nearest land. Perhaps I should say before, as the " croaker "[1] has lately appeared in the mythical seven days' deluge, related by Sisit (Xisuthrus), and was a very cannibal from the beginning, as well as a bird of augury and

---

[1] Raven—old German, Hraban; modern, Rabe; Icel. Hrafn (*pron.* Hrabn); Anglo-Saxon, Hræfn; Dan. Ravn; and Slav. Vran—is derived (says Max Müller, " Science of Languages," Longmans, 1862) from the Sanskrit Rn or Krn, " to cry," whence "raucus," and other kindred words. Like the pigeon, the genus Corvus (Corax and Cornix) crops up in all mythology, even where least expected; witness the Hierocorax of Mithras and the marvellous changes by which Apollo and Athene became crows.

sagacity. Sir William Thompson has thus ably discussed the
question of raven *versus* magnet: " We have no certain information of the directive tendency of the natural magnet being known
earlier than the middle or end of the eleventh century (in Europe,
of course). . . . That it was known at this date and its
practical value recognised, is shown by a passage from an Icelandic historian, quoted by Hanstien in his treatise of Terrestrial
Magnetism. In this extract an expedition from Norway to Iceland in the year 868 is described; and it is stated that three
ravens were taken as guides, for, adds the historian, 'in those
times seamen had no loadstone [1] in the northern countries.'
This history was written about the year A.D. 1068, and the
allusion I have quoted obviously shows that the author was
aware of natural magnets having been employed as a compass.
At the same time it fixes a limit of the discovery in northern
countries. We find no mention of artificial magnets being so
employed or even known till about a century later. In a curious
old French volume by Givot de Provence, of which the MS. is in
the Royal Library at Paris, there occurs the following very interesting passage, which is the first allusion extant to the use of needles
in place of the natural magnets for the compass: ' This same
(*i.e.*, the Polar star) does not move, and mariners have an art
which cannot deceive by the virtue of the magnet, an ugly brown
stone to which iron *adheres of its own accord.* When they look
for the right point, and when they have touched a needle on it,
and fixed the needle on a piece of straw lengthwise in the middle,
and the straw keeps it above, then the point turns just against
the star undoubtedly. When the sea is dark and gloomy that
you can see neither star nor moon, then they bring a light to
the needle, can they not then assure themselves of the position
of the star towards the point? By such means the mariner is
enabled to keep the proper course; this is an art which cannot
deceive.' This passage shows clearly that magnetised needles
were actually employed for nautical purposes as they are at
present in the twelfth century." This interesting quotation

---

[1] The very word is Norsk, "leiðar- (Anglo-Saxon, lád) steinn," not "lapis viæ,"
but leading stone (að leiða), or lode-stone; like lode-star and lodesman, "a pilot."
It is also called Sólar-steinn, or "sun-stone."

concerning the Marinière or *La Grenouille,* was obligingly sent to me by Principal D. M'Farlane of Glasgow.

About one P.M. the sea became unaccountably smooth, and as the wind drew round to the north, we judged that we were under the lee of the land. Presently it was whispered that a white gleam of shore had appeared and disappeared over the weather-bow, and that we were running into shallow water, rendering lead more necessary than look-out, whilst upon all ears fell ominous sounds:

"the surf that sings,
The bar-that thunders, the shale that rings."

The fog suggested the old traveller's description, " subito collapsi sumus in illam tenebrosam rigentis oceani caliginem, quæ vix oculis penetrari valeret;" and the sea became a "mare tenebrosum" of the most repulsive aspect. We had intended to make our landfall at the southernmost extremity of Iceland, Portland Head, some forty-five miles to the west. But at six P.M. the water, blackened by the uliginous discharge of an unknown stream, and the dimly-seen pale-grey breakers furiously lashing the low-lying strand, and blurring it with water-dust, told us where we were. Immediately in front of us lay the carse, or alluvial lands, the *déblai* of those scarped walls that first issued from the deep: here begins what is technically called the Siða, " side," or sea-shore, the long narrow strip of habitable land between the mountains and the beach. Its western limit is the river Kuðafljót : this, the broadest in the isle, and ridiculously termed " Nile of Iceland," derives its name from Kúði,[1] the little Norwegian boats which ascended it in the olden day.

We now ran cautiously westward. The southern shore, harbourless as the corresponding part of Sicily, has in many parts, like Norway, two coasts, an inner and an outer ; the latter composed of reefs and islands, and somewhat resembling the true or old, and the false or new, shores of tropical Africa, for instance, about Dahome and the Slave Coast. Slowly rose on high, towering through the mysterious gloom, the grisly, black, and scarped form of Hjörleifshöfði, a ghostly castle upon a Stygian strand.

---

[1] Cleasby derives it from Kúði or Kóð, the fry of trout and salmon.

But such weather would deform the fairest face that earth can show—would reduce the approach of Venice and of Wapping to an absolute level: as I afterwards saw it in clear sunny weather, Hjörleifs Head is by no means without a certain grim beauty of expression. The huge escarpment is a noble monument to him, who "fell by the basest of slaves" (Irishmen) because he "did not sacrifice to the gods."

The scene now develops itself and becomes imposing in its cruel hideousness. We are off the eastern Jökull, so called in contradistinction to the western Jökull, now best known as Snæfellsjökull. It is truly Iceland, "everlasting frost," as oft-quoted Pindar sings, "and fountains of unapproachable fire." Beyond the ghastly greenish waves, and the low base of black, bleak, and barren shore, appears a contorted *silhouette* of broken basaltic blocks, a line of "Kárá Bábás" (Black Papas), rising in towers and battlements, and setting off the dead whiteness of the hogsbacks above, gleaming whiter still from their background of angry, watery, purple cloud-rack. The mighty mass starts from the south with the Mýrdals (mire-dale) Jökull, a tract of eighty-four square miles, which often gives a name to the whole; it then connects with the Goðalöndjökull, running east and west about fifteen to twenty miles long, by twenty to twenty-four broad, and utterly unexplored, save only the Kötlugjá;[1] thirdly, rising some way to the westward, the Eyjafjalljökull floats in air, the mighty beacon which guides to his landfall the sailor voyaging from the south. Here the southern or

---

[1] Several Icelanders (see Dr W. Lauder Lindsay) have visited the rift which engulphed Katla, the murderess and suicide; a name well known by the translation of Powell and Magnússon. "G. H. C.," before quoted, who explored it in August 1874, after being misled by the map, found on the southern face "a deep circular indentation where black volcanic sand could be seen uncovered by snow and ice." We can now explain by the usual method the glacier which, according to Professor Steenstrüp, was torn from its moorings in 1721 by water within or below: evidently the heated ground melted the whole of the upper *calotte* and caused the catastrophe. Other traces were concealed by the snow-fall which, consolidating into glacier-ice, accumulates annually twenty feet, and fourteen years have elapsed since the last eruption. The guides were surprised that "their natural foe should present phenomena of a character no more startling and tremendous. What had they expected to find? Perhaps a vast yawning gulf, over whose edge might be watched the spirit of Katla, whirling like a second Francesca di Rimini in the sulphurous depths below." Yet Henderson could descry from Skaptafell "the aqua-igneous volcano *Kötlu-giá*, whose tremendously yawning crater was distinctly visible" (i. 264).

warmer exposure, which Dr W. Lauder Lindsay saw almost bare as late as June 13, shows snow only in the huge rifts gashing its black tormented flanks; whilst its head is crowned with a silvery aureole, possibly the reflection of the northern side, and contrasting sharply with its canopy of slaty-blue sky. The aspect of all this *nevada* makes the discoverer's heart beat fast, but the tremendous chasms in the basalt suggest peculiar difficulties.

Still our weary skipper, indefatigable withal, was doubtful about his position, when Professor Paijkull's volume lying open upon the deck enabled all to recognise the southernmost point, Portland Head (W. long. G. 18° 54'; N. lat. 63° 22'). The broad and high escarpment is faced by three diminutive outliers, and the largest of these is known as Dýrhóla-ey, door-hill-isle ; the Napoleon book translates Dýrhólar by *tumulus des arches*. Except that the port-holes number two, it exactly resembles the Doreholm of our Shetland Islands, prefixed by Pinkerton to John Brand's " Brief Description." A little to the east lie the Reynidrángar (rowan-needles), a sister formation of drongs, but curving south-eastward and not south-westward.

The freezing wind evidently blew directly from the mighty mass of snow-roofed glaciers lying immediately behind the shore, and it was midnight before we had covered the thirty to thirty-four knots separating Portland Head from the Vestmannaeyjar archipelago. The only sensible remark made about these "Irishmen's islands " was by an ancient seaman who, transferring his quid to the other side of his cheek, declared that they were exactly like a "toon with ill-liggit sta-a-cks." A small but enthusiastic knot of passengers did not turn in before five A.M. ; they were rewarded by seeing sundry cockle-shell craft, the Norwegian steamer making southwards, and a peak which they determined satisfactorily, for themselves at least, to be Hekla.

*June 8.*

The morning, if we can so call it where night is negative, not positive, broke clear and cold, the north-westward savouring strongly of Greenland; and under the rosy sky the western horizon was a white streak, as though the gleam of an iceblink,[1] adding a strange Polar charm.   After Eyjafjall there is a complete change of feature; the sea faces a great alluvial plain cut by many broad streams, which breaks inland into waves of rolling ground, with dots denoting hill and hillock, and which ends northwards in blue-black ranges jagged with many a detached peaklet.   A host of gulls and terns[2] put in an appearance: I afterwards passed twice along this line, and found it almost desert of feather.   Our Cockney gun again amused himself by slaughtering and maiming as many unfortunates as he could— it is only fair to own that this wanton cruelty was not looked upon with a favourable eye.   The sable-crested and silver-breasted eider ducks with their brown wives fell easy victims. The same fate overtook the black diver (*Colymbus Troile*) and the Lundi[3] or puffin (*Mormon Fratercula* or *F. Arctica*), called sea-parrot, probably from the disproportionate painted beak which, however, does not lodge a talking tongue.   They could hardly rise in the smooth sea, for their wings are short as if they were a transition to the penguins; but they scuttled away, paddling with their web-feet as fast as we approached them. The feathers of the Lundi are collected for stuffing, despite their prodigious growth of pediculi.   It is the Shetlanders' Tommie or Tom Noddy, the Norie of the Orcades, the Priest of Scotland, and the Pope of Cornwall.   Some travellers strongly recommend puffin-pie stuffed with raisin pudding and baked, but the oily flesh has a bad name as diet: its chief uses are fuel and fish-bait. Yet the "pope" or "priest," the half-fledged bird, is pickled and eaten in our islands.   The Arctic Skúa (*Lestris Thuliaca*, Prey., or *Stercorarius parasiticus*), the Shetlanders' Bonxie, kept out of our reach as it chased and plundered its feathery brethren. It derives the opprobrious "*Stercorarius*"[4] from a mere scandal,

---

[1] In Iceland the reflection of field-ice is brightest, but yellow; new ice is grey, and drift-ice is purest white.  The use of "blink" is not happy: Ross employs it in "ice-blink" to denote a cliff or barrier; others talk of land-blink, *i.e.*, the reflection of the sky upon the earth.

[2] The English "tern" is from the Icel. Therna (*Sterna hirundo*).

[3] Hence "Lundy" in the Bristol Channel.

[4] Baring-Gould (pp. 418, 419) gives four kinds of skuas—*Catarrhactes* (great skua), *Pomatorhinus*, *Parasiticus* (Arctic skua), and *Buffoni*.   He makes "Kjör" the Icel. name for No. 3: I heard it so applied, but the Dictionary gives "a sea-

and "*parasiticus*" from its habit of harrying the tarroch (*Rissa tridactyla*) and the " graceful sea-swallow," which Mr P. Miles holds to be game (*Sterna macrura*). The Icelanders call this " víking of birds " from its cry, Kjói (pronounced *Kiowi*) ; and the Færoese Tyovi, " the thief." The white-robed Dominican, with its black scapular, has a strong wing, and the sharp, crooked claws which garnish the web-feet, make him a raptor addicted, they say, to attacking newly-dropped lambs. The gannets or solan geese (*Sula Bassana*, whence. probably Sulisker, the Suleskerry or flat, insulated rock never awash) fell before the shot, but after a short sickness they rose struggling, and winged their way towards land. These interesting birds, made conspicuous by their cream-coloured heads and black primaries, form Indian files or wedges when travelling from place to place, and separate where the tide-rip shows the sea to be unusually fishy. The " *Pelicanus Bassanus*," though connected by name with the Bass Rock, abounds about the Cape of Good Hope and Madagascar. It is a fowl of many titles. Here it is termed Súla or Haf-súla (deep-sea Sule); whence our solan, misnamed goose ; and the Dutch know it as Jan van Genter—whence our " gannet " (?) Its fine shape and flight have probably given it a place amongst the " *singularia naturæ et providentiæ*," with which the good Bishop Pontoppidan has supplied these northern regions. Hence, according to Meyerus (*de volucri arborea*), the *conchæ avitificæ seu anatiferæ*, birds growing like African oysters on trees : this fable finds a pendant in Los Pateros of Manilla, duck-hatching establishments where men incubate the eggs. Mr James Wilson, speaking of the Solan goose (*Sula alba*) of St Kilda, computes that the 200,000 birds forming the colony consume . between March and September 214 millions of herrings. Jerome Cardan (Travels in Scotland) found the " Soland, perhaps Pliny's sea-eagle," a bird of general use. In spring they supplied the garrisons with fuel, to say nothing of fish ; they patiently endured their young to be taken from them ; they have quantities of fat

---

bird of the tern kind; Hill's Sterna." We find the family mentioned by Pigafetta, the circumnavigator (A.D. 1519-22), under the libellous name " Cagassela " or " Caca uccello," and he himself oftentimes witnessed the practice which survives in the term Stercorarius. It is an Antarctic as well as an Arctic " pirate of the seas."

under the skin used for dressing wool (*hac lanas inficiunt*), and a " certain small gut " yields a grease which is excellent for pains in the hip-joint. " The profit this bird gives is manifold, viz., from sticks, feathers; fat, and young ones; and it is said to amount to 500 golden crowns yearly "—an extinct industry !

We ran along the shore of Krísuvíkrberg, with precipices some 200 feet high fronting the leprous splotch upon the conical and jagged highlands that denote the Krísuvík Sulphur Mountain. This formation accounts for the sandstrips, which look notably yellow after the black lowlands to the east; and the colour is rendered brighter by quantities of comminuted sea shells thickly spread on the shore. This south-western projection is one vast " Hraun,"[1] or cold lava-field, a land seemingly afflicted with " black death," yet it rejoices in the title of Gold-breast Canton (Gullbringu Sýsla); the plentiful fisheries representing the precious metal. At nine A.M. we ran by the "Karl" (carle or old man),[2] a detached mass standing boldly out from the lava-crested coast; it has a ridge and steeple, which, especially when seen from the west, justify the English " Church Rock." Here, like the great lava lip beyond, its flanks are white with the guano of the Filungr or Fulmar[3] (*Procellaria glacialis*), foulest of sea-fowl. Beyond it is a bunch of volcanic cones and tumuli, spiracles and hornitos, all bare rock, or clothed with lapilli; one grass-clad crater appears to be of considerable size, and we easily count four distinct *coulées* or discharges spilling over the Palagonite cliffs.

Behind the leprous Karl lies Reykjanes, or Reeky Naze, so named with a reason. A puff of steam rose high in the air, suggesting, as I read with astonishment in the *Scotsman* (June 17th),[4]

---

[1] A term of daily use, derived from " að hrynja," to flow, to stream down; its pronunciation (*Hroyn*) induces the facetious traveller to call it the "road to ruin," and Henderson wrote as he spoke, Hroyn. "Gullbringu" is usually translated gold-bringing; but Cleasby, sub voc. "bringa," derives the word differently, and makes " Gull-bringur" signify the Golden Slopes. In Sect. VII. of Introduction a third signification has been given.

[2] Hence the country word " Kaarl Cat," for tom cat, still preserved in heraldry. The Icel. Karl is pronounced *Katl* or *Kadl*.

[3] Farther south the Fulmar is called the Mollie-moke; hence the " mollie," or mild orgie on broad northern whalers.

[4] The following is the whole text of the letter upon the " Expected Eruption of Mount Hecla" (which did not take place):

"MANSE OF ARBUTHNOTT, *July* 2, 1872.

"SIR,—Will you permit me to add the following to your paragraph with the above heading in the *Scotsman* of to-day? While doubling Cape Reikianess, the south-west

that " a new Geyser had burst out at a point a short distance inland, and about twenty miles in a south-westerly direction from Reikiavik, throwing up a vast column of water to a height of at least a hundred feet." The " same outburst was observed in full play on the homeward voyage of the ' Queen '" (June 11, 1874), and was held to be " premonitory of an eruption of Hecla." Had the writer looked at the large map of Iceland, he would have seen four blue circlets placed behind Reykjanes to denote warm springs; they are supposed to be the work of the Skaptarfells eruption, which, in 1783, threw up Nyöe, " the new island." The map of Iceland in Pontanus (1631) shows at this place a " fons commutans lanas nigras in albas." I may observe that in the first place we saw only steam, not water, or rather that we were too far off to distinguish anything but the former. Secondly, the weather was exceptionally still and rainy; and the damp air, deficient in barometric pressure, allowed vapours to rise high, whereas, under opposite conditions, they would be dispersed, or hug the ground. The Geysirs are said to rage more furiously in wet than in dry weather; and on arrival at Reykjavik we distinctly observed the fumes of Laugarnes, which suggested the name " Reeky Bay,"[1] standing up in a tall, transparent column—

---

promontory of Iceland, on the morning of Saturday, June 8, we saw a remarkable Geyser a few miles inland, shooting up water at regular intervals of about five minutes to a height of at least 100 feet. All on board who had ever heard of the Great Geyser, so graphically described by Madame Ida Pfeiffer and others, but which is sometimes so unpolite as to keep sightseers waiting two days before it favours them with an exhibition, were amazed at a spectacle so remarkable, and yet so unremarked by any who before us had visited Iceland.

" After attending service at the church of Reikiavik on Sunday, I did myself the honour to call upon the Bishop of Iceland, an excellent, courteous old gentleman, who, if he does not dwell, like the Psalmist, in a ' house of cedar,' dwells, like his flock, in a house of Norwegian fir. He could not speak English, but he spoke French well. To him I mentioned the phenomenon we had seen, believing that he was as likely as any one to know whether or not it was new. He told me that he knew the district well, but that there was no Geyser there at his last visit; that what we had seen, therefore, was quite new. In answer to my inquiry whether there had been any recent volcanic disturbance in the island, he informed me that there had been a violent earthquake in the northern region about the middle of April. This outburst of a new Geyser (which we observed in full play on our homeward voyage on Tuesday, June 11) and the earthquake in the north, seem premonitory of an eruption either of Hecla, or of some other of the other seven mountains which Keith Johnston, in his Physical Atlas, marks as active volcanoes. I hope we shall shortly have a description of any such occurrence, if it do take place, from the graphic pen of Captain Burton, whose society made our outward voyage a rare treat.—I am, etc.

"(Signed)      R. M. SPENCE."

[1] Reyk = reek (Kelt. Ruagh, Reác, and Ruah, the German Rauch), seems to be a word common to the Aryan and Semitic families. Old philologists derive it from the Hebrew Ruach, Arab. Rûh or Rîh, wind, breath, mind, spirit. Spinoza,

it was not seen from the town during the rest of my three months' stay. I twice voyaged past the site of my friend's "new Geysir;" every glass was pointed shorewards, but none succeeding in detecting the least trace of water or vapour. In 1862 Mr Symington (p. 46) observed " steam rising from a hot sulphur spring on the coast" near Reykjanes. Finally, as will be seen, Icelanders who have visited the spot describe the features as " Hverar," caldrons, boiling fountains; or as " Laugar," baths, tranquil waters.

The Fire Isles being hidden by fog, our attention was drawn to the mosquito flotilla of fishing-boats around us, each confined to its beat by the various buoys and buckets. The general appearance of the craft is that of the Shetlands; Mr Spence compared them with the " Westræ skips," but the Icelander is not nearly so solid as ours. The largest carry two low masts, both strongly supported by backstays; they are clinker-built, high at stem and stern, with a sharp projection for the rudder, which fits loosely into two iron eyes, and which often proves worse than useless. A transverse section forms the letter V; the planks belly out little, probably for facility of hauling up: the latter process, especially when the sun is hot, renders them exceptionally leaky, and want of care causes them to last for a very short time. There is no such thing as a decked boat in sight; the total of sixty-one to sixty-three which exists in the whole island being almost confined to shark catching on the north coast, whilst there are 3092 open boats, with from two to twelve oars. Row boats are preferred on account of the number of hands they feed; and hence the unusual loss of adult males, which is said to average forty per cent. drowned. At all times the crews must run three to six miles out before arriving at their ground, and repeat the task after work—a vast waste of time and toil. The craft has plenty of what the French call *pied*, and will not hesitate to cross the Faxa Fjörð, some fifty miles broad. The ballast is composed of basalt blocks, and the numerous sails are mere strips of cloth, for greater convenience of lowering. The oars are remarkably narrow, the rule even in

---

the Hebraist, translates, apparently with reason, " Ruach Elohim" (the Spirit of Elohim or Gods, Gen. i. 2) by " a strong wind."

"The Islands,"[1] a precaution rendered necessary, it is urged, by the strong currents. I strongly suspect it to be the mere effect of "father-to-son" principle. Below the handle, the shape is a heavy square, on the principle of the Rhine and the Kaikjis on the Bosphorus. The oars fit into coarse thwarts, lined with hoop-iron, or they play upon rude wooden pins doubled to the fore. The stroke is very long and slow, hardly to be recommended for Oxford and Cambridge; and of course feathering is impossible. Iceland nets are ridiculously small, and are floated by gourd-shaped bottles of Danish manufacture, closed at the mouth: these glass balls are also used by Norwegian fishermen. At the capital there are no lighters; farther north they will show themselves, shaped like the fisher-boats, but many-ribbed as herrings. Evidently the first want is a decked vessel of from twenty to thirty tons, which would employ fewer hands, and show better returns.

The smaller craft are four-oared, and at the landing-place we shall find two-oared boats: not a gig is to be seen, and the highest authorities must embark and disembark, if they cannot borrow from a man-of-war, in these receptacles of slime and filth. The seat is a mere perch, decidedly not comfortable; baling with the little wooden scoup is hardly ever thought of, and all are equally wet and greasy. We read in the Sagas of "long ships," of dragon ships, and of merchantmen, whose common complement was some thirty oars: the figure-heads of the Vikings were so fright-ful that they terrified the Land-vættir, or local genii; and the decks were protected by awnings, and "girdled for war" by shield being laid to shield on rims or rails.[2] Truly, the mariners of Iceland have lost much by staying at home in ease; and piracy evidently had its advantages.

The crews of these outlandish "skips" are as degenerate as their craft. Silken kirtles, gilded helms, and spears inlaid with gold, are as unknown to them as the "Bisons" and "Serpents"

---

[1] "Eyjar" is often used of the Western Isles, Orkneys, Shetlands, and Soder or Suder (Suðr-ey, south isle, whence the diocese of Soder and Man). In south Iceland it is also applied to the Vestmannaeyjar.

[2] One of the earliest forms of armour-plating, the old defence still survives in the nettings of our bulwarks.

which caused " a furore Normannorum libera nos, Domine !" to
be inserted into the monkish litany. The men are good for fine
weather, but in danger all become captains; very different from
the Danish sailor. The comfortable primitive costume is gone;
the Stakkr, hide blouse or jacket, extending from the neck and
fastened round the waist; the large Sæskór, or water-boots;
and the Leistabrækr, or stocking breeks, also lightly laced about
the middle. The moderns are clad much like our fishermen;
they have, however, sensibly preserved the long-flapped " sou'-
wester," now " out of fashion" in Great Britain. They seem to
rejoice in wet feet, wearing three or four pair of coarse woollen
socks, which serve to retain the water. The only peculiarity of
their dress is the Iceland glove, which even the shepherd and
the mountain-guide will never doff. For the convenience of a
dry and clean side near the palm, it has two thumbs, one projecting from the little finger, as if all were *sexdigitati*, like the
Shaykhs of the Fazli clan near Aden. Little or no provision is
taken on board, and the chief luxury is snuff, the pinch being
spread in line from the root of the thumb upwards, somewhat
after the style of the original Scotch " sneeshin' mull;" at times
the flask is raised to the nose, and poured in till that member,
which ought here to be placed bottom upwards, is filled. These
water-ousels reap golden harvests of cod during the season, sometimes clearing per diem ten rixdollars a-head; and if you hire a
Reykjaviker two-oar for the afternoon, you will not pay less
than $5. They are rarely long-lived. Privations, fatigue, and
hardships, wet feet, poor food, and defective hygiene soon get
the better of the " *triste laboureur de l'ocean:*" weakened by
psora and ascarides; by obstinate coughs, measles, and hypo-
chondria, he soon becomes a victim to chronic rheumatism,
which will bend the fingers permanently back, and he dies
early of visceral or pulmonary affections, gout, or paralysis.
Better a life of a canvas-back shooter on the banks of the
Susquehanna.

After Reykjanes we bore north (magnetic) along a shore
exceptionally populous: farmsteads and chapels, each perched
upon its own knoll, and not unlike the clachans of Lewis, formed
a straggling line, black and gloomy, surrounded by walls of dry

stone. We turned eastward off "Skagi Point,"[1] a long thin lingula with a beacon at the tip, and with a dwarf *enceinte* of dry stone inland, probably a look-out in the old Víkingr days. Steaming across the big back-bay towards the next headland, Suðrnes, afforded us for some moments an agreeable surprise. Right over the gulf called Faxa Fjörð, and distant some forty miles, rose a long broken dorsum of snow-range, not unlike the Friuli section of the Carnian Alps, the continuation of beautiful Cadore, as seen in winter from the Rive of Trieste. Here, however, the projection, a sister to that of Reykjanes, was terminated by the crescent-shaped head of Snæfell, the western Jökull, whose two cusps at once denoted the extinct crater-cup. The *névé* towered in the lift, catching a golden gleam which beautifully burnished the virgin silver, whilst above and below it slaty clouds were based upon a darker sea now smooth and mirrory as oil. The travelled few on board pronounced the spectacle grander than Mont Blanc from the Hôtel de la Russie, Geneva, but the fair vision was transient, and presently a *bonnet de nuit* of chilly lowering mist settling down made it a "Pileatus." To the north-east, and far nearer, stretched the long sea-arm Hvalfjörð, an inverted arch, with its two giant steeples Akrafjall and Esja, whilst the scarps of Skarðsheiði formed the bottom of the great *cul de sac*. Passing clouds of pseudo-columnar shape, here a common feature, simulated volcanic smoke; mountain head and shoulders were streaked with snow, whilst at their feet brooded the sea-fog, a horizontal line of blue mists broken and detached. Presently the rain came on again, and perforce we confined our attention to the features close ahead.

The pilot now boarded us, leaving his cockleshell in charge of his mate, an angry water-rat with otter-like features, the usual fishy eye, and gold ear-rings, the general usage. We made straight for the little archipelago, which in this weather appears part of the mainland. The nearest item was Akrey: as craft in harbour can be seen to the south-east, and that direction leads straight to shipwreck, "Cornfield Isle," a mere grass-grown bulge of rock, has an outlying buoy to the north-east, warning

---

[1] English tautology. Skagi (in Shetland Scaw or Skaw, *e.g.*, the Skaw of Unst) is a low cape opposed to Höfði, a high headland (Cleasby).

us off its long projecting point. The next feature left to port is
Engey of the eider duck, a mound provided with the long,
curving and knobbed tail of a scorpion. Then came Öffirs-ey,[1] a
bit of turf-clad basalt, in places sub-columnar: a red buoy,
" stone-men " and a beacon, give warning that its spit is also
dangerous. About Öffirs-ey and Akrey are two islets, the Hol-
mar: the larger and outer, bombé and slightly grassy, is the
Sker (skerry), or Selsker (little-farm-skerry); and the other,
dignified by the name of Grand Holmr, connects, like Öffirs-ey,
with the shore at low water by a traversable natural causeway.
The other islets are Viðey (wood or withy eyot), which we shall
presently visit, and Lund-ey (puffin eyot), at the mouth of Kolla-
fjörð (ewe firth): there are also sundry shoals and banks scattered about to the north and west, making the outer roads of
Reykjavik safe enough except when the storm-wind blows from
the north-east or the east-north-east.

The amount of shipping surprised us when we remembered
that the first steamers appeared here in 1854-55. In the roads lay
a French frigate, " Le Cher," Capitaine Alfred le Timbre, looking
taunt and gay: her consort, " Le Beaumanoir," Capitaine Maylet,
will soon come in from the east. The Danish gun-boat " Fylla,"
the waiting-maid of Frygga, had lately been outside sounding
in preparation for the telegraphic cable: she is a sister ship of
the " Diana," which also flies a pennant, and which to-morrow
will land the governor of the island. The " Jón Sigurðsson " had
just left, and the " Yarrow " lay inside amongst eight square-
rigged ships bearing the flags of various nationalities, whilst,
drawn up ashore, was a Noah's ark, in the shape of a Danish
galliot, almost circular, like the old Dutch dogger or the modern
Russian monitor. Five to six steamers in port argued well for
progress within the last twenty years, and presently we shall see
the " Heimdall," called after the giant foe of Loki.[2] This school-
ship for the Danish navy is a frigate (Captain Skowstrüp),
freighted with thirty-six cadets—a rather noisy lot. An English
yacht which floats like a sea-bird will also astonish the
natives.

---

[1] Originally Örfiris-eye, which has been explained under Orfir of the Orkneys.
[2] Heimdall was the doorkeeper of the gods, who kills and is killed by Loki.

The aspect of Reykjavik from the sea is more unlike its description by travellers than, perhaps, anything that I have yet seen—even Humboldt's Tenerife. One expects, after the Haurán-like profile of the coast, to see a "Giant City of Bashan" rising from the waves. Old sketches suggest the "negative features" of John Barrow, the miserable show of a few tarred pent-roofs topping the black shingle, but free trade has changed all that. Even on this dull day, when it looks its worst, we cannot call its aspect "*triste, morne, désolé.*" Where, again, are the gaudy colours noticed by Mr Bryson? We see nothing but dingy-white, dull-gamboge, verging on rhubarb, slate-grey, and tar-black, a perfect contrast with the Norwegian town—

"Where tawdry yellow strives with dirty red."

At both extremities, east and west, the ground is stony, and rudely-formed basaltic pillars line the water, guarding ragged scatters of fishermen's huts. The right point (west) is called the Hliðar-hús (lith-house), a classical name. On the left a grassy earthwork and a flagstaff still remain to remind us of a quaint passage in local history. Icelanders are much given to boasting that their island, which contains the population of a third-rate English town, was never conquered; that Thule is still *invicta.* Yet in 1809, Mr Sam. Phelps, of London, a soap boiler, who considered himself aggrieved by the authorities, landed a dozen jail-birds from Gravesend, and forcibly took possession of the capital. He established an independent republic under the wing of England; and his Cromwell was a Danish seaman, Hr Jörgen Jörgensen, "Protector of Iceland, and Commander by sea and land." This Dictator, a bad Masaniello, seems to have acted with peculiar energy: he threw up the redoubt; armed it with six small cannon, brought from Bessastaðir; and hoisted over it the flag of independence, three slit cods (stockfish) argent in an oval garland, on a champ azure. Better, at any rate, than Yarmouth, with its three bloaters! The ridiculous affair was squashed by an English frigate, the "Talbot" (Captain Jones): the earthwork was disarmed, and the guns were thrown upon the beach; whilst "Mercator Phelps," as Bishop Pètursson calls him, Jörgensen, & Co., were removed to England. It was the second time that the island, "bound in with the triumphant sea," nearly fell to the "Britishers'" lot.[1] Christian II. was upon the point of pledging it, as the Orkneys and Shetlands were temporarily transferred to the Scottish Crown, but he was deposed before the bargain was struck.

Between the points lies the inner or boat harbour, clear water in which floats a crop of "sea-ware," especially the long, tufty hair of the Hoy or Haar-teari (*Fucus aculeatus*) : it is supposed by some to have named the Færoe Islands. But, however clean the water, it is considered too cold for *uso esterno;* and the English eye at once misses the machines and sheds and other appurtenances of a bathing place. The ripple is confined by unclean black sand, strewed with boards, nets, and offals of all kinds, especially thorsk or cods' heads. There are fair landing-places, plank pierlets, kept steady by caissons full of stones, and not removed in winter: the traveller may see the same style all round the coast, and perhaps he will remember making Venice through the "Murazzi." The principal buildings, beginning from the right as you face the town, are the Glasgow House, the Bridgehouse, the Post-office, the Club, the merchant stores, and the coal-depots belonging to the Government and to Mr Slimon. Behind rises the steepled Dóm-Kirkja (cathedral), and we see with pleasure that the College, *alias* the Latin School, is larger and more important than Government House. The tenements mostly face the beach; the roofs, pitched steep against the snow, are slated or boarded; tiles are common, and turf is preserved only by the poorest. They are built of planks like Valparaiso, earthquakes being not unfrequent; but I could hear only of one fire—a notable contrast to the "Vale of Paradise," where the stone house is impossible, and where being burnt out is purely a question of time. Above the west point is the Catholic chapel and a windmill; the winds can never be very violent, or this thing would soon be blown up like a tent high in the air. The opposite rise is garnished with another windmill, also lacking steerer; and with a double-storied tower of solid masonry, called the Observatory. The surface of the upper country has that dull, dark-green tint, so difficult to shoot against, and so characteristic

---

[1] I dismiss the " Iceland Revolution" in a few lines, for Baring-Gould (Introd. xlii.) has given a very complete account, borrowed from Hooker and Mackenzie.

of the Emerald Isle in early autumn. The people complain that the rains have been scant this year, that hay will be scarce and dear, that the fishing season has been bad, and so forth. The inland view is bounded by a long, unbroken range, which we shall see on the first clear day.

All Reykjavik assembled to gape and chat upon the shore, whilst a torrent of strangers poured on board. They were assailed with questions by the tourists, and the answers were satisfactory as usual. The Hotel had been abolished. The Club did not receive guests; never a room was to be had for love or money. We must pitch tents upon the beach—pleasant during this weather, a bad November in England! There was hardly a riding-pony within fifteen miles, although some four hundred were awaiting embarkment. Guides were unprocurable, all hands at Reykjavik being thoroughly engaged, and the telegraph scheme making even the idlest unwilling to take temporary service. No one would change sovereigns for rixdollars. At the same time, if we would put ourselves unreservedly in the hands of our kind and courteous informants, who were of the horsiest, we might possibly find lodgings, ponies, guides, dollars.

Before landing, I discipline myself severely. From London and Edinburgh, even from Leith, the fall to Reykjavik being heavy, the traveller's eye is apt to view everything through a jaundiced medium, and the consequence is undue depreciation. Everywhere, and at all times, it is difficult to find a standing point of comparison from which to prospect persons and things, and which shall be fair to the subject, and intelligible to the reader. One man sets out with "the City" in view, and is called a "Cockney traveller;" another and a numerous class looks at matters through the spectacles of civilised life in England, perhaps the easiest way when writing for Englishmen; whilst those who have seen much of the world make themselves unintelligible and unpleasant (myself, alas!) by drawing parallels between scenes unknown or unfamiliar to their Public, who resents the implied slight accordingly. Hence it is generally said that works of exploration are mostly read only because they must be read, and that the book which treats of the land best known to us is that which gives the highest enjoyment. For

here we have the pleasure of comparing the impressions made
by the same things upon the writer's mind and upon our own,
a process far more personal and more satisfactory than mastering
mere discoveries or pursuing a tale of extraordinary adventure,
which we often only half believe. And when reading travels in
absolutely new lands, we feel that we are reading the opinions
of another man, without the concurrence which alone càn check
them. But the veteran voyager is a practical "Pantisocrat,"
and he must especially adopt the advice of Juvenal:

       "Audeat ille palam qui vidit, dicere vidi."

And nowhere is greater càre required than in studying a mother-
city, the characteristic of its race, the living photograph; the
manifest expression of its manners and customs, and especially
of its short-comings. "Capitals represent doctrines." Apply
this to the old drab-coloured utilitarian London, now happily
passing away, with its boxes of mean brick and of hideous
"stone-colour," where every man's house, reckless of order,
regularity, and economy of space, was his castle, small, dull, and
dry as the educated mind; with its Belgravian "palaces" and
wretched porticos, which an hour with a crowbar would demolish, expressing a rental more than sufficient for a "*hôtel entre
cour et jardin*" in Paris, Vienna, or Rome; with its utterly taste-
less and artless works of art which sadden the civilised eye,
looking, a foreigner observed, as if the foul fiend had scattered
them flying; with its slushy and greasy streets, the richest
population in the world being apparently too poor to keep them
clean; and with its shops exposing, even in Bond Street, corpses
of poultry, sheep, pigs, and cattle for the use of carnivorous
denizens. We can hardly wonder when the "wild-cat corre-
spondent" of the Yankee paper describes it as "a vast wilderness
of dingy brick and stone, of huge half-empty palaces and roaring
torrents of humanity—a money-snatching metropolis where vice
and poverty herd and breed in filthy alleys behind the abodes of
the great and wealthy."

We bid adieu to the "Queen,"

       "That white-winged monastery moving still,
       Of rugged celibates against their will."

She leaves for England on the sixth day, and thus five of our fellow-passengers hardly find time for the shortest scamper across country. Her captain and her crew have claims upon our gratitude; we are unanimous in declaring that all are good men and true, and in recommending them to the author of "Ship, ahoy!" The old traveller ever prefers the English steamer, even at a sacrifice of comforts. He will find fair-weather sailors all the world over, but in the day of danger he will repent having added unnecessary risk to his travels. The French decision upon the conduct of the "Ville de Havre"—a disgrace to a civilised people—is another reason for carefully avoiding foreign craft. Under English, of course, I include Scandinavian and American (U.S.), and carefully exclude the average Latin race. Yet it is only fair to say that the P. and O. boats in the Mediterranean have found it an excellent plan to engage Italian sailors, officered, of course, by Englishmen. The crews are quiet and trustworthy, thrifty, and hard-working; a strong contrast with the turbulent, drunken, ne'er-do-weel which in these days too often represents the old man-o'-war's man. In England, a sentimental regard for the name "Jack" prevents our seeing the immense deterioration of the class owing to the mixture of "tailors" and good-for-nothing landsmen: my colleagues of the Consular Service will, however, I think, agree with me that foreign port-towns would be benefited if many of the so-called "British sailors" were never allowed to put foot ashore.

# CHAPTER III.

REYKJAVIK[1]—THE SUBURBS—THE LODGING-HOUSE—THE CLUB AND
THE WAY WE SPEND THE DAY.

THE latitude of Reykjavik—the residence of the governor and
the Supreme Court of Judicature, the episcopal see, and the
chief mercantile station—is N. 64° 8′ 26″,[2] a little higher than
Norwegian Trondhjem (Thrándheimr),[3] which English books
and maps will write Drontheim, and about that of Archangel.
In the map of Pontanus (1631) it does not appear. About A.D.
1760 it became the chief port, although till seventy years ago it
was a mere scatter of fishermen's huts sheltering some 700
human beings. Travellers of the last generation, Hooker (1809)

---

[1] Reykjavíkr in the nominative sing. is an abstract linguistic fiction, from
Vík (feminine), a bay, a wich (e.g., Greenwich). Travellers neglect the Icelandic
termination, and even English literati omit the -r or -ur as superfluous and
strictly correct only in the nominative, e.g., Leif for Leifr. From Vík, a bay,
comes Víking, a baying-voyage, or seeking the shelter of bays, and Víkingr, a
baying-voyager, or a voyager from the fjords. This word, sometimes written
Vi-king in English, suggests a wrong etymology. Cleasby warns us that the
termination -wick or -wich is Norsk only for maritime places, the inland "wicks"
derive from the Latin vicus. Local names beginning with Reyk are unknown
to Scandinavians, and peculiar to Iceland where the pillars of steam must have
struck the colonist's eye.

[2] Taken at the cathedral. The longitude (G.) given by Norie is W. 21° 51′ 3″,
by Raper 21° 55′ 2″; Norie gives the lat. 64° 9′ 0″, Raper 64° 8′ 4″. The variation
of the compass is roughly 35° off Berufjörð; 35° 15′ off the eastern Jökull; and
45° off Reykjavik : it was in 1814 (Henderson, i. 250) "two points towards the
west ;" in 1840 (French charts) it was W. 43° 21′. M. Lottier (1838) made it
43° 14′ ; and in 1871 (Admiralty chart, by Captain Evans) it was 44°, still increasing at the rate of 5′ per annum. Consequently the people have two norths—north
by compass and true north, the latter at Reykjavik fronting the mountain-block
Akrafjall. The inclination (dip) of the magnetic needle (French chart of 1840)
is 76° 45′. The vulgar Etablissement du port (Hafenzeit, high water at full and
change), French chart, is at 5h. 0m. ; and the maximum height of the tides 5m.
35 cent. The Admiralty tables give spring-tides a rise of 17½ feet and the neaps
13¼.

[3] The Dictionary translates it " home of the Thronds " (Thrændir).

and Mackenzie (1810), show the extent of improvement: in their day the townlet had only two streets—much like the Cowgate and Canongate of the last century. One line of buildings fronted the sea and another set off from it at right angles. Now we have a fair north-of-Europe port. It has lately risen from the 1000 or 1600 which travellers generally give it; the stationary population, according to the census of 1870, was 2024 souls; at this season, when the fair is approaching, we may add as a maximum 500. I need hardly say that the 50,000 of our hydrographic books is a misprint.

The sacred pillars of Ingolf's Hall (öndugis súlur[1]), unduly translated "door-posts," or "wooden door," probably chose Reykjavik because it is the largest anchorage-ground in this "Canaan of the North," and his thralls were justified in reproaching their lord for preferring so rugged and barren a corner to the more fertile regions farther east. The harbour is dangerous only when the wind blows off the Esja *massif*, forcing ships to run out seawards, and the tides of late years have not flooded the town. The picturesque background will be described when we can see it. The site is on the northern side and near the point of the Seltjarnanes (Seal-tarn-naze), a peninsula, whose lowlands are digitated by the prevalent winds and driving seas. Henderson very poorly describes the town as "situate between two eminences that are partially covered with grass:" it is built on both gently-sloping sides of a dwarf river-valley draining the Tjorn (tarn), a lakelet to the south, about 800 yards long by 400 broad. The ditch which has evidently been much larger, and which some propose to deepen into a port, is crossed by some half-a-dozen bridges, one with iron rails painted vermilion; it is in

---

[1] From "And," opposite, and "Vegr," an "opposite seat," a "high seat." In the old timbered hall the benches (bekkr) were ranged along the walls with the two seats of honour in the middle facing one another. The northern, fronting the sun, was called Öndvegi æðra, first or higher high-seat, reserved for the master, and the other was Úæðra, the lower or second, kept for the chief guest. In England the master and the mistress sitting opposite each other at table, may be a remnant of the old Scandinavian custom. The sides of the high seat were ornamented with uprights (öndugis súlur) carved with figures, such as a head of Thor : these posts were regarded with religious honour and were thrown into the sea as guides. When a man of rank died, the son, after all rites performed, solemnly sat in his father's seat, as a sign of succession, but this was not done if the paternal murder remained unavenged (Cleasby).

the foulest condition; but here cleanliness is not next to godliness. Throughout Reykjavik a smell of decayed fish prevails, making strangers wonder how it escapes pestilence and plague; and the basaltic dust raised by the least breath of wind causes hands and face to be grimy as at Manchester or Pittsburgh.

The mass of the settlement lies in the dwarf hollow of the streamlet, somewhat protected from the blasts, and straggles up both slopes of the rivulet-valley. But for this it would be unpleasantly windy; and, as is said of Landudno, between two waters is nearly as bad as between two fires. The neighbourhood is a lean neck of flat and barren ground, with the sea to the north and south, whilst, in the former direction, the great Hvalfjörð inlet sharply cutting the Esja and the Akranes blocks, and backed by the snowy Skarðsheiði, acts as a wind-sail. The same reason makes the rains exceptionally heavy. The shape is long-narrow for sea-frontage rather than deep, and the orientation is puzzling as that of Hebron.[1] I shall call the right flank of the valley east and the left west, although the correspondence is by no means exact. Along the shore runs Harbour Street (Hafnar Stræti), with the north side open to the bay: here are the chief stores and shops, the warehouses and coal-depots, the Club and the Post-office. At right angles, and to the west, a High Street (Aðalstræti) stretches some four hundred yards to the tarn: it begins from the head of the chief pierlet, passing under the archway of the Bryggju-hús (bridge- or pier-house),[2] a place of customs, whose occupation long gone is now returning to it. Broad enough to dwarf the houses, macadamised and straight, like all the best thoroughfares which cross one another at right angles, it sounds hollow to the tread, as if walking upon a boiler—the "Rimbombo,"[3] as Italians call it, not uncommon in newly made ground, which propagates sound. It is traversed

---

[1] There is a plan of Reykjavik, but the size of the scale keeps it in MS. Baring-Gould and others give ground sketches, which are now obsolete.

[2] In Icel. Brú is a bridge in our sense of the word; Bryggja is a landing-place as well as a bridge.

[3] This hollow sound may be remarked even in the new town of Trieste, where a passing omnibus shakes the substantially-built stone houses. Such soil must be always the most dangerous in case of earthquakes, which are comparatively harmless on the adjacent hill-slopes.

here and there by impure gutters, which are unwisely covered
with iron-cramped boardings: I rejoice to hear that they were
cleaned out for the royal visit. High Street abuts upon a
square and whitewashed wooden building, labelled Hospital in
white letters on a blue ground: here is the chief pump which
works a well 12 feet deep, and revetted with dry stone. The
first aspect of the gabled *tout ensemble* strongly suggests Alder-
shot.

Turning to the left we reach the Austurvöllr,[1] or Eastern
Square, a kind of Parsons Green, with three built sides, the
fourth being still open towards the tarn. It is the regular
camping ground for inland travellers who pitch their dwarf tents
and peg their ponies where a handful of grass can be nibbled.
Here is the "Cathedral," whose adjoining cemetery has now
disappeared. The houses are built with the scant regularity of
a Brazilian village; they face in every direction towards the sea,
or towards the rivulet-valley, and rarely southwards as they
should do for the benefit of sun. With rare exceptions, they
are all wooden frameworks of joists, filled as in Germany with
basaltic slabs, and mortar blue with dark sand; the walls are
boarded over, as without the stone they would be unsupportably
cold and hot. They are short-lived like the "skips," requiring
frequent repairs, and rarely lasting beyond thirty or forty years:
their endurance depends greatly upon the quality of the wood;
the maximum of age would be nearly a century, but only when the
timber is not mixed with turf and peat, which, crumbling under
sun and frost, causes early decay. Barents' house (built 1597),
"in the wilde, desart, irkesome, fearfull, and cold countrey" of
Novaya Zemlja, was lately found (Captain Carlsen, 1871),
uninjured by the dry air. On the other hand, the excessive
damp renders danger of fire nugatory, compared with the wooden
match-boxes called houses at Constantinople. It is to be wished
that the tenements could be "telescoped" during the hot weather,
as most families pass the whole year in town. Many of them

---

[1] The word Völlr (plur. Vellir, and gen. pl. Valla) means a field, and is akin
to the German Wald. It often occurs in the plural, *e.g.*, Reyni-vellir (Rowan
plains); and "Thing-valla," the foreign way of writing, is properly Thingvellir.

are revetted on the weather-side with imported slates, and all are numbered, even as the thoroughfares are provided with names. There is far more open ground than building, each "plant-a-cruive" being girt with planks or rails, useful for drying clothes, and showing no want of wood. The best plots are surrounded by wire, often a single strand, which has extended to the country parts, or by walls of dry stones; the latter shelter the sterile dock, with here and there a stem of angelica, not unlike a wild artichoke. The land, neatly hoed in straight lines drawn between two pegs, and raked by the women, is planted with " Garden sass," especially parsley and fennel, kail and turnips; fine cauliflowers, cabbage and potatoes; the latter will not ripen till the end of August, when snow has left the mountain-tops. Radishes must be set in boxes guarded by wooden hurdles or by nets to keep off the birds; they are fair-sized but hollow and flavourless. The rare flowers are chiefly geraniums and fuchsias, pansies and marigolds; but as in Norway and the North generally, flora flourishes best in pots behind the little half-blinded windows; here the oleander will be a whole foot high. Of fruits, we find chiefly the hardy currant, and a few gooseberries and strawberries, with a southern exposure, mostly protected by glass. In 1810, it will be remembered, there was "not a single garden or vegetable of any kind growing in the place."

On the right side of the main drain, and higher than the " Pelouse," rises the Latin School, ridge-roofed, tiled, coloured rhubarb-yellow, and provided with a shallow façade of three windows, as many being pierced in both wings. To the south is the College Library, a plain building of large basaltic blocks, partially whitewashed; the glass panes look as if they carried the dust of ages. Farther down stream, and a little above the right bank, is Government House, a substantial barn, also of white-washed stone, fronted by a well drained slope, and a bit of meadowland, courteously called a garden; its dignity is denoted by a tall flagstaff. It was originally an almshouse, and a tugt-hús (jail); old travellers tell us that, as the poor preferred its comforts to their wretched homes, it was not easy to keep certain citizens out of it. Count Trampe, a governor whose hospitable name is well remembered, especially by travellers, left it a one-storied building; the present occupant added a second floor. The houses on a level with the open drain below are to be avoided; the air during a sunny day is like that of a hot-house without the perfume, and the nights are stifling to an extent for which a stranger is not prepared. Here is the photographic establishment of Hr Eymundsson, who saves his guests expense as well as trouble.

The houses of the " honoratiores," the " upper ten," are in the sole of the valley, and the east is here the " West End," boasting of the Palace, the Library, and the High School. Lower down lie the Bishop Pètur Pètursson; the Chief-Justice Hr Jonassen; the Land-Fógeti, or treasurer, Hr Thorsteinssen, who is also Bæar-Fógeti (Danicè, By-foged) or mayor of the city; the Land-læknir, or head physician of the island, Dr Jón Jónsson Hjaltalín; the French Consul, M. Randrüp; the editor of the local paper, Hr Procurator Guðmundsson; the Postmaster, Hr Finsen; and the college professors. The principal building on the west or left bank of the river-valley is the old " Glasgow House," which has passed through various phases. It was originally built by Messrs Henderson & Anderson for a dwelling-place and warehouse, as shown by the belvedere, the crane, and the dwarf tramway. When that firm came to grief by trusting to native agency, it became a hotel: hence the " Iceland Reader," by Hr Lund says:

" Thar er gestgjafa hús " (here you will find a hotel);
"Thað er ekki slæmt" (it is not a bad one).

But the hostelry followed the rule of all such civilised appliances in these regions—failed, and was sold to a Norwegian house. It fetched $6000 (rixdollars), and was a good bargain to the purchaser; various debts were recovered, to the tune, they say, of nearly double the value. It is too big, the ceilings are too high, and the windows admit far too much air.

The most characteristic part of Reykjavik are the suburbs of the Tómthúsmenn,[1] or empty-house men, mostly fishermen who have no farms, and consequently no cattle. We will visit the

---

[1] Tómr, empty, is the Scotch "toom."

west (not West) end built between a swamp abutting upon the sea, and the normal knobbed meadow-land, where a few cows fight against starvation. It is cut by a bit of made road, and another runs east to the Laxá or Salmon River—these are the only Macadams in the island. The by-streets of our suburb become mere lanes, and the *impasse* is far more common than the thoroughfare. The few good houses of wood are raised upon foundations of basalt or brick laid edgeways, which keep out the damp like the piles of Fernando Po. They are entered by dwarf ladders, instead of the usual sandstone flags imported from abroad. These "magalia" will float off to sea unharmed, like Gulliver's cage, and not break up for a long time. The empty-house men, who far outnumber all the other classes, adhere to what represents the Irish shanty, the cabin of the Far West, and the Eskimo's earth-covered hut. The primitive fashion, preserved even in the capital, is an oblong parallelogram of basaltic blocks, alternating with peats by way of mortar—*cespite pro cœmento adhibito*—where tons of mussels and shell-fish[1] cumber the shore. The houses look as if shoving shoulders together against the wind, rain, and snow. The walls are sunk in the surface to the extent of a few feet, beyond which the ground is never frozen;[2] they are raised three or four feet high, with the same thickness as at the base, and battering a little inwards. One of the short ends is left open for a doorway; sometimes additional defence against wind is secured by a side-adit, a small, wooden, pent-roofed sentinel, like the office of an East Indian tent. This shell supports an acute-angled or equilateral triangle of wood: formerly birch boughs were used, now pine planks are largely imported from Denmark, as we see by the stacks scattered over the settlement. The steeply-pitched slopes, revetted with peat sods a foot square, yield a superior crop of grass—a hint of what may be done by "scalping" and draining. The gable generally shows the wood well daubed with blistering tar, which soon turns red and rusty; here are mostly two single-paned, white-framed windows, the larger

---

[1] I particularly remarked the beautiful shell, striped white and brick-red, the Hörpu-diskr, *Pecten Islandicus*, or Iceland clam. The krákuskel, or *Mytilus edulis*, is eaten by foxes.

[2] Native authorities differ as to the depth where frost extends. I heard a maximum of eight feet, even in the lowlands.

one lighting the gun deck or lower floor, and the smaller the upper deck, loft or garret. The old chimney was a tub; now there is an iron tube or a square pipe of bricks : a cowl like a " fly-cray," two bits of flat wood attached to a perpendicular, and moving with the wind, cures smoking; and where there is a weather-cock, it is the bird that warned Peter of his fall. Some of the larger establishments will have four or five of these pointed gables ; and the smaller are often so small that we admire how human beings can get into them.

COTTAGE IN REYKJAVIK.

The characteristic building of the fishermen's quarter is the Hjallr,[1] or "wind-house," acting like the Skeo of the Scoto-Scan-dinavian islands; which, however, is a mere shed of dry stones. Here it is mostly an open cage of wooden uprights and stretchers, roofed over against the weather—a superior style of drying fish,

---

[1] The word Hjallr, the Færoese Kiadlur, is akin to Hjalli and Hilla (English hill), a shelf or ledge in the mountain-side, and hence a scaffold ; the full term for the fish-shed is Fisk-hjallr (Cleasby).

especially cod. The body is either hung upon a line (hengi-fiskr or flattr-fiskr), or salted and stretched upon a rock (harðr-fiskr).[1] When dry and ready for embarking, it is heaped up on the beach and covered with stone-weighted boards. Even more unpleasant features are the vats and pits in the ground, where sharks' livers[2] and cods' sounds and bladders are left to form, with the addition of a little iodine, cod-liver oil. After this we cannot complain of the salting operation, done usually in some old ship's tank.

The beach is the normal scene of a European fishing village, a chaos of anchors, old masts and spars, nets and wooden floats, clothes and waterproofs hung up to dry; blue petroleum barrels from Scotland; big piles of wrack-thatched turf, and drawn-up boats, the sails being left, whilst the rudders are taken home. We see some three carts in one place. Travellers in the early nineteenth century tell us that not even a wheelbarrow can be found at Reykjavik: now hand-carts stand in every business street, and at times a carriage drawn by two ponies, and full of people, attracts every head to the window. When the made road shall be prolonged east and west, the settlement will become civilised, as our Accra on the Gold Coast.

The rude succedaneum for the wheelbarrow, which still lingers even at Trieste, is a straight stretcher carried by two men. But the race is thoroughly unmechanical, as we might expect from its social state. A local philanthrope gave one of the peasants a small sledge, to save him from trudging under a heavy box over the deep snows; the consequence was that the box was slung to the back, whilst the sledge depended down the breast. This reminds me of S'a Leone, where a British negrophile sent sundry wheelbarrows for the benefit of the "poor black" navvies: the barrows were duly filled with earth, and hoisted

---

[1] Henderson confounds the "Klip-fish" (Danish, Klippe, a rock), which is cleaned, salted, and stacked, with the stock-fish or dry-fish, simply split, washed, sunned, and turned by the women. The latter forms the national staff of life, and is not exported. "Fiskr" in Icelandic is especially applied to cod, trout, and salmon.

[2] The Maskat Arabs eat shark-meat, but they never apply the oil to the skin, considering it a caustic; rubbed into ship bottoms, it is supposed to defend the wood from worms.

upon the negro's head, where he wisely carries everything, even his toothpick. Many of these fishermen have been sailors, and the chances are, that if the Cockney traveller chaff them with, for instance, "How did you leave the old 'ooman?" they will straightway reply, "A' right, s'r!" They touch their hats as strangers pass, but this patriarchal custom will soon disappear before the presence of steamers. The children clamber about the boats, and swing by cords from the masts even as Bedawin boys play upon camels' backs; they toss up with fish tails; they chase the black cats like the denizens of Lilliput-Land; they bully the dogs, and they harness a pig on the rare occasions when one lands. "Gi' me a skilling!" the "Gie me a yap'ny" of Wales, is sometimes heard—in fact "bakhshish" is not utterly unknown in these hyperborean lands. Yet it is only fair to confess that not a single professional beggar is to be seen at Reykjavik.

Our hunt for lodgings ended in a short and sharp run in. A young Englishman, who had spent some time here, led us ashore. After rejecting the noisy tavern, and vainly seeking shelter at the Hospital,[1] whose civil matron was once the handsomest woman in the island, we presently found cover under the roof of Frú Jonassen, sister of Geir Zoega, the guide, and married to a Dane, whose over-affection for Bacchus confines him mostly to his couch. The house deserves description: it is the normal bourgeois dwelling-place of the capital, very different from that of the country. The little box is revetted with rhubarb-coloured boarding, and covered by a black tarred board-roof. Its entrance debouches upon a hall no bigger than a bird cage, with a door to the right and the left; you must duck head as you enter them, and—never forget this precaution in Iceland. The first *pièce* is a bedroom some 15 feet long by 8 broad and 8 high; the single window has a half blind, but neither curtains nor shutters. Strangers complain loudly of such an unnatural thing as the broad glare of day at midnight, and indeed the effect of a horizontal sun, impinging upon the ground, is not very unlike the noon of

---

[1] There was one corpse at the Hospital; the death had been caused by delirium tremens.

an English November. At first, we envy those on board ship who can darken their cabins. Sound sleep is difficult under the stimulus of light which allows you to read the smallest print; presently we secure it by hanging up one of the dame's flannel petticoats. The people, and especially the children, seem to take their rest at and till any hour: the maternal admonition "Ten o'clock, go to sleep" is here unknown; the "early to bed" of the proverb, and the doctor's dictum about the benefits of slumber before midnight, are clean forgotten. I puzzle myself to divine how a Moslem would time his prayers in Iceland.

The bedroom contains two apple-pie-shaped box-beds, some three feet long, which startle the traveller till he sees them drawn out; they are covered with the familiar eider-down coverlet of Germany, under which you may perspire and freeze to your heart's content: no wonder when, next to hare's fur, it offers the greatest obstacle to heat-transmission, consequently you always kick it off. Presently we shall exchange the vile cider-down pillows and coverlet for a clean waterproof blanket, and dislodge our pests by means of the insecticide powder invented in near Dauphiné, and consequently derived by commercial humbug from distant Persia. The "B flat" at once put in an appearance, and the people accounted for it by some German musicians having lately been their lodgers: we afterwards found that the pest is not indigenous, and similarly it has been imported into the Færoe Islands from Copenhagen. The livelier animalcule is well—too well—known. The sitting-room inside is also wainscotted, and of the four shutterless windows, only half of one is made to open; they are never doubled, which shows that the cold cannot be intense; yet at times the wind must whistle through them as through a summer-house.

Each room has a stove, backed by a blackened wall, the best are the tall German cylinders, and fire is the *côté faible* of the capital. A little heap of peat smoulders in the kitchen behind the bedroom, and thus hot water, a prime necessary, is very scarce. The furniture consists of a central drugget, a round dinner-table, a square writing ditto, a work-table, a commode, a tall armoire, and sundry horsehair chairs, with a sofa, which must often act bed. In the rear of the kitchen is a microscopic pantry wherein it is not good to peer. Above us, a grenier occupies the sharp angle under the roof; here the family lives, and there is no sleep between 6.30 A.M. and 11 P.M.; they seem always to be clearing the decks for action. At the back of the house a yard reeks with impurities, and on both sides cages for drying fish give the well-known ancient smell. That human beings can live and enjoy health in the "stifled filth" of Damascus; of Mile-end, Old Town, or of Trieste (Città Vecchia), argues, they say, peculiar excellence of climate, and the deduction certainly applies to Reykjavik.

The comely middle-aged dame, who speaks a few words of English, has no children except those whom, after popular Icelandic fashion, she has adopted. An aged Cinderella, a bundle of waste dry-goods, hardly human, haunts the kitchen, whilst Christiana, an artificial daughter of the house, is the Kellnerin. She is a good-looking lass with the fresh complexion and the *blond cendré* hair, one of Iceland's charms, which are here the rule; her dress is fine Wadmal of dark colour; and her large feet, which terminate solid supporters, are encased in the island slippers, giving a peculiarly lumping tread: a bright plaid apron and a grey woollen shawl for visiting, complete her toilette. She never knocks at the door and she slams it with a hideous noise —the neat-handed Phyllis and the light fantastic toe have not yet come so far north. When serving us she ejaculates mechanically "Værsgu," the Danish "Vær saa god"—be so kind—extensively used throughout Scandinavia, and now imported into Iceland. Mightily dull of apprehension she appears, especially after the sharp-witted Syrians, and the dialogue with us Anglo-Indians is frequently as follows:

"Here you, Kitty, heitt vatn. . . . Why, you don't know your own language! Water hot!"

Answer passive and stolid: "Hvað?"

"Oh what a girl you are! Samajtá? You almost deserve to have a vote. I say, 'water hot!'"

"Hvað segið" (what say ye)?

"Will you have a drink, Kitty? Where's mamma? HOT WATER, I tell you."

" Hvað segið thèr " (what do you say) ?
And so forth, *ad infinitum*. Yet in Iceland Jomfru (Icel. Jung-
frú) Christiana is the gem of a waiteress, and in her leisure
moments she will act *bacheliere ès lettres*—in fact, she readily
adapts herself to our little bachelor ways.

Frú Jonassen agrees to lodge and find us in " small breakfast "
or early coffee, and big breakfast at ten A.M., for $1, 3m. 0sk. (say
3s. 5d.) per diem, and for an equally reasonable sum to house
our spare goods when travelling. Washing is of course cheap
where there are so many feminine spare hands.[1] The tea is vile,
having been drunk at least once. Water is almost throughout Iceland excellent, cold, clear, and slightly flavoured with
iron, like the sparkling produce of the Haurán and other basaltic
lands. Coffee and brennivín (schnapps) may be called the national
drink, and the people pride themselves upon the former : after
our senna-like potions farther south it is admirable, but it must
not be compared with that of the nearer East. The bean is
never good, even England cannot afford the true Mocha monopolised by the United States : still it is never stinted,[2] and it
lacks the odious *chicorée* so popular across the Channel. It is
burnt black instead of brown as in Arabia; it is milled in lieu
of being pounded, and the brew is made in a venerable flannel
strainer-bag placed where the kettle's lid should be. The consumption is even more extensive than in Germany : large cups
and sometimes bowls are served strong and hot several times
a day, and are always offered to the stranger guest. Some find
fault with the excess, but they forget that coffee prevents waste
of tissue, and that a heating drink is necessary in cold, damp
climates where the diet is poor. The sugar is white loaf, and
the cream thick as curds, we never see such luxury in England;

---

[1] The " boiled shirt " costs 12 skillings = 3d.
    Flannel        ,,    8   ,,   = 2d.
    Socks and collars   ,,   3   ,,   = 1½d.
    Kerchiefs and white ties  2   ,,   = 1d.
You must be pretty careful, however, unless you wish your linen to go the way of
all washing in all lands.

[2] I was once asked at an English country-house to show how coffee is made in
Arabia ; the housekeeper's only remark was, " It is easy to make coffee like Captain Burton if one may use so much ! " But the Arab system, though simple as
it is scientific, cannot be learnt without long practice.

sheep's milk is kept for cheese, and Reykjavik ignores the national Skýr.

At seven A.M. we have *café au lait,* rusks, white bread and brown, or rye loaf, which we all prefer. Breakfast is substantial as in northern Scotland. The staple is fish, notably cod, boiled or grilled, but all poor, small, and watery: a "head and shoulders" equal in size or flavour to those of our own country is rare as the *Spatium admirabile rhombi* farther south. "Tout ce qui vous plait—mais pas de poisson" is the frame of mind which soon follows pure ichthyophagy. Meat is always mutton, the liver and kidneys being apparently preferred; "Carnero no es carne," says the Gaucho, and at last we sigh for the Murghi (fowl) at which the Anglo-Indian turns up his sybaritical nose. Hens' eggs are equally uncommon; those of the cider-duck, boiled hard, are rarely wanting at this season. They are about as large as turkeys', with dirty-green shells, and very white albumen; the stranger enjoys them at first, but, like the Pallo fish of Sind and the "palm-oil chop" of Guinea, they are too rich; they pall upon the palate, and they are pronounced to be rancid and *gluants;* besides which they are rarely quite fresh, the one virtue of an egg. Potatoes are not always to be had; those grown in the island are waxy and taste like soap; the best are imported from Denmark and even these cannot be praised.

It must be observed that the Reykjavik lodging-house has a great advantage over that in England, which exists by petty overcharges and by small robberies. Here also a strange tongue and foreign habits conceal that fearful caricature of "society" ever prominent at home. The chief bane of poverty is not so much that it renders man ridiculous, as that it brings him into contact with a life-form of which only Mr *Punch* can make fun. I envy the *richard* in civilisation only because the talk of the Vestibule does not reach the Peristyle: his wealth removes him from all knowledge of what is going on within a few yards of him, the mean jealousies, the causeless hatreds, the utter malice and uncharitableness which compose " high life below stairs."

By way of simulating civilised existence we converted the tavern into a club, and dined there daily. It is the usual little

board-house in the High Street, and the northern wall backs
a couple of trees some five feet high, the Sorbier, or service
apple (*Sorbus aucuparia*). Another may be seen in the governor's " compound," but apparently one-half of it has lately paid
the debt of nature. The dining-room is a stuffy little box, and
it is useless to open the windows as they will at once be shut.
Often some unwashed and burly traveller from the country precedes us for a feed; a sewing-machine awaits our departure, and
we are serenaded by the monotonous croon of the nurse above.
Sometimes she breaks out into " Champagne Charley," with the
true British " rum-ti-tiddy " style of performance. The capital
has evidently forgotten the " beautiful lullaby," Ljúflingsmál,
composed by a calf-father, and sung at the window; but we
have an abundance after this fashion :

*Et sic ad infinitum.*

On the other side of the hall is the drinking saloon, and beyond
it the billiard-table, a highly primitive affair in which the slower
balls describe graceful segments of circles : the Russian game is
the favourite, and " the price is a penny—it is no more." The
dingy little room is mostly crowded in the evening, peasants and
visitors in rags act wall-flowers, whilst the *jeunesse dorée* per-
forms in the centre—yet note that neither Kirkwall nor Lerwick
owns a billiard-room. Groups gather at the tavern door, and
there is more life than usual in the High Street. Women flock
to the large pump and bear away their full pails with a square
fender of lath, like a falconer's cage; the long bearded and ragged
water-carrier is a local *curio*, and the one carriage sometimes
passes. Young ladies, escorted as in France by the *bonne*,
troop by to shop or to pay visits; and now and then an
" Amazone," very unlike her Dahoman sister, ambles by on her
little " sheltie."

The proprietor of our club was Hr Jörgensen, a Dane, formerly valet to Count Trampe; he began by hotel-keeping at the Hospital, but when that failed to keep him he wisely took the pothouse which paid well. He was an independent landlord, disdaining to tout for new comers, and not even advertising himself by means of a sign-board: in fact, he cared for nothing as long as he could tap a barrel of beer per diem. At the end of the season he sold the house and goodwill for $12,000 to Mr Askam, a Yorkshireman, and returned to his native country a " warm man."

You dine at Hr Jörgensen's *café beuglant* for the very moderate sum of one rixdollar per diem, including even coffee and *petit*

THE ANGLO-ICELANDIC HOST.

*verre*, but not including the " cheap Gladstone " which would be distasteful to the Oinomathic Society of Edinburgh. The hour is three P.M.; you fight for five with the good-tempered mistress and often you lose the battle. Appetite is never wanting near the North Pole, and Reykjavik is a thirstier place, the result of evaporation, than even the banks of Brazilian Sâo Francisco. High spirits, fine air, and free ozone—if such a thing there be— are proof against the excessive greasiness of Icelandic cookery where, however, it must be owned that melted butter now takes the place of tallow. The people have learned the use of salt, which formerly they ignored like the Guanchinets (Guanches) of Tenerife, not to say islanders generally: it is hard to see the hygienic value of the condiment amongst eaters of fish and meat, however necessary it may be to a vegetarian race like Brahmans and Banyans. Icelanders still prefer spices: the nutmeg, clove, and cinnamon which are mixed, in place of pepper, with sorrel or scurvy-grass (*Rumex acetosa*); and the sugar which is added, even to cabbage, gain for the cook anything but our blessings. Rice pudding with a sauce of currant jelly and water by way of molasses or the Syrian "dibs" (grape-syrup), often after the fashion of Dotheboys' Hall, precedes soup, and the latter is not rarely milk-soup, or Sod Suppe, the sweet broth of Norway, a slab compound of sago, dry cherries, raisins or plums, coloured with the juice of the imported Tyttebær, *Vaccinium myrtillus* and *vitis-idœa*; the Bláber of the Færoes and our own bilberry or blaeberry, red whortleberry or cowberry.

The salmon is excellent, firmer, finer, curdier, and leaner than with us; unfortunately it is cut up into slices. We make ample acquaintance with Australian and other preserved meats, and as might be expected, we find baking in lieu of roasting which seems now almost confined to England — the *rationale* of the regretable change is that it saves fuel. The cheese is certainly not from Cheese-shire; it is about as good as bad Gruyère: there is a dark sweet stuff called Mysust (*mysa*, whey, and *ostr*, "yeast" cheese), made of pressed curds, which the traveller will certainly not prefer to the Gammell ost, the "old" or common cheese of Denmark.

There is a tolerable beer misnamed Baiersk (Baerisch), and imported from the Continent—I do not know where Metcalfe learned that barley brew is made at Reykjavik. The Schoppe costs threepence, whereas the Rödvin, or Vin-de-pays, much like vinegar, and by courtesy called claret, fetches five marks or nearly a rixdollar per bottle. The people avoid the ancestral ale because it is supposed to give neuralgia, and prefer "Brazilian wine;" here Brennivín, korn-schnapps, or rye brandy which is always drunk raw. English travellers declare that they cannot enjoy it on account of the harmless, or rather the beneficial, aniseed with which it is flavoured: so Sir Charles Napier, the sailor, ordered casks of Syrian Raki to be started overboard because it must be poisonous, as it whitened the water—simply the effect of the condiment. The sensible traveller will prefer this unadulterated spirit to the vile potato brandy from Canada, coloured with burnt sugar and perhaps flavoured with an infinitesimal quantity of mother-liquor, the impostor which now passes itself off to the world as Cognac.

The tavern and *table d'hôte* have now passed under the rule of Jón Zoega, No. 7 High Street, and his pretty wife works hard to secure a clean house and good cookery. The stranger on landing should at once ask for the "head guide," Geir Zoega, who can always find bed and board at his brothers or his sisters. Other lodgings are by no means so comfortable, especially those fronting the ditch, by courtesy called a canal.

The day at Reykjavik is simple. Sleep is sound as appetite is hearty, and assimilation of food expeditious. When the infantry overhead opens its eyes, you proceed to the "chhoti háziri" (little breakfast), and you pass the time in reading and writing till the real affair about noon breaks the neck of the day's work. A visit or two and a long walk land you at the dinner hour—there is no better plan for the student-traveller than to make himself thoroughly familiar with a single section of the country which he is learning, so that during his field-work he may confine himself to the observation of differences. After dinner—at five or six P.M. if possible—another and a shorter walk, weather permitting, prepares for a few hours' reading before bed-time. The monotony may be varied by picnics and excursions, gun or fishing-rod in hand, more, however, for the sake of doing something than in view of sport. Were I a Reykjaviker my rule would be to hybernate, to be "bedded in," during the eight months of cold season:

> "Me levant tard, me couchant tôt,
> Dormant fort bien;"

and to be "potted out" with late spring, so as to pass as much as possible of the summer wide-awake and in the open air. Yet winter here is the "season," the gay time, when balls last from six P.M. to six A.M.; and "society" at the capital apparently looks forward to the "disease of the year."

# CHAPTER IV.

SUNDAY AT REYKJAVIK—DRINKING IN ICELAND.

*Sunday, June 9.*

THE Iceland Sunday begins at six P.M. on Saturday, and ends at following six P.M.; this precession is the case with the days in general; thus Sunday night here is the Saturday night of Europe. Apparently Scandinavia is the only part of the Western World which preserves a chronometry directly imported from the East. We find it everywhere amongst Jews and Moslems; and Genesis (i. 5) tells us that Arab or Gharb (evening) and Bakar (morning) formed the first day or period before the sun came into being. The old Germans and Gauls computed, we know, by nights, and not by days; and the Teutons probably borrowed it from the Celts: it survives amongst ourselves in such terms as sen'night and fortnight. At Reykjavik we distinguish the "Sabbath" by the amount of flying bunting; every store has its flagstaff, and the merchants as well as the consuls claim a right, as in the Brazil and Zanzibar, to sport their colours, which are, however, always Danish. The "church-going bell" begins to ring, and the doors to open, about 11.15 A.M.: the people much prefer the lively measure of their own summons to the monotonous system of England, whilst the chimes of the Royal Exchange, a national disgrace, provoke their contempt. Service does not commence till near noon, the usual time in the island where many of the congregation have long and rough rides.

The Dómkirkja (cathedral) in the Austurvöllr has often been described externally and internally; the "Napoleon book" and others, however, make it all of stone instead of being partly brick. The older basaltic building may be seen in Mackenzie, and the last additions bear date A.D. 1847. Its outside is shabby as the

People's Palace at Sydenham; the unclean yellow plaster has fallen from the distempered walls, the result of mixing salt sea-sand with the mortar; and the same is the case with the College and the College Library. "Rispettate la Casa di Dio" should be writ large upon every corner of this nondescript. A clerestory, with double windows, partly stained, those on the ground floor being single; a low-tiled ridge for the chancel; a higher pent roof for the nave and aisles; and a tall wooden tower, revetted with boiler-plate, compose what the polite call Gothic, the uncivil "Bastard Nothing." Utility is consulted by a weather-cock and a clock, serviceable to regulate time where no gun, even for saluting purposes, must be fired, lest H.H. the eider-duck take fright. The front, which is turned west, with a highly orthodox regard for orientation, shows the three windows of Roman Catholic architecture; and the Lich-gate,[1] never wanting in

THE LICH-HOUSE, CEMETERY, REYKJAVIK.

Iceland, is the normal house-hall: it is flanked to the right and left by flights of steps leading aloft. And the roof is now water-tight.

---

[1] The lich-gate proper in the cemetery is, or rather was, called Sálu-hliŏ, or souls' gate.

The inside is better kept than the outside. The ambulatorium
and wings are all hard benches, with stiff, straight backs, but
not divided into pews. The upper galleries along the long walls
are supported by square and round wooden beams and pillars;
the tint is characteristic salmon-colour. Over the entrance is
the succedaneum for the Narthex-gallery, an organ loft, a cage
like that used for women in the Melchite churches of Syria.
On the left side of the nave hangs the board showing the lessons
of the day; on the other and outside the chancel is a pulpit, with
gilt gingerbread work. The holy of holies is very Lutheran, the
usual blending of Catholicism with Protestantism, which marks
the first step when consubstantiation took the place of tran-
substantiation. There is an altar—not a communion table—
surmounted by a full-length figure of the Saviour, with a sleeping disciple and a Roman soldier as usual unusually alarmed;
its frame supports a cross, and the *tout ensemble* is an evident
derivation from the Iconastasis or Rood-screen. Upon the altar,
besides an open Bible and a chalice, with pall but without
bourse, two brass candlesticks of ecclesiastical aspect bear lighted
tapers, and eight medallions of the popular cherubim adorn the
boarded wall. The railing is of brass perpendiculars, with
wooden horizontals, and a cushioned step is knelt upon by com-
municants receiving the wafer. The gem of the building is the
font of Bertel (Albert) Thorvaldsen, whose features, figure, and
character prove him, though not born in Iceland, to have been
essentially an Icelander.[1] The font has been described as a
"low square obelisk of white marble:" it is the ancient classical
altar, with basso-relievos on all four sides, subjects of course

---

[1] According to Professor J. M. Thiele (Copenhagen, 1832), he was descended
on the spindle side—where, by-the-by, almost any descent can be established—
from the royal blood of Scandinavia. The family, once settled at Óslandshlíð in
Skagafjörð, sank, and his father Gottskálk emigrated to Copenhagen, where he
lived by carving figureheads for shipwrights. His mother was a clergyman's
daughter, and he was born November 19, 1770. Finn Magnússon (Antiquitates
Americanæ) has also drawn up his pedigree.

His first order from his northern home was, according to Thiele, a font which
Countess Schimmelmann and her brother Baron Schubarth wished to present to
the church of Brahe-Trolleberg in "Funen," as we write Fyen. It was adorned
with four bas-reliefs—the Baptism, the Holy Family, Christ blessing the children,
and three angels. After being exhibited and admired at Copenhagen, it was sent
to its destination, and a copy, we are told, was offered by the artist to the deserted
land of his forefathers, to be *placed in Myklabye church.* A note informs us that
this font was bought by a northern merchant, whereupon the artist immedi-

evangelical; on the top an alto-relievo of symbolical flowers, roses, and passifloræ, is cut to support the normal "Döbefad," or baptismal basin. Some have blamed its un-Christian shape, without taking notice of its use; others have reported that the inscription has been erased; unhappily we still read such latinity as "TERRÆ SIBI GENTILICIÆ . . . DONAVIT." The sacristy contains some handsome priestly robes, especially the velvet vestment sent by Pope Julius II. to the last Catholic bishop and martyr (?), Jón Arason, in the early sixteenth century, and still worn by the chief Protestant dignitary at ordinations. All have been carefully described: they reminded me much of the splendid vestments displayed in the Armenian convent at Jerusalem during Holy Week, and of the specimens of old embroidery, of rich stuffs, rare and interesting, that are worn at certain parts of the Protestant service by the officiating clergyman of Transylvanian Kronstadt. "It is a strange contradiction," says Bonar, "to the spirit of Lutheranism; and the rich, almost royal, robe ill accords with the studied plainness of the other parts of the dress, in which is not a trace of colour, of flowing lines or beauty. But the dissonance to the feelings is greater, for one could not but feel it as such, to see the magnificent chasuble which the priest had worn at the altar—so highly prized as only to be used on the most festive occasions—now employed for some everyday purpose unconnected with any holy mystery."

ately began another in Carrara marble. It is not said whether the third edition actually reached Myklabye church or is the one bought by Lord Caledon—evidently we have found it in the cathedral.

The "Patriarch of Bas-reliefs," as the Italians entitled him (ob. 1844), has been called a "handsome young Dane," when he was peculiarly Icelandic in body and mind. It was his misfortune to belong to the day of manufacturing sculptors, amongst whom he was the first and no more. But what can the artist expect from such inspiration as Jason, Anacreon and Cupid, Mars, Bacchus, Apollo, can give? The Icelander was pure and simple, free from the Gallicisms of Canova, an improvement upon Sergell the Swede, but cold, lacking life and interest; in fact, an imitator. I would rather in these days settle as an artist amongst the Kru-boys of the west coast of Africa, and attempt negro subjects, than copy the classics.

Richard Cleasby, who, by the by, killed himself with Cures, or rather Kurs, had a wide experience of men and manners in Europe, and his criticisms are sometimes sharp, but he left Thorvaldsen "with the impression of having been in the company of a great man." The peculiar Icelandic traits in his character were an ultra-Yankee 'cuteness in making a bargain, and a love of money, which led him into that ugly business of Madame d'Uhden. Still he amply deserves the statue for which the Municipal Council of Copenhagen has voted $6000, in honour of the Iceland Millenary.

Six votive tablets of silver metal hang against the wall, in memoriam of departed dignitaries.

Presently enters the Rector, Hallgrímr Sweinsson, attended by Sira Guttormr, a candidate for ordination. He has walked to church in black robes, with the broad and stiffly-crimped white ruff, the Fraise à la Medicis, which is seen from Iceland to Trieste: the poorer clergy in the island, as in Norway and Denmark, do not use it on account of the expense. His close-cut hair and peaked beard give him the aspect of an old family portrait dating from the days of the Stuarts. Presently, assisted by a bustling clerk in a white surplice, he dons the purple vestment with a yellow cross down the back—it will be remembered that the cope and the vestment were long retained by the Reformed Church in England. Sira[1] Hallgrímr thus attired stands up and intones with rotund mouth and a good voice somewhat like a Russian papas: he has been seven years in Denmark, yet he speaks no French, and very little English. The congregation, which is certainly not crowded, first joins in a long, a very long, hymn; after this come the prayers of the Lutheran rite; and finally, a thirty-minutes sermon for the benefit of the nodders and the noddees. The service lasts at least two hours, therefore the people rarely sit through it: the men especially disappear for a few minutes, and return when they please with a faint aroma of tobacco, which no one remarks; whilst many strangers see it through by instalments. The governor, who was visiting, did not attend, nor did the bishop, who was unwell.

The first aspect of the congregation was a novelty, especially after reading sentimental descriptions of man, whose " œil est pensif; son attitude nonchalante et sa démarche engourdie," and of woman, whose " traits respirent la douceur et la resigna-

---

[1] Síra is more commonly, but not so correctly, written Séra, and by foreigners Sjera; and I have heard it pronounced *Shera*. It is a Romance word, originally Senior, hence Seigneur, Signore, Senhor, Señor, Sir, Sir-r (Richardson), Sirrah, and "Sir-ree." Icelanders still keep up our fashion of Shakespeare's day, and apply it to clerks with the Christian name only, as Sir Hugh. *Magister* was the university title of the M.A. in our fifteenth century : *Dominus* (the Dan of Chaucer and his contemporaries, and the Don of modern Italian priests) was, and still is, the B.A., entered as Sir This or Sir That (the surname) in some of the college registers down to the time of Queen Anne, and, I believe, even in our day. Hence, possibly, the origin of the French Sir Brown and Sir Jones.

tion." The latter are naturally far more numerous than the former; firstly, the ceremony is in their line, and secondly, they preponderate in the population. They mostly affect the left aisle, whilst both sexes are mixed in the right. Few of the men sport broadcloth and chimney-pot hats; and these latter, when worn, are mostly of the category known as "shocking bad." The usual habit is a Wadmal paletot, the creases showing "store-clothes," and a billycock or wide-awake; the students carry caps, and the general look is that of the Bursch, without his swagger and jollity. The distinguishing article is the "Islandsk Skór," Iceland shoon, of which I have deposited a specimen at the rooms of the Anthropological Institute. It is a square piece of leather —sheep, calf, seal, or horse—longer and broader than the foot; the toes and heels are sewn up, the tread is lined with a bit of coloured flannel, and the rim is provided with thongs like our old sandals. It corresponds with the Irish "brogue," as shown in heraldry; the Shetland Rivlin, or Rullian; the Revlens or Revelins of the Scoto-Scandinavian islands; the Red Indian Mocassin; the Pyrenean Spartelle; the Zampette of Sicily; the Roman Cioccie; the Opanke of the Slavs; and the Mizz, which Egypt and the nearer East, however, are careful to guard with papooshes. It is one of the very worst *chaussures* known; it has no hold upon snow; it is at once torn by stone; being soleless, it gives a heavy, lumping, tramping, waddling gait; it readily admits water; and being worn over a number of stockings, it makes the feet and ancles look Patagonian, even compared with the heavy figure. There are a few specimens of "Lancashire clogs" from Denmark and the Færoes; chumpers or sabots are unknown; and the civilised bottine is not wanting.

The women at first sight appear tall compared with the men, but not so notably as in the case of the little Welshman and his large wife. They are, as they should be, better looking than their mates, whilst the chubby and rosy children are better looking than their mothers. The expression of countenance is hard and uncompromising. We involuntarily think of "those chilly women of the north who live only by the head;" and they gorgonise us into stony statues. Regularity of features is hardly to be expected so near the Pole. Even amongst the Ger-

man races we look for complexion and piquancy to take the place
of that classical beauty which is exceptional beyond the lovely
Mediterranean shores.   The congregation showed many a pretty
girl, but not a single face that would be remarked farther south.
The hair is admirable, and requires no chignon—the invention

ICELAND WOMAN—SUNDAY WEAR.

which conceals the Englishwoman's chief defect, her *capiglia-
tura*.   It is either *blond-cendré*, dark red, or light chestnut-brown,
as in older Denmark; farther south, but not here, brown-black is
by no means a rarity.   Plaited in two large queues, which hang
down the back at home, it is gathered up when abroad under

the Hufa or cap. This article is a caricature of the Fez, as the Skór are of the Mizz, and it has every defect except that of ugliness. The material is elastic black web woven by the women. The old style is to wear it large, like the night-cap of former days: the juniors prefer a mere apology for head-cover.

ICELAND WOMAN—MONDAY WEAR.

ing, much smaller than the thing now called a hat in England. It is provided with a Tuskana, a long tassel of black spun silk brought from Copenhagen; and the latter is ornamented at the base by a short cylinder (Hólkr) of silver, gilt-silver, or brass made in the country. This tassel serves for not a little by-play;

usually it. depends. upon the right or left shoulder indifferently, but when bending, for instance, it may be held under the chin for coquettish contrast of colours. The whole affair, which costs some six rixdollars, is kept in position by hair-pins, and, as it gives no protection against cold, it is covered out of doors with a shawl, mostly grey, striped white or chocolate; in fact, women rarely leave the house, even in what we consider warm weather, without being muffled to the ears; and the men are not less effeminate. There is only one specimen of the old Falldr or Skott Falldr (galeated cap), which seems to be growing obsolete; the day is windy, and this curved and

" High-peaked head-dress of snowy white,"

which corresponds with the "Roide Cornette" of ancient Holland, and of which modifications may still be seen in Normandy, could hardly be worn. I' shall reserve a description of the crested and helmet-like affair which strangers compare with a flattened cornucopia, with a cap of liberty, or with a dragoon casque, ultra Amazonian: here let me merely premise that it is a larger edition of the Lapp head-dress; that, within the memory of man, it was worn in the Orkneys; and that the whole costume somewhat resembles that of the Oberland Bernois. The few hats and bonnets accompany more modern attire, and even the crinoline and the Dolly Varden are not wholly unknown. In Iceland dress denotes the station; in Europe it is only the most advanced society that escapes from this outward show. The sensible Yankee travels in his "Sunday best," because it procures him respect and attention where he is unknown; we reverse the rule, and notably so on "the Continent"—which is uncivil and breeds incivility. Most of the elderly women are in black Wadmal; the juniors prefer fine, dark bottle-green stuff, with plaid or rainbow-coloured aprons. I at once remark the absence of the γυνή πυγοστόλος, called. "bussle-wearer" by our grandmothers. Those in the island-costume wear a narrow band of gold embroidery round the skirt, which resembles the costume of the Slav women about Trieste. The bosom is no longer flattened as much as possible—was this the result of a savage decency which taught the sex to mask nature? On the contrary, about the middle of the jacket a *soupçon* of white chemisette is now allowed to peep forth. But these coy dames have still to borrow a hint from the young Irish person who wore

> " every beauty free
> To sink or swell as heaven pleases. "

"Sabbath" in the "moral north" passed away as usual. The respectables, masculine as well as feminine, sat at the windows opposite one another, the former smoking vile Hamburg cigars, the latter devoting themselves to the serious and exhaustive study of street scenery. The German mirror placed to reflect the thoroughfare is still a rarity, and therefore the prospector must display herself as *chez nous*. The commonalty leaned against the walls and railings, much like the Irish peasantry of the present day, whose poetry, wit, and humour, once so famous, appear, like art in Italy, to have been crushed out of life by a generation-long course of "patriotism," politics, and polemics. There was a little more apparent drunkenness than usual, men staggering about, peasants supporting one another, and all jostling whatever they met in the streets. This unpleasant process of "rubbing up" seems to be here the rule, and we can hardly complain of it when we remember the lower orders, and not only the lower orders, of the Lowland Scotch: as the Yankee is the Englishman with the weight taken off him, so here the people, like the scenery, are Caledonian intensified. In the evening, thus to speak, when the dissolute sun, instead of keeping the regular hours of the tropics, does not turn in before eleven P.M., the sexes paired, and one gentleman accompanied his "lady" in carpet slippers. The day ended without a brawl. On St Monday, however, there was a tavern quarrel, when one of the strongest men in the town had his face cut open by a stone. We were assured by all that such things are very rare. Yet on the following Wednesday one of the couthless Calibans from the country, whom tangle-leg had made "drunk as an auk," thinking that he was derided by a party of Englishmen, slipped up behind one of them and hit him a rounder, in popular parlance a "regular slogdolager." The Briton, thus unexpectedly assaulted, soon recovered him-

self, and, though the peasant bundled away, rolling like a bolt-
ing bear, Mr A—— succeeded in lodging a couple of sound
lashes with his horsewhip. A small crowd gathered; of course
it took part against the strangers, and a free fight became imminent. This was prevented by the chief constable, whose
badge is the tallest hat I ever did see, and who commands a

THE HEAD CONSTABLE.

body of three men, armed with the "Northern Star." When
appealed to, however, the dignitary distinctly refused to take his
fellow-countryman into custody; hence, perhaps, the freedom of
the jails from jail-birds, a peculiarity strongly insisted upon by
complimentary writers, and quaintly corresponding with our
"gratifying diminution of crime." This is not what we read

about Iceland and the Icelanders. It of course will be said that fair time is approaching, and that we are at Reykjavik, a centre of dissipation, where men are eagerly looking forward to the arrival of a grind-organ.

This appears to be the place for inserting a few remarks upon the subject of drinking in Iceland compared with that of England and Scotland. I had asserted in the *Standard* that "more cases of open, shameless drunkenness may be seen during a day at Reykjavik than during a month in England and Scotland." A gentleman interested in the matter writes to me: "According to the only official returns of Icelandic statistics ('Skýrslur um landshagi (resources of the country) á Íslandi, gefnar út af hinu islenska Bókmenntäfélagi,' Kaupmannahöfn, 8vo), from 1865 to 1869, the date of the last publication, the consumption of intoxicating drinks has been steadily decreasing. Thus in—

1865 the amount of 2 gallons 6½ pints were drunk per head.
1866    ,,     2 ,, 1 ,,      ,,
1867    ,,     1 ,, 6 ,,
1868    ,,     1 ,, 4 ,,      ,,
1869    ,,     1 ,, 3 ,,      ,,

In 1869 the gross total used in the island was thus one gallon and three pints per head. In Scotland the consumption of spirits alone for 1870 was a fraction of a gill less than two gallons a head (Parliamentary return for 1870 relating to spirits, beer, and malt spirits), and in the United Kingdom one gallon a head. I have not been able to ascertain the quantity of wines consumed, nor the proportion contributed by the secret stills of Scotland and Ireland; but of beer and spirits together, the consumption in the United Kingdom was no less than thirty gallons per head per annum. You must remember that the Icelanders have no spirits equal in strength to whiskies and French brandies. You must also remark in connection with the drunkenness observed by you at Reykjavik that you were there during the trading season, when people flock to the capital. They have not tasted, perhaps, a drop of intoxicating liquor during nine or ten months, and they make up for their sobriety by a fortnight or so of indulgence. I have known several peasants who bought a keg of Danish brandy at the trading-place, and who made free use of it during their homeward journey, and as long after as the supply lasted. Then they did not taste a drop till the next season, for the very good reason that they could not get it. It would therefore not be quite fair to state, as a general condition of the Icelanders, what might be observed at Reykjavik during the fair, from about the middle of June to the end of July. It would be equally unjust to show up the condition of Londoners on Boxing Night, or of the Scotch on New Year's Day, not to speak of every Saturday night."

To this I reply. In 1834 the consumption was only 2 bottles of spirits per head; on the whole, therefore, there is an increase. Between 1849-62 (Paijkull[1]) the imports had increased 79 per cent., and in the latter year the consumption per head was of 6·7 Danish pots or quarts, when Scotland uses 1½ gallons per head. Mr Consul Crowe (1870-71, p. 648) shows that the consumption is "about 24 quarts annually for every adult male, without counting ale, wine, rum, punch extract, and other spirituous drinks imported." My stay in Iceland lasted not till the end of July, but till September the first. I found drunkenness prevail not only in the capital, but in the farm-houses; and, as the trading stations and market-ships are now scattered all round the coast, there is no difficulty in obtaining spirits throughout the year. Since 1869, the practice has apparently increased with the growth of commerce. As regards the figures, they are like facts perfectly capable of misleading as well as leading. The statistics of a sparse and scattered population can hardly be expected to be correct; for instance, the fleet of French fishing vessels smuggles a quantity of cognac which does not appear in the returns. The Consular Report (1870-71, p. 650) adds, "The consumption of ardent spirits in the island is very great, being as 490,000 imperial quarts annually (or 490,000 : 70,000), and of this large quantities are landed by the foreign fishermen, who barter it with the natives for their fish and other raw produce." We all issued from the "Queen" with more or less whisky, about which nothing was asked or said; and this may counter-balance

---

[1] This author also tells us that Sweden annually produces 38,000,000 of pots of Korn-schnapps, of which 6,000,000 are used for technological purposes.

even the large produce of the "secret stills" existing in Ireland,[1] but rare in England, Wales, and Scotland. Also what is consumed in Iceland is almost entirely drunk by the men—I never saw that disgrace of our great cities, a drunken woman.

The actual state of things is not what is shown by the figures. An eminent Icelander openly asserted that he had dived into the gin-palaces of London and Edinburgh, yet that he had seen more drunkenness in a day at Reykjavik than during his whole visit to Great Britain. This comparison with a nation which derives £13,000,000 of revenue from spirits alone, and which has "drunk itself out of the Alabama difficulty," is telling. There have been repeated attempts to establish teetotalism, but none have succeeded—perhaps a whisky war might lead to victory. And here hard drinking is apparently a little reprobated practice. A party of English travellers lodged at the house of an educated man, who, fresh from a visit to Denmark, expressed the *dulce domum* and domesticity sentiment by loud and late striving in strong liquors. The same tourists engaged a guide, who kept himself sober during the march, but afterwards broke out in a way which prevented his re-engagement, sleeping *unter freien himmel*, and so forth.

That our vices like our virtues are regulated by our "media," no traveller can doubt. Thus in England, out of an annual total of 150,000 souls "drunk and disorderly,"[2] the number proceeded against in the south (not including London) was 3·2 : 1000; in the Midland district, 4·0 : 1000; whilst in the north it rose to the extreme ratio of 10·8 : 1000. These figures show, if evidence be wanted, that "as we go north drunkenness increases." The classical Scandinavian and the Northmen generally were deep topers, quarrelsome withal; their wives always removed their weapons when they sat down to drink; and they looked forward to a Houri-lacking and *pro tempore* paradise, where the dead rode forth daily to cut one another to

---

[1] In 1872 no less than 1100 cases of illicit distillation were detected in Ireland, against 21 in England, and 8 in Scotland.

[2] The irrepressible statistician of the *Figaro* assigns annually to England 50,000 deaths by drunkenness, of which 12,000 are women ; 40,000 to Germany ; 38,000 to the United States ; 10,000 to Russia (? ?) ; 4000 to Belgium ; and 1500 to virtuous France.

pieces, and rode back to gorge nasty boiled pork and swill vasty draughts of bilious mead. In the south, take Europe for instance, men hold wine to be the ἰατρεῖον ψυχῆς, and prefer to over-nourishment gambling, or what we call immorality, in the confined sense of the word. Race, again, heredity and atavism, or the habits bequeathed by forefathers, modify climate: the Slav, for example, who occupies the same latitudes as the abstemious Turk and Italian, is a hard eater and wine-bibber. And I have a conviction that spirit-drinking is becoming common in countries where it was formerly almost unknown. During a late ride to Ronda in Spain, two drunken men were seen in one day, and three appeared at an Italian country-fair—these are instances out of many which might be quoted.

In England, on the other hand, drinking in society has been modified not solely, as we flatter ourselves, by better taste or by a "higher tone," but also by the increased use of nicotine—an axiom which will be grateful to the readers of *Cope's Tobacco Plant*, and unpleasant to gentlemen of the happily defunct Palmerstonian school. In the age of Queen Anne apparently all Englishmen smoked. The Continental war made the practice "un-English," and an increase of snuff was the result. At Oxford, shortly before I matriculated, some youth of heroic mould, who deserves a statue if any one does, lit a cigar almost immediately after the hall-dinner. He was called hard names, but he persevered, and he found imitators: the consequence was a notable curtailing of the "wines" which used to last from seven to eleven P.M. In 1852 I was objurgated, and not unfrequently cut, for smoking a manilla in the streets of London. Very shortly afterwards a ducal reformer spread his plaid under a tree in Hyde Park, produced a briar-root, and expected his friends to do likewise. I need hardly say that they did.

After this little experience of life, man will be careful how far he allows local custom to modify his comfort and his convenience.

# CHAPTER V.

VISITS—CONVIVIALITIES—THE CATHOLIC VIEW OF THE "REFORMA-
TION"—SURTAR-BRAND—THE HOME-RULE PARTY.

THE Reykjavikers may be distributed into four classes: the official, ecclesiastic, and civil; the merchants; the fishing-class; and the paupers. The visiting hour begins with noon. You open the outer door of the diminutive hall and rap at either side-entrance: but generally the left, otherwise the gynæceum may be sorely disturbed. The rapping possibly lasts for five minutes; the servant hears you or not, and if she condescends to open she usually stares, backs, and leaves you on the threshold. This class in Iceland appears to me the worst in the world—practical communists with the rude equality of the negro, worse even than the Irish help in the United States, or the servitor at Trieste, where the men are either louts or rogues, and the women are cheats, bacchanalians, or something worse. The domestic agrees to live with his employer for a certain sum, finds little to do, will do nothing but drink and be dissolute, refers frequently to the contract, tells the master, with true northern candour, to serve himself, and finally retires to the house of his brother's wife's third cousin. So the Greenlander gives warning by "Kasu-onga" (I am tired of you). Throughout the country it appears a dishonour to do household work. Most of the farms, even when in debt, have some article of the kind, but generally it is an aged and feminine body, perhaps connected with the family and liable to starve when turned off.

On the other hand, if after knocking you enter, there is probably a startled rise and rustle of petticoats, like a flushed covey of partridges, the home-toilette, as in the nearer "East," being the one all-sufficient cause. At this season well-to-do Reyk-

javikers rise at eight A.M.; breakfast substantially at nine or
ten, and sally forth after noon to walk, ride, or call upon friends.
The islanders dine at two P.M.; the Danes at four, and sometimes, when parties are given, at five—already an approach to
civilised hours. A supper, mostly cold like the breakfast, is
taken at eight P.M.; and thus, as in the homely parts of Austria
and Italy, the evening visit is impossible. There is no better·
contrivance for cutting up society.

As on the Continent of Europe, the stranger makes the first
call, and of course he begins with the governor. H. E. Hilmar
Finsen, despite his Danised name, Finsen for Finnsson, is an Icelander of old and well-known stock, and he worthily keeps up
the hospitalities of the late Count Trampe, whom so many
English travellers have cause to remember with the liveliest
gratitude. The family is a little hurt by the Napoleon book,
which gives (p. 160) the genealogy of Vilhjalmr Finsen, in 1857
" magistratus " (mayor) " Reykjavicæ," through Adam, Noah,
Saturn, Jupiter, Priam, and " Odinn, rex Asarum." The table
was sent to the prince as a specimen of an Icelandic tree, and
French sense of humour could not let pass the opportunity of
taking it *au sérieux* and printing it *in extenso*. After all there
is a fine Old World flavour in it: so a Greek eupatrid found in
his genealogy, either paternal or maternal, all his country's gods
both of Olympus and of the other place. Governor Finsen's
great-great-grandfather was the celebrated Bishop of Skálholt
(1754) and editor of the Landnámabók, Finn Jónsson, who loved
to latinise himself into Finnus Johannæus; his "Historia Ecclesiastica Islandiæ," though much decried by Catholics, continues
to be a standard work. The portrait of this worthy, in ruff and
gown, is found everywhere; and the fine oval face, straight features, and serene blue eyes have not left the family.[1] His son
Hannes Finsson was the last Bishop of Skálholt, when shortly
before 1800, Danes, for motives of economy, fused together the
two sees, in the person of Geir Vidalin, first primate of Iceland.
About this time the patronymic began to be exchanged for the

---

[1] Bishop Pètursson has a section (No. 3, p. 448, et seq.), "De regiis Islandiæ
Satrapis," amongst whom was a Count Ehrenreich C. L. Moltke. Chap. II. (p. 474)
treats " de Finno Johannæo ; " and Chap. III. (p. 479) "de Johanne Finnæo."

family name ; the son of Bishop Finsson was called Ólafr (Olave) Finsson, and, he being a Danish official, a judge in Jutland who never saw Iceland, Finsson became Finsen. The present governor's title, Stiftamtmand (Icel. Stiptamtmaðr), has been lately changed to Landshöfðingsi (Danish), a higher grade without extra rank or salary ; and the mayor (Bæarfógeti) has similarly been advanced to Landsskrifari, or official secretary. Hr Finsen is a civilian—admirals and naval officers are no longer the privileged ruling caste, and Iceland has gained by the loss. He speaks French, but prefers Danish; whilst his very young looking wife, whose six stalwart boys and girls suggest brothers and sisters, knows only her native tongue. We talked of the mysterious volcano in the depths of the Vatnajökull, whose flames were first seen about the end of August 1867 : he advised me strongly to attempt the south-eastern corner of the island viâ Berufjörð ; Professor Gunnlaugsson did the same, and the only dissentient voice was Hr Procurator Jón Guðmundsson. The governor was, I shall show, right.

The second call should be paid to Bishop Pèter Pètursson, who is also agent for the Bible Society.[1] This dignitary was most obliging in giving me information, and he presented me with a copy of his work, alluded to in the Introduction. He was then (1841) licentiate of theology, " toparchiæ Snæfellensis et Hnappadalensis Præpositus" and " Pastor Stadastadensis." I asked him why he did not bring it up to the present day, and he replied, with excellent sense, that to write contemporary annals is a hard task ; and that De vivis nil nisi bonum, though a fine Christian precept, is a prescription for composing history of very dubious value.

The approaching departure of " Le Cher," and the presence of a Danish cruiser, and the mail-steamer, officered by the Royal Navy, caused an unusual outburst of hospitality. The first dinner where I " met the surly Dane," and found him an uncommonly good fellow, was at the house of the good M. Randrüp,

---

[1] I made the mistake before leaving England of buying the Biblia published in the German character at Copenhagen in 1747, and found the language old-fashioned. The Oxford edition of the Bible Society, which sells for four marks, is certainly an improvement.

Consul de France, a Continental, whose devotion to the interests
of his native country has considerably " exercised " the political
section of the islandry. I cannot refrain from expressing my
gratitude to this gentleman and his family; he was ever ready
to assist me and, indeed, all travellers; whilst madame and
mademoiselle made visits peculiarly pleasant. A Danish house
is always known by pictures and engravings of Copenhagen and
other home scenes, in addition to family photos and loyal portraits of King Christian IX. and his queen; of King Frederick
VII., who travelled in Iceland and left there the best of names;
of the Prince of Wales and the Princess Alexandra, who has
warmed every heart; and, perhaps, of the battle of " Schleswig-
Holstein meer-umschlungen." One enjoys even the artificial
presence of trees, which look like the portentous growths of the
Brazil or Central Africa, after the stunted vegetation in and
around Reykjavik. The Icelanders sing or are supposed to sing:

> " From the midst of Copenhagen's smoke,
> We all yearn for home ;
> Long, dearest, again to behold thee.
> The noisy din irks us ;
> Revelry tempts us in vain ;
> And the fool grins contemptuously at us
> In the streets of Copenhagen."

The Danes slily remark that a good appointment and the easy
temptation of rixdollars greatly modify all this athumia and
nostalgia; and there is much truth in what the Napoleon
book says, " Chose étonnante ! il n'y a pas de patriote islandais,
lorsqu'il est de retour dans son pays, ne caresse l'idée de s'en aller
vivre dans un pays à végétation sérieuse " (p. 157). In a certain
stage of civilisation, there is no place like home; about the end
of the last century we find Ireland, that " mild and sedimentary
Iceland," styled the "kingdom of the zephyrs," and grandilo-
quently described as a " country particularly dignified by the
magnificent hand of Nature, whose liberality has denied it
nothing that is necessary to constitute a great and happy
nation." A fallacy lurks in the well-worn quotation :

> " So the wild torrent and the whirlwind's roar
> But bind him to his native mountains more."

The Switzer readily leaves his *mère patrie*, but ever cherishes the hope of returning, a wealthy man, to lay his bones in the place which gave him birth. The Englishman, whose native mountains are mole-hills and whose wild torrents are mere " cricks," does exactly the same. The Frenchman, also an inhabitant of the plains, tears out his heartstrings whilst bidding adieu to " beautiful France," but when comfortably settled abroad seems to care little for seeing her charms again. Perhaps I should speak in the past tense, for railways and steamers are levelling these differences.

All the guests spoke English and French, and all were very charming. They were curious concerning Bláland, the country of the blacks; and they asked about Dr Livingstone, whose name is known in every farm-house which owns a few books. They inquired if I belonged to the " Jökull Klubb " (Alpine Club) : apparently in a mountainous country an Englishman must study mountains not mountaineers. The table is always *à la Russe;* flowers and fruits have been to our "groaning boards " what the cigar and the pipe were to the dessert and " wine ; " only those who remember the last generation can appreciate this relief from endless side dishes and the barbarous hospitality which prided itself upon pressing an indigestion upon the *conviva* '*satur.* The flowers are mostly artificial— I wonder why the tender and beautiful island heaths are not more generally used. The salmon from the Laxá and the sea-trout are undeniably better than ours. The venerable custom of drinking healths is still preserved : it descends directly from the " full," or tumbler, quaffed in honour of Odin and Njord, Frey and Braga. Christianity converted these toasts to the Father, the Son (Kristsminni), the Angels, especially Michael, and the Saints ; and modern conviviality has devoted them to present and absent friends. The habit is to " cap out " after bowing, and then to tilt the wine-glass slightly toward the compotator, with a second bow. When you help your neighbour from a fresh bottle, you first pour, as in the Brazil, a few drops into your own glass ; and at a certain stage of the proceedings you do not administer a bumper. The sole toast was to Justisrað Bojesen, the governor's venerable father-in-law, who was on a visit to the island. After a dessert of the *studentenfutter*, cold pudding, dates, prunes, and olives, all rise and, whether introduced or not, bow or shake hands, especially with the host and hostess, saying "Velkomme," not "welcome" but "prosit," a hearty old Danish, or rather German, practice, not indigenous to this part of Scandinavia. There is no sitting when the smallcoats leave the table; and probably from the scantiness of accommodation only men dine out.

The next banquet, being at the governor's, was more official, only four black coats appeared, and even the mayor was dressed in uniform, gold-embroidered cuffs and collar of green velvet. Toasts were numerous, beginning with the French and Danish nations, which were duly acknowledged: and the two strangers, a young Englishman and myself, replied in French—not in Latin. After dinner we smoked and drank coffee, whilst the juniors, despising the damp cold, repaired for croquet to the "lawn." At the bishop's there was a strong muster of the clergy from the outstations, in honour of the Rev. Guttormr Vigfusson, who had that day been ordained. Here, and here only, we saw snuff taken at table, and a use of the knife in the matter of peas and gravy, which still lingers amongst the best society in parts of Europe—it would be insidious to specify—but which Beau Brummel and his cloth have completely banished from England. It is only in the "Regimen Mensæ honorabile," that we still read:

> "Sal cultello capia-
>       .      .      .      } tis."
> Modicum sed crebrò biba-

The bishop's wife dined with us, and went through the laborious process of dispensing soup and meat to some two dozen guests; there was no room for the two pleasing daughters, nor for the adopted child—certainly the best looking of maidens at Reykjavik. We separated early, and after the Homeric proportions of the banquet a long walk was judged advisable.

The evening's conversation taught me how thin-skinned are Icelanders upon all subjects connected with their country and themselves. I could not but think of a canny people farther south, who hold praise to be an impertinence, whilst dispraise, if it were not so truly contemptible, would be the one offence never to be condoned. Madame Ida Pfeiffer's angry book was duly sat upon, all declared that she has misconstrued almost everything she observed. The fact is, that the poor authoress, when flitting through the country on her "weird visit," was utterly misunderstood by the people, and showed her resentment by the use of her especial weapon. Even the genial and amiable owner of the yacht "Foam," who, so far from wishing to hurt the feelings of any reader, has passed over in silence many things which ought to have been told, is not forgiven for the Latin speech beginning with "Pergratum est"—"chaff" is unknown in Iceland, and gives terrible offence to this painfully sensitive race. Chambers is a *farceur ;* Prince Napoleon is harsh-judged for writing anything that might not please Icelandic readers; Forbes never rounded Snæfell; the late Professor Paijkull is a prejudiced foreigner, whose views about the sheep disease are simply ridiculous; and even Baring-Gould is incorrect in his details. For science, we are referred to Sir George Mackenzie; and for geography, manners, and customs, to Dr Henderson. It is only fair, however, to state that sensible Icelanders, who have lived out of this "living and antiquarian museum, recalling, as far as material and practical progress is concerned, the Europe of a century ago," agree that Henderson praises them beyond all measure, and recommend to all Englishmen Professor Paijkull, as the fairest and the least exaggerated in general statements.

I already felt the growling and the bursting of the storm upon my devoted head. But the traveller who would do his duty to the Public must think as little as possible of blame and praise. The reader, and also the critic, enjoy high spirits, persistent optimism, and especially the "burying of all animosities, and condoning of all offences"—in fact, every tale of travel must be a Chinese picture, all lights and no shades. The end of a journey, like the resignation of a ministry, should cause a general whitewashing. If we tell the truth, we are sure to be assured that our pictures are forbidding or "bilious in tone." My only reply is, that under certain circumstances they can be nothing else, if, indeed, they are to be portraits, and not fancy sketches for a Book of Beauty. I own to feeling a personal grievance against a writer who spreads before me all the sweets, and who hides under the table all the sours and bitters of his experience.

The next invitation was from Capitaine Alfred Le Timbre, of Saint-Malo, a pleasant, gentlemanly man, who spends his summer in looking forward to September, when the "Cher's" head will turn south. To an Englishman the most companionable of French-men is generally a sailor, and a Breton is all but a compatriot. Capitaine Le Timbre and his consul have no slight task in con-trolling some 3000 French fishermen, distributed amongst 250 vessels: the foreigners are bound not to land, and, indeed, not to approach the shore within the normal score of miles. This law is much broken; the men are often obliged to be invalided, and are sometimes wrecked with considerable loss of life: the under-writers after August add 1 per cent., and 0·50 per cent. for every subsequent fortnight. I afterwards travelled with nineteen of them on board the "Diana," and found them by no means a "rough lot." The people buy smuggled goods low, and sell pro-visions uncommonly high, and the results are frequent free fights between the strangers and the islandry. The former complain that they are always wrong in the eye of the law, and that their own authorities are ever the most severe in the matter of fines and imprisonment. As has been said, the Reformation made salt cod more valuable to Catholic lands; still sundry of our fishermen, when they fail at the Færoes, where the fish is better and more easily carried home alive, try Iceland: the Grimsby men are said to be the worst, the Hull men the best. An occasional cruiser is much wanted to keep the ruffians in order: Forbes recommended the measure years before H.M.S. "Valorous," Captain Thrupp, appeared in August 1872. No English man-of-war deigned to grace the millenary festival of 1874—the successful effacement of Great Britain should be a matter of heartfelt congratulation to us; but *gare* the recoil of the spring. The evening was pleasant, as usual on board a ship of war, and the belongings wore a home look, a civilised aspect, which made it more than normally agreeable—I felt again at home. The traveller cannot help remarking one effect of rail-roads and steamers upon European society: in dress and manners we all seem to be forming one great nation. One of the guests was a Hr Grímr Thomsen, who is favourably mentioned by Messrs Dasent and Newton: after being employed in sundry consulates, this gentleman of "grim cognomen"[1] has taken a pension, and settled at the old college of Bessastaðr, where he attends to agriculture, and looks after the fishing. From him I heard how far superior to Arab blood are Iceland ponies, and a curious local grievance—it must serve for a better—namely, that strangers come to the island under the impression that they cannot break their necks in it. He first showed me the popular habit of making unpleasant and antipathetic, if not rude, remarks: this mordant tone is still a mania in Iceland; it descends from the days of the defamatory songs, which spared neither gods nor men. And now, having dined out, we will turn elsewhere.

The Klafter (chat) Klubb is an institution even more primitive than that of Madeira, which, greatly to feminine and connubial satisfaction, used to close at six P.M. The many-windowed wooden building in Hafnarstræti is the store kept by Hr Möller, who manages the club, and allows it three small rooms somewhat higher in the ceiling than usual. It opens only on Wednesday evenings, when the principal merchants congregate to drink "toddy." The yearly subscription is $12; and strangers, after being presented, may visit it three times gratis—unless the usual sharp practice rule otherwise. In such matters there is a conventional honesty; even in London the secretary will sometimes do for the institution what he would not think of doing for himself.

At the first opportunity I called upon M. l'Abbé Baudouin, now the only Catholic missionary in the island, which formerly had two. The road leads past the Hospital, and we can inspect the tarn whose southern bank is the Paseo for "beauty and fashion" —I rarely met any there but English. The little piece of water in former days was covered with wild. fowl; now it supports nothing but yellow-green weed, especially when it shrinks in July and August. It drains large peat bogs at the southern or

---

[1] Grímr and Grímnir are names of Odin, from his travelling in disguise: grímu-maðr is a cowled man, "Mutalassam," or "face-veiled," as the Bedawin say.

inland end, and when swollen it passes to the sea by the foul
ditch before mentioned, fit only for stickle-backs. In winter it
serves for skating, but it is not always frozen over, another
proof of unexpectedly mild climate despite high latitudes. Of·
course it is very variable under the influence of the volcano and
the iceberg: in 1845, the last eruption of Hekla covered the
adjacent valleys with abundant vegetation; in 1869 and 1873,
the greater part of the island was ice-bound for months.

On the western bank of the tarn are two targets for rifle
practice, one at 95, the other at 112 paces. I never saw shooting there; in fact the only soldiering known to Reykjavik
is when the Danish "Fylla" disembarks her short, stout, dapper,
little crew, averaging twenty-two years of age, for drill under
a tall quartermaster. On the other side of the road is the
cemetery, guarded by posts and rails; the mortuary chapel,
with its dwarf steeple, all wood, and lighter than those of the
Sienna country, faces east. Crosses are everywhere, from the
deadhouse to the *parva domus*: some of the tombs are not to be
despised, and the epitaphs beginning with "Hver Hvílir" (here
lies) are not the comedies of our country churchyards. It is a
peculiar custom to keep the dead unburied sometimes for three
to six weeks; and the measure can hardly be precautionary, as
the bodies are screwed down in the coffins, and stored at the
solitary cemetery. A resident foreigner lately exposed himself
to prosecution because he interred his servant only six days after
death.

Turning rightwards we pass a windmill to the south-west of
the town. On its eminence the people assembled in May 1860
to see the flames and flashes proceeding from the "aqua-igneous"
fissure of Kötlu-gjá, which, distant some eighty miles, shot up,
they say, a pillar of smoke, steam, and scoriæ some 24,000 feet
high (?). From this point also, we are assured, the gleam of the
Vatnajökull volcano could be detected in 1867. The country
beyond the mill is a barren stretch of stone, where dodgy plovers
lay their eggs, and where swarms of gnats put the promenader
to flight. A few steps lead us to the house of M. Baudouin, which
is the best in the island; it was built by Bishop Helgi Thordurs-
son, predecessor of the present dignitary, and the use to which it

was converted gave some scandal. The Abbé fenced himself in with a railing and turnstile, levelled the warts, and manured the ground—the shells and the sea-wrack offer excellent compost, but they are never used. This was done seven years ago, yet double crops are still produced: the inordinate price of labour, $2 a day being the wage of a field hand, prevented further operations. Truly a few Trappist establishments scattered over the island would do an immensity of good.

M. Baudouin then built to the west of his dwelling-place a cross-crowned chapel, and preached to full congregations, who attended regularly—I should mention that he is an excellent Icelandic scholar. This proceeding aroused the wrath of the Reformed. Strange to say, in this section of the nineteenth century, a country which boasts of "liberal institutions" will not permit -version; and, although the Althing has been strongly in favour of extending everywhere freedom of faith, propagandism is allowed only to commercial settlements. The house being out of town, Monsieur l'Abbé was warned that he was not en règle: the code of Denmark authorises a "subvention" to those who build places of worship, but "subvention" was altered by Icelandic interpretation to "permission," and thus the good missionary was assured that he required permission to do what the law permitted—which is absurd. His opponents then tried to revive against him the obsolete tyrannical ordinances of the old Protestant world: he is an outlaw, he may be flogged, and even killed with impunity, whilst harbouring a Papist is punishable by a heavy fine—six ounces of silver doubled every day.

The Abbé wanted nothing better than to be a martyr, but of course he wanted in vain. Laws in Iceland are somewhat flexible things, exceptionally applied at times, and liable to be broken with impunity: so in England "law" contrasts pleasantly with the rigidity of "la loi" of France. In this island, where people cannot afford paupers, families are dispersed even more cruelly than in our inhuman workhouse system, and each member is transferred to his or her Sýsla (county): the country, however, can plead necessity for these severe conditions. M. Baudouin chose to lodge and board an unhappy household subject

to forcible separation.  Thereupon the mayor imposed upon
the paupers a fine, which they refused to pay, and lastly,
he ordered their protector to expel them.  The Abbé stoutly
refused, and asked what would result if the affair came
before Chief Justice Thorður Jonassen?  The reply was, "It will
be as he sees it."  Presently, the authorities perhaps remembered that when something of the same kind happened in the
north, the case was quashed by the Court of Cassation in Denmark—nothing more was said.  As Rome proposes to establish
a Vicar Apostolic for Scandinavia,[1] M. Baudouin bides his time.
For two years he has been in bad health, and wears a frost-
bitten look; he now proposes to sun himself for a time in France,
and after his return, to preach in Icelandic when he pleases and
where he pleases.  The Protestant party boldly hopes never to
see him again.

I was pleased to hear from the Abbé a Catholic version of the
Reformed movement which followed the proclamation of Christian III. in 1540, and more especially of the murder or just
execution of that "illiterate and turbulent prelate" who ended
the "dismal ages of papal darkness," Jón Arason (Are's son),
whom foreigners call Aræson and Areseni, the last occupant of
the northern see, Hólar.[2]  His enemies declare that at eighty
he had a concubine; that he unmercifully seized and otherwise
persecuted, his opponents; that he never went south without an
armed retinue of two hundred bravos; that he refused to go to
Copenhagen, and that he was a rebel against the Crown.  His
friends refute the charges preferred against him; deny the hólm-
ganga or duel which he is fabled to have fought with Bishop
Ögmund; assert that the "Historia Ecclesiastica" contains no less
than three contradictions, and persistently declare that J. A. was
simply a martyr to Catholicism.  The Reformers, acting under
the Danish Government, were headed by Oddur Gottswálksson
and Gizurr Einarson.  The former, a son of the Bishop of Hólar,

---

[1] I see by the papers that Father Stub, the Barnabite, on his return to Berghen
in Norway, opened a Catholic church, to the great satisfaction of the people.

[2] This common name of places in Iceland means Holts, hills; it is the plural
of Hóll, but most writers put it in the dative plural, Hólum, as it would stand in
composition "í Hólum" at Hólar.  Possibly the intention is, despite grammar,
to apply Hólum to the bishopric and Hólar to the other sites.

when studying at Wittenberg, had been strongly imbued by Luther and Melancthon with the spirit of the new faith; he afterwards became the first translator of the Bible, and lawyer for the northern division of the island till he was drowned in 1556. The latter was in turn secretary to Ögmund, Catholic Bishop of Skálholt, Lutheran priest, and, finally, first Lutheran bishop of the southern see. They suborned against J. A. one Daði, a peasant of Mýra Sýsla, in the Borgarfjörð; and Judas, as usual, pretending to be his friend, betrayed him to his foes. The house in which he was arrested is still shown a little south of the Kvennabrekka chapel: he was carried to Skálholt, the southern see, already Lutheran, and was incontinently beheaded.

Followed the usual scenes of persecution and destruction: we might be reading a History of England. The Reformers became deformers. Cruel laws were passed against the priests; the churches were plundered of their wealth; the various religious houses,—four monasteries, two priories, and two nunneries,—each of which, after the excellent fashion of El Islam and its mosques, had a school attached, were suppressed, whilst the lands were either sold, vested in the Crown, or made over to Lutheranism. It was a case of "non licet esse vos," and the proceeding was exactly that of our Act of 1537.

Let me briefly remark that in treating of matters which happened three centuries ago, both Catholic and Protestant writers are too apt to look upon them from the stand-point of the present. Catholics see only the use of their establishments; they will not accept the consequences of defeat, and yet they know that by the rule "Væ victis" they would have dealt, had they been conquerors, the same measure which was dealt to them. Protestants note only the abuses which marked the age; they look upon the old system with a jaundiced eye, and they misrepresent, undoubtedly, often without knowing it, the state of the ancient Church. Thus, we find it chronicled that many of the Icelandic bishops were married, without being told that they might have been married before they were ordained. And if there is anything in the present day which draws English Protestants to Catholicism, it is the fact that honest inquirers find they have been brought up in gross ignorance, to say nothing more, of the rival creed.

The Abbé Baudouin is strong in the belief that by virtue of the jewel Fair Play he would soon revive Catholicism in one of its old seats. And looking at the lukewarm action of the Lutheran faith, the scanty hold it has upon the affections and the passions of the people, the laical lives of the clergy, the prevalence of the "squarson," and the growth of "free thinking," I cannot but agree with him. Indeed the revival of Catholicism is one of the phenomena of the later nineteenth century, which time only can explain. Is it a steady flame or a fitful flicker preceding the final darkness? Its statistics are wonderful. During the last eighty-five years in the United States, it has risen from 25,000 to 9,600,000, a proportion of 1 : 4 of the population; whilst *the* faith of the nineteenth century, spiritualism (R. D. Owen), numbers only 7,500,000. In Holland, the very cradle of the Reformation, Catholics and Protestants are now about equal; and, whilst the census of Victoria gives 121 religions to less than three-quarters of a million, Catholicism in England seems bent upon forcing men into the extremes so distasteful to the English mind, upon dividing the country into two great camps, Catholicism and its complement Methodism. In Iceland the result of free propagandism would probably result in making all the people Catholics or Rationalists.

It was generally regretted that Dr Hjaltalín the Archiater, who was preparing for a trip in the "Diana" to Europe, did not take part in the festivities. I need say nothing about the scientific acquirements of this well-informed and most obliging Icelander, whose writings are known throughout Europe. He has travelled extensively in his own country; and I was the greatest loser by his departure, as otherwise he might have led me to the unexplored regions in the south-east. He was especially interested about coal, a subject which seems now to be undergoing revival in the north: a fresh impetus has been given to its exploration in Norway and Sweden: even in the Færoe Islands a Danish company proposes to exploit the beds. An expedition, accompanied by Professor Jonstrüp and a Silesian engineer, lately returned to Copenhagen, and revived the views of Professor Krazenstein, who in 1778 examined the Pröste-fjeldt in the island of Suderoë. The report is that the people have used their coal as fuel for a century; that although not so easily fired as the English, it gives a stronger and more lasting flame, and that it is free from sulphur and other minerals injurious to the fabrication of steel and iron. But, after settling its calorific properties, the grand question is, whether the veins are in the real carboniferous formation, whose beds are thick enough to work profitably. Seams which occur in the nummulite-hippurite Jurassic formation mostly lead to loss, witness those which have been worked near Trieste, on the Adriatic coast, and in parts of the Libanus.

Dr Hjaltalín was sanguine concerning the coal lately found in the regions about Norðrá, a northern influent of the Western Hvítá River: the exact position is between the little tarns Vikrafell and Herðavatn in Norðrardal. He expects soon to settle a long-disputed question, "Has coal been produced *in situ?*" and the sister formation of the Færoe Islands, where a Danish officer, Captain Dahl, has bought a vein seven feet thick for $50,000, ought to aid in solving the mystery. It is found associated with the Surtar-brand,[1] a semi-mineralised lignite, common ˉon the western coasti of the island. Uno Von Troil tells us that cups and plates which take a fine polish are made of it at Copenhagen: this reminds us of the bitumen "finjans" from the Tomb of Moses, near the Dead Sea.

Uno Von Troil, Sartorius Von Waltershausen, and Professor Silliman maintain this Devil's or black fuel to be a local produce of forests buried by ashes, and ripened by the superincumbent sand and humus. On the other hand, Professor Steenstrüp and M. Gaimard declare this "brown coal" to be flotsam and jetsam from the Gulf of Mexico. Professor Paijkull found in it some thirty kinds of growth: the vine and platanus, the tulip-tree and mahogany, associated with oak, elm, willow, alder, birch, walnut, fir, and other resinous vegetation. These items, if grown *in situ*, as they appear to be, suggest a change of temperature utterly unknown to historic times, and belong-

---

[1] The name has been discussed in the Introduction (Section VII.).

ing to the flora of the upper Miocene, *e.g.*, Madeira. Halley explained the intense cold of Behring's Straits, by placing the Pole there before the earth's axis had altered its direction. Others have attributed the change to the diminution of eclipti- cal obliquity, the excentricity of the earth's orbit, the precession of the equinoxes, and the revolution of the apsides. Similarly the Markgraf F. Marenzi (Fragmente über Geologie) cuts the Gordian knot, by supposing an altered obliquity of the ecliptic, which may have acted, he says, in past ages even as the present ever-increasing excentricity of the orbit will in some 210,000 years produce another Glacial Period, and render Northern Europe uninhabitable. On the other hand, he remarks that however torrid may have been the hyperborean climates, they must ever have lacked the fructifying insects, peculiar to temperate, sub-equatorial, and equatorial zones. Judging from Miocene Greenland, the reverse would appear to be fact.

It is impossible to stay a week in Reykjavik without finding out that the world is split into two divisions, strongly marked as were our Whig and Tory of the last generation. The Danes are in the minority: they represent the utilitarian, the cosmo- politan, and, perhaps, the metropolitan side of politics; and they complain that whatever the mother country does for her distant dependency, the latter is ever clamorous for more. The majority is the Icelandic party, for whose political aspirations I can find no better name than "Home Rulers,"—warning readers, how- ever, that the comparison must not be strained and identified with that of Ireland. The main difference of the movement, as far as I can see, appears simply this. Iceland is actually 1600 miles distant from Denmark, as far as London from Jamaica, and practically, when the post goes only seven times a year, as far as Australia from England. Again, the proportions of Iceland to Denmark (1,800,000) are 1 : 35, and the population is 1 : 25·70. England certainly would not refuse Home Rule to the Irish if they lived in New Zealand and numbered about 750,000. No wonder then that Iceland objects to be treated like a " Crown colony of a rather severe type."

The islanders show a growing dissatisfaction with the Danish Government, which they declare to be, though mild, meddling and unintelligent—in fact, perpetuating the petty, "nagging," and annoying policy which lost the duchies. They might respect whilst they hated a strong despotism; but perpetual interference they despise as well as hate. They are urgent as Mr Butt, for leave to stand on their own legs, to manage their own affairs; the Danes have tried, they say, for centuries to govern them, and progress could hardly be less were they left to themselves. The worst that could happen to them would be to starve, in which case they would deserve their fate, and could blame none but themselves. They complain, and I think with justice, that individually the Dane is not sympathetic to them; whilst Icelanders learn Danish, which, however, they pronounce with their own accent, Danes disdain their language and will not even attend their church. Residents of twenty years declare that they never read the theogenic, cosmogenic, and mythic Eddas,[1] because they are literally "grandams' tales;" whilst the Sagas or Sayings, moral and dogmatic, epic and historical, are a tissue of inventions, monotonous, moreover, sanguinary, immoral, and barbarous. The actual leader of the opposition, or Home Rule party, is Hr Jón Sigurðsson (nat. 1811), now in Denmark, a far-famed Norsk scholar, and an *employé* of the Danish Government. "White John," as the popular nickname is, shows his clean shaven face everywhere, photographed for the patriot party. He owns advanced opinions, but he rests within constitutional limits; his followers, of course, go further afield, and not a few of them may be called republican. He has the honour to appear in the Millenary lithograph with the following notice: "President of the Althing, President of the Icelandic Literary Society, President of the Icelandic Thjóðvinafèlag; has distinguished himself as an uninterested and faithful champion of the national and political rights of the Icelanders; besides he has made himself conspicuous as a thorough scholar in the history and legislation of Iceland."

There is also a small and uninfluential Norwegian faction which seems bent upon drawing the islanders to itself, chiefly, it appears

---

[1] Moðir is mother ; Ammá (evidently a Sanskritic form), grandmother ; and Edda is Proavia, or great-grandmother. Of course the derivation is disputed.

to me, because Naddodd and Ingólfr discovered and colonised Iceland, and because she still speaks the Norræna-Túnga: a few distinguished names, literary and political, belong to this political category.

In the Introduction I have offered a few remarks on the pros and cons of Home Rule in Iceland. But the history of the world generally, and especially that of Italy, teaches one great lesson—how easy it is to divide and how hard to "unify" a country. The line between local and imperial measures is difficult to draw and facile to be overstepped at all times of popular excitement: a manner of dismemberment is proposed at the time when the condition of Europe seems to demand centralisation. Diets in Great Britain will only assimilate her with Austria, which exists by a political necessity: statesmen say that if she were not she would have to be invented. We can all distinguish the dim form which stands behind Home Rule in Ireland, and I venture to predict that in Iceland it will be the shortest path to separation from the mother state, and to the re-establishment of the old Norwegian Republic.

END OF VOL. I.

*M'Farlane & Erskine, Printers, Edinburgh.*

WS - #0043 - 050724 - C0 - 229/152/22 - PB - 9781332468560 - Gloss Lamination